THE PACIFIC RAINCOAST

DEVELOPMENT OF WESTERN RESOURCES

The Development of Western Resources is an interdisciplinary series focusing on the use and misuse of resources in the American West. Written for a broad readership of humanists, social scientists, and resource specialists, the books in this series emphasize both historical and contemporary perspectives as they explore the interplay between resource exploitation and economic, social, and political experiences.

John G. Clark, University of Kansas, Founding Editor
Hal K. Rothman, University of Nevada, Las Vegas, Series Editor

THE PACIFIC RAINCOAST

Environment and Culture in an American Eden, 1778–1900

Robert Bunting

 University Press of Kansas

© 1997 by the University Press of Kansas
All rights reserved

Published by the University Press of Kansas (Lawrence, Kansas 66049), which was organized by the Kansas Board of Regents and is operated and funded by Emporia State
University, Fort Hays State University, Kansas State University, Pittsburg State University,
the University of Kansas, and Wichita State University

Library of Congress Cataloging-in-Publication Data

Bunting, Robert.
  The Pacific raincoast : environment and culture in an American
Eden, 1778–1900 / Robert Bunting.
     p.   cm. — (Development of western resources)
  Includes bibliographical references (p. 207) and index.
  ISBN 0-7006-0805-2 (alk. paper)
  1. Human ecology—Northwest, Pacific—History.   2. Man—Influence
on nature—Northwest, Pacific.   3. Northwest, Pacific—History.
4. Northwest, Pacific—Environmental conditions.   I. Title.
II. Series.
GF504.N87B86   1996
333.7'09795—dc20   96-9655

British Library Cataloguing in Publication Data is available.

Printed in the United States of America

10 9 8 7 6 5 4 3 2 1

The paper used in this publication meets the minimum requirements of the American
National Standard for Permanence of Paper for Printed Library Materials Z39.48-1984.

Dedicated to

Janet Bunting, my wife, and
Janice Bunting, my mother

CONTENTS

Acknowledgments   ix

Introduction   1

1   The Native American Landscape   5

2   Fur Trade Society   22

3   Nature's Society   36

4   Settler Society and Native Americans   51

5   Settlement   72

6   Settler Society   89

7   Living on the Land   104

8   Settler Society and the Forests   120

9   Transforming the Forests   135

Epilogue   159

Notes   165

Bibliography   207

Index   223

(photo insert follows page 50)

ACKNOWLEDGMENTS

In undertaking this volume I have received support and encouragement from many persons and organizations. Staffs at the Oregon Historical Society, the special collections department in the University of Oregon, and the manuscripts and archives division at the University of Washington were particularly helpful. Richard Hanes and Pete Teensma, Bureau of Land Management; Ken Bierly, Oregon Division of State Lands; Dennis Peters, U.S. Fish and Wildlife; and, especially, Jerry Williams of the U.S. Forest Service provided me with important printed materials and unpublished papers of their own. Scientists working in the private sector, like Ed Alverson, Marc Boule, and John Cristy, were also generous in sharing their materials and knowledge.

I experienced firsthand that a "community of scholars" truly exists, as numerous persons shared with me their ideas, research, and themselves. Scientists Patricia Benner, Bob Frenkel, and Bill Romme patiently answered the inquiries of a social scientist while supplying me with papers that I would not otherwise have known about or had access to. Portions or all of this book in its numerous forms were read by Forrest Bond, James Brooks, Dick Brown, Janet Lee Bunting, Dan Calhoun, Bob Ficken, Paul Goodman, David Johnson, Bill Lang, Bill Robbins, Bill Romme, Jim Ronda, Ruth Rosen, Carlos Schwantes, Michael Smith, and Don Wolf. Their criticisms saved me from egregious errors, and I unabashedly appropriated their insights as if they were my own. The intellectual debt that I owe those people can never be repaid. That is particularly true of my mentor, friend, and running companion William G. Robbins; no person has done more to shape this work than he.

Nor can I ever repay the support I have received from family and friends. My parents, Ralph and Janice Bunting, as well as friends Forrest Bond, Thomas P. Henry, Lloyd C. (Chuck) John, Marianne Keddington, Bill Lang, Bill Robbins, and David and Pamela Watson offered not only encouragement but their homes. Marianne Keddington did double duty, because she not only nourished me with wit, lodging, and fine meals, but took time out from her own busy schedule to edit the manuscript. Much of whatever clarity the work possesses is due to her and to the guiding hands of Michael Briggs, Nancy Scott, and Susan Schott at the University Press of Kansas. To chronicle what I owe colleague, friend, and running mate

Duane A. Smith would require a separate book. He and Gay are two of Colorado's great treasures.

Finally, I feel both privileged and obliged to acknowledge publicly those who have influenced this work by shaping me. My father continues to be my guide in word and action and the best man I have ever met, but four extraordinary women have most affected me and my scholarship. My grandmother, Louise (Nana) McDevitt, and aunt, Hazel Hilliker, did not live to see this work completed but would take as much pride in it as they always did in everything I undertook. But it is my mother, Janice Bunting, and my wife, Janet Lee Bunting, who are models for what I only hope to become, who daily enrich my life, and who remind me of what is truly important. To them, I gratefully dedicate this book.

THE PACIFIC RAINCOAST

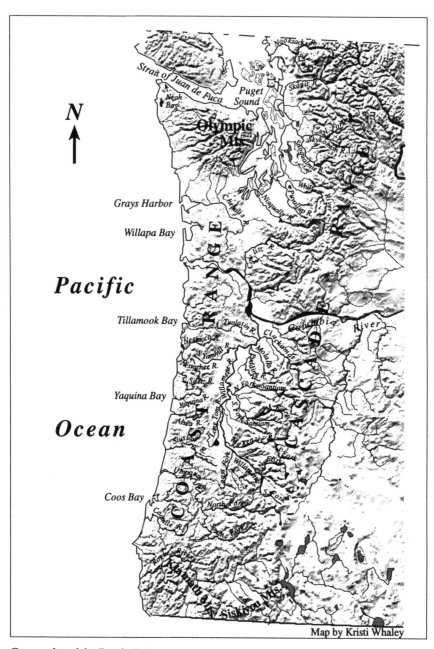

Geography of the Pacific Raincoast

INTRODUCTION

The history of Euroamerican settlement in the Far West has most often been told as a tale of heroism, but over the last quarter century that heroic narrative of material progress, democracy, and social improvement has been revised to reflect the destruction and exploitation of both the land and the native people. But neither interpretation—the ascent from wilderness to civilization or the descent from a pristine, harmonious natural world to social chaos and environmental suicide—adequately captures what took place. Euroamerican contact, settlement, and early industrialization did profoundly alter the land and the native people. But the world into which Euroamericans came was a landscape already used to change, because for centuries Native Americans and ecological systems had adapted and changed as they interacted with each other. The differences in the change wrought by Euroamericans were its vast scope and limited time frame.

The changes have resulted in a very different landscape from the one the first white men saw. If the early explorers returned today, they would still be greeted by Native Americans, fertile valleys, mountain ranges, forests, and volcanic peaks. Salmon still swim in the streams, birds still fill the sky, herds of deer and elk continue to roam the land, and evergreen trees still line the roadways. But it is a transformed landscape with weakened and reduced links. The Douglas-fir forests themselves no longer house a rich variety of species and genetic diversity. Today the Douglas-fir region of western Washington and western Oregon possesses little of its old-growth forests, and the estimated 6 percent that does remain is fragmented into islands and threatened with logging operations. Native peoples, plants, and animals have been eliminated, reduced, or marginalized. Species and genetic reductionism threatens to push the region into ecological disaster. Reforested tree farms rather than biologically diverse old-growth forests dominate the region's evergreen species. How is it that the world's greatest temperate rain forest, seemingly inexhaustible, has been so reduced, and what are the biological and social consequences of this reduction?

Such questions, and their answers, require looking beyond present conditions, policies, and attitudes. They necessitate a journey into the past. An understanding of the region's physical environment and how various groups of people have viewed this land, lived upon it, been shaped by it, and struggled to possess it goes to the heart of Pacific Northwest history.

The Pacific Raincoast, then, is a book about how natural and human history have interacted to shape the region. It is a tale of relationships and an attempted conquest that was not always intended and never completed. The Euroamerican invaders to the Northwest sought to systematize society and the physical world according to a cultural script that was supposed to enhance their economic, social, and political freedom and to bring a measure of control and security to their lives. The strategies and structures that systematization took were shaped by what Donald Worster has called a "culture of capitalism," a culture that holds to an ethos of cash-value exchange, self-interest, competitive materialism, freedom as a function of possession, the rational calculation of success and failure, unlimited expansion, contractual relationships, and private ownership and accumulation. Relationships in a culture of capitalism are commodified so that subjects are turned into objects. Nature is viewed as a capital resource to assist in the accumulation of wealth while nature's interdependent functions are ignored in the economic calculus.[1] A "capitalist culture of systematization," therefore, captures both the Euroamericans' cultural vision and the values by which they sought to order society and nature as well as how they lived on the land.

For many emigrants to the Northwest, opportunity resulted in a better life, but never was it a life lived independent of the environment and other people. The new regionalists found themselves not only shaping their world but being shaped by it—by indigenous people, the land, and the consequences of their own actions. The power to shape their lives and the resulting benefits were not, however, shared equally by everyone. Moreover, attempts to systematize the landscape involved costs that were not distributed equitably. Generally, the environment and the least powerful members of society bore the burdens, and only occasionally were the most powerful citizens not able to ignore the consequences of what they had done. Ironically, in trying to ensure a measure of security and predictability, the new society undermined the very order it sought to achieve. At first, geography, technology, and population forestalled some of the costs. But gradually, as technology improved, population increased, and market penetration deepened, changes were more radically recast. Recognizing a problem was not a solution, and reform brought little real change. Lacking the cultural and economic information to generate another model of behavior, the new people of the Northwest sought answers within the cultural understandings that had created the problem in the first place. A capitalist ethos, a sense of national destiny, and a land of abundance continued to govern how most people lived, and the result altered life for all who lived in the Northwest. By the beginning of the twentieth century, many of the region's defining elements and processes were clearly in place.

This study reaches from 1778, the period of sustained Euroamerican contact in the Northwest, to 1900, when Frederick Weyerhaeuser purchased

900,000 acres of Washington forestland, completing one of the largest land deals in American history and symbolizing the forces of industrial capitalism that would increasingly shape the region's ecological and cultural landscape. The story's protagonists are mainstream dominant white males who settled in the Northwest from the 1840s to the 1880s. Many traditional Western themes appear in this story: native peoples, fur trappers, settlers, Indian-white conflicts, extractive economies, colonial dependency, and the role of government. The story line does not, however, follow a well-scripted stage play of heroism or brutality, and older themes and historical categories are placed in a new regional and environmental framework.

Regionalism is nothing new, certainly not for historians of the West. They have set regional boundaries with reference to geographical, economic, political, and cultural patterns, with geopolitical boundaries being the most prominent. But few have used bioregional boundaries to frame their histories. A bioregional approach regards region as a physical and cultural ecology of place, where ecological and cultural systems interact to shape one another. Through this relationship, cultural structures and meanings can be discerned, biotic processes understood, and historical change traced.

The bioregion of western Oregon and western Washington was largely a coniferous montage of spruce, cedar, hemlock, pine, and fir—the world's largest temperate rain forest, covering 90 percent of the land in the late eighteenth century. The Douglas-fir bioregion, named for the region's dominant tree, extends along a north-south axis from southwestern British Columbia to northwestern California and eastward from the Pacific Ocean to the western slopes of the Cascade Range, with western Oregon and western Washington constituting the heart of the region. Within those boundaries lie the Klamath and Olympic mountain provinces, the Coast and Cascade mountain ranges, and the physiographic Willamette–Puget Lowland province.[2] It is also where the Pacific Northwest's economic, political, and demographic forces of power are located.[3]

But why study the Douglas-fir region of western Oregon and western Washington? Whether portraying a colonial, dependent section or a romanticized place of western lore, many historians have marginalized the West. The Pacific Northwest in particular has been seen as a mere backdrop to the American pageant. This treatment is particularly puzzling given the immense changes in historical methodology and focus over the past twenty years. Formerly marginalized groups—whether structured according to gender, class, race, or ethnicity—are now seen as important creators of our history. Yet certain "elite" states, sections, or areas are still at the center of the American story. Just as the colonial American South is as central to the shaping of America as colonial New England, so too the Douglas-fir region is as informative about the character of the American experience as are more heavily studied areas.

Moreover, the Douglas-fir region has been much more at the center of the American experience than many have recognized. International empires contested for power on the far Pacific coast during the eighteenth and early nineteenth centuries. Furs from the Northwest provided East Coast Americans with capital and financed the importation of goods from Asia. The end of the trail for Lewis and Clark, the Oregon Country was central to the American imagination and the political debate over expansionism from the years of the Jefferson administration until the 1840s. As settler society gave way to industrial society in the 1880s, the Douglas-fir region became a center for the new timber industry, conservationism, and the growth of the bureaucratic nation-state. Even notwithstanding these significant issues, the region would still warrant study. As much can be learned by studying those who are at the end of the cracked whip as from those who are cracking it.

Land and its seemingly inexhaustible nature forms the heart of American history. An abundant natural world supplied a cornucopia of resources that sustained Americans' physical lives for generations. Nature also provided white Americans with natural monuments that rivaled European cultural artifacts and gave the young nation a past reaching back thousands of years. Moreover, nature's abundance seemed to confirm the status of the United States as an exceptional republic, providentially destined to re-create the world in its own image. Americans clearly conceived of their country, in Perry Miller's apt wording, as "Nature's Nation."[4] And no place appeared more like Eden than the Far West, where myth and reality seemed to be so closely linked.

How did people interact with a land of plenty, and how did they seek to maintain that abundance? By what myths did people order their lives? How did experience of place and transported ideas interrelate, and how did physical and cultural geography shape the region's history? What were the environmental attitudes of settlers? Why did two states that share a similar forest province develop so differently? Ultimately, what are the connections between exploitation of land and human exploitation? How are environmental change and social change connected? Finally, how are current environmental and social conditions connected to a longer past? These questions take us to the heart not only of Pacific Northwest history, or even of American history, but of a world transformed by what William H. McNeill labelled "the great frontier" of European expansion.[5]

This is a history of how a place is physically and culturally mapped. Although the region's history shares much with other places in the United States, timing and place gave to the Pacific Northwest a particular environmental and cultural configuration. Thus, the Pacific Northwest reflects regional distinctions that are closely tied to place, even as its larger commonalities give the Pacific Northwest context and meanings that transcend the borders of the land dominated by the Douglas fir.

CHAPTER ONE

The Native American Landscape

Somewhere around 70,000 years ago the Bering-Chukchi platform connected Russia with Alaska, allowing waves of plants, animals, and peoples to cross over into North America.[1] Descendants of these migrants continued to move across the North American continent in a southerly direction. Following the retreating ice, during the last period of glaciation in about 10,000 B.P., Amerindian peoples moved along the Columbia River, crossed over the Cascade mountain range, and entered the Douglas-fir region.[2] As groups expanded throughout the region, available resources and cultural choices (including existing technologies) framed peoples' lives.[3]

The difficult process of adaptation was eased not only by cultural continuities but also by the environment. The forested landscape was a place of abundant plants and animals, and the Northwest coast would eventually support one of the most densely populated nonagricultural populations of Native American people in the precontact world.[4] Plentiful rainfall, an ocean seascape, and snow-capped mountains that fed numerous streams watered the landscape. Pacific Coast natives chose to live along these river systems and estuaries, making them very much a "people of the water."

Native peoples drew their most important sources of food from the Pacific Ocean and Northwest streams. Some of this fare came from the sea mammals that seasonally inhabited the region's waters. Harbor seals traveled along the coast and up inland rivers, sea lions and harbor porpoises frequented coastal waters and estuaries, and sea otters and whales migrated up and down the Northwest coast.[5] Although none of these mammals occupied a position of primacy in the Indian economy, they did play an important secondary role. Particularly significant was the supplementary role that whales played. While only the Makah, Quileute, and Quinault in northwestern Washington hunted whales south of de Fuca Strait, whales were often swept ashore, where they were an important source of meat, fat, bone-tools, and oil.[6] Coastal residents also gathered marine invertebrates such as clams, mussels, oysters, mollusks, and sea urchins.[7] They also ate dentalium, found off the west coast of Vancouver Island. The shell from dentalium was also a highly prized trade item that served as a display of wealth, a medium of exchange, and ornamentation.[8]

River otter and beaver abounded in Northwest estuaries and freshwater streams, and river environs supported a variety of albatross, brants, cranes, ducks, geese, herons, swans, and loons. John Ball, writing in 1835, observed how the "incredible numbers" of "*Swan*, brown and white geese and ducks of many kinds" literally "whitened" the lower Columbia River. William Clark, while encamped along the lower Columbia, was less sanguine, complaining that the densely populated waterfowl created such a "horrid" noise that he was kept awake most of the night. The moderate climate and abundant food sources kept some waterfowl in the area year-round. Others were transients, passing along the Pacific flyway, stopping only long enough to rest and refuel. Migratory or resident, waterfowl were an important part of peoples' diet, for their size, their close proximity to riverine peoples, and their congregating habits, which concentrated immense numbers within a limited area, made waterfowl easy targets for hunters' nets, spears, and arrows.[9]

Pacific waters yielded not only mammals, invertebrates, and waterfowl, but they also provided native people with their dietary staple, fish. According to Father Pierre-Jean De Smet, SJ, who visited the area in 1845–1846, "As the buffalo of the north, and deer from north to east of the mountains, furnish daily food for the inhabitants of those regions, so do these fish supply the wants of the western tribes."[10] Freshwater species, such as rainbow trout, inhabited Northwest waters, but the most important fishes for Pacific Northwest natives were saltwater and anadromous species, including sturgeon, lamprey, and eulachon.[11] Most significant by far was the salmon. Five species of salmon, differing in size and each with its own migratory pattern, breed in Northwest streams, migrate to the ocean where they mature, and then return to their place of birth to spawn and die. From the spring through the fall Indian northwesterners planned their activities around the salmons' spawning migrations.

Native American fishing techniques reflected a keen sense of environmental adaptation. Fishermen harpooned sturgeon from canoes and harvested herring and smelt with rakes. They took salmon from estuaries and calm areas of freshwater streams using seines and gill nets, but the best fishing was found at waterfalls and riffles where the salmon were most concentrated and exposed. Fishermen at those locations hunted with hooks and spears but most commonly caught the salmon with v-shaped weirs and scoop nets. At the opening of the apex, the men stretched a net between two canoes. Then, like a funnel, the weir directed the fish into the waiting nets. At a falls, fishermen stood on natural precipices or constructed platforms and caught salmon with scoop nets as the fish tried to leap up the waterfall.[12]

In addition to being a people of the water, Northwest Amerindians were also a people of the forest. Given the region's forested landscape, it could hardly have been otherwise. Extensive waterways may have provided food, acted as transportation corridors, and determined where people lived, but the forests shaped that riverine environment. Along Northwest streams, dense forest canopies shade the water, helping to ensure the cool temperatures that fish require. The root system of streamside trees spreads like fingers to grasp and hold the soil, preventing erosion and siltation that could smother eggs or choke off the air and food sources that fry and mature fish need to survive. Streamside trees deposit needles, leaves, stems, and limbs on the ground, where they decompose and cycle nutrients back into the soil. The enriched soil can then support a heavy growth of vegetation, which promotes soil stability. Some of the litter shed by streamside trees falls directly into the water, adding nutrients to the stream. Occasionally, as a result of disease, insects, windthrow, or rushing currents, an entire tree may fall into the water. The vast amount of organic debris added to the water and the tree's position in the stream alter the stream's physical and biological character to promote habitat stability. The result is the same whether there is an individual log or a lower river jam of entangled downed trees and woody debris that has been swept downstream by floods.[13] All of this organic matter translates into a stabilized, biologically diverse stream environment.

Streams interlaced with downed trees do not flow at an even pace or depth, but instead they form a complex pattern of shallow riffles and quiet pools where a diversity of life can flourish. Pools—where the energy of flowing water dissipates, gravel for spawning beds accumulates, sediments become trapped, and nutrients are housed—create the habitat necessary for rearing fish, particularly salmonids. During brief flooding periods, these slack water refuges also offer protection against moving sediment and the swift currents that can sweep young fish downstream to their death. Riffles provide the ideal feeding habitats for underyearling steelhead and cutthroat trout. But even steelhead and cutthroat prefer pools once they start to mature. Trout require rearing sites where food is plentiful and little effort is required to hold a feeding position against the current. Deep pools also provide protection from terrestrial predators and offer layers of water where diverse species and age classes can coexist.[14] Thus no single environment fully supports the needs of all fish or even the habitat requirements of a single species of fish throughout all stages of its life course. Genetic and species diversity requires habitat variety.

Like downed trees, large log jams and beaver dams structure streams and creek habitats though with a slightly different twist. Larger obstructions increase watershed storage and nutrient retention, and drift jams and beaver dams sometimes create new habitat areas. When streams are particularly high, dams can divert water onto previously dry lands. But whether creating or sustaining wetland areas, log jams and beaver dams enrich overflow land soils with organic materials and create a habitat that aids bear, muskrats, elk, waterfowl, and countless other animals. Fish, particularly salmon, benefit from larger stream obstructions, which provide protection against storm-induced floods in the main channel, predator protection from under-cut banks, overhead vegetation, downed log cover, and insect food sources. Juvenile coho salmon, for example, spend approximately the first eighteen months of their lives in freshwater streams like Oregon's Coquille River. There, in an estuarian habitat of backwater pools, channels, and sloughs, juveniles develop more quickly than smolt do upriver, ensuring an abundance of salmon in those river systems.[15]

Downed trees may provide a stable source of nutrients, give streams a complex structure, and promote habitat diversity, but not all trees make an equal contribution to a habitat. The age, size, and species of standing and downed trees are a function of a forest's age and make-up and act differently on a stream environment. For a number of nutritive and structural reasons, old-growth coniferous forests create and sustain long-term habitat stability best. First of all, the large dead trees that old-growth stands make available provide more nutrients to be recycled back into the ecosystem than do small dead trees. In addition, old-growth conifer debris decays at a much slower rate than a deciduous species like red alder, which characteristically grows along young-growth streams. Moreover, younger stands, regardless of species, provide less cover and fewer deep, slow-moving pools of water than old-growth stands—and cover to regulate stream temperature and pools for food and shelter from enemies are all structural requirements of salmonid. A genetically and species-rich fish population depends upon a diverse aquatic environment, which in turn is linked to a forest ecosystem of genetic, structural, and spatial complexity.[16]

Whereas fish reigned supreme in the native diet, with salmon dominating the hierarchy, the health of fish remained connected to the forest ecosystem. Like a thread hanging from a sweater, trees are a crucial constituent of the larger whole. To cut the thread off is to weaken the entire fabric. To pull on the thread without understanding its connectedness to the entire garment is to unravel the complex weaving that is the sweater. Individual species, human or otherwise, do not live a segmented existence, they exist in the context of an ecological whole.

The forest ecosystem also supported an abundant and diverse biotic community on the land. To the human inhabitants that diversity meant a bountiful and easily procured fare. The more than forty kinds of berries and fruits that grew throughout the area had a mineral content comparable to cultivated berries and fruits and provided an important source of sugar and vitamin C.[17] Native people consumed rhizomes from licorice and a variety of ferns such as bracken and sword. Vegetable greens were in the form of horsetail, cow parsnip, wild celery, skunk cabbage, and stinging nettle, while most starches came from the tuber of wapato and camas root.[18] Wapato, found in abundance around ponds in Columbia River valleys, closely resembled the potato in size, shape, and taste. Unlike many other Indian foods, it remained edible throughout the year, though it was most often harvested during the fall. For those who lived in the region's moist interior areas, camas root provided a stable and nourishing fare. Gathered in the late spring, camas resembled onions but tasted like a potato when cooked.[19] Some groups collected mosses to use as condiments, while others south from the lower Columbia supplemented their diets with acorns.[20]

Native people used nets and snares to capture grouse and other fowl. Because of the forest ecology, more mammalian species were available in the Douglas-fir region than in any other North American locale except California's Sierra Nevada range. Black-tail deer ranged from the region's northern boundaries through western Oregon, while its white-tail relative foraged in the lower Columbia valley and western Oregon south to the upper Rogue River valley. Elk lived throughout the region.[21]

Both deer and elk depend heavily on an extensive forest ecosystem for forage and cover and require large expanses of land. Deer travel individually or in small family groups, ranging seasonally over an area of 320 to 640 acres. Elk, which are larger and live in herds, require a more expansive land area, from 1,000 to 6,000 acres. More than space is required, however, for the way that space is biotically constituted and arranged is also important. Forest cover offers protection not only from hunters and predators but also thermal cover during cold and hot weather. A mixed-stage forest that permits enough sunlight for the growth of ground vegetation yet sufficient forest cover to ensure protection provides the best habitat. Old-growth forest is particularly important during winter months in the Cascade and Olympic mountains, where the forest provides both thermal cover and a source of maintenance forage.[22]

People were not unmindful of the bounty. Hunters used bows and arrows, snares and pitfalls, and game drives to bring down their quarry. Although they preferred deer and elk, native people also hunted black bears, raccoons, foxes, bobcats, gray wolves, marmots, and other smaller animals.[23]

The forests framed the people's material culture as well as their physical sustenance. In 1841, U.S. naval officer Charles Wilkes marveled at the ability of native women to make buckskin clothes and footwear that he judged to be the ideal dress for traversing the Northwest. Natives made ingenious mats, baskets, and hats from cattail, cedar bark, and beargrass. Important tools were fashioned from bone and horn, and trees provided the necessary material for fuel, spears, bows and arrows, pipes, bowls, and baskets. Some clothing was made by weaving threads of inner bark fiber, and homes were built from hewn planks. Plants and roots were endowed with cultural-religious meanings and medicinal powers.[24]

Native societies did not rank all tree species equally. Except for use as firewood or saplings for weirs, Douglas firs and western hemlock stood largely undisturbed. But Sitka spruce was extensively used: root fibers were harvested for fishing nets, and the tree's gum served as a healing agent. The sugar pine of southern Oregon yielded a sugarlike substance that natives used as a sweetener; its dried seeds were pounded and baked into cakes. People peeled the yellow pine and ate its cambium. Craftsmen preferred big-leaf maple and Oregon ash for canoe paddles, alder for masks and eating utensils, and yew for bows and arrows. The most desirable tree, however, was the western red cedar, a choice guided by nature as much as culture. Western red cedar was light, strong, easy to split, and rot resistant. From those trees came the wood for house planks, posts, beams, carved monuments, rope, baskets, mats, baby diapers, floats for fishing nets, and canoes. Not surprisingly, given the tree's material importance, strong spiritual properties and power were also attributed to western red cedar.[25]

The sources of physical and material culture were all related to the forests. The wooded environment, in the words of one modern writer, provides "those very elements that are 'Indian'—power, ritual bathing or swimming areas, berries, fish, and deer, among other things."[26] The forests provided native people with such a diverse and bountiful fishing, hunting, and collecting economy that agriculture was unnecessary.[27] Through environmental adaptation and a reliance on a variety of natural resources, Indian exploitation avoided monoculture dependency or the overharvesting of any particular species. Adaptation, however, required an intimate knowledge of the land, its seasons, and physical mobility. Place and stability, culturally and ecologically, were not divorced from mobility. Movement and belonging to the land were not inimical.

Native settlement was characterized by "satellite patterning," with a main settled village surrounded by a cluster of temporarily occupied sites. Generally, people wintered along the lower river valleys, where they found shelter from winter winds and occasional snows and still had access to water and wood supplies. By February and into March, fresh eulachon and sturgeon supplemented the natives' diet of largely preserved foods. During those months the larger village split into smaller units to collect nuts and berries and to hunt game. In April, the spring salmon run reached its peak, and people from the coast and interior congregated at rapids and falls. At preeminent fishing spots like Celilo Falls on the Columbia River, Willamette Falls near what is now Oregon City, and coastal streams, Indians took great numbers of salmon, performed ceremonies, played games, and exchanged goods. Similar gatherings and ritual reenactments greeted subsequent salmon runs.[28]

As the salmon migration waned, natives close to the Cascade Range moved into the foothills and the mountains, where they established trail stations and seasonal camps. The women moved over the land digging roots while the men hunted. In June or July, most people returned to the rivers for the second salmon run. During the late summer months, families divided their time between hunting, collecting, fishing, clamming, and preparing foods for storage before the fall salmon migration again took the bulk of their energies. Along with fishing, fall witnessed a return to hunting game and harvesting berries in the mountains. As winter came on, family and band members once more returned to their winter villages, where they constructed and repaired material objects, fished and hunted, arranged marriages, and performed important ceremonies.[29]

Each native group, of course, had its own migratory habits, resource priorities, population concentrations, and cultural constructs. A broadly shared forest ecosystem framed the larger region, but people depended on the resources that were most plentiful and predictable. Consequently, microecosystems created differences among groups. Those who lived near estuaries or by riverine fisheries relied more heavily on fish and had less developed hunting skills than their more removed neighbors. Some people lived in moist interior areas, where it was common to find fields with ten or twelve acres of camas, yielding sometimes twenty bushels an acre.[30]

Physical and cultural adaptions interacted to shape one another. The Cowlitz Indians of western Washington, for example, lived near Cowlitz Falls, which restricted the migration of salmon. As a result, Cowlitz natives were primarily prairie-oriented people.[31] In western Oregon's Willamette Valley, Willamette Falls was a physical and cultural line of demarcation that divided southern from northern valley natives. The high water of springtime provided enough flow for chinook salmon to surmount the falls, but the falls height restricted earlier and later salmon runs. In addition, even the spring chinook were apparently limited to the larger tributaries of the Cascades, such as the North and South Santiam and the McKenzie rivers. The western tributaries of the Willamette River, which were smaller and warmer, remained free of spawning salmon. Consequently, southern Willamette Valley Kalapuyans relied less on fish and more on collecting and hunting than the Indians who lived north of the falls (or other natives who resided along the coast or on anadromous-fed streams). Moreover, the availability of salmon not only divided groups materially, culturally, and socially, but linguistically as well, into a Chinookan-speaking people north of the falls and Kalapuyan-speaking people south of the falls to the Calapooya Mountains.[32]

Native Americans might have interacted with different microenvironments to shape a distinct geography and culture, but they harvested no plant, animal, or fish exclusively enough to endanger its existence. For example, the number of salmon taken by native people has been variously calculated, but recent estimates indicate that Indian fishing "was fully comparable to the Columbia River commercial fishery during its heyday in the late nineteenth century."[33] Although the numbers indicate that fishermen harvested large quantities of salmon, the species' population was not endangered.

Two structural factors have been advanced by modern scholars to explain the phenomenon. One explanation suggests that Indian fishing actually ensured salmon reproduction by culling the salmon population and preventing overpopulation, thereby ensuring an adequate breeding ground for reproduction.[34] Another argument runs that while certain advantageous fishing spots existed, native fisheries remained generally dispersed throughout the region, lessening the likelihood that particular spawning grounds would be destroyed.[35] Neither factor, individually or together, however, offers an adequate explanation. The first argument disregards nature's economy and only seems applicable when salmon runs outrun spawning environments, something that does not appear yearly. And, although dispersed fishing grounds may have made exploitation more difficult, it did not guarantee protection.

The fact remains that indigenous people apparently possessed the population and skill to have decimated the region's salmon, yet they looked for security and safety in extensive relationships with the land and other peoples.[36] Fishing beyond a certain limit was simply irrational. As the numbers of fish decline, the yield per effort also declines, making it more productive to switch to other food sources.[37] Through intermarriage and gift exchanges with groups from other locations, native peoples increased the diversity of available food and other resources while lessening the intensive exploitation of local habitats. Security was the peoples' goal, and diversity allowed them to meet it. The question remains, however, why native peoples did not exploit plants and animals to a greater degree than they did. The answer resides within the larger Amerindian cultural landscape, for, although cultural particularities among Native American groups existed, people shared a broadly similar cultural landscape throughout a common bioregion.

Although Northwest Indians adjusted their economic and cultural patterns to nature's abundance and seasonal offerings, they were not passive to an environmental determinism. Nor were they protoecologists who left the ecosystem unaltered. They killed animals, collected plants, and removed trees. Nature may have framed the choices people made, but the conscious ways that people shaped the environment to enhance their physical well-being were in accordance with cultural prescriptions.

Natives used a number of instruments to shape the land, but fire was their most important tool. When David Douglas and Alexander McLeod journeyed through the Willamette Valley in the 1820s, they noted how much land had been burned. In 1841, Wilkes Expedition botanist William Dunlop Brackenridge commented on burnt woods and complained that smoke from a grass fire prevented his seeing beyond a quarter of a mile.[38] Setting fires aided survival in a number of ways. Burns gave people protection from hostile groups that might seek to approach unseen and served to discourage and impede whites from crossing their land during and after the actual fire.[39] Fire was also an intricate part of hunting. Indians set fires to keep down the growth of underbrush in forest areas, to mask the visibility and scent of hunters, and to drive deer herds into tightly bound circles where they could more easily be killed.[40] The following description indicates how the Kalapuyans used fire to hunt, as well as their measures for conserving some of the animals: "When the circle of fire became small enough . . . the best hunters went inside and shot the game they thought should be killed. . . . The true hunter knew the animals that should be preserved for breeding purposes and was careful not to injure such."[41] Fishermen speared fish at night by using fire, and hunters used pitch pine fires in the bows of their canoes to stupefy swans, making them easy prey.[42]

Fires were set to create and preserve habitat areas that would attract game, particularly deer and elk. Although prescribed burns did not destroy oak trees, they did increase oak acorn production, a favorite food of deer and bears. Fire also created a rich grass habitat. Late-summer and early-fall burns fertilized the ground with ash and fostered a luxurious growth of grasses following the first rain. Without those annual burns, grassland areas would have been circumscribed, as well as the large deer and elk populations that depended on the grass for winter feed. An Indian told one Washington settler that deer were so plentiful and tame that they could be killed with stones and clubs. Furthermore, in the Willamette Valley indigenous grass species tend to be tough and unpalatable, and fire created a more tender young grass feed for fall grazing animals and migrating birds. Thus, by using fire, the region's inhabitants created "edge" environments that functioned very much like a managed domestic hunting preserve.[43]

Northwest Indians also used fires to simplify the gathering and harvesting of plants. Low-intensity valley fires not only furthered oak acorn production and protected trees from worm infestation but also facilitated acorn gathering by removing brush. Jesse Applegate described how the Kalapuyans near Yamhill burned the prairies in late autumn to assist the harvesting of tarweed. George Riddle reported similar practices by the Umpquas on Cow Creek. Fire burned the sticky resin of the tarweed but left the stalks standing. Women then collected the seeds into a basket by striking the dried pods.[44] Burns not only made gathering easier but, as with acorns, increased the productivity of tarweed seeds, hazelnuts, wild onions, wild carrots, bracken, and camas by removing competing woody species. Natives also torched mountain meadow areas to produce berry patches. Rogue River Indians in southern Oregon collected sap from the fire-created cavity of the sugar pine. Willamette Valley Indians told David Douglas they used fire to gather wild honey and grasshoppers. Some Amerindians may even have fired the land in a ritual observance to ensure an abundant salmon run.[45]

Fires set by natives certainly altered the region, but without impairing a biologically diverse ecosystem. Lowland fires were largely controlled, annual, low-intensity burns. Fires in the more heavily forested upland areas were apparently set during the spring or early summer when flames burned at a reduced intensity and could be extinguished by rainfall. These burning practices not only created the ecotones natives wanted, but they also lowered the chances of a major conflagration by reducing the ground fuel buildup.[46] Fire both destroys and renews the landscape, a paradoxical relationship that is particularly evident in the forests of the Pacific Northwest. Like all of nature's interactions, the relationship between fire and forests is complex and tied to a specific landscape. Climate, weather, elevation, soil, and a forest's composition all frame the fire regime. The overall regional interaction between fire and forests was a patterned landscape of species and genetic diversity.

As Northwest conifers grow, they shed limbs, twigs, and needles much as deciduous trees drop their leaves. Over time, depending on climate, weather, and elevation, the litter begins to decompose and to dry out. The result is a tinderbox of kindling that can be ignited by one of the region's natural fire starters: spontaneous combustion, volcanic eruptions, and, most commonly, lightning. Dry areas at higher elevations are most susceptible to lightning-induced fires. Thus, the Cascade Range, particularly its southern portion, is more vulnerable to fire than the moister Coast Range.[47] Once ablaze, the ecological effects vary according to the fire's intensity and type: crown, surface, or ground fire.

A catastrophic crown wildfire can actually kill numerous trees and yet remove little litter, so that the fire's most profound consequences may be delayed a few years. These fires actually add to the forest's biomass, thereby increasing the amount of fuel available to kindle a reburn. In addition, forest openings created by such a fire contribute to a probable cycle of reburns in the same area, for biomass desiccation is accelerated when it is more exposed to the wind and sun. Such a process virtually ensures the creation of a fire regime.[48]

A surface fire can also run through a forest, do little damage to the mature trees, and yet sweep the forest floor clear of litter. This form of housekeeping not only removes unsightly clutter but reduces the likelihood of a reburn. Unlike rare ground fires that burn through the organic matter and the soil itself, other important ecological results also follow surface fires. Rather than eliminating litter, fire serves to decompose it and release nutrients, enriching the soil. Because not all litter and woody debris are usually consumed, the remaining organic matter serves as a longer-range source of nutrients for soil enrichment and plant growth. These burns also aid forest regeneration by releasing seeds from cones.[49]

Actual burns, of course, seldom fall neatly into these types. Major fires often kill the overstory in some places, destroy only thin stands of trees in other places (through underburning), and completely pass over other areas, leaving patches of forestland relatively undisturbed. Though messy, this less-than-orderly burn pattern contributes to a healthy forest ecosystem.

Fire also affects particular tree species differently. The Northwest's dominant tree, the Douglas fir, offers an insight into this relationship. *Pseudotsuga menziesii* are subclimax, shade-intolerant trees that depend on a disturbing agent like fire to kill less fire resistant and shade-tolerant species like western hemlock and to open up areas where they can grow unobstructed by climax trees. Without disturbances, the densely shaded understory provided by mature canopy trees will choke out Douglas-fir seedlings. But if properties of the Douglas fir make it unsuitable to be a climax tree, other qualities aid its dominance at a subclimax level. While the western hemlock is very susceptible to fire and the cedar only a little less so, the Douglas fir possesses a resilient thick bark that protects the tree's living tissue, making it much more resistant to fire than the climax species. The Douglas fir's shade intolerance becomes an asset in an open environment, allowing it to establish a position of dominance. Because of insects, windthrow, and, most notably, fire disturbances, Northwest forests are consequently dominated by this false fir.[50]

Native American burning practices may not have severely damaged the forest ecosystem, but the same cannot be said for the Indian people. Ironically, in using fire to sustain themselves, native peoples inadvertently facilitated their eventual displacement and dependency. The parklike landscape that fire produced and maintained created a "garden" that appealed to Euroamerican aesthetic tastes and a cleared, fertile landscape that met settlers' practical farming needs. Moreover, by increasing regional fires, Northwest natives ensured the dominance of the Douglas fir, which would become the commercial centerpiece of the Northwest lumber industry.

Fire was only one of many ways that the geography of culture sought to shape the geography of place; for example, Indians also occasionally drained marshlands to produce more ground for root crops. According to legend, the Stillaguamish Indians tore apart the Sauk Prairie beaver dam to create more horticultural land for themselves.[51] Still, Indian resource management practices remained restricted, whether they involved draining marshlands, fishing, hunting, or using fire. Their restraint does not reflect so much a mystical ecological insight but the way Northwest Indians ordered their lives.

Northwest Amerindians operated within a communal culture that saw the world as organic.[52] This perception did not mean an absence of lines of demarcation; indeed, the cultural geography of native life was an ordered map with well-drawn economic, political, religious, and social boundaries. Boundaries radiated inward in concentric circles from the outermost limits of the village to the band, family, and individual. European notions of centralized leadership and a nation-state (in the form of tribes) did not exist. Political authority did not extend beyond the village and band level and seldom resided in a "chief."[53] Within the larger group structures were drawn the various internal lines of sociopolitical demarcations, the most basic of which involved a geographical bounding by gender. Men focused their energies on fishing and hunting, and women largely devoted themselves to gathering food, processing and preserving foods, making clothing, and doing other domestic tasks. Although this labor division increased productivity and the skill and knowledge of both men and women intersected to sustain the whole, men still dominated the system.[54]

Native American social ordering ranged from "nobility" to "slaves," but, despite this hierarchy, native society was not a caste system.[55] Although leadership positions remained generally hereditary, power could also be accrued through merit. Social mobility was possible, and personal leadership traits constituted an essential ingredient in possessing and exercising power. To be sure, leaders had power, but custom and personal traits of persuasion circumscribed the exercise of that power, and although leaders might intervene to mediate quarrels or provide military guidance, their power rested on their ability to influence, not on their attempts to command or coerce. Notions of personal freedom and a politics of kinship restricted centralized political power. As Hudson's Bay's George Simpson commented: "Every Flat Head [Chinook] Indian who is possessed of a Slave considers himself a Chief."[56]

Kinship established the social and political bonds of Indian society. Familial ties came most directly through blood, but fictive kinship also existed. Villages, then, were not homogeneous but a composite of various family groupings who had relatives in other villages. What strengthened or created those bonds of kinship was an exchange system that tied them together.

Giving gifts bound people to one another in social relationships of mutuality and obligation, expressing communal bonds in a very tangible way. The exchange, however, also conveyed power, for gift giving created an asymmetrical patron-client relationship. Exchange was not, therefore, narrowly economic. The dispossession of goods to others signified status and was the way a person discharged responsibilities and incurred obligations. The more wealth a person conferred, the greater his status and power. Here, distribution rather than economic accumulation demonstrated social standing and political power, and links between power and mutuality were forged. Because it took place within this gift-exchange system, trade was not primarily designed to obtain the fullest material advantage possible but to claim and exercise political power and social standing and to meet peoples' need for aid, security, and meaning.[57]

Perhaps the foremost example of ritualized gift giving among Northwest Indians was the potlatch, where ceremonial hosts gave gifts of wealth to formally invited guests. To Euroamericans, the potlatch seemed a wasteful ceremony of status display, the consequence of a rich environment, and a gesture unrelated to problems of livelihood. A gifting ritual of dispossession, so antithetical to capitalist values, made little sense to them.[58] Whites overlooked the fact that potlatches created obligations and extended social relationships that bound people to one another and offered a blanket of protection against enemies and material need. Euroamericans also failed to see that gift giving distributed wealth so as to keep resources constantly flowing within the society; that it thwarted scarcity, that it allowed possessions to sustain community relationships rather than divide community members, and that it lessened ecological intrusion.

The potlatch was only one of a number of native cultural practices with "conservation" overtones. Population and land-use control also promoted a sustainable landscape. Birth control practices of abortion, infanticide, and extended lactation, as well as intercourse taboos, all functioned to maintain a balance between population and resources while implying an awareness of limitations.[59]

Individuals, families, bands, and villages set boundaries that governed land use. For example, lower Columbia River natives did not wander freely in search of food but went annually to particular places where families and groups held proprietary rights. The land was not, however, individually owned with a privatized right to use or convey that land as the "owner" saw fit. Landholding existed more as a form of trusteeship that mirrored communal notions about society. Individuals gained access to the land through the group, and group controls regulated its use. Individual entitlement remained, in Paul Tennant's words, "derivative rather than primary." By "possessing" the land, the group also possessed a sense of ownership and the ability to exclude others. It was a system of use rights that not only reflected a communal culture but also contained consequences for environmental conservation. Although this kinship form of property ownership provided no guarantee against land abuse, it did create a favorable situation for limiting environmental intrusion, especially when other cultural values and structures were ordered in a conservative direction.[60]

Potlatching, population control, and familial property holding expressed cultural understandings that carried environmental consequences. Yet those practices were also shaped by the environment. Where people lived, group-living arrangements, food-collection patterns, movements of dispersal and coalescence, sociopolitical structures, concepts of property, and even social practices like potlatching depended on nature's abundance. The ways that people went about structuring their daily lives reflected the choices the environment gave them. They organized their lives according to what seemed most obvious about their environmental reality and their technology, relying on a variety of plants and animals. Native gift-exchange was just a more ritualized expression of that same quest and contained an analogous strategy for attaining security.

Adaptation to nature may also have informed Indian material culture, but the legitimation and meaning for those cultural practices came out of a particular worldview. The Indians' myths, beliefs, and values were in consonance with their physical surroundings and social ordering. Represented and strengthened in ritual, native cultural and cosmological understandings drew a symmetrical map of the natural world as a communal-organic whole. The Northwest native landscape was not a bifurcated world that distinguished rigidly between culture and nature, spirit and matter, domestic and wild. The Indian world was more integrated, and indeed the native cosmology was animistic, viewing all life forms as possessed of active spirits that could be both dangerous and helpful. Ethnobiologist Eugene Hunn captured the heart of animism and its moral claims: "People, animals, plants, and other forces of nature—sun, earth, wind, and rock—are animated by spirit. As such they share with humankind intelligence and will, and thus have moral rights and obligations as PERSONS."[61]

Belief in a spirit-filled world of powerful forces that could protect or harm a person was structured into native life. One powerful manifestation of the belief was the vision quest of adolescents. After a preparatory period of cleansing that could involve fasting, meditation, bathing, and scrubbing one's body with conifer boughs, the teenager left the village to meet the sacred. The destination was not a specific place shared by all initiates, although a mountainous forest environment was common. Most important was that the place of the encounter be clean and sacred, a space where a spirit helper would come to the initiate through a particular form of nature, such as a raven, and convey specific knowledge or special skills. Depending on the type and extent of the power conferred, a person could gain status and the means of asserting control over others. But power was not accorded just for the benefit of the individual: obligation and responsibility attended power, and it was exercised within communal bonds.[62]

The spiritual realm of Northwest Indians, no less than the physical reality of their lives, remained unpredictable and beyond human control. Stability depended on maintaining a good relationship with one's own guardian spirit and the guardian spirits of nature's creatures. To mistreat a life form moved the violator outside the mutual community of respect binding all creation together and invited punishment—possibly severe— at the hands of the spirit protector. The Snoqualmie Indians say that, according to tradition, salmon once spawned far up the Snoqualmie River. One day the people placed a fish weir across the stream. Moon witnessed the abuse and turned the weir location into Snoqualmie Falls, preventing the salmon from ever again benefiting the people upstream.[63] Humility, respect, and cooperation with nature—not egotism and domination— ensure health and well being. Just as gift giving sustained cultural ties, it also maintained the bonds between human and nonhuman life. Hunters and fishermen entered into a gift exchange with the animals and fish. Animals gave themselves up to the catch when a hunter-fisher showed proper respect and followed ritualistic ceremonial practices.

The treatment of salmon in the first salmon ceremony offers an insight into this way of looking at the world. In a carefully prescribed ceremony, the first salmon of the season is cut and eaten so the fish spirit will not be offended and thereby continue to inhabit the waters. Astorian Alexander Ross wrote:

> When the salmon make their first appearance in the river, they are never allowed to be cut crosswise, nor boiled, but roasted; nor are they allowed to be sold without the heart being first taken out, nor to be kept over night; but must be all consumed or eaten the day they are taken out of the water; all these rules are observed for about ten days. These superstitious customs perplexed us at first not a little, because they absolutely refused to sell us any unless we complied with their notions, which of course we consented to do.[64]

On May 2, 1833, Hudson's Bay Company physician William Tolmie was traveling upstream on the Columbia River from Fort George to Fort Vancouver when he stopped at a Kuhelamit village: "They had six fine salmon in a canoe, but superstitiously refused to sell any, because they were the first caught this season and it is their firm belief that if the first caught salmon are not roasted in a particular manner, the fish will desert the river."[65] U.S. Naval Lieutenant Neil Howison witnessed the ceremony and termed the practice "superstitious," but he also caught its logic and implicit conservationist consequences:

> When it is remembered that the many thousand Indians living upon this river [Columbia], throughout its course of more than twelve hundred miles, are almost entirely dependent upon salmon for their subsistence, it would lessen our surprise that these simple-minded people

should devise some propitiatory mean of retaining this inappreciable blessing.[66]

This animistic world did not preclude human use or abuse of nature. Indians cut trees, fired the land, fished, hunted, and gathered plants. Native Americans understood that one of life's great paradoxes was that to sustain life another life must be ended. Yet an animistic worldview placed limits on the rightful use and abuse of nature, whether or not these limits were always observed.

Conceptions of property embedded in native landholding and potlatching practices, then, represented deeper myths and values that constituted Indians' view of the world. By not drawing a rigidly bounded line between people and nature, nature was not objectified into "the other." Even less did Native Americans regard nature as a privately owned commodity created for trade. Animals, fish, and plants could be used, but they were not regarded as "things" or "resources" that an individual could possess. Personal ownership rights remained mostly restricted to what one produced. Accumulation beyond a certain point made little sense. Property conceptions that only seemed to "assign a nominal value to property of every kind" both startled and offended Euroamerican commentators, but to indigenous people the logic seemed sound.[67] The cultural map of indigenous Northwesterners overlay the region's ecological map, and the ecological and cultural landscapes followed common patternings. As nature and people with dynamic cultures interacted to shape one another, changes occurred but they did not disrupt the sustainability of either the cultural or the ecological systems.

The landscape that greeted Euroamericans was not, as they thought, a "virgin wilderness." Indians had long fished its waters, hunted its animals, cut down its trees, fired its forests, and collected its fruits, berries, and roots. It was a natural landscape recast by people but not genetically and biologically simplified. The human changes in the landscape flowed from a number of factors: limited technology, a restricted population base, subsistence economic practices, social structures of control, an animistic worldview, and a people generationally rooted to place. They directly experienced a dependency on nature, and their cultural structures of production and reproduction shaped and were in turn framed by the region's forest ecosystem.

Within two centuries, Euroamericans would radically transform the forest and cultural ecology of the Douglas-fir region. The changes they made so altered the web of life in the Pacific Northwest that their coming can best be termed an invasion. Native American people, along with plants and animals, found themselves transformed, severely reduced, or destroyed. Ironically, Indians who lived in locations that afforded the greatest material abundance and security were the most endangered. Groups residing along riverine systems and estuaries were most likely to have contact with Euroamericans and the most likely to be victimized by disease, competing access to the natural bounty, and land theft. With the Euroamerican invasion, life in the Douglas-fir region changed drastically, and the invaders not only transformed the indigenous landscape but themselves.

CHAPTER TWO

Fur Trade Society

Beginning in the sixteenth century, explorations to the Northwest coast by Spanish, Russian, and British ships resulted in an occasional formalized claim of sovereignty and a few observations about the land.[1] Visits, however, remained sporadic until Captain James Cook entered the Douglas-fir region in 1778. Cook inaugurated a sustained European expansion, setting in motion changes that redrew the landscape. Dramatic, even cataclysmic changes were not new to a land sculpted by glaciation and volcanic explosions, but the Europeans initiated a radically different form of change, qualitatively and quantitatively. Albeit less dramatic in its immediacy than a rain of fire and ash, the changes would prove eventually to be more powerful.

Captain Cook's voyage was part of a larger thrust outward by an England interested in global market exchanges. London and Liverpool merchant interests, as well as the crown, launched numerous global fact-finding explorations. Cook was dispatched to search for the fabled Northwest Passage, make claims on the land for England, and report on the area and its people. After locating the Hawaiian Islands, Cook sailed eastward. Bypassing both the mouth of the Columbia River and the Strait of Juan de Fuca, Cook reached Nootka Sound on Vancouver Island in 1778. He remained for about a month before journeying along the Alaskan coast and finally proceeding back to Hawaii, where natives killed him. When the ship reached England in 1780, much more than a well-traveled crew arrived. The adventurers brought information that spurred an invasion of the Northwest coast, an invasion led in many cases by persons who had first gained knowledge about the area as members of Cook's party.[2]

The information that drove Europeans to the Pacific Coast was not that the long-sought Northwest Passage had finally been located; it remained a mystery. What directed white sails to the Pacific Coast was the knowledge that the Northwest provided a natural treasure chest of wealth waiting to be opened. The most readily apparent treasure came wrapped in fur. Cook's crew, while trading with Northwest Native Americans, had exchanged European goods for sea otter pelts. Stopping off in China on their journey home, the crew received the phenomenal price of $120 for each prime fur, representing an 1,800 percent return on their investment.[3] Less apparent, but no less significant in the long run, was the Northwest's forests. Cook's men were the first Europeans to enter those forests and to fell trees for masts. Subsequent coastal traders followed Cook's lead, cutting trees for fuel and ship repairs. Eventually, when the fur trade declined in the early nineteenth century, maritime traders supplemented their fur sales with planks and spars taken from Northwest trees.[4]

With the publication of Cook's journals in 1784, the natural bounty of the Northwest became known. The isolation had ended. European contact with the region became a sustained engagement, as profit-seeking entrepreneurs sought wealth in the fur trade and competing nations struggled over ownership of the land. By the 1790s, the nations vying for the land had narrowed to two: the United States and Great Britain. Beset by European concerns and internal problems, France and Spain had largely withdrawn from the Pacific Northwest.[5] Russian enterprises, while significant along the northern coast of Alaska, remained marginal within the Douglas-fir region. That left the British and Euroamericans. Over the next half-century, the protagonists would battle for regional control.

Commercial interests from Britain may have preceded the merchant capitalists of the newly independent United States, but it did not take long for Euroamericans to enter the fray. By the late 1780s, American merchants involved themselves in a triangular Northwest trade. New England trade goods were brought to the Northwest and exchanged for furs. The furs were traded in China for a variety of items, including tea, textiles, and porcelain. Finally returning home, the Chinese products were sold to American consumers.[6]

The year 1792 proved particularly auspicious for the Pacific Northwest. British and American parties of trade and exploration drew increased attention to the area as they mapped the landscape and staked out national claims to ownership. Captain George Vancouver, acting under orders of the British government, explored the Pacific seacoast and the inner coastal waters of Puget Sound and British Columbia. Vancouver sought to bind the Northwest to England by drawing maps, claiming possession, and giving English names to the land's geography. Alexander Mackenzie of the Canadian North West Company mapped the interior as he made the first continental crossing of North America that same year.

The individual most responsible for spurring American awareness of the Pacific Northwest was former revolutionary ship captain Robert Gray. Outfitted by New England merchants, Gray made his initial voyage to the Northwest in 1790 as part of a trading venture, during which he became the first American to circumnavigate the world. On his second journey to the Northwest in May 1792, Gray entered the Great River of the West, which he named after his ship, *Columbia*. The Columbia appeared to be the hoped-for great western river whose source lay deep within the interior and that might be the natural corridor that tied the continent together. News that Gray had located the river aroused U.S. interest in the Far West and drew

American fur traders to the Pacific Northwest.[7] Just over a decade later, a U.S. expedition led by Meriwether Lewis and William Clark crossed the North American continent by land. The party descended the Columbia River and wintered on the coast at Fort Clatsop in 1805–1806, near the mouth of the Columbia, before returning to the East. Lewis and Clark did not accomplish their main directive: to find a direct and practical waterway across the continent for domestic commerce and trade with Pacific rim markets. Nonetheless, the two leaders put the best interpretation they could on that failure. If the Corps of Discovery's commercial passage proved illusionary, it did bring back new information about the people and the land of the Pacific Northwest. Increasingly, knowledge about the Douglas-fir region began to take shape as Euroamericans mapped the physical landscape according to personal and cultural expectations.[8]

The British and U.S. citizens who came to Northwest shores existed as individual competitors, but they also represented competing nations with important differences, one aspect of which was the economic structure within which the traders operated. British traders functioned inside the parameters of mercantilism. The North West Fur Company and, after 1821, the monopolistic Hudson's Bay Company structured and directed the British fur trade in the Northwest. Americans possessed no similar land-grant entitlement. Most merchants who took part in the coastal trade were New Englanders based in more of a laissez-faire market than their British competitors. National differences, however, were not as marked as their commonalities: representative forms of government, market economies, and Anglo-European cultural heritage. Thus a common stock of shared influences and ideas from the larger world shaped Pacific Northwest history.

Although competitors, "King George Men" and "Boston Men" operated within a common landscape of geography and market exchange. Each nation's commercial adventurers were components of an expanding capitalist economy, and they saw the Northwest as an unowned land filled with extractive goods. Personal and national histories certainly colored the lens through which individual traders viewed the Pacific Northwest, but the rivals shared cultural understandings that framed what they saw when they looked at the Northwest landscape. It was a vision that often differed from the view held by the land's native inhabitants.

Maritime explorers and traders took a particular interest in mapping the region's rivers, bays, and harbors. Moreover, being traders, they also directed their attention toward cataloging "resources" that nature seemed to have so lavishly bestowed on the Pacific Coast.[9] Although soil and weather were not the focal points they would be for settlers, they did receive attention, especially when fur companies began to establish trading settlements. Most early Euroamericans drew a clear distinction between the coast and interior areas. Few people found the coastal weather appealing, but the drier inland valleys drew favorable comment, including the following observation by Alexander Ross: "The climate of this [Willamette] valley is salubrious and dry, differing materially from that of the sea-coast; and the heat is sufficiently intense to ripen every kind of grain in a short time."[10] Less rain was not the only reason to favor the country's interior valleys. Euroamericans were comfortable with the physical and mental geography the valleys provided; over and over again, they extolled the mixed landscape of water, woodlands, and grass. Beauty lay in structured diversity, where clear boundaries of harmonized distinctions seemed to establish control and order.[11] Besides, a well-watered, fertile land that was open and parklike promised material rewards with a minimum of labor. In 1838, Hudson's Bay Company's James Douglas remarked: "The aspect of the country, in its natural state is strikingly beautiful. The intermixture of woods & fertile plains, peculiarly adapts it for the residence of civilized man, affording lands easily tilled, excellent pasture, fuel and building materials of the best quality."[12] In contradistinction to this ordered physical and mental landscape stood the region's forests. Like the sea or the prairies of the Great Plains, Pacific Northwest forests presented an undifferentiated landscape.

Never before had the fur traders seen such dense undergrowth and trees of such size. Felling those giants severely tested even skilled woodsmen, and the trees clearly overmatched the men attached to the fur trade. After two months of labor and two workers injured by falling trees, barely one acre of ground was cleared at Astoria. Alexander Ross's 1811 vivid description of the work, dangers, and problems associated with cutting down the huge trees typifies forest land clearing in the Pacific Northwest during the early nineteenth century:

> After placing our guns in some secure place at hand, and viewing the height and the breadth of the tree to be cut down, the party, with some labour, would erect a scaffold round it; this done, four men—for that was the number appointed to each of those huge trees—would then mount the scaffold, and commence cutting, at the height of eight or ten feet from the ground. . . . Indeed, it sometimes required two days, or more, to fell one tree. . . . So thick was the forest, and so close the trees together, that in its fall it would often rest its ponderous top on some other friendly tree . . . giving us double labour to extricate the one from the other, and when we had so far succeeded, the removal of the monster stump was the work of days. The tearing up of the roots was equally arduous, although less dangerous: and when this last operation was got through, both tree and stump had to be blown to pieces by gunpowder before either could be removed from the spot.[13]

Even for those not directly involved in the arduous task of trying to cut down the immense trees, the forests of the Pacific Northwest seemed a barrier and a threat. The ubiquitous forests virtually eliminated land travel and often hampered water transportation as well. Underbrush of chinquapin, devil's club, 15- to 20-foot-high rhododendron, salal, and 3- to 10-foot-high ferns, dense tree growth, and downed trees in varying stages of decay made traveling through the forest next to impossible. Trunks and branches of downed trees obstructed streams. Some obstructions reached enormous proportions, such as the upper log jam on the Skagit River that measured a half-mile long.[14]

When Euroamericans looked out on the Northwest forests, therefore, they did not see an ecosystem that sustained the "resources" they valued. Instead, sojourners to the Pacific Coast saw a massive green barrier that they described as monotonous, interminable, gloomy, somber, dark, wild, and savage.[15] Physician William Tolmie, journeying on the Columbia River from Fort George to Fort Vancouver, captured those sentiments in a May 2, 1833, journal entry:

> The scenery along the banks has been of a monotonous character—a dense & unbroken forest of pines covers them and the surrounding hills—the only interruption to this is where low sandy points project, these clothed with stunted willows & bushes, afford by their verdure a pleasant relief to the eye tired with the sombre gloominess of the wilderness in the background.[16]

Without clearly differentiated lines, forests were not merely a barrier but a place, in the words of early Washington pioneer George Savage, where the "silent maddening Solitude of the unbroken forests . . . seemed to scare you and fill you with an unspeakable dread and terror."[17] Lacking perceptible, distinct boundaries, forests seemed chaotic and dangerous, perhaps even harboring wild people and animals. The forests not only represented a threat, but their lack of differentiation provided such a blurred vision that Euroamericans often did not see the forest for the trees. Indeed, they did not even see trees. What they saw was timber.[18] But forest exploitation had to wait.

During the late eighteenth and early nineteenth centuries, competition between American and British traders for sea otter and beaver skins was intense. The trade was a maritime enterprise, which, by 1800, the Americans would come to dominate. After 1811, the pattern began to change. In that year, John Jacob Astor sponsored the first American land-based trading enterprise to Northwest shores. Near where Lewis and Clark spent their Oregon winter, the American Fur Company established a fort named Astoria, after the company's owner. Fort Astoria turned out to be a short-lived enterprise, beset with internal problems and bad timing. The War of 1812 broke out shortly after the fort was established, making the isolated and unprotected enterprise vulnerable to the British navy. Aware of its precarious situation, American Fur Company employees sold the post to the North West Company in the fall of 1813. The Montreal-based, Canadian-fortified North West Company—which renamed the post Fort George—had better luck than its predecessor. Throughout the decade, the company extended its control over the inner reaches of the Northwest (although American maritime traders continued to dominate the coastal trade). By the early 1820s, that American presence had faded before a well-orchestrated British onslaught that reached a crescendo in 1821 when the North West Company merged with the powerful Hudson's Bay Company. Individual Americans simply could not compete against the company's capital and expertise. Although American maritime and land-based traders would subsequently penetrate the Northwest, their ventures would never seriously challenge the company's hegemony.[19]

Control of the fur trade was not confined to the struggle between the United States and Britain. Early on, ultimate control rested with the native peoples who lived on the land. Only because indigenous people were willing participants in exchange did a fur trade exist at all. Charles Wilkes captured a degree of truth when he commented that the "self-interest of the Indians is . . . the true safeguard of the white traders."[20]

The exchange of goods was nothing new to Northwest people, who long ago had established extensive trade networks along which people and goods traveled.[21] Trade with merchant capitalists seemed merely to be an extension of existing exchange patterns with the expectation of new, highly desired goods. The number and range of those new trade articles were limited and were not intended to transform traditional society but to complement and enhance existing cultural patterns, for the use and meanings attached to the goods were not Euroamerican but native. The exchange itself occurred within a traditional context of gift giving primarily conducted by traditional leaders. The goods traded symbolized social standing and, more important, usually carried a utility value that made life easier: fabrics that were both colorful and warm; molasses that sweetened foods; metal tools that held a sharp edge; guns; glass beads; and pieces of iron and copper that could be used for decoration.[22]

If control over the fur trade was not restricted to Euroamericans, neither was trade competition. Native groups vied among themselves to control access to traders. By securing a monopolistic intermediary position between Euroamerican traders and native groups, prospective native middlemen hoped to extend their power and material wealth. Middlemen sometimes physically kept other Indians from directly trading with Euroamericans, or they spread frightening tales about Euroamerican practices to dissuade possible rival groups from direct trade with whites.[23]

Euroamerican traders quickly discovered that Northwest peoples were very astute bargainers. The Indians demanded that white trade items be of high quality. Noting the sharp rise in the cost of British manufactured goods since 1836, for example, Governor George Simpson suggested that the Hudson's Bay Company trade a lower-quality blanket for furs. Chief Factor John McLoughlin successfully opposed the strategy, acknowledging native people's independence and high standards. Native Americans were also serious about obtaining the highest return possible for their trade goods. In 1831, McLoughlin reported that Columbia District returns for 1830–1831 had declined from the previous year because "the Indians exerted themselves more than usual in 1829/30 in consequence of the reduction of the price of Goods." In addition, Northwest Indians skillfully exploited the British-American rivalry to obtain high fur prices and independence. The problem with this system was that it lasted only as long as the competitive situation prevailed. Nevertheless, even when the Hudson's Bay Company exercised a virtual fur trade monopoly in the Northwest, the Indians' bargaining position was only weakened, not destroyed.[24]

The early fur trade, then, developed partially because of mutuality. Native people prized Euroamerican trade items, and whites valued Indians as trading allies and sexual partners. Historian Richard White has termed this situation "the middle ground."[25] Chinook Jargon, a trading vocabulary formed from a linguistic blending of many languages, typified that "middle ground." Coastal Indians developed Chinook Jargon to facilitate trade among themselves even before Euroamericans entered the trade.[26] The new language and self-interest allowed Native American and Euroamerican to meet on a common terrain. Conflicts and misunderstandings occurred, but basically the traders adopted an accommodating position toward one another for their mutual benefit.

Market forces impinged upon the lives of native people, but they did not become avid trappers or dependent on Euroamerican goods. Limited needs and cultural ideals, including the value of competitive play, kept Indians from maximizing their hunting efforts. Isolation from trading posts was also a factor. James Douglas of the Hudson's Bay Company acknowledged that "we have few opportunities of acquiring influence over [the] . . . minds" of native people who lived far from the company's forts.[27] In fact, the abundant natural resources that made profits possible also checked natives' interest in profit making. The Indians were able to have food, shelter, and clothing with a modicum of work. British and Anglo-American commentators were quick to acknowledge the association between the land's abundance and native work habits, a link they consistently decried. Alexander Ross wrote:

The productiveness of their country [the Willamette Valley] is, probably, the chief cause of their extreme apathy and indolence; for it
requires so little exertion to provide for their wants that even that little
is not attended to; . . . the Indians throughout are so notoriously lazy
that they can hardly be prevailed upon to hunt or do anything else that
requires exertion.[28]

American naval purser William Slacum agreed, lamenting that "the ease
with which they procure food, fish, and fowl, . . . the 'Wapspitoo' [Wapato]
and 'Kamass' engenders the most indolent habits among these people."[29]
James Douglas wanted his workers to "endeavour to rouse the Indians to
more active habits, and train their energies to useful pursuits"—that is, helping to increase company profits.[30] Douglas's desire went largely unfulfilled.

With an abundance of plants, animals, and fish, Native Americans sustained a vibrant subsistence economy. Indeed, Euroamericans often
depended on the Indians for articles of sustenance rather than the other
way around. More importantly, because native peoples' resource base was
rich and continued under their control during the period of fur trade, they
did not become dependent on the market economy.[31] The exchange of furs
for Euroamerican goods was just one part of the extensive trade relationships they had long used to enhance their lives. Security meant obtaining
food and other goods from diverse sources and alliance networks. To find
safety in a life devoted to intensive market hunting did not seem reasonable, nor did it seem consonant with animism. New York lawyer John Ball,
who served as Oregon's first schoolteacher and farmed briefly on French
Prairie between his arrival in 1832 and his departure the following year,
may have only implicitly grasped that point, but he certainly caught its
environmental implications:

On the streams, especially in the mountains region, we found land
otter, mink, rats, and the sole object of the traders long journey to that
region—the Beaver—These were very numerous till, their number has
been diminished by white trappers—the business of which people is
always to exterminate every native animal—for the Indian spare the
young and take not life wantonly—unless sometimes their captives.[32]

But the Indians' control of the trade was short-lived, and the benefits
of exchange were eventually overwhelmed by the costs, some of which
were absorbed, delayed, or disguised, but one of which was implacable
and inescapable: disease. Coastal traders transported disease organisms to
the Pacific Coast as unconsciously as they brought their culture. European
trade and death, however unintended, proved to be synergistic arrivals—
materially and symbolically, physically and culturally. The importation of

trade goods and disease proved costly, and those costs were borne by the native population.

Not that native peoples were free from medical problems prior to white contact. Chinook peoples of the lower Columbia River, for example, suffered from strokes that quite possibly were related to their rich, oily marine food diet. But the deadly pathogens of smallpox, chicken pox, malaria, influenza, dysentery, whooping cough, typhus, typhoid fever, and measles, along with venereal disease, were unknown to Native Americans before the coastal trade.[33] The Amerindians had spent an extended period in a semiarctic environment, and the cold had killed the pathogens that had accompanied them to North America from Asia. In addition, the harsh, far northern environment had eliminated people who were weakest and disease prone. Native peoples then lived and propagated in isolation for generations, further distancing themselves from foreign microbes. As a result, the Indians lacked an immune system of antibodies with which to combat the biological invasion that occurred alongside the Euroamerican cultural invasion. Thus disease facilitated Euroamerican military, economic, and cultural dominance over the Pacific Northwest.[34]

The spread of diseases among Pacific Coast natives during the late eighteenth century was like the species harvesting of the trader society, destructive but limited. Smallpox, which apparently first broke out during the 1770s with the onset of maritime contact, is conservatively estimated to have killed about 30 percent of the native population. Its reintroduction among a new generation of Clatsop Indians in 1800–1801, according to William Clark, took another heavy toll.[35] Then, starting in 1830 and continuing through 1836, an "intermittent fever" that was probably malaria struck the Fort Vancouver area every summer. The fever created widespread sickness among the white population, but it killed the Indians. John McLoughlin estimated that 75 percent of the native population in the Fort Vancouver area died during the first summer outbreak of the fever. Subsequent annual appearances of the fever killed many more. On May 19, 1833, Doctor Tolmie wrote in his diary that the fever had "almost depopulated [the] Columbia R. of the aborigines." William Slacum visited western Oregon in the mid-1830s and wrote that of forty descendants of the great Clatsop leader Concomly not one was still alive.[36] In 1835, John Kirk Townsend painted a similarly bleak picture:

> Probably there does not now exist one, where, five years ago, there were a hundred Indians; and in sailing up the [Columbia] river, from the cape to the cascades, the only evidence of the existence of the Indian, is an occasional miserable wigwam, with a few wretched, half-starved occupants. In some other places they are rather more numerous; but the thoughtful observer cannot avoid perceiving that in a very few years

the race must, in the nature of things, become extinct; and the time is probably not far distant, when the little trinkets and toys of this people will be picked up by the curious, and valued as mementoes of a nation passed away for ever from the face of the earth. . . . It seems as if the fiat of the Creator had gone forth, that these poor denizens of the forest and the stream should go hence, and be seen of men no more.[37]

Roman Catholic priest François Blanchet, writing a decade after McLoughlin, estimated that 90 percent of the Indians had died of disease. In the mid-1840s, Father Pierre-Jean De Smet, SJ, guessed that 67 percent had perished. Modern scholars estimate that between 1830 and 1841, Indians from the lower Columbia River suffered a 92 percent loss of population due to disease. People north of the river could not escape the microbes either. James Douglas reported that a large percentage of Indians had died at the Hudson's Bay Company Cowlitz establishment, and Charles Wilkes reported a similar decimation of the native population around Nisqually.[38] Euroamerican traders aggravated the situation by passing on syphilis to the natives and by giving them alcohol. The exchange of disease and goods, then, held out important environmental and cultural consequences for the people of the Douglas-fir region.

One immediate result of the introduction of disease was a shift in control over territory and trade. Native northwesterners already had more than a passing familiarity with the appropriation of territory by one people from another. Territorial boundaries between native groups existed as fluid lines that had long ebbed and flowed. What Euroamerican-introduced diseases touched off, however, was a new process of territorial adjustments. Decimation and weakness of some native groups meant opportunity for others who had survived the epidemics with substantial numbers intact. Disease created an ecological niche into which those pioneering Indian groups moved. Sometimes, one group would move onto land vacated by a group that had simply died out. At other times, a disease-weakened people would be physically displaced by a stronger group.

The Klickitats are a classic example of conquest and displacement. Prior to Euroamerican contact, the Klickitats lived east of the Cascade Mountains in southeastern Washington. Although Klickitats journeyed to Celilo Falls on the Columbia River for salmon and traveled to the Cascades to hunt and gather berries and nuts, they were basically a mounted people of the Columbia Plain.[39] When disease took its toll on westside natives, the Klickitats saw their opportunity to expand into the resource-rich Douglas-fir region. What they had previously obtained through trade they could now gain through conquest. People reduced and weakened by disease proved no match for these mounted, skilled gunmen from the east who swept over the Cascades in the 1830s.

The Klickitats established a village along the Columbia River, on Sauvie's Island (west of present-day Portland), and entered the Willamette Valley sometime after 1839. Eventually, they extended south to the Umpqua River and north as far as Mount Baker. The Klickitat presence had environmental consequences. As a horse culture, the tribe placed a new domestic grazer to the land. There are also indications that Klickitats hunted deer and elk more extensively than the previous residents had. They enriched themselves through environmental extraction and by seizing control of the lucrative east-west trade along the Columbia River. By the 1840s, Klickitats were one of the richest Indian people on the Pacific coast, and they remained so until their ordered removal from the Willamette Valley by U.S. Indian Superintendent Joel Palmer in 1854.[40] Disease thus inaugurated changes between Euroamericans and Amerindians and brought intergroup adjustments as well, thus altering a landscape that created new paths and deepened and redesigned older ones.

In the 1820s, Hudson's Bay Company ordered its field representatives to exterminate valued fur animals. It was a conscious policy of destruction designed to forestall U.S. competition, to ensure company control over the Northwest fur trade, and to secure profits. By creating a fur desert around the boundaries of the Pacific Northwest, the company hoped to dissuade American land-based trapping parties from moving into the area. This plan would leave the country, especially the interior north, free of fur competitors. Governor George Simpson summarized the policy in a July 1827 letter to Chief Factor McLoughlin:

> The greatest and best protection we can have from opposition is keeping the country closely hunted as the first step that the American Government will take towards Colonization is through their Indian Traders and if the country becomes exhausted in Fur bearing animals they can have no inducement to proceed thither. We therefore entreat that no exertions be spared to explore and Trap every part of the country.[41]

Sovereignty and profits were closely aligned in the company's policy of destruction. U.S. geopolitical interests in the Pacific Northwest had been growing during the early nineteenth century and by the 1820s seemed to supersede those of Great Britain. With the 1818 joint-occupation agreement between Britain and the United States set to expire in 1828, it was increasingly likely that the Columbia River would mark the geopolitical territory with the United States claiming land to the south and Britain taking the land to the north. As a result, Hudson's Bay Company believed that it made good economic as well as political sense to thoroughly hunt an area that might fall under American control. In 1825, the company's Columbia Department was instructed "to work the southern portion of the Country as hard as possible, while it continues free to the subjects of both Nations." Governor Simpson was told that "it is extremely desirable to hunt as bare as possible all the Country South of the Columbia and West of the Mountains." John McLoughlin suggested increasing the number of trappers south of the Columbia River so that an estimated 12,000 beaver might be killed each year before the joint-occupation agreement expired.[42] As it turned out, joint occupancy was not resolved by 1828. On August 6, 1827, British and American negotiators signed an agreement to extend joint occupation into an indefinite future. But that political decision and the final resolution of the boundary line in 1846 lay in the future. What the Hudson's Bay Company faced in the 1820s was an uncertain present.

Political machinations and decisions concerning economic markets thousands of miles from the Northwest had a profound impact on the region. In 1806, Meriwether Lewis wrote that beaver and otter were "tolerably plenty" near the coast and along inland creeks and rivers. Five years later, Alexander Ross remarked on the abundance of beaver in the Cascade Range. Within two decades there was a noticeable difference. By 1825, British botanist David Douglas was struck by the scarcity of beaver in a Willamette Valley area where they had once been abundant. Subsequent visitors to the Northwest similarly commented on the absence of fur-bearing animals. James Douglas noted that the decline was particularly extensive from Fort Vancouver to northern California, where "of late years, [the land has been] closely hunted and is now greatly impoverished."[43] Areas north of the Columbia River and east of the Cascades also experienced a sharp decline in marketable fur animals, even though the Hudson's Bay Company controlled most of the fur trade in those areas.

By the early 1840s, the Pacific Northwest fur trade was clearly in decline, the result of new consumer preference for silk over beaver hats, low reproductivity of beaver and otters, and overhunting. The demise of the fur trade did not come as a complete surprise to the Hudson's Bay Company. George Simpson reported that the number of beaver pelts traded at Fort George and Fort Vancouver fell from 6,000 in 1822 to half that number in 1827. William Tolmie observed on May 12, 1833, that the North West Company, with a restricted land base, exported more furs in 1792 than HBC was presently sending from all of Canada despite "an almost exterminating system of hunting."[44]

As the decline set in, maritime traders began to supplement furs with a variety of exchange items from coastal Indians. Hudson's Bay Company began exporting a greater diversity of items, but it also developed organizational and market strategies that included marketing a diversification of the animal skins.[45] Hunting was intensified in an attempt to compensate for a declining animal population, further ensuring animal extermination and ecological change. This assault upon a few targeted species might seem myopic from the ecological perspective of the late twentieth century, but it did make sense from a market-directed, short-term, profit-maximizing vantage point.

Competition could easily be made the culprit in this tale of destruction, and some commentators have made that claim. William Slacum in the 1830s and Charles Wilkes in the following decade implicitly linked the overexploitation of beaver and other fur-bearing animals to competitive ruthlessness. Wilkes contrasted the situation in the south with that in the north (above the 48th parallel), where the monopoly control of the Hudson's Bay Company seemingly prevented such destruction.[46] A modern investigator into the British Columbia fur trade has more clearly linked competition with devastation and monopoly landownership and control with conservation.[47] Other analysts have noted a similar pattern. What these researchers collectively detail is the "tragedy of the commons," popularized in the 1970s by biologist Garrett Hardin. When resources are held in common and controlled by no one, Hardin contends, overexploitation and ruin are inevitable because there is little incentive for restraint. Even when there are individuals who limit their use of a resource, other competitors simply move in to use that resource and gain an advantage.[48]

Clearly, the Pacific Northwest offered a commons to Britain and the United States. With both nations claiming rights to the land but with neither wishing to push their claims to a point where armed conflict could arise, the joint-occupation treaty formalized a competitive situation that muted economic structural differences and guaranteed that the land and resources would be free for the taking. Here was an open land, rich in natural resources and unencumbered by rental costs. Conservation or concerns about future species reproduction made little sense in the midst of resource abundance, a "commons," and market imperatives. The results closely resembled Hardin's scenario.

Although regulatory restriction seems important in preventing environmental disruption, neither private property rights, state-held property, nor even communal property holding guaranteed ecological protection. The cultural values and beliefs that underlay property relationships is critical, for property ownership offers little protection against exploitation wherever profit maximization governs decision making.[49] Overexploitation occurred even where the Hudson's Bay Company, for example, held a monopoly, for the company tied promotions and pensions to profits, thereby encouraging resource exploitation.[50] The exploitation of beaver and otter in the Northwest was more than the "natural" consequence of contending political and economic forces over a "commons"; the exploitation was grounded in its historical and cultural context.

Both Euroamericans and Native Americans desired security, safety, and prestige, but they went about achieving their goals differently. Native people sought those ends through extensive practices of subsistence, alliance, and wealth distribution. Euroamerican traders pursued their goals by intensive hunting, selling furs, and accumulating wealth. Each group's practices held an internal logic. Native Americans followed a logic of adaptation, diversity, extensive relationships, trade, and animism. Euroamerican fur traders, by contrast, adopted a market logic. This geography of capital framed the way early explorer-traders imagined the land and legitimized its invasion. First it was animal species; later it was faunal and floral species. Market calculations left little room for other values. The worth of a species did not rest in its own structure and function as part of an ecological whole but in its extracted economic worth. The market was natural; human dominance was natural. Nature was a passive object, awaiting fulfillment. Completion came when nature was extracted, transformed, and made into something purposeful. Like humanity itself, natural species were objectified and measured according to economic worth. Ecologies of nature and culture were mirrored in these changes.

Otter and beaver felt the consequences of the changes most severely, but native people also experienced an altered world with the arrival of the Euroamericans. During the fur-trade era, however, the ecological and cultural changes were withstood. A bountiful and resilient ecology along with a small Euroamerican presence that extracted a narrow range of species limited the loss of habitat and restricted ecological intrusion. That fact, combined with Native Americans' ability to direct hunting-trading activities and their lack of reliance on beaver or otter, also slowed cultural impairment and dependency during the early period of contact. Not until the 1830s did disease, death, alcohol abuse, intensified social stratification, and a limited dependency on external political-economic forces begin to be widely seen.[51] As tragic as those experiences were, they were less a sign of cultural collapse than a harbinger of future tragedy. The trader society had prepared the way for a succession of Euroamericans who would settle on the land. Those newcomers would order and define the land in new and different ways, transforming once again the cultural and physical landscape of the Pacific Northwest.

CHAPTER THREE

Nature's Society

Settler society in the Northwest began during the 1840s with sustained migration and settlement of Euroamericans in the Douglas-fir region. Settlers would dominate Northwest life until the 1880s, when their culture would give way to an industrial society of transcontinental railroads, industrial lumbering, large-scale capital investments, urbanization, metropolitan control over hinterlands, and the bureaucratization of business and government. Not even industrialization, however, would displace settler cultural patterns, which governed the region's culture into the twentieth century.[1] Northwest settlement was the westernmost extension of an expansionist nation that viewed itself as exceptional, called by God to be a "city upon a hill." Americans thought of themselves as a covenanted people who inhabited a promised land of abundance—but nature still had to be subdued. Settlers turned the environment that Leo Marx termed a "gardened middle landscape" into what might be more aptly termed a "systematized landscape."[2]

The fur-trade society had prepared the way for settlers. From the region's first Euroamerican settlement at Astoria, Hudson's Bay Company reached out and established settlement posts in the hinterland. The company built a short-lived fur trading post along the Umpqua River in the early 1820s. By 1837, crops, cattle, and swine were being raised there.[3] The company also moved north into present-day British Columbia, establishing posts at Fort Langley on the Fraser River in 1827 and Fort Victoria on Vancouver Island in 1849, where agricultural and grazing enterprises defrayed costs and secured a measure of independence from the Indians.[4]

"Free trappers" from the Astoria enterprise and a few former North West Company men settled at French Prairie in the Willamette Valley between the fall of 1827 and 1830. Retired Hudson's Bay Company employees joined them around 1830. Until then, the company had opposed former workers' settlement in the Northwest. Terms of their employment actually required their return to eastern Canada when they completed their service. Former French Canadians, however, had married local native women and wanted to remain in the region. Chief Factor John McLoughlin came to believe that any forcible attempt to return the men to Canada would only create a hostile and disgruntled cadre who might enter into common cause with Anglo Americans. The company agreed, and retirees became an important counterweight to Anglo-American influence in the region.[5]

As the fur trade declined, the Hudson's Bay Company's Columbia District developed an increasing interest in farming and animal husbandry. Both John McLoughlin and James Douglas concluded that the company's future in the Pacific Northwest lay in crops and livestock, not fur. During a Sunday ride with McLoughlin on May 12, 1833, William Tolmie wrote in his journal:

> [McLoughlin] thinks that when the trade in furs is knocked up which at no very distant day must happen, the servants of Coy, may turn their attention to the rearing of cattle for the sake of the hides & tallow, in which he says business could be carried on to a greater amount, than that of the furs collected west of the Rocky Mountains.[6]

McLoughlin's views no doubt sprang from his awareness of the lucrative tallow and hide trade in Mexican California.[7] Douglas echoed the same sentiments in 1838: "If we could succeed in covering the plains of the Columbia with flocks of sheep, we may provide a valuable succedaneum for Beaver, and open a much more extensive trade than the present."[8] In 1839, the Hudson's Bay Company established the Puget's Sound Agricultural Company. A de facto subsidiary of its parent but a legally separate enterprise, the new company had posts on Puget Sound at Nisqually plains and Cowlitz prairie.[9]

Cowlitz was an arable, level, undulating prairie of camas, flowers, and coarse grass. It was a land, wrote Charles Wilkes, "ready for the plough," a place that seemed "to invite the husbandman." The first furrows at Cowlitz prairie were turned in 1839, and, by 1841, 600 to 700 acres were under cultivation. Wheat yielded particularly well, averaging about 20 bushels per acre, for a total of 7,000 bushels. In 1847, at its most productive, Cowlitz farm produced 10,000 bushels of wheat annually and supported 700 cattle, 130 horses, and 2,000 sheep. The Cowlitz prairie area would become a mecca for former Hudson's Bay employees north of the Columbia River.[10]

The Nisqually plain was a 30-square-mile area between the Cascades and Puget Sound, bounded north and south by the Puyallup and Nisqually rivers. Terraces 10 to 40 feet high, interspersed with parklike groves of poplar, aspen, ash, maple, and a few pines and oaks, dotted the level land. The Hudson's Bay Company had established the first Euroamerican settlement in the area when it built Fort Nisqually to tap the Puget Sound fur trade in 1833. At the fort, agriculture and grazing supported the fur trade, and, by the winter of 1840–1841, most company property holdings at Nisqually were transferred to the Puget's Sound Agricultural Company. The soil at Nisqually was light and dry, but it did produce a nutritious, short, tender grass that made the area well-suited to rearing stock. In 1841, Nisqually farm supported approximately 4,530 sheep and 1,000 cattle; by midcentury, the numbers had risen to nearly 10,000 sheep and 6,000 to 7,000 cattle. At its height, the enterprise grazed perhaps 17,000 sheep and 8,000 cattle.[11]

The Cowlitz and Nisqually farms formed the settlement wheel spokes of Hudson's Bay Company's Columbia District. The hub, and the region's dominant farming-ranching center, was Fort Vancouver. Until 1825, Fort George had been the region's fur depot, but in that year Hudson's Bay moved its central establishment one hundred miles to the east. George Simpson chose the north bank of the Columbia River for the new fort in anticipation that the United States–British North American territorial boundary would be drawn along this natural divide. The removal to Fort Vancouver placed the company entrepot closer to the interior fur trade and nearer the Willamette River drainage system and provided a locale where farming and grazing could be carried on to defray company food costs.[12]

The Fort Vancouver herd started with 3 bulls, 23 cows, 5 heifers, and 9 steers. By spring 1837 that number totaled 229 cows, 58 bulls, 178 oxen and steers, 61 heifers, and 159 calves. There were also 15 rams, 361 ewes and wethers, and 142 lambs. The company divided the herd in 1838, keeping one portion at Fort Vancouver, another group pastured eighteen miles to the west and on the south bank of the Columbia, and others removed to Sauvie's Island where the company operated a dairy. Imported breeding stock improved the quality of the animals, and by 1841 Fort Vancouver had some 3,000 cattle, 2,500 sheep, and 300 brood mares. To avoid predators, the stock was penned at night, and, to further soil fertility through manuring, the pens were moved every night. The company also sowed and harvested grain crops that were ground into flour or distilled into whiskey—until 1836, when McLoughlin had the distillery destroyed because it produced "bad effects." By 1846, at the end of joint U.S.-British occupancy, the Hudson's Bay Company cultivated 1,420 acres of land near Fort Vancouver.[13]

The Hudson's Bay Company and the Puget's Sound Agricultural Company's pastoral and farming enterprises gave a different face to the land. Manuring and crop rotation sustained soil fertility, but they also displaced indigenous plants and animals with a new "nature" of domesticated crops, animals, and grasses. Perhaps even more important, Hudson's Bay's successes drew settlers into the region. The company offered support for incoming emigrants who might have otherwise perished and provided the newcomers with imported goods at reasonable prices.[14] It was a prologue to and an impetus towards the future.

The American fur-trade enterprises, too, demonstrated a direct link between trader and settler society. Fort Astoria's agricultural pursuits had been directly tied to the fur trade. Subsequent American ventures followed that pattern, with land-based settlements emerging to support and extend the trade. Following the Astoria experience, Nathaniel J. Wyeth made the next American attempt to establish a settlement in the Douglas-fir region, first in 1832 and again in 1834 at Sauvie's Island. Like Astor, Wyeth intended settlement efforts to be an auxiliary to his fur-trade scheme. And though Wyeth's economic enterprise failed, it was successful in drawing Americans' attention to the region, popularizing the land route over which most overlanders entered Oregon (the Oregon Trail), and establishing an American presence at a time when few of the members of the 1834 Wyeth party chose to settle in the region. A group of Methodist missionaries led by Jason Lee joined those initial American settlers in 1834, erecting a central mission and various satellite posts throughout the Willamette Valley. Congregational and Presbyterian missionaries soon followed to establish posts on the Tualatin Plains in 1840–1841. Protestants achieved little in the way of converting native inhabitants, but they did succeed in adding to the farming population and the U.S. presence in the Northwest. Anglo-Americans increased over the next decade and, with the nascent British population, formed the core of early Northwest settler society.[15]

Early emigrés both populated the Northwest and popularized the region. The published writings of government-sponsored exploration and survey parties to the region, lectures by adventurers who had visited the North Pacific Coast, and American emigrant letters to family and friends generally described the country in glowing terms. In the border states of Missouri, Iowa, Illinois, and Indiana, John Minto remembered, "Lewis and Clark's journal was read and passed from hand to hand for information till worn out."[16] Dartmouth College graduate John Ball came to Oregon with the Wyeth expedition in 1832, remained until October 1833, and then returned to Troy, New York, where he practiced law and gave lectures about Oregon. Philip L. Edwards lived in Oregon from 1834 to 1838 before returning east where he, too, stimulated an interest in Oregon colonization. George Riddle remembered that his father, William, decided to emigrate after hearing the glowing account of Oregon that Illinois neighbor Isaac Constant gave upon his return from the Northwest. Few proponents, however, matched the efforts of Hall Jackson Kelley. Through lectures, writings, and memorials to Congress, as well as by organizing the American Society for Encouraging the Settlement of the Oregon Territory, Kelley sought to popularize and colonize the Oregon Country.[17]

Personal correspondence about Oregon often reached an audience beyond friends and family by being printed in local newspapers. Some, like settler-promoter Peter Burnett, wrote letters designed to appear in the *New York Herald*, the *Ohio Statesman*, the *St. Louis Reporter*, and the *Washington Globe*. Books, broadsides, and travel guides appeared throughout the 1830s and 1840s, drawing people west and shaping their ideas about

Oregon. Phoebe Judson and Michael Luark acknowledged that their first acquaintance with the region came through reading Methodist minister Gustavus Hines's book on Oregon before coming overland in 1853. All these writings circulated widely, mapping the Douglas-fir region into the lives and imaginations of the American public. Even addresses by people who had never even been to Oregon inflamed people's imaginations and desire to migrate.[18]

In 1840, Joel P. Walker's family became the first to travel overland for the expressed purpose of settlement. The Walker emigration is a fitting symbol of transition from fur to settler society, for leading Joel's party was his famous brother, trapper and explorer Joseph Walker. Few Americans followed the Walkers until the "Great Migration" of 1843. Amid a rising tide of "Oregon fever," Americans swept westward under the banner of "manifest destiny," with around 800 Americans moving into the Willamette Valley that year. By the fall of 1845, 4,000 to 5,000 Americans were living in the Willamette Valley.[19]

The overlanders had regional and cultural characteristics. Most emigrants living in the Willamette Valley by 1850 had been born in the border states of Arkansas, Iowa, Missouri, Illinois, Ohio, and Indiana. The overwhelming proportion of former border state residents, 85 percent, were rural Oregonians. The predominantly single, male Mid-Atlantic and New England emigrants dominated the towns.[20] A similar pattern also prevailed outside the Willamette Valley. New Englander Silas Plimpton proudly wrote that in Rainier, Oregon, "all our business men . . . are Yankees." Massachusetts newspaperman Samuel Bowles, traveling through Oregon in the mid-1860s, observed that "the agricultural population are largely Missourians, Kentuckians, and Tennesseeans." But "Eastern men . . . of whom there are indeed many," noted the decidedly biased Bowles, "are mostly in the villages and towns, leaders in trade and commerce and manufactures, as well as in the professions." During the early 1850s, this settlement pattern was observed north of the Columbia River, as well.[21]

Emigrants to the Northwest sought both an escape from their current situation and an opportunity to gain something they did not presently possess. People came, in the words of 1847 emigrant Ralph Geer, "for the purpose of finding a better country to live in."[22] In pursuit of that better life, emigrants were pushed and pulled by a variety of motives and inducements that reflected personal experiences, family background, and cultural hearths.

Those seeking homesteads were drawn to Oregon by hints of generous government land grants. In 1821, Senator John Floyd of Virginia had been the first to introduce into Congress a large land-grant provision to attract settlers to the Oregon country. Later Oregon bills contained land-grant proposals for up to 1,000 acres. In 1843, a bill granting 640 acres plus

160 acres for each child in a family passed the Senate. Despite its defeat in the House, it "afforded great encouragement to potential emigrants." Colonel Michael T. Simmons, who would go to Oregon in 1844, believed the Donation Land bill "or a law like it, will pass, and I am going to Oregon anyhow." From Oregon, William Shaw later commented that the "bill in Congress . . . was the first start that set me to thinking of coming here." Similarly, 1850 emigrant Mary Hayden remembered "hearing my father talk about the Oregon land grant as early as 1844, when it was being agitated in Congress."[23] Chauvinistic desires to secure U.S. title to the Oregon Country and to advance civilization were constant refrains. The Pacific Northwest was the newest "west" of opportunity, inspiring the latest march in the westward course of empire where open space and opportunity were said to allow the fullest development of character, social equality, political democracy, and economic improvement.[24]

Another factor in emigration was the urge to flee the institution of slavery. The largely free, white working-class that migrated into Oregon desired independence and competency. They were a people who wanted to avoid competing against slave labor, and to escape the degradation of labor that black slavery symbolized.[25] In Oregon Country, those settlers dealt with the paradox between freedom and slavery with legal statutes of exclusion and racist appeals to biological imprinting.

Some settlers traveled to Oregon to escape the chains of debt and failed relationships; still others sought escape from the midwestern climate.[26] The seemingly constant floods and periodic malarial fevers that plagued people along the Ohio and Mississippi rivers induced a number of people to move west. Others did not want to endure another cold winter. The Pacific Northwest promised not only a healthful climate but an Edenic retreat into a fuller and longer life.[27] Willamette Valley settler Joseph Eagon expressed these sentiments from his claim near Milwaukie:

> I have 23 acres of prairie under good fence and shall raise plenty this season. . . . I have not got rich By coming to Oregon But I have got all I come for that is health and a healthy country and So far have had plenty to Eat and good appetites to Eat it. I consider it quite fortunate for me that I got a claim where I did. I am in a good Settlement handy to market and a good School kept handy for our Children to go too.[28]

Romance and adventure also propelled some people west. Young, well-educated people such as Francis Parkman and George Catlin wanted to experience the wilderness and Native Americans before they both disappeared. But the west also pulled on less renowned young people, such as John Minto, whose reading of James Fenimore Cooper's *The Pioneers* had early inflamed his desire to visit the frontier. John Ball remembered his "desire to see men in an uncivilized state and still greater to see the vigitable and mineral productions of a part of the world where they had been so little observed."[29]

Nationalism, profit, cheap land, bankruptcy, unhappy relationships, health, adventure, and romanticism all brought people West. Their choice of the Northwest had to do with the region's physical landscape and the cultural landscape of the emigrants themselves. White Americans' sense of mission and the natural world made the Douglas-fir region a place of destiny. But if mission impelled and justified empire in the Northwest, nature's abundance appeared to ensure its success. The region offered a mild climate, fertile soil, plentiful forests, and numerous pure streams.[30] "Everything," one visitor observed, "seems planned on a gigantic scale of twice the dimensions of which we have been accustomed." Theodore Winthrop, descendant of Massachusetts Bay Colony Governor Jonathan Winthrop, agreed: "Civilized mankind has never yet had a fresh chance of developing itself under grand and stirring influences so large as in the Northwest."[31]

The environment inspired an unending chorus of praise throughout the nineteenth and twentieth centuries. Most directly, the land's abundance offered a life free from material wants and a demonstration of God's power and providential care, a sign to settlers of blessing bestowed on a chosen people and a covenanted nation. This description of the Pacific Northwest was formed in the larger context of white Americans' perceptions of the nation as a whole. Nature endowed a young nation with "natural monuments" and a natural history that rivaled Europeans' cultural artifacts and history. Americans were assured of their own goodness and innocence by being a people that was close to nature. As the Northwest publication *West Shore* noted:

> It is true that we may not be able to point to ivy-robed ruins resplendent in story, massive cathedrals with age that are hoary, castles enshrined in weird legends so gory, nor tombs that recall petty tyrant's vain glory, and yet we have simple scenes, replete with pathos, that are as potent to purify the mind and elevate the soul, as those in foreign lands.[32]

If America was "Nature's Nation," no place looked upon itself more self-consciously as "Nature's Region" than the Northwest. One Northwest newspaper trumpeted:

> we have larger ranges, greater plains and valleys, and far mightier rivers than the land of the Swis, or than all Europe itself. The enormous forests which clothe the rugged flanks of our great range would

cover the whole country of William Tell, and spread over a good part of the fair land of France besides. The Columbia is larger than any European river.[33]

Today, you can hear these distant echoes from northwesterners who still refer to the Douglas-fir region as "God's Country."[34] Chauvinism aside, that perception demonstrates how closely intertwined are the environment, the material lives, and the regional self-understanding of northwesterners.

Nature might have provided Americans with a sense of history, demonstrated God's design, and assured the country's destiny, but this natural world was nonetheless in need of transformation. Just as Christians believed that God's gift of faith had to be appropriated, changing the believer from sinner to saint, so, too, God's gift of nature had to be appropriated and transformed into something Americans judged to be humanly purposeful. Only then could nature find its intended end, Americans fulfill their material and ethical potential, and the United States achieve its destiny.

But the very abundance that seemed to signal Americans' chosen status also endangered the character of the beneficiaries. In 1848, Absolom Harden observed that little effort bore extraordinary results in Oregon: "You can sit in your house or Shop land work or play for it is the best Lazy mans countery in the known wourld people works hear the least of any place I ever saw in the wourld no man works hear in the winter that is if he has bin hear one year So as to raise a crop then he is Safe."[35] Other observers offered similar observations of Oregon as a "land of ease and plenty."[36] Roselle Putnam, Jesse Applegate's oldest daughter, wrote that in Oregon's Umpqua Valley "all the necessities of life" could be enjoyed "with less labor than they can be produced in any other country."[37] Charles Wilkes reported: "In comparison with our own country, I should say that the labor required in this Territory for subsistence and to acquire wealth is in the proportion of one to three, or, in other words, a man must work through the year three times as long in the United States to gain the like compensation."[38]

Settlers seemingly faced a conundrum: the region's very abundance might lead to dissipation, unproductiveness, and unpleasant behavior. Many residents quickly brushed aside those concerns. Peter Burnett, writing from Linnton, Oregon, in 1844 claimed: "Lazy men have become industrious, as there is no drinking or gambling here among the whites; and labor meets with such ready employment and such ample reward, that men have more inducements to labor here than elsewhere." Other settlers supported Burnett's views. Clatsop County settler Tallmadge Wood reported: "At present almost every man that arrives here, is at once filled with enterprise, and dives heels over head into something."[39]

Northwesterners went one step further, enlisting the prevailing belief that nature itself played a role in shaping people's character. Given the region's moderate climate, bourgeois values were certain to be nurtured in the Northwest, a position residents continued to emphasize into the early twentieth century.[40] In an ironic twist, Peter Burnett, who would be the first governor of California, contrasted the different ways the climates of Oregon and California shaped character: "The climate of that country [California] is to warm for men to have any commercial enterprise. . . . A very warm climate enervates mankind too much."[41] John Ball communicated similar sentiments, also bordering on environmental determinism:

> For it is doubtless the character of a country, that usually gives character to its inhabitants—The Britons are Meritiure, the Swiss agricultural—where the climate is warm and means of subsistance easy indolent—Our varied climate Ocean and extended rivers give to us that energy & enterprise of which we are so vain.[42]

Should arguments from nature fail, northwesterners also took other steps to ensure that new migrants to the region held to a bourgeois character ethic. Like the old New England town that warned out a poor itinerant, the regional press cautioned any people from coming into the Northwest "who . . . come here to prosper without labor." "Drones succeed no better here than elsewhere," warned a columnist in the *Oregon Statesman*. "We want, and want only, busy, active, stirring settlers—men and women."[43] Settlers knew what kind of society they wanted to create, and it called for an industrious, independent, white population.[44]

The Northwest thus seemed a big land awaiting a people who could match the landscape. Out of this confluence would supposedly come a hardy, prosperous people who in shaping the land would shape themselves. Northwesterners saw in the environment a basis for regional pride, an assurance of material success, and a foundation for good character. The land seemingly existed as both the repository of American's dreams about independence and freedom and the instrumental means for achieving them. Dreams and means abounded, but deeds were also required. As settler Michael Luark noted in his diary, independence resulted from "good land [and] . . . lots of hard work."[45] The land's resources appeared unsurpassed and limitless, the future was open, and control was within the grasp of any individual with the desire and discipline to order nature and others according to his will. In a mixture of expansionism, imperialism, and teleology, a Washington territorial newspaper declared:

> The restless spirit of conquest, and the wonderfully ingenious turn of the Anglo-Saxon race, is rapidly effacing the old lines on the map of the world, and giving an impetus which will yet enable the Caucasian race to infuse its peculiar energy into every part of our vast continent,

and eventually homogenize and reduce all jarring elements and national idiosyncrasies into one complete and perfect harmony. . . . In fact, it requires no very prophetic eye to foresee and foretell the existence of a vast Republic, reaching from the Arctic to the Antarctic.[46]

Americans saw nature and culture as linked, but the former was clearly subordinate to the latter. Settlers in the Pacific Northwest did not regard their intrusion into the natural world as a distortion of nature but as a redemptive undertaking. Nature found its purposeful completion, settlers believed, in being fully utilized. Indeed, throughout the nineteenth century most Americans praised pioneering efforts for having "redeemed [the land] from the wilderness."[47]

For Americans, process predominated over place; thus the processes by which settlers transformed the land were seen as more important than the place itself. Modern scholars, such as David Lowenthal and Robin Winks, have examined the cultural meaning of this point. Winks concludes that Americans preserve a place where something significant happened even if the physical landscape has been changed, suggesting that Americans value what occurred rather than the place itself. Lowenthal makes the point explicitly: "Most pioneer villages aim at process rather than landscape; what people did matters more than the structures and locales that sheltered them."[48] Yet place should not be overlooked. The natural landscape of any place frames the actions people take, provides for their physical existence, and informs cultural understandings. Carrying physical and metaphorical meanings, nature provides a symbol system into American culture. Albeit individual mood, social circumstances, physical location, and gender shaped the way people viewed nature, a few generalizations are possible.

Americans possess a broad lexicon of terms to express their attitudes about nature, ranging from adversarial to appreciative. "Wilderness" was the negative extreme, "garden" its polar opposite. In discussing those extremes Americans employed words like "gloomy," "dark,""beauty," "sublime," and "picturesque." Maintaining the distinctions is important. In addition to respecting past meanings, it prevents us from using the words "nature" and "wilderness" without considering the nuances of those terms.

To most settlers, the natural world was a didactic expression of the divine.[49] God had ordered the natural world according to well-defined precepts, they believed, and the dominant social group possessed the instructions for reading God's revelatory order. Cultural norms were defended as divine prescriptions, and encroachments were violations of "natural law," but there were few admonitions about adapting to the natural world itself.

The nature that people came to regard and know was made up of properties that served particular material or aesthetic purposes. God might want humans to understand nature, but only so they could shape the landscape according to their will. Value lay in instrumentality rather than intrinsic worth.[50] Humans stood at the summit of a creation, "the lord[s] of an inanimate world."[51] Nature, as reported in the March 3, 1866, *Washington Standard*, existed "to minister . . . to the wants of man": "It is . . . sublime, to view atom after atom of the whole creation unceasingly changing place, that man, the lord of creation may be abundantly supplied with all his comforts and luxuries; to see the lilies of the field, and the insects of the earth and air, living and dying for man's sustenance and adornment."[52] Without human intervention, nature lay "wasted" and "dormant." The land awaited settlers who would domesticate and "improve" nature, ordering the landscape for civilized purposes.[53]

Nature, much like woman, was to remain subordinate to man and find its fulfillment through man. Not surprisingly, nature was perceived as female. Only occasionally was nature depicted as male, and then most often as a gendered pairing that held the female subordinate, such as when William Tolmie described the sun as masculine and the moon as feminine.[54]

Americans prized an ordered, systematized landscape that promised security. When views were restricted or there wasn't enough light, as in a dense forest, people lost their sense of control. A nature that was constant and orderly seemed most secure and was, therefore, preferred. As Theodore Winthrop concluded, while once again demonstrating how nature was related to a gendered belief system: "Caprice is out of the question with Nature, although her sex be feminine."[55]

Because emigrants valued a gardened, systematized nature, undisturbed natural landscapes received no more favorable responses from settlers than they had from the fur traders who had preceded them. Wilderness seemed unrestrained, unruly, and irregular, the very antithesis of security. Caroline Leighton recorded on October 30, 1860:

> We saw, along the Cowlitz Valley, marks of the havoc and devastation caused by the floods of last winter. The wild mountain stream had swept away many familiar landmarks since we were last there. . . . It gave us a realizing sense of the fact that great changes are still in process on our globe. . . . We mourned over the little place at Monticello, where for eight years a nice garden, with rows of trim currant-bushes, had gladdened the eyes of travellers, and the neat inn, kept by the cheery old Methodist minister, had given them hospitable welcome.[56]

Generally, any romantic observations of the wildness of nature quickly dissipated under dangers, real or imaginary.[57]

For the settlers, wilderness did not so much mean uninhabitable as uninhabited, except by Native Americans and wild animals. Indeed, white Americans sometimes equated Indians with wild animals and wilderness. As John Kirk Townsend watched domestic animals being unloaded near Portland from Nathaniel Wyeth's ship in 1834, he said the scene before him made it "difficult to fancy oneself in a howling wilderness inhabited only by the wild and improvident Indian, and his scarcely more free and fearless neighbors, the bear and the wolf." The wilderness was a savage space awaiting domestic cultivation, where waste would be converted into productivity, chaos transformed into order, and the wild growth turned into a garden.[58]

Wilderness and garden not only represented physical realities and psychological needs, but also a social, political, and cosmological order. Nineteenth-century Americans believed in republicanism, a mixture of traditions and experiences that nonetheless had some general precepts. A republic was to be composed of free citizens who were industrious, frugal, simple, and disinterested property holders, attached to civic virtue (the common good), and ever vigilant against a concentration of power. Americans understood history as cyclical, with republics rising from a condition of virtuous simplicity and independence before declining into an overcivilized condition of social and political corruption, luxury, selfishness, tyranny, and dependency. Nineteenth-century Americans' view of nature paralleled and symbolized their republican beliefs. Nature and civilization could be enlivening, but they could also be corrupting, chaotic, and dangerous. The solution seemed to rest with being "natural" rather than "wild" and being civilized without becoming overcivilized, a vision that implied a gardened, systematized landscape.

Settlers in the Oregon Country insisted that the Northwest was such a garden—ordered but close enough to nature to inspire, heal, and offer a testing ground for human achievement: "In the backwoods such a child will grow up with tastes so pure and simple, habits so near and refined, and affections so elevated, as to give all the highest results of a most finished education, without going through any of the fashionable forms of city instruction."[59] In the Pacific Northwest, the virtuous yeoman freeholder would garner independence and competency, create a gardened landscape, and thereby maintain the republican structures necessary for sustaining and extending the American republic.[60] The Northwest garden conveyed materialist meanings as well. Phoebe Judson summarizes the experience many settlers must have felt as she describes her first winter (1853–1854) at Grand Mound prairie in present-day Washington:

We longed for spring, that we might make [a] garden, having been so long without vegetables or fresh fruit, caused us to be exceedingly visionary in our plans for raising great crops the coming season; and our air castles, within whose walls, were stacked potatoes, onions, cabbages, beets, peas and beans, towered high.[61]

For material, emotional, and social reasons, park, flower, and mountain landscapes figured prominently in settler accounts, testifying again to the power of a systematized landscape. Parklike landscapes of prairies and scattered tree groves provided emigrants and travelers alike with comforting emotional and psychological references.[62] John Minto acknowledged that he was "attached to the 'lay' of this country [Salem, Oregon, area] because it resembles the country in England that I was raised."[63] J. G. Cooper, author of the botany report for the transcontinental railroad survey, noted:

With all this magnificence there is not wanting scenery of a milder and more home-like aspect. The smooth prairies, dotted with groves of oaks, which in the distance look like orchards, seem so much like old farms that it is hard to resist the illusion that we are in a land cultivated for hundreds of years, and adorned by the highest art, though the luxuriant and brilliant vegetation far excels any natural growth in the east.[64]

Like Charles Wilkes, who found it "impossible to realize that . . . nature, not art, had perfected the landscape," Cooper was not aware that the lovely park groves and prairies were the result of annual burnings by the native people.[65] Moreover, a preference for parks, like the garden metaphor generally, had a material as well as a psychological hold. James Douglas's discussion of the Willamette Valley gets at the material basis of the parklike landscape: "The intermixture of woods & fertile plains, peculiarly adapts it for the residence of civilized man, affording lands easily tilled, excellent pasture, fuel and building materials of the best quality."[66]

Flowered scenes, too, elicited appreciative responses. Fields of flowers conveyed a garden image, reassuring settlers that their labors would bring success while evoking sentimental memories of people, places, and events. Flowers evidently held a special place in pioneer women's lives; their beauty helped compensate for adversity and connected women to a remembered world of friendship and domesticity. Men, too, shared this interiorized world and found in nature, particularly flowers, compensation for their sacrifices and a way of closing the space between themselves and loved ones left behind. Indeed, any aspect of nature imbued with memory and personal meaning was singled out for attention, as when Caroline Leighton celebrated a particular sky because it reminded her of home.[67]

The mountains of the Northwest also received a great deal of attention and almost universal praise. To a romantic, educated man like Theodore Winthrop, mountains exalted and inspired human endeavor. As "nature's nobleman," mountains represented "our grandest emblems of divine power and divine peace." Similarly, Reverend Gustavus Hines commented "that the works of art sink into insignificance, when compared with the stupendous works of nature [Mount Hood and Mount St. Helens]." But mountains were even more than impressive monuments. They provided recreation and health, they serviced settler society emotionally and physically, and they posed little direct threat to the settlement enterprise. Writer A. B. Guthrie, Jr., saw it this way: "In the company of mountains, among the everlasting hills, we are supported and consoled by the thought of permanence, by our impermanent fellowship with permanence. . . . The mountain is, and so am I, forever and forever."[68]

Finding beauty in nature, however, involved no renunciation of utility. Implicitly paired, utility and beauty occasionally became explicitly linked. "Beautiful" was how Oregon settler Absolom Harden described his wheat field and how William Tolmie viewed the Hudson's Bay Company's cattle herds.[69] In promoting emigration to the Oregon Territory, an 1852 newspaper noted that the territory's "one continuous pasture" was dotted with "cotton wood, maple, fir, and oak groves, of singular beauty, and furnishing ample timber for all necessary fencing, building and domestic use."[70] A bird's-eye view of Olympia, sketched forty years later, shows that this mingling had not lost its hold on the popular imagination:

> It is a beautiful picture. The clear, sparkling water, the shores covered with forests or green fields to the very water's edge; the mountains with their eternal crown of snow in the distance; the steamers, sailing vessels or tugs passing up or down, busily engaged in developing the resources and commercial interests of Washington's great inland sea.[71]

Indeed, the quest for security often left little room for sentimentality, natural processes, or ecological understanding. A gopher might aerate the soil, but this benefit was lost on a farmer whose garden was being invaded.

Nature, then, carried a variety of meanings, but settler society retained an attitude and practice of conquest and domination over nature. If the Northwest existed as nature's region, it was a segmented, extracted, nature that was most prized—a nature whose value lay in its market worth rather than in its biological or intrinsic worth. In a mix of boosterism, hyperbole, and racism, newspaper editor Thomas Jefferson Dryer captured the settler enterprise:

> Forests are fast yielding to the axe of the adventurer, and the ground heretofore trod by the wily savage, or inhabited solely by the wily

beasts of the forest, now produce, by the application of industry, rich rewards to their occupants. The Indian retreats before the march of civilization and American enterprise; the howling wilderness is fast becoming fruitful fields, and ere long this isolated country will be far in the advance of many portions of our republic of a century's age.[72]

This 1899 photograph of an old-growth Douglas fir, measuring 39.1 feet in circumference, shows the long-handled, double-bitted axes and platform springboards loggers used to fell the region's giant trees. *(Courtesy Gerald W. Williams)*

Using yoked oxen to haul logs was the common method for transporting cut trees overland to mill or yarding sites until the onset of industrial logging in the 1880s. *(Courtesy Gerald W. Williams)*

The steam donkey helped revolutionize logging in the 1880s. It made the harvesting of larger trees possible; extended tree cutting into previously inaccessible forests, for example, into areas where steep inclines had provided problems for bull-team logging; speeded up the pace of logging; and made clearcutting an efficient method of logging. *(Courtesy the Oregon Historical Society, #47547)*

This 1910 Booth Kelly Lumber Company photograph shows a typical splash dam, this one on the Rolling Riffle Creek in Oregon. In the background is the millpond where logs were held; the center foreground shows how logs were released and indicates the water velocity that carried the cut trees downstream. *(Courtesy Gerald W. Williams)*

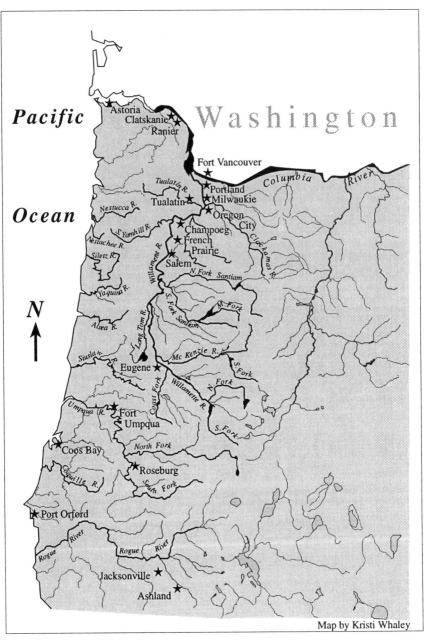

Historical Places of Oregon

Map by Kristi Whaley

Historical Places of Washington State

This photograph shows a sawmill and the flume that carried lumber from the sawmill to a planing mill four miles away in Bridal Veil, Oregon. *(Courtesy Gerald W. Williams)*

The torrents of water and cut trees on Washington's Wind River demonstrate why log drives created such havoc with riverine environments—cutting away embankments, sweeping away gravel spawning grounds, and, in general, destroying fish habitat. *(Courtesy the Oregon Historical Society, #86528)*

The refuse in this 1929 picture by Ralph Penniwell Cowgill is just one example of the refuse dumped into regional waterways by sawmills. The pollution shown here below the Booth Kelly lumber mill at Springfield, Oregon, later entered the Willamette River. *(Courtesy the Oregon Historical Society, #93594)*

This 1888 sketch of the Chehalem area in the Willamette Valley, Oregon, shows the transformed systematized landscape that northwesterners desired and prized. *(Courtesy the Oregon Historical Society, #35543)*

Henry J. Warre's 1845 sketch of a New England—looking Oregon City, entitled "The American Village," presents an Edenic landscape of order and American progress. *(Courtesy the Oregon Historical Society, #791)*

CHAPTER FOUR

Settler Society and Native Americans

The invading emigrants to the Pacific Northwest possessed little knowledge of Indians. Settlers gradually acquired information, but an understanding of native peoples' culture eluded them. What they did understand was that the native population was both a potential labor force and a barrier to white advancement. The means for turning the problem into opportunity lay in reducing Indian landholding. By controlling the land and undermining Native Americans' subsistence base, whites gained access to both Indian land and labor. If fur society had sought a middle ground, settler society claimed the ground itself.[1]

Northwest settlers felt entitled to the land. In this newest "west," they expected the "excellent vacant land" to fulfill their dream of independence and prosperity.[2] Settlers observed that Indians occupied very little land and that most of it lay vacant. Because Northwest Indians were not horticulturalists, according to a labor theory of value, they were nonproducers who created no wealth and held no rights to the land. Moreover, the land was not defined, surveyed, and registered in a document that established proof of ownership. As Harvey Scott, long-time publisher of the Portland *Oregonian*, explained in 1909:

> Native life in this country at the time when the pioneers came was adjusted strictly to the environment. The Indian probably had reached his limit of progress. Without assistance from outside sources, man in America could have got on no further. He had not the means of additional attainment. It was necessary to have help from a world beyond him.[3]

For similar reasons, settlers also challenged Hudson's Bay Company's claims to the vast lands it did not occupy. Nothing seemed so inimical to the public good in the Age of Jackson than monopoly. Imbued with a sense of destiny and mission, Americans aimed to redeem the Northwest from British and Indian monopoly. The treaty in 1846 rescued the land from the British; redeeming the Northwest from the Native Americans would take longer.

Redemption required that native peoples be removed and the land transformed into an American vision of civilization. Protestant missionary

Marcus Whitman might initially have wanted to save Indian souls, but he resigned himself quite happily to taking Native Americans' land, particularly in light of his less than overwhelming success in "civilizing" them. Indian removal should not cause Christians undue concern, Whitman observed. Whether to avoid lingering self-doubts or to express the certainty of a true believer, he justified the disposition of native peoples with an appeal to providence and progress. On May 16, 1844, he wrote his parents: "I am fully convinced that when a people refuse or neglect to fill the designs of Providence, they ought not to complain at the results. . . . The Indians have in no case obeyed the command to multiply and replenish the earth, and they cannot stand in the way of others in doing so."[4] Subsequent settlers elaborated on Whitman's rationale. Elwood Evans told an audience in 1869:

> While the Indian makes no fixed habitation, really occupies no land, and surely reduces none to production, yet he seeks to exclude others to whom it may be beneficial, not because he needs it but because it has been his hunting range, here he has required subsistence, his dead are gathered here. Our race, following their destiny in obedience to God's great law that this earth shall be made to contribute to the benefit of His creatures, appropriate it to useful purposes. Upon this principle earth has been reclaimed to civilization. Christianity and human progress have advanced.[5]

James Swan echoed those attitudes in his characterization of Native Americans who lived on Willapa Bay, Washington:

> Their property consists in movable or personal property. They never considered land of any value till they were taught so by the whites. . . . All the value they set upon their grounds is for hunting and fishing, and the only bounds are such as they set between themselves and neighboring tribes. All such property is common stock, each member of the tribe owning as much interest in it as the chiefs, although, when dealing with the whites, the chiefs assume to own the whole.
>
> They were glad to have us settle on and improve their lands. They knew they could not do so themselves, and they were content to be paid for the land so used by what the settlers saw fit to give them of the potatoes or wheat raised.
>
> What they consider as property is any thing they can exchange or barter away for articles they desire to possess.[6]

To whites, settlement meant "redeeming the wilderness from the wildness and savageness of barbarism."[7] Settlers saw their invasion not as imperial conquest but as the expansion of freedom and civilization. America's greatness, as one early Fourth of July orator made clear, was

> not tarnished with blood, or stained by conquest. . . . But our greatest conquests and noblest victories have been achieved with the ax and the plow. With these we have changed the forest into fruitful fields— with these we have made happy homes for freemen, and extended the blessings of civilization across a continent. Freedom, stimulates enterprise and discovery. These have pushed our people westward . . . checked only by the Pacific's wave.[8]

Although the republican vision was inherently expansionist, depending as it did on an ever-expanding land base, few Americans saw their actions as imperialistic. When they did acknowledge blood and conquest, Americans offered legitimating arguments about mission and destiny to dispel any cognitive dissonance that might have existed. Whites continued to view their expansion as a limitless civilizing empire of liberty commissioned by God.[9]

As part of a colonial pattern, the idea of mission had been transformed during the revolutionary era and the early republic from a tribal Puritanism to a national sense of being the chosen people. That heritage had infused the new nation's sociopolitical structures with the republican ideals of individualism and independence. Although older notions about republican independence were maintained, American culture removed republicanism from its hierarchial, deferential, and community moorings. An increasing emphasis on individual political rights, abstracted from family and community, furthered a movement toward liberal concepts of personal autonomy and freedom.

Individualism and independence, however, seemed impossible without the right to secure and maintain personal property. Consequently, the federal constitution contained safeguards like the contract clause and provisions giving the national government the power to quash populist uprisings that might threaten established notions of property and the wealth of property holders. But Americans did not conceive of government's role in securing property to be confined to protective safeguards. Government also existed to promote individual independence by removing impediments to the private accumulation of wealth and by actively supporting private economic activity. The political party system that arose structured itself around these same notions. And although the different parties might have debated whether development should be extensive or intensive, all agreed that government should dispense economic opportunities rather than restrict economic behavior.[10]

Increased geographical mobility and the growth of urban areas aided the movement toward increased individualism. As individuals became less tied to place and moved to more populated localities, greater anonymity became possible. The external constraints of community norms began to unravel, and traditional communal restraints increasingly gave way to notions of individual freedom. The expansion of a market economy only served to accelerate this process. An ethic of internal restrictions, constructed around bourgeois values, came to be seen as the socially limiting bounds of behavior. The only limitations to individual success and possessive independence lay with personal will and the moral failure to inculcate and follow internal standards of discipline and control. Northwesterners drank deeply from the cultural stream that lauded male character traits of independence, industriousness, and willpower.[11]

The geographical expanse of the United States, its rich resources, and its isolation from foreign attack only furthered ideals of limited government, individualism, control, opportunity, optimism, freedom, and destiny. The relatively free security that the United States enjoyed following the War of 1812 enabled American development during the nineteenth century to be more extensive than intensive in form. It also placed fewer restraints on individuals, allowing people to go wherever their finances permitted and their dreams dictated.[12]

Emigrants saw themselves as extending these ideals to the Pacific Northwest. Personal and national destiny converged in the Oregon Country. Northwesterners believed that industriousness and enterprise brought progress and that the individual could be re-created. In a July 4, 1855, "Oration," Washingtonian Edward Evans told his listeners that "the road to preferment" remained open, even for the humblest American. For Evans and his audience, America was the "bright exemplar" to the world, a "disinterested democracy of liberty, knowing no rich or poor, but open to the enjoyment of all."[13] Marching across the continent, Americans felt that destiny had secured the future. "Human vision," as an early Washington newspaper trumpeted, "can see no limits to this American progress."[14] Here was a republican empire "marching onward . . . as only the conquering can march, with heads up and colors flying, our bugle note shall be that of defiance of all who envy us, or would retard our progress."[15] On October 1, 1858, Olympia's *Pioneer and Democrat* proudly proclaimed: "Ten years ago Washington was a terra incognita. . . . [Now] the Pacific is covered with the most industrious and enterprising people on the face of the globe—all contributing to extend the area of European and American civilization."[16] Native Americans could not be allowed to block civilization's progress.

In reducing the Indian barrier, the settlers' best weapon, however unintended, was disease. The spread of pathogens begun during the fur-trade era accelerated and broadened as more settlers came west. By 1853, the Chinooks, once the largest tribe along the Columbia, had been virtually eliminated through smallpox and alcohol. Other Indian groups suffered a similar experience. Methodist missionary Gustavus Hines estimated that the Kalapuyans in the Willamette Valley had declined from 8,000 in 1836 to 600 by 1840. In Oregon's Umpqua Valley, Roselle Putnam wrote that "where there were hundreds eight years ago there are only one or two left in eight years more the race will probably be extinct." J. G. Cooper recorded on July 18, 1854, that "few of the Indians knew anything of the trail [from Willapa Bay to Puget Sound], as it had not been used for twenty years, or since the whole tribe of Willopahs inhabiting the valley were exterminated by smallpox."[17] Samuel Hancock, who had constructed a trading establishment at Neah Bay, Washington, graphically described the devastation wrought by smallpox in 1853:

> In a few weeks from the introduction of the disease [from a San Francisco ship], hundreds of the natives became victims to it, the beach for a distance of eight miles was literally strewn with the dead bodies of these people, presenting a most disgusting spectacle. Eventually they abandoned the idea of remaining away from this dreadful enemy and in their distress concluded I might afford them some relief, and as soon as they would feel the symptoms of the disease, they would come about my house and lie down in the yard to die. They continued this until the dead were so numerous I could scarcely walk about around my house, and was obliged to have holes dug where I deposited fifteen or twenty bodies in each. Still they continued to come about me to die, in such numbers that I finally hauled them down to the beach at a time of low tide, so they would drift away, and even the dogs, during the prevalence of this pestilence, became fat on the bodies of their deceased masters.[18]

New pathogens arrived as settler migration accelerated during the 1840s. Dysentery made its appearance along the lower Columbia in 1844 and spread down the Willamette Valley. Measles entered the Oregon Country with the 1847 emigrés, with predictably fatal consequences for Indians. The measles epidemic worked its way north, striking Victoria, British Columbia, in 1848. According to Hudson's Bay Company's John Work, the disease spread over a large area and proved more fatal to the Indian population than the smallpox epidemic of 1836. In the 1850s, scarlet fever, diphtheria, and the reappearance of smallpox devastated the remaining native groups.[19] Venereal disease seems to have been particularly destructive, according to settler Absolom Harden:

> But they are the pourest indians [the Klikitat and Kalapuya] in all the wourled and they are decreasing as fast as if the Smallpox was a mangest them for they have A more fatel desease then the Small pox

for it is called the Oregon Each. But it is in truth the Bad desorder they caught it from the Sailors on the Ships sam years a go and they are dying as fas as Sheep with the rots[s].[20]

Within a century of sustained Euroamerican contact, the Northwest native population had been reduced by more than 80 percent.[21]

The widespread death severely disrupted Indian cultural patterns of organization and authority. Pathogens weakened survivors, and labor shortages affected subsistence economic practices. Distribution systems broke down. The inability of native medicines and healers to halt the spread of disease and death subverted traditional knowledge and authority, sometimes costing failed shamans their lives. Death took both leaders and slaves. The loss of leaders, at the very time that native societies were undergoing internal strains, further weakened Indians' ability to maintain cultural patterns. The death toll left native people often hopeless and increasingly powerless to resist the invasion of settlers.[22]

Alcohol further eroded Native Americans' health, subsistence systems, and cultures. It also increased Indian impoverishment, interfering with the pursuit of traditional subsistence patterns or wage jobs and stripping people of their wages and property. Hetley Kanim, a subchief of the Snoqualmie, told Michael Simmons: "Liquor is killing our people off fast. Our young men spend the money that they work for liquor; then they get crazy and kill each other, and sometimes kill their wives and children." The victim's death in an alcohol-related slaying often initiated an escalating spiral of murders. There were few goods to give to a murdered individual's family as a traditional offering of compensation, which ensured more violence and social instability.[23] American John Ball grasped the consequences of what was happening: "The natives already here begin to feel the exterminating effects of the whites—*Bear, Deer* and elk which were formerly very abundant begins to grow scarce, and they also feel the deadly effect of new diseases—and the evil of new created wants, that they have not the ability to meet."[24]

Not that the demise of the native people particularly bothered emigrants. Most early settlers shared Washington pioneer Henry Coonse's view that Indians were "feeble minded and uncivilized." To most of settler society native peoples were "a cowardly, thievish, indolent race of beings, subsisting almost entirely on Fish."[25] They bore little resemblance to the noble savage portrayed in romantic writings. Nor did the settler enterprise of conquest lend itself to romance. Settlers had little reason to romanticize the real dangers and obstacles that Indians presented. George Savage thought that his great grandfather, James Fenimore Cooper, "who writs Lo the poor Indian . . . must have been somewhat of an idealist although very nice it is hardly practical when applied to everyday life."[26]

In contrast to fur traders, who spent more time with Indians and needed them to be successful in the trade, few early settlers recorded positive reactions to the indigenous population. Territorial and state legal codes barring intermarriage embodied those attitudes.[27] The reduced conditions of native people by the 1840s and 1850s made empathy or understanding even harder.[28] For the Reverend Gustavus Hines "the hand of Providence is removing them to give place to a people more worthy of this beautiful and fertile country."[29] Whether providentially directed or not, most settlers agreed that the speedy elimination of the Indians would be best, rather than "dragging out to the bitter end their wretched existence."[30] Indians "must yeald as they always have done," concluded settler Silas Plimpton in 1855, and a Washington newspaper mixed pragmatism with guilt expiation:

> I saw a set of bipeds represented to be human beings, the "red men of the forest; I thought of 'Low, the poor Indian!'" and felt persuaded in my mind, that the sooner they *vamosed the ranche* on "terra firma" the better—as it will save sympathy on the part of the whites, and degradation and misery on themselves. Poor devils! their "brief candle" will soon flicker out, and Ned Buntline, and the contributors to the popular magazines of the East will have to look somewhere else for heroes and heroines, for their lofty strung and highfalutin novels.[31]

A few individuals, such as Presbyterian minister Wilson Blain, decried the changes that settler society inflicted on the Indians:

> The case of these por savages is a hard one. They have been the mark for the white man's rifle ever since white men have been among them. In very many instances they have been shot down in the merest wantonness. They have never been treated as human beings, and if a righteous God ever makes inquisition for the blood of American Indians, Oregonians will have a bloody reckoning to answer for in the wrongs of the untutored and degraded savages of Rogue River Valley.[32]

But Blain was in the minority. When the public learned that Indian agent F. M. Smith, stationed at Port Orford, Oregon, denounced the killing of Lower Coquille Indians in 1854 and John Beeson protested the lynch-mob mentality that arose in 1855 at Jacksonville, Oregon, both men had to flee for their lives.[33] Women seemed particularly sensitive to the Indian issue. Phoebe Judson, for example, who had many direct contacts with Indians, demonstrated a sensitivity toward native people and an awareness of their unjust treatment. When some Indians camped at the Judson's homestead at Grand Mound prairie in Washington, Judson asked:

> How could they realize they were trespassing our rights, when no doubt this spring had been one of their favorite camping places and hunting grounds, as well as that of their forefathers for generations.
>
> The earth with its haunts, and trails, had been as free for them to roam, hunt and fish as the air they breathed, and we, in reality, were the interlopers.[34]

Settlers' children, particularly in reminiscences written in the late nineteenth and early twentieth centuries, also generally wrote sympathetically about native people. Raised in proximity to Indians and often with Native American playmates, many young people had an appreciation for native culture. They most often blamed the vagrant, avaricious men attracted to mining districts for the mistreatment Indians suffered. "A class of white men," settler George Riddle said, who "acted upon the principal [sic] that the Indian had no rights that a white man would respect." Riddle and others were right. Miners did perpetrate some of the most egregious examples of anti-Indian behavior, but insensitivity came from among the settled members in society as well. Even sympathetic reminiscences overlooked the ways in which early and permanent settlers, the "home builders," had contributed to the injustices.[35]

In general, there were few early voices of concern for the Indians, particularly if they asserted themselves in any way. When Indians interfered with a government survey party between the Puyallup and White rivers, claiming that the land belonged to them, for example, the *Washington Standard* called them "savages" and "devils." That attitude continued to be heard throughout the settler era. The January 18, 1879, *Washington Standard* editorialized: "The improved Order of Red Men in Oregon, is made up of white men; a facetious individual in this place says an improved red man in this Territory is a dead Indian." Eight years later, the same newspaper judged that the Indians of western Washington possessed only one good trait: "They are all perfectly harmless and never interfere or worry the whites, provoke quarrels or fight them."[36] In 1882, *Harper's* reported that a "spirit of intolerance" prevailed throughout the region, particularly among "the old settlers and their sons." The magazine published a stinging rebuke:

> To that sort of man (and unfortunately he is in tremendous force among the people still influential in Oregon) the Indian is merely something to be kicked out of the way. He is never spoken of save as a "damned Injun," and never conceded to be "good" until dead. The man who asserts the red man's humanity and immortal worth in the eyes of his and our Creator goes flatly against the theory and practices

of this class, and must expect much the same treatment as martyrs to other unpalatable truths have received.[37]

As the nineteenth century wore on and settler society began giving way to industrial society, disparaging remarks about Northwest Indians became less frequent. The Native American population had dramatically declined, their land-holdings had been reduced, and they were no longer perceived to be a threat or barrier to the dominant society. An alternate Indian image began to gain strength. Wealthy, educated urbanites were especially prone to romanticize Native Americans. Indians could now provide an image of a free, simple, innocent people in touch with nature and nature's god. For Americans who felt increasingly uneasy over America's industrializing processes during the second half of the nineteenth century, the new image had appeal, though it did not dislodge older prejudices.[38] In 1892, the *Washington Standard* made some common distinctions:

> The "Horse Indians" . . . are far handsomer race of people than the bowlegged, fishing tribes of lower Columbia and Puget Sound. The "fish story" that the brain is developed and higher manhood reached by fish eating people is certainly reversed in this case. Upper Columbia Indians lived by the chase, made annual journeys across the Rocky mountains to the "buffalo country," and lived on horseback. Exercise, war, the chase—environment made them alert, quick, straight and strong, and probably no finer specimen of manhood exists than Chief Joseph, a Nez Perce warrior and statesman, who is a typical "Horse Indian."
>
> The "Canoe Indians," on the contrary, lived on the beach and spent a great part of their lives squatting on their bent legs in a damp canoe. They lived upon fish and clams . . . and few demands were made upon them for violent exercise.[39]

As non-Indian Americans became concerned about conservation and wilderness, Native Americans were increasingly romanticized as conservationists if not protoecologists. A few individuals, largely informed by romanticism, empathized with the Indians and acknowledged the harm done them. One wrote:

> I do not wonder they look with jealous eye[s] upon the movements of the whites. His touch to them has been contamination, and here among their mountain fastness, amid the grandest works of the Great Spirit they so humbly worship, this child of nature who—"Looks through nature up to nature's God," beholds with dread the march of

civilization, that civilization which to his fathers has been death and to himself despair.[40]

Oregon pioneer chronicler Samuel Clarke observed in his 1905 history:

> What he [called Jo Hutchins by Clarke, but who was really Santiam Kalapuyan Joseph Hudson] told of the modes of supplying winter meat is of interest as showing their wisdom and good management, also their economical use of the gifts of nature. Under the reckless waste of the whites the buffalo were slaughtered for their robes and the meat was wasted; before our race the deer, elk, buffalo, and bear—all the wild game—became practically extinct on the immense ranges they had occupied; beaver, otter and fur seal disappeared from the land and the sea. But the Indians preserved all these with a wisdom and economy we may at least respect, so prudently and wisely that the supply remained intact as surely as are the individual flocks and herds so well cared for in civilized lands today.[41]

White women like Caroline Leighton proved especially receptive to this perspective. An upper-class, well-traveled woman with educated tastes, Leighton judged that U.S. Indian policy had failed, especially when compared to the treatment accorded Native Americans in British Columbia. But Leighton's perspective was based more on romantic literature than on firsthand knowledge. When she observed that Indians conformed to the romantic image of the noble savage, Leighton rhapsodized poetically, but those who did not conform came in for condemnation. This often placed Leighton in the ambiguous position of desiring a "civilized" Indian who yet held on to certain tribal ways, such as handicrafts.[42]

For Caroline Leighton, Native Americans were caricatures who served her needs, not a people she truly understood. Yet, like other well-to-do Victorian women she also felt constrained within a gendered system. Consequently, Leighton often depicted Indian women's lives as a projection of her own needs and desires. On July 1, 1873, for example, Leighton recorded a recent encounter she had with "a female chief, Yaquina," while crossing the Cascade Range in western Oregon. In a telling passage, Leighton uses Queen Victoria as a masked alter ego: "She [Yaquina] was mounted on a little pony, and riding along in a free and joyous way, looking about at the green leaves and the sunshine. I thought of Victoria with her heavy crown, that gives her the sick headache, and wondered how she would like to exchange with her."[43] Leighton was not unmindful of the hardships that Native American women endured, yet she envied their hardiness, self-sufficiency, and freedom to move outdoors.[44]

Leighton's ambivalence was shared by most nineteenth-century reformers. At heart, reformers retained a mentality of conquest—intent on preserving what they judged important without reference to the way that the culturally valued and valueless functioned to sustain the whole. Even reform-minded women like Caroline Leighton had little desire to understand, appreciate, or help sustain a self-directed Indian people. What Leighton and other reformers sought to conserve and praise were those aspects of Native American life that met their needs and conformed to their ideals of what Indians should be.

However much writers romanticized native people, settlers felt few compunctions about displacing Indians. Settler and Indian differences over property, ownership, and land use led to increased conflict. Whites constantly complained that Indians stole their vegetables, livestock, grass, and timber, as well as killed the game that settlers wanted. Not surprisingly, those who settled on or near traditional Native American land experienced the most depredations. Willamette Valley settler Judge Comegys occupied land that native people used as a summer and fall camping ground. From the Indian vantage point Comegys was the violator whose presence infringed on their rights to use the timber and other resources in the accustomed manner; that use certainly did not constitute theft.[45]

Increasingly, the framework within which Indian people shaped their lives was constricted as social, political, and economic disruptions washed over them. Even active resistance could not stem the tide. Those who managed to survive disease and armed conflict were confined to reserves or lived in areas far removed from white settlement.

Whites wanted Indians removed from lands they coveted, but attempts to create the first reserves met local opposition from settlers. Reservation treaties made with Willamette Valley Indians in April and May of 1851 excited widespread settler hostility. The treaties negotiated by commissioners Alonzo A. Skinner, John P. Gaines, and Beverly S. Allen were a "farce," settlers claimed, and a squandering of public monies on "a handful of filthy, squalid Indians, such as burrow about our towns and rivers." Moreover, they argued, the reservations themselves were far too extensive.[46] The *Oregon Statesman* complained:

> Skinner made treaties, reserving to miserable, filthy Indians, large tracts of land adjoining, and in the midst of settlements, thus not only retarding the growth of the country, but entailing a nuisance and curse upon the inhabitants. . . . There is nothing more farcical and grossly wrong than to treat with such miserable specimens of humanity as the Indians of this [Willamette] valley, (no more competent to contract than the wolves of the prairies) for lands to which they have a nominal title, and pay them heavy sums of money therefor. It results in not one particle of benefit to the Indians. . . . We hold it to be the duty of

our government for all time, to take care of these Indians where they cannot take care of themselves, to supply their necessities and prevent suffering, so far as suffering can be prevented among such beings. There its duty ends.[47]

The 1851 treaties and those subsequently negotiated by Territorial Superintendent of Indian Affairs Anson Dart never received Senate ratification. Treaties arranged in 1853 by Dart's successor, General Joel Palmer, with the Umpqua Cow Creek band and the Rogue River (Takelma) Indians were ratified the following year. Palmer concluded reservation treaties with other inland southern Oregon bands in 1854 and saw those ratified in 1855. Treaties made with Oregon coast Indians in 1855, however, were never ratified. In the newly created territory of Washington, Governor and ex officio Superintendent of Indian Affairs Isaac I. Stevens quickly concluded a number of treaties with western Washington bands during the winter of 1854–1855. Congressional approval, however, came slowly, with ratification, except for the Medicine Creek Treaty, coming in 1859.[48]

The treaties did little to halt Indian-white conflict and actually contributed to the violence. Episodic conflicts partly grew out of misunderstandings about what the treaties meant, Congress's inability to quickly ratify the agreements, and the government's failure to meet treaty stipulations, including keeping whites off Indian land. Each side felt aggrieved and believed the other party could not be trusted. Indians were particularly angry. In addition to the treaty-related problems, settlers and miners injured native people with personal insults and physical assaults, introduced stock that rooted up camas fields, and reduced fisheries by polluting streams with mining debris. Unwilling to tolerate the situation any further, a number of Indian groups in Oregon and Washington took up arms. In 1855, there was a major outbreak of hostilities.[49]

The fighting of 1855–1856 brought death and change to Indians and whites alike. Although the changes that settlers underwent pale in comparison to what Native Americans experienced, as whites sought to make sure there would be no "nits to make lice," settler society was nonetheless disrupted. The disruption was more severe in Washington than in Oregon, but generally the Indian war retarded the overall economic development of the Northwest. Hostilities interfered with farming and trade and, perhaps most importantly, contributed to the region's slow population growth during the 1850s.[50]

That a war had to be fought to gain control of Indian-held lands was bad enough from the settlers' perspective. That it hampered regional growth was worse still, and that it was fought and concluded as it was seemed outrageous. Settlers turned much of their rage not just toward the Indians but also the federal government. For some time, settlers had been disgruntled at the government's failure to remove native people from their midst. Their discontent was not lessened when the U.S. military refused to pursue a policy of Indian extermination. In a letter to his half-brother, Silas Plimpton charged:

> The United States troops are nothing but a damnable curse here, and the Volunteers ought to serve them the same as they do the Indians. They have protected the red skins long enough for they would not consent to have them punnished when they realy deserved it. The blood of many families has gone unavenged.[51]

No other large-scale armed attacks took place west of the Cascades after the 1855–1856 conflicts, but fears could still be stirred by "sassy" Indians.[52]

Settlers regarded the war-related treaties they imposed on native people to be embodiments of "justice" and "honesty" and their treatment of Indians as just and superior to that experienced elsewhere.[53] The coercive nature of the treaties, including forcing Indians who had never killed any settlers to sign away their lands and move to reservations, were further attempts by settler society to systematize the Northwest's cultural and physical landscape.

For the less well-intentioned, restricted land holding and segregation allowed Indian-held land to be seized and brought into a "civilized" state. Those who were sympathetic to the Indians saw reserves as enclaves where native people could be protected from hostile whites while being acculturated. Consequently, treaties sought to eliminate Indian collectivism and extend "civilization" by providing for farming, schools, industrial training, and landownership in severalty.[54] Reformers designed those policies to bring Indians within the boundaries of what whites understood to be the human community. All that native people had to do was to shed their own culture. Even the most enlightened Indian policy was a method of social control that amounted to "imperial benevolence." In either case, native people were being placed on the periphery of society, with the social and ecological landscape being ordered according to white American cultural standards.

Treaties made with Washington Indians created numerous, smaller reserves that left some space for traditional native practices, including the right to hunt, fish, gather, and pasture horses on common places not owned by whites. The arrangement lowered government costs, provided a cheap reserve labor force, and assured whites an inexpensive means of procuring fish and game.[55] Being nonagriculturalists, few western Washington Indian groups were concerned about keeping arable lands for farming. What they valued was the right to remain in their homelands and follow traditional production practices. People in the Neah Bay area, for example, relied primarily on fishing and possessed little arable land. The short-term result of a treaty reserve for them was a life modified by the white power structure but still a world in which they lived in their homeland, followed established practices, and maintained a degree of independence. As Indian Agent C. A. Huntington reported: "The Indians generally are unwilling to work in civilized [agricultural] pursuits. Their main dependence is upon fishery, the productions of which give them means of trade for all needed supplies."[56] Not all groups were so fortunate. Even Neah Bay agency bands had become more dependent on whites by the late nineteenth century. After all, acculturation, not the preservation of native peoples' traditional culture, was the goal of U.S. Indian policy. Whites intended reserves and traditional Native American practices to pass out of existence. The plan was for Indians to exchange communally owned land and food-quest patterns for a life of farming privately owned parcels of land.

Few people within the dominant society considered the Native American perspective and thought about how disruptive removal reservations life was. Particularly for most Oregon bands, a reservation meant being displaced from traditional homelands of memory and resource extraction. Treaties with Washington's native peoples created a number of smaller reservations, but Oregon Indians were placed on a few large reserves. Benjamin Wright, subagent for the Port Orford District, explained:

> The Indians on the coast will be much harder to persuade to give up their homes and country than those in the interior from the fact of their traveling so seldom and never more than 30 or 40 miles therefore their knowlege of any other place is limited the idea of leaving the houses where they were Born in and the Stream where they have fished in all their lives for a home only a Short Distance from them would be Something that with their limited knowlege they would not Readily Sanction.[57]

The forced migration of Indians to the reserves was traumatic. When the southern Oregon Umpquas arrived at the Grand Ronde reserve they were a visibly shaken refugee people suffering from cold, ill health, and a loss of personal possessions, including their land. Joseph Jeffers, superintendent of farming at the reserve, reported that the Umpquas "dayley prodused sutch a wild and dolefull lamentashion that it wold almost overcum my better judgment in sympathy for them, in droping a tear of pitty for degraydid and suffering humanity."[58]

The government offered "bounty contracts" to whites who would track down and capture Indians who would not go to the reserves. Regional volunteers had a simpler solution, hunt the recalcitrants down and kill them. Indeed, a fear of being murdered by whites probably induced a number of Indians to go to reservations. L. P. Day, who the government engaged to find scattered groups in Oregon's mountains, did not feel it would be a difficult task. Indians knew, Day wrote, that there were a number of people who "would kill them . . . if they could get a chance." He was right, as a recalcitrant party of Rogue River Indians found out in 1857. Only a few Oregon bands were allowed to live on traditional lands. The once extensive Indian societies of the Northwest found their lives increasingly proscribed; whether placed on reserves, granted permission to remain where they were, or removed far enough from settler society that the government neglected them.[59]

Reserves may have been created for what whites perceived was Native Americans' own good, but reservation life did not always produce the ends that even the reformers desired. Some Native Americans thought that their removal was only temporary. Others may have been willing to make some adjustments, but they had no desire to abandon their culture. When one or both of those expectations were not met, people sought escape. Occasionally, particularly in the early years, those who planned to leave a reserve actually announced their intention. John, chief of the Applegate Rogues, informed Special Agent J. Ross Browne: "I will consent to live here one year more; after that I must go home."[60] Most of the time, people simply slipped away. Many were captured and returned to their reserve. Even those who eluded capture faced a life that was different from the one lived before the Indian war.[61]

Whites' expectations of the reservations were altered in other ways as well. Eventually, native people from various tribes began to interact in ways that gradually allowed shared meanings and new ways of being "Indian" to emerge. However, a pan-Indian identity was neither a design nor an immediate consequence of reservation policy. The most immediate effect of bringing people together who had been geographically and socially separate was conflict. Forced proximity created a violent-prone milieu where old animosities were readily acted out and where groups attempting to preserve their identity struck out against traditional opponents who seemed to threaten cultural preservation. Siletz Reservation Agent Courtney Walker recorded: "The [Eucha Port Orford Indians] are still discontented about the placing the Rogue Rivrs near & with them, they have a fight every day or so."[62]

Conflicts were fueled by other conditions as well, as Indians acted out their new way of living in an altered physical landscape. The severe restrictions that reserves imposed on Native Americans' land base deepened dependency and frustration. Congregated in a confined area, Indians fought over easily procured food sources as need, competition with "outsiders," and societal breakdown eroded traditional sources of restraint. Alcohol exacerbated the situation.[63]

The situation was particularly acute on Oregon's executive-order reservations, where native peoples not only lacked treaty-reserved rights but also suffered other limitations on their way of life. Interior Indians were moved to a wet, cold coastal climate to which they were unaccustomed. Little wonder that Southern Oregon Indians called the reserve land a "bad country."[64] In addition, the new landscape often lacked traditional food sources and contained plants and animals with seasonal patterns different from what the people knew. Spring salmon runs did not occur in any of the Siletz Reservation streams, and game was scarce. Moreover, interior people, who relied on fish and game, were reluctant to gather shellfish, the one bountiful food source at the coastal reserve. Only "as a last resort," would they eat mollusks.[65] But few whites regretted the situation. Those who hated Indians were not sympathetic, and humanitarians who viewed the people's hunger as unfortunate did not feel badly about their loss of traditional food sources.

Reservation policies not only did little to ameliorate Indian suffering, but they also failed to accomplish their intended ends. Annuities, tools, and training in agricultural techniques, guaranteed by treaty, were inadequate and sometimes nonexistent. Corrupt or unqualified agents only aggravated the situation. Native people on reservations generally faced an uphill struggle against hunger, disease, dependency, and death.

Early reservation reports of sickness and death became a familiar feature of Indian life as native populations continued the decline inaugurated with Euroamerican contact.[66] One leader summed up the situation: "My heart is sick; many of my people have died since they came here; many are still dying. There will soon be none left of us." Warned that any attempt to return to their homeland would mean death, the Rogue leader called Sam articulated his people's desperation: "We might as well be killed as die here."[67] Siletz Indian Agent J. H. Fairchild correctly observed that it was "Little wonder . . . that these Indians, thus brought together, continually fighting among themselves, and required to subsist on food to which they were wholly unaccustomed . . . rapidly disappeared."[68] Each year, the death rate exceeded the birth rate on the Siletz and Grand Ronde reserves from their creation until the twentieth century: the Siletz population declined from 2,026 in 1856 to 438 in 1900, while the Grand Ronde population fell from 1,826 in 1857 to 298 in 1902. Not until the 1920s did the Native American population begin to stabilize.[69] "It is not your wars," remarked the Rogue leader John, "but your peace that kills my people."[70]

Moreover, the reservation sites chosen to make native people into agriculturalists were often some of the least desirable farming lands available. Reservations had been selected not only because they were remote from white settlement but also because of their apparent uselessness for farming.[71] James W. Nesmith and J. W. Perit Huntington, who both served as superintendents for Indian affairs in Oregon, made explicit the "worthless land thesis." Nesmith, writing in 1858 to U.S. Commissioner of Indian Affairs Charles E. Mix, reported that "for agricultural pursuits" the Siletz reserve was "worthless." Huntington agreed, telling how the Siletz Reservation was created "at a time when the Western Slope of the coast mountains had been but partially explored, and was supposed to be nearly or quite worthless." The common belief, according to Huntington, was "that the rugged nature of the coast range of mountains would forever debar the population of the Willamette Valley from using the harbors which are found at the estuaries of the Siuselaw [Siuslaw], Alsea, Tillamook and Yaquina rivers."[72] Later events altered that judgment.

By the early 1860s, pressures began to build for reducing the Siletz Reservation in the Yaquina area. Whites who wanted access to Yaquina Bay's rich oyster beds at first simply tried to take what they wanted. Judge Stratton of the U.S. Circuit Court for Benton County ruled in 1864 that Ladlam and Company of San Francisco had no right to oyster at Yaquina Bay because the beds lay within the Indian reservation. Stratton said that only persons licensed or employed by the Indian Department had a right to be on reservation property.[73] The petitioners were not pleased and continued the fight by finding common cause with other whites interested in gaining control over the Yaquina area.

A route over the Coast Range that linked the Willamette Valley with Yaquina Bay had been found by the 1860s. The passage allowed valley residents to transport freight more quickly and cheaply to and from San Francisco than on the Columbia River. The major obstacle to using the route, however, was the Native Americans at the Alsea Agency, south of Yaquina Bay, who controlled the land. To overcome this "problem," the Oregon Superintendent of Indian Affairs recommended moving the people north of Yaquina. There, between the Siletz and Yaquina rivers, according to the superintendent, Indians could find adequate subsistence. Besides, that land seemed of little value to whites: "It is densely wooded, portions of it rugged mountains, and other portions worthless swamps, and none of it likely soon to be wanted for settlement." The *Oregon Statesman* agreed and readily lent its support to the proposal.[74]

In the Douglas-fir region, as elsewhere, Indian reserves could not be allowed to stand in the way of white "progress." By executive order, Siletz Reservation land was opened up for settlement by non-Indians on December 21, 1865. Ten years later Congress closed the Alsea subagency with a March 3, 1875, act that allowed whites to settle the entire southern portion of the reserve and permitted settlers to take up land from the Salmon River to Lookout Point on the reserve's northern end. Consequently, between 1865 and 1875, Siletz Reservation lands were reduced by two-thirds.[75] And the reduction did not end there.

As more "worthless" reservation lands were coveted by late nine-teenth-century Anglo Americans, particularly timbermen interested in forest stands, reservation policy was increasingly labeled a failure.[76] Whites denounced Indians, like those on the Quinault Indian reservation: "They are superstitious, beastly, ignorant and lazy, and have but three ambitions in life, namely: to gratify their vile passions, to exist without labor, and to prevent their children from embracing civilization through the means of education provided for them through the Government."[77] The desire to reduce or eliminate reserves was the result of well-intentioned reformers and avaricious land grabbers. Washington Territorial Governor William A. Newell's address before the legislative assembly in 1881 sounded a familiar refrain: "They [Indians] cannot make proper use of these vast domains, and do not appreciate their advantages, whilst its possession and occupation are lost to a large body of Americans, who, by cultivation, would make it highly productive."[78] An 1887 newspaper article, in a tone reminiscent of the 1840s, made an even more blatant defense for taking reservation lands:

> The Indian reservations in Washington Territory are 17 in number and contain 6,332,885 acres of the best land of the whole country. These vast holdings, as they now stand are but little benefit to any one, but are positive injury to the prosperity and growth of our future great State. Something should be done by Congress to eliminate these extensive and almost useless reservations. If the Indians were given annuities, and these lands turned over to white men the country would lose nothing in the end.[79]

Three years later, those sentiments again found expression:

> About the only prairie land in this northwest country suitable for agricultural purposes and not yet taken up by white men, is on the Quinault Indian reservation. About ten miles from the coast there are several large prairies that are very similar to the Quillayute prairies and contain several thousand acres. These prairies are used by the Indians only to hunt elk on, and it is a shame, that the government does not throw them open to settlement, as the Indians will never use them for any other purpose.[80]

Under regional pressure and the provisions of the 1887 Dawes Act, Congress reduced the Siletz Reservation from 225,280 acres to 46,000 acres with the Siletz allotment agreement in 1892. Grand Ronde underwent a similar reduction. Following a 1901 allotment agreement, the reserve's land base declined from 33,148 acres to only 25,791 in 1904. Once again, reserves had proved to offer little protection against powerful forces that wanted

Indian-held land. In the same spirit, white Americans dismissed Indian treaty fishing rights when whites moved into commercial fishing during the late 1880s.[81]

Still not understood, Native Americans saw their numbers and land base eroded and their culture reduced. Whites told Native Americans that if they hoped to survive, they had to cast off their traditional culture and adopt an Anglo-American cultural ethos. In one of the most critical parts of that transformation, native religion must give way to Christianity. Conversion pressures intensified when President Grant's peace policy during the 1870s placed reservations under the agency of Christian churches. Indian "indolence" also came under severe attack. To encourage a work ethic, Indian agents were instructed in 1875 that "all able-bodied male Indians between the ages of eighteen and forty-five" were "to perform service upon their respective reservations to an amount equal in value to the supplies to be delivered."[82] That directive was often translated into working under white supervision both on and off reservations. Where could Indians better learn to work hard than in service to white employers? In a region of labor scarcity with a high wage scale, Indians could supply cheap labor while being tutored in proper work habits.[83] For Indian young people, assimilation meant anglicized education. Children were separated from their parents and tribal elders, something that Superintendent of Indian Affairs Joel Palmer had argued for in the 1850s.[84]

Native people who adapted most readily to the changes, who learned to speak English correctly, and who practiced agriculture received praise. Those who showed a reluctance to adopt the work habits and values of the dominant culture were labeled "dull," "indolent," "superstitious," and "uneducated."[85] Living patterns on the reservation corresponded to those cultural labels. Native Americans who lived near agency headquarters were said to have "better kept and cultivated" herds of cattle and horses, grain fields, and vegetable patches. Few of those living farther from the agent's supervision farmed, however, and they were considered lazy, dirty, "loafers and stragglers."[86]

If Indians most closely associated with whites seemed to advance (with the exception of those who came under the influence of degenerate whites), proximity was a double-edged sword and Native Americans remained caught up in an Anglo-American paradox. On the one hand, settler society desired Indians as cheap labor and believed that Native Americans only advanced when placed in contact with "civilization." On the other hand, close proximity offended whites, particularly when an Indian presence seemed to threaten land values or a white urban image of advancement.[87]

The situation became even more complicated from the Anglo-Americans' viewpoint because Native Americans pursued their own route to adaptation. Medicine healers continued their practice, for example, and traditional rituals surrounding death were maintained (and regrettably found far too many opportunities for expression). They also continued to dispose of the dead person's material goods as part of the burial ceremony, which not only offended the dominant culture's value system but also further impoverished the people by reducing their property. The Indians also continued the traditional potlatching. Although whites made inroads on these practices, Lieutenant Philip Sheridan overstated his claim to have "completely suppressed" such actions. Still, the traditional functions these ritual forms served had been altered. The potlatch, for example, survived, but the native economy and cultural system had been so disrupted that the practice no longer retained its crucial role in native society.[88]

Both reservation and off-reservation Indians continued to provide food for themselves through fishing, hunting, and collecting plants. They also labored as farm hands and loggers, and worked in hops fields, sawmills, and canneries. They were road builders and boatmen and sold berries, wood, fish, and animal skins to Anglo Americans. Native women provided a sexual outlet to a white male population and worked as domestic servants for Victorian white women. Some Indians even adopted agricultural practices, particularly potato cultivation, which no doubt increased as camas and wapato became less available.[89] Traveling up the Cowlitz River in 1871, for example, a party of whites entered a remote area, where they encountered a small Indian group of about fifteen adults who, in addition to fishing and hunting, cultivated vegetables that included potatoes, peas, corn, and turnips.[90]

Despite pressure to become "white," Native Americans continued to adapt to new conditions according to their own values and understandings. Potato growing did not seem that distant from wapato and camas digging. Moreover, agriculture remained secondary to traditional pursuits of fishing, hunting, and gathering.[91] Most jobs that Indians undertook were seasonal or short-term tasks that could be done within the preexisting context of Native American seasonal labor practices. In addition, Indians exercised a degree of control over their own employment, especially when labor was scarce in the Northwest. For example, they recognized the hops growers' dependency on Native American labor and pressed for higher wages. According to Washington hops grower Ezra Meeker, "The Indians are quick to perceive the situation and ready to profit by the anxiety of growers and to drive the best bargain possible."[92]

Indians adapted religion, too, in their own way. Some Indians rejected Christianity, and others embraced it. Most interesting, however, was the blending of Native American and Christian religious traditions into a syncretistic form that expressed itself in the Ghost Dance and the Earth Lodge cults, prophetic movements of the 1870s to 1880s. The blend of the two religions took on a more institutional form in Indian Shakerism, founded in 1882 by a Squaxin, John Slocum. Scholar Cesare Marino's conclusion about western Washington Indians may be less precise for those in western Oregon, but it is nonetheless applicable: "Traditional patterns of subsistence, kinship networks, and intervillage ties persisted, fostering Indian values and the maintenance of Indian identity."[93] Although cultural patterns persisted, Indians nonetheless inhabited a changed world. Economically, socially, and politically, Northwest Native Americans had been marginalized.

By 1900, this description of Lummi and Nooksack life in Washington applied to other Northwest Native Americans as well:

> In place of plank houses stood white-style houses. . . . The Lummi . . . had land in the production of agricultural crops. New systems of government were imposed. Areas which had been used for generations by both the Lummi and the Nooksack were no longer available for use. As a result of the white settlement patterns and the confusion over the rights of the Indians to homestead, much of the fishery above Ferndale was lost to the Nooksack.[94]

Settler society sought to impose order on untamed nature and Indian people. The reservation system was an attempt to domesticate the "wild" Indians, to redeem the land and its people, and to transform the Douglas-fir region into a "civilized," managed landscape. The reduction of the Indian barrier transformed native peoples and the land itself, for Anglo Americans lived on the land differently. The ecology of the Douglas-fir region was now increasingly shaped by the social and cultural changes brought by settlers.

CHAPTER FIVE

Settlement

By restricting Indian land holding and population, white America broke down one of the barriers to reordering the Northwest's landscape, but the land still awaited transformation. National mythologies, government policies, a market economy, and Euroamerican perceptions of nature would be influential factors, but the process was not one of simple cultural imposition. What occurred was a mixture of conquest and adjustment as settlers found themselves both shaping and being shaped by the ecological system they found. The changes amounted to an ecological revolution.[1]

Travel guides and dreams of success may have brought Anglo Americans to a place of new beginnings, but the past also made the journey west. Settlers sought not so much the creation of a new society as the re-creation of an older, familiar one that allowed them to advance their fortunes. Emigrants wanted to transform the Douglas-fir region according to a familiar text. When James Clyman gazed on the Willamette Valley in 1845, he envisioned it transformed into "grain fields and . . . hills covered with flocks and herds of Domestic animals."[2] Clyman's visionary landscape was not an idiosyncratic or isolated dream. Washington settler J. W. Goodell offered an even more ambitious expression of that future landscape in an 1856 Fourth of July oration at Fort Davis:

> These immense forests have disappeared and in their place I behold well cultivated farms, adorned with fields of golden wheat. Around our numerous water-falls, I hear the hum of machinery, converting the various products of our forests, our soil, and our flocks, into the comforts of life. Numerous steamers are ascending and descending our numerous rivers, and I hear the shrill whistle of their engines as they lay along side of the many flourishing towns which have been built along the banks, to discharge or receive freight. . . . I behold large cities, with . . . their streets teeming with busy thousands, and their numerous wharves crowded with immense steamers and ships from all parts of the world, receiving and discharging their immense cargoes. I turn my eyes eastward, and behold an immense train of rail road cars thundering down the inclined plain of the Cascade[s].[3]

Like their Indian predecessors, whites settled close to waterways at French Prairie and Scappoose Plains in what became the preeminent area of settlement, the Willamette Valley. As emigration increased, settlers followed this early pattern and began filling up "the sweet Arcadian valley of the Willamette."[4] Bounded on the west by the Coast Range and on the east by the Cascade Mountains, the valley that Matthew P. Deady called "the prettiest country I had ever seen in my life" slopes gradually north from what is currently the Eugene area to the Columbia River. The flat surface and sedimentary rock floor of the low lying alluvial plain has a scattering of 80 to 250 foothills, but only the 1,000-foot-high hills transecting the valley south of Salem show any significant elevation. Fed by tributary Coast and Cascade mountain streams, the Willamette River flows the length of the valley before emptying into the Columbia River near Portland.[5]

Early settlers and visitors thought of Willamette Valley as the perfect "garden" environment. By the mid-1860s, this garden metaphor had not lost its hold. According to visitor Samuel Bowles, the Willamette "garden" was a "paradisiacal valley." Never, the editor of the Springfield, Massachusetts *Republican* maintained, "were my bucolic instincts deeper stirred than in this first outlook upon the Willamette Valley." Nor did the praise or garden lexicon diminish with time.[6]

The Willamette Valley that Euroamericans entered in the early 1800s was a mosaic of foothill forests, oak openings, riverine woodlands, marshlands, and prairies. Shaped by moisture, soil, and fire, Willamette Valley was a physical landscape that settlers deeply appreciated both materially and perceptually. Foothill conifer forests of grand fir, ponderosa pine, incense cedar, sugar pine, western red cedar, and the dominant Douglas fir surrounded the valley. On the valley floor were woodlands of Oregon white oak, California black oak, Pacific madrone, bigleaf maple and, because of Indian burning practices and their own fire-resistant properties, the Garry oak and Douglas-fir dominants. Beneath the prairie's interspersed oak-grove openings was an understory vegetation mixture of grasses; forbs like American vetch, coast strawberry, western buttercup, and the common woolly sunflower; and shrubs such as California hazel, swordfern, Saskatoon serviceberry, mazzard cherry, and common snowberry.[7]

Appealing as the parklike oak openings were, however, the most abundant forest communities in the valley existed along the floodplains. Dominated by Oregon ash, black cottonwood, Douglas fir, bigleaf maple, white alder, red alder, and willow, these woodlands extended along the length of the Willamette River. Where major tributaries flowed into the Willamette, riparian forests could reach up to 6.5 miles from the river's edge, but generally averaged from just under 1 mile to 2.25 miles in width. Those bottomland forests oversaw understory species of Oregon grape, salmonberry, elderberry, and ferns.[8]

Most of the Willamette Valley, however, was over a million acres of grassland prairie composed of clover and luxurious grasses such as blue wildrye, Idaho bentgrass, California oatgrass, California danthonia, and needlegrass. Red fescue was the characteristic bunchgrass on well-drained soil sites, while the tufted hairgrass, which grew high enough to touch the belly of a horse, dominated the valley's extensive, poorly drained soils. Camas flourished on land where low elevation, high water tables, and seasonal flooding created marshy valley areas. Extending sometimes over ten to twelve acres, the pale blue of the flowering camas gave the land "the appearance of a beautiful blue lake" during spring.[9]

Initially, emigrants chose to settle in upland areas rather than along the gallery forests of the Willamette River. The necessity of clearing cottonwood, ash, maple, alder, and fir might have deterred some settlers, but that laborious task does not seem to fully explain the lack of settlement in floodplain forests. The gallery trees did not present a barrier comparable to the daunting evergreen forests, nor were they much more formidable than the forests the settlers had recently left. To border-state emigrants, the floodplain forests must have seemed somewhat reminiscent of their former home, since they so "closely reproduce[d] the appearance of the Upper Mississippi lowlands."[10] The reason why the emigrants did not settle in those gallery forests apparently lies elsewhere.

The fertile alluvial soil of the floodplains was a creation of poorly drained soil, topography, and climate. Mountain streams that enriched the alluvial valley soil with sediments could bring torrents of floodwater as well. Particularly when warm winter rainstorms melted the snow, rivers and creeks overflowed their low embankments and raised the Willamette River 20 to 25 feet beyond its normal level. While the 1.5 to 3 miles of floodwater enriched the floodplain soils with organic nutrients, sustaining a luxurious vegetation that fed numerous land animals and abundant waterfowl, it also meant marshy conditions throughout much of the year on the 400,000 acres of poorly drained soils and the over 400,000 acres of soil types without good natural drainage. Those floodplain and poor drainage conditions were of special concern to the large number of Oregon emigrés from the flood-ravaged areas of the Mississippi and Missouri rivers.[11]

Occasionally, unfamiliarity with the country and an unusual season of high water brought floods that caught settlers unaware. In February 1843, the Willamette River rose "higher than it had been known for thirty years."[12] Gustavus Hines described the consequences: "Farms were swept of their fences, and farmers suffered heavy losses in grain, the water rising several feet deep in some of their barns. . . . The flood coming so suddenly upon the valley, the herds on the bottom lands had not time to make their

escape. Horses, cattle, hogs, etc., were swept away and drowned."[13] Due
to abnormally high levels of snow and precipitation, the Willamette River
and its tributary systems brought a similar swath of destruction to valley
settlements in December 1849 and 1861. In 1861, according to Isaac and
Margaret Smith, the Willamette rose "ten feet higher than ever known by
white men." Sweeping away farms, drowning stock, and damaging towns,
the flood did an estimated property damage of several million dollars.[14]

Streams, however, were not to be completely avoided. Water was critical for agricultural and domestic use as well as transportation. Whereas settlers sought to escape lowland areas subject to overflow, upland riverine
locations, with spring water, abundant grassland, rich soil, and nearby timberland, seemed ideal. Offering resources for construction, food, power, and
transportation, these areas were most quickly settled. More than 90 percent
of the farms established in the Willamette Valley were in these grassland
areas, with the remaining homesteads located in oak openings and other
sparsely timbered sites. By the mid-1850s, the most accessible Willamette,
Umpqua, and Rogue River valley lands were occupied, and settlers began
to penetrate more remote, smaller valley areas where they claimed similar
edge environments and carefully avoided floodplains and forests.[15]

Like the region's Native American people, few Northwest settlers tried
to establish homes in the forests. Part of the reason settlers avoided the
forests was that so much arable land was available; even more significant,
however, was the nature of Northwest forests. Clearing forestland was an
overwhelming task, particularly in the Douglas-fir region, where undergrowth and trees formed a barrier contemporary J. Ross Browne described
as "impregnable" as "the great Chinese Wall."[16] Pacific Northwest forests
dwarfed those in the East and Midwest. Eastern and midwestern emigrants
had "never before seen such formidable obstacles to be overcome in order
to redeem land to cultivation."[17] When Horace Holden arrived in Oregon
Country in April 1844, he observed that there was "to much timbered country" here. Another pioneer ruefully noted that if Oregon was "not now
under the control of the 'Fur Company,' it [was] at least largely encumbered
by the 'Firs.' "[18] Before 1850, fewer than a dozen farms had been attempted
in the dense forest land in the western area of what would become Oregon.
Those few settlers lived for years on that land without bringing "more than
10 to 15 acres under cultivation." Heavily forested areas in Washington also
remained sparsely settled throughout the 1850s. In Kitsap County, Washington, for example, land claims involved extractive activities of milling,
logging, fishing, and mining, not homesteading.[19] William Keil's description of the Willapa River area offers an explanation for this phenomenon:

> In the forests . . . the soil is covered three or four feet . . . [with] decay-
> ing tree trunks, moss, parasitic plants and underbrush so that it is

impossible for man or beast to penetrate the forest. . . . I would scarcely risk penetrating into the forest to a distance of a mile with the hope of getting back before night. . . . Such forests are found in the whole territory and all prairies are surrounded by such forests.[20]

Little had changed by 1880. George Wheeler noted that "there seems to be a positive mania among immigrants to locate almost anywhere except amongst 'the big timber,' of which, although it is one of our chief blessings, they all seem to be very much afraid." Throughout the settler era and well into the industrial period, people rarely lived anywhere but on prairies.[21]

Settlers both north and south of the Columbia River shared their avoidance of the forests, but farm settlement was less immediate and more restricted in what is today western Washington. The vastness of the Willamette Valley and Oregon's other good-sized interior valleys provides a partial explanation. But other reasons also account for the slower growth north of the Columbia. The presence of the Hudson's Bay Company certainly slowed American movement into Washington and the province of British Columbia. Prior to 1846, it was uncertain where the boundary would be drawn, although the Columbia River seemed a real possibility. As long as there was a chance that the area north of the river might become British, Americans showed an understandable reluctance to settle there. Not until an immigrant party led by Michael Simmons settled near Tumwater in 1845 was there a permanent American settler population in Washington, and only after 1850 did a substantial influx of Americans settle in Washington. Even after the boundary line was set, however, there were few farm settlements in western Washington. Washington's mountain ranges were no more conducive to agriculture than were Oregon's, and settlers avoided those areas just as their neighbors to the south did.[22] The real physical differences between the two places lay in the lowlands.

Besides the Willamette Valley, the other major regional lowland in the Northwest is the 30- to 40-mile-wide Puget Sound Trough, which extends north 225 miles from the Columbia River floodplain. Several Cascade-fed rivers flow over the lowland and empty into the waters of Puget Sound, a u-shaped body of long channels, inlets, and islands that connect to the Pacific Ocean through the Strait of Juan de Fuca. Unlike the landscape south of the river, which formed as a river system drainage basin, Puget Sound is a glacial depression that created an environment little suited to farming. Throughout much of the Puget Trough, glaciation had left a poor, sandy, and gravelly soil. Streams flowing into the sound did create an enriched soil by depositing sand and silt near river mouths, but the land was subject to overflow. Fertile agricultural land, consequently, was largely restricted to estuaries and river valleys.[23]

Other barriers to agriculture existed as well. The area's dense forests and thick growth of ferns reaching eight feet in height restricted farm settlement even in readily accessible prairie areas adjacent to Puget Sound. The flooding that made farming on the rich alluvial soil possible in the first place could also sweep a farmer's efforts away. Moreover, because it was river overflows that produced rich bottomlands, much of Washington's best and most easily cleared agricultural land lay in remote, small valleys, which meant that settlers were isolated. Not surprisingly, as Michael Luark noted, "these parcels are at present not much sought after, generally being out of the way."[24] Consequently, rich soil and extensive land parcels—even in the 15-mile-wide, 70-mile-long Chehalis Valley—were not enough to ensure rapid settlement. Not until steamboats worked the Chehalis River in the late 1860s could settlers move easily into the area. With the new form of transportation, farmers had access to markets and found a way to combat social isolation, making the valley more appealing to a growing white population.[25]

Mining often provided the catalyst to move settlers into those valley areas. California's gold rush created a thriving timber industry in Washington that stimulated a growth in the area's economy and population. Closer to home, the Fraser River strike in 1858 brought a flood of miners to Washington, bolstering market sales and adding substantially to the settlement population. Numerous erstwhile miners never reached the Fraser River gold fields, largely because of difficulties on the overland trail. Others failed to strike it rich. In either case, many gold seekers, now broke, took up government land in Washington, particularly on the San Juan Islands and in the Snohomish Valley. Unlike earlier Washington settlers and Oregon's farming population, however, most of these men were single, at least until they cohabitated or married a native woman. Homesteads increasingly appeared in the Snohomish, Skagit, and Nooksack river valleys during the late 1850s and early 1860s. During the 1870s, the population in those and other side-stream locations grew, attracted by the "good wild land to be had as homesteads & preem[p]tions." By 1879, the *Washington Standard* observed: "The settlements in Skagit river valley, only recently a howling wilderness, now comprises a population of eight hundred industrious people."[26]

Upland areas from navigable streams like the Puyallup, Chehalis, and Duwamish rivers might have offered settlers rich soil and an escape from seasonal floods, but those lands were not without their own problems. Locations with the best soil were often heavily forested. Boosters, seeking to increase the region's population, wrote about the building material that the giant trees afforded and the revenue settlers would receive from mills for the trees they logged as part of land clearing. But the rhetoric outran reality. Joseph Dugan's statement about the homestead his father took up near Goble, Oregon, was closer to the truth: "In those days timber had very little value so the first thing my Father did was to clear enough land so they could grow things to eat."[27] Besides, few farmers possessed the means to profitably log their land. Other ways of obtaining arable land, apart from trying to clear heavily forested areas, had to be found, and it was not long before settlers began draining and diking the wetlands.

Tideland prairies provided excellent soil and produced grass from two to four feet high. But wetlands also provided fish and wildlife with critical habitat. In addition, wetlands exercise important hydrological and soil functions: helping maintain groundwater supplies and water quality; acting as a floodwater storage shed for holding and processing nutrients; regulating drainage flow rates; and controlling shoreline erosion.[28] Altered wetlands, consequently, wrought significant changes in the Northwest landscape.

W. B. Moore became the first white man to dike and cultivate tideland on Puget Sound when he diked 140 acres between 1865 and 1866. Other enterprising settlers followed his example. Diking and draining the Stillaguamish tide flats and wetlands along the lower reaches and at the mouths of the Snohomish, Skagit, and Nooksack rivers began during the late 1860s. By the early 1880s, approximately 30,000 acres of Puget Sound marshland had been diked. In 1889, 20,000 acres of tideland (Swinomish flat) near the mouth of the Skagit River was "reclaimed." Similar projects were under way along the lower Columbia River by the 1860s. Oregonian David Warren created several hundred acres of hay and pastureland in 1878 by diking tidelands along Skipanon Creek near Astoria. Bottomlands in Columbia County provided good pastureland, following June overflows, and these too were drained and diked during the late 1880s. Ditching to drain the wet Willamette Valley lowlands was underway by the 1870s, and farmers were ditching some of Washington's lowland marshes by that time as well. Moreover, settlers throughout the region drained beaver ponds to reclaim arable farmland with rich peaty soils.[29]

Sometimes the efforts to redesign the landscape set in motion uncontrollable processes that settlers neither envisioned nor desired. Willamette Valley pioneer John Minto destroyed a beaver pond in an effort to create more arable land. Instead, Minto's actions ruined a trout pool and opened a niche for forest growth that threatened to overtake the "natural sheep pasturage" that the beaver had created.[30] Minto may have been somewhat unusual in his understanding of the environmental changes he had unleashed, but the destruction of beaver ponds, along with diking and draining projects, commonly resulted in a loss of riparian ecosystem and wildlife habitat. Under the new American landscaping, farmers reduced the number of natural duck ponds and the fringe environments of willow, ash, alder, aspen, and green grass that ducks, snipe, curlew, woodcock, plover, and crane used for breeding and that fawns employed for protection. They also destroyed estuary systems that estuarine-dependent chum, chinook, and coho salmon utilized. The subsequent clearing of log jams from rivers to further water transportation and travel also acted to not only alter hydrology and stream habitat but also to reduce wetlands as well.[31]

The loss of wetlands has only begun to be studied, but the processes begun with settlement accelerated during the twentieth century and have resulted in vast wetland losses. Wetland acreage in Washington and Oregon declined by 31 percent (1,350,000 to 938,000) and 38 percent (2,262,000 to 1,393,900), respectively, between the 1780s and 1980s. The most desirable locations underwent the highest amount of reduction. In Oregon's Tualatin Basin, for example, there has been a 61 percent loss in wetlands below the 600-foot level. Agricultural reclamation between 1880 and 1940 reduced the pre-settlement 10,000-acre Snohomish estuary by about 90 percent. Other western Washington areas also show reduced wetlands. The lower Columbia River estuary between Westport and the Pacific Ocean declined by 25 percent from 1870 to 1983, but this comparatively low percentage is misleading because it incorporates deep and shallow water acreages. A truer picture of change is indicated by the 65 percent loss (46,200 to 16,150 acres) in swamp and marshlands, due largely to diking.[32]

Even aside from the unintended consequences, efforts to drain the land were not always successful. At times, the raw forces of nature simply overwhelmed human-engineered barriers. Restructuring nature, farmers learned, was neither simple nor cheap, as floods and high tides occasionally swept diking away and ruined fields. From 1871 to 1877, there was a spurt in reclamation in order to take advantage of soil-rich unclaimed wetlands and the rising prices of grain crops. But this investment proved costly in terms of capital, labor, and machinery. Those who were well-capitalized developed some of the most productive farms in Washington State. Others, however, were not so fortunate. Many farmers borrowed money, gambling that projected profits would cover their indebtedness. With a net average profit of $35 a ton for oats on the San Francisco market during 1877, the gamble seemed to be paying off, until an economic downturn between 1878 and 1880 saw the average price for oats fall to about $16 per ton.[33]

There were other costs as well. John Minto observes that wildlife seldom benefited from the endeavors: "To me it seems easily unbelievable by a person coming here now, to state the quantity of waterfowl, cranes, curlew and snipe which wintered on the grasses and roots of the damp lands of the valleys and the sloughs, ponds and streams sixty-four years ago."[34] Minto lamented the change:

> The Willamette Valley has largely ceased to be the home of the crane, curlew, gray plover, and even the snipe, as well as the beaver, muskrat and wild duck. These damp-land and water fowls and animals, which once found here their breeding places, have gone forever, unless farm-

ers in the near future construct artificial fish-ponds, and reservoirs for irrigation when needed.[35]

However much Minto may have regretted the changes, he was nonetheless intimately involved with bringing them about.

Human alterations in the Douglas-fir country were nothing new. Native Americans and fur traders had certainly recast the environment, and settler society appeared to be just the latest agent of change. After all, both Indians and whites fished and hunted, gathered vegetation, cut trees, used fire, and utilized the waterways for transportation and communication. Yet settler society differed qualitatively and quantitatively from Native American society.

Whites used fire to shape the region's vegetation, but the location, the frequency, and the areal extent of burns differed from Indian fires. Settler society acted both to suppress and to extend the frequency of fires. Fewer fires were set in valley settlement areas, but the number and the extent of forest fires increased. Between 1845 and 1855, a period of heavy emigration, approximately seven times as much land was deforested as in any of the three previous decades. Other studies show a similar pattern of white settlement and increased forest fires.[36]

Native Americans had employed prescribed, low-intensity burns to create the valley landscapes that Euroamericans so idealized. In the fall of 1844, Jesse Applegate wrote a vivid account of one such fire in what would become Polk County, Oregon:

> We did not yet know that the Indians were wont to baptise the whole country with fire at the close of every summer; but very soon we were to learn our first lesson. This season the fire was started somewhere on the south Yamhill, and came sweeping up through the Salt Creek gap. . . . The flames swept by on both sides of the grove; then quickly closing ranks, made a clean sweep of all the country south and east of us. . . . The Indians continued to burn the grass every season, until the country was somewhat settled up and the whites prevented them; but every fall for a number of years, we were treated to the same grand display of fireworks.[37]

As Applegate and others noted, settlers had forced the Indians of the lower Willamette Valley to discontinue their burning practices by 1850. Elsewhere, too, settlers curbed Indian fire.[38]

With notions of fixed, privately held property that included livestock and crops, Northwest settlers saw fire as destructive rather than regenerative. Like the region's predatory animals, annually set prairie fires appeared more a threat than an aid in securing peoples' well being. Fire could be useful when domesticated, but wild fire seemed as chaotic and threatening as any other aspect of the unsettled landscape. Consequently, wild fire declined in areas of settlement.

In places like the Willamette Valley, white settlement and the suppression of Indian wild fires reduced prairie lands and increased tree and brush growth in the surrounding hills. Largely unproductive for row crops and open to invasion by Douglas-fir and oak seedlings, much of the better hill land became pastureland. By the late 1870s, according to Matthew Deady, oak and fir, 20 to 40 feet high, grew on vast acres that had been prairie land when he had emigrated to the Willamette Valley in 1849.[39] Other accounts, including Joseph Brown's observation about the change since his migration from Illinois in 1847, supported Deady:

> The country then was entirely different to what it is now [1878]. It was new and their was more prarie. It was more open than it is at the present time. This growth of oak and fir has grown up since pretty much. . . . When I came to Salem 30 years ago you could ride these hills anywhere. The trees have all grown up since.[40]

Suppressing Indian-prescribed burns may have also produced another unintended consequence. Native Americans had used fire to harvest grasshoppers, but what they thought was a delicacy, settlers considered a pest. In the mid-1850s, grasshoppers invaded the Willamette Valley, injuring the grass, crops, gardens, and orchards. The invasion may have been directly linked to the curtailment of Indian burning practices in the valley.[41]

This does not mean that settlers were against the use of fire. They disdained it only where it threatened their property. By the 1870s, affluent settlers hired Chinese workers to clear their land. But most settlers prepared their own land for cultivation and regarded fire as their most beneficent tool. Isaac Smith wrote his siblings in 1854: "It is not a big a job to clear land here [Oregon] as one might suppose. They do the most of it with fire. They can burn up the green timber roots and all."[42] And burn they did. "I set some fires in the woods," Washington settler Michael Luark wrote in 1865, "which spread from tree to tree over about 20 acres of land . . . making some of the most sublime sights I ever witnessed of that nature."[43] Decades later, a critic of that land-clearing technique testified to its continuing use: "The fire is the peculiar weapon of the settler here. Elsewhere the ax has been the weapon of progress, . . . it has led the march of the pioneer in the conquest of America. . . . But here it is laid aside. The woods no longer ring with its stroke. The deadly insidious fire works in its stead."[44]

To remove alder, vine maple, and other deciduous trees, farmers used girdling and an axe. But to clear the land of the larger, evergreen Douglas fir, cedar, hemlock, or spruce often called for fire and an axe.[45] Phoebe Judson detailed the process used near Lynden, Washington, in the 1870s:

> They were not all felled by the axe—some were brought down by fire. With a large auger two holes were bored into the tree—one sloping slightly upward and the other downward, to make them meet, thus creating a draft. After a few burning coals were dropped into the holes [and then fanned with a bellows through the downward made hole], it usually required four to five days to burn them down. Often they burned only to the sap, leaving a hollow shell, when a few strokes of the axe would bring them to the ground—some of the largest ones making the earth tremble, as though shaken by an earthquake. Felling them was a small part of the work. Their giant forms now cumbered the ground and must be disposed of in some manner, and the auger was again called into use, holes were bored at regular intervals the whole length of the tree. In the holes fires were set to burning, which were kept blazing night and day until the tree was consumed.[46]

Sometimes, as Judson noted, settlers burned a tree where it fell. At other times, depending on the species, they used portions of downed trees for farm construction or fuel and burned the rest as slash.[47]

Inherent in using fire to clear the land was the possibility that fire would spread into the surrounding woods, creating a "booming" sound "like artillery" as falling trees crashed to the ground and burning large areas of forests before dying out. Michael Luark described a conflagration that grew from a slash burn he started: "I burned the Slashing on the hill above the house and barn getting a good burn on all the east end the wind carrying the fire among the trees to the East." On another occasion, Luark recorded how two spruce trees he fired fell "and the fire run up the big spruce and spread from that to others until the woods was all ablaze."[48] For farmers who could "not get the heavy growth off the land in any other way," fires that might burn surrounding forests were not an evil. As Frances Fuller Victor commented, forest fires could reveal "fine level benches of land fit for farming" that otherwise would have remained hidden.[49]

Farmers also used fire to rid their land of troublesome weeds and tenacious ferns that often reached 8 to 10 feet in height.[50] Oregon settler Absolom Harden explained the difficulty farmers faced:

> Thear is one pess in this country that is the fern it groes Spontainously near the fawls and all over the twality plains and a greatdeal of it groes on the East Side of the wilamett for 60 milies a bove the city and this

fearn is like the winter fearn in the States and they Say it is heard to kill and it Smuthers wheat and wheat dont do so well in fearn Land."[51]

For most settlers, the arduous, back-breaking work of clearing land was something they took great pride in having accomplished. Skagit County, Washington, settler Thomas Hastie expressed the feelings many homesteaders must have felt: "I cleared up 160 acres out of that bottom land and never let a contract to do it. Did it all myself. There was heavy timber on it, but you wouldn't know by looking at it to-day that a tree ever grew upon it. They have better ways of clearing the land now with their dynamite. But I did it with only team, grub, ax and fire."[52]

Americans also used fire to clear trails, build roads, and construct railroads. Again, nature proved difficult to control. Fires set for the purpose of clearing transportation routes sometimes spread well beyond the intended path into the surrounding forests.[53]

Wherever and whenever Americans traveled, fire threatened. Campfires were a common source of conflagrations. The great Yaquina and Nestucca burns in Oregon during the fall of 1849 probably resulted from goldseekers camping on their way south toward California. Samuel Clarke wrote: "Those who lived here in the summer of 1849 tell of seeing the heavens flame-lit until a pall of smoke settled on the world that almost smothered communities."[54]

Years later, as hunting, fishing, and tourism increased during the nineteenth and into the twentieth century, so did the frequency of fires. Hunters, cognizant of how a forest-grassland ecotone attracted game, started fires to make hunting more productive, much as Indians had done for centuries. Hunters were also known to set fires to burn away the thick undergrowth that impaired their vision and travel. Stockmen and sheepmen, using the forest "commons," burned forested areas in the Cascade Mountains to promote grasslands and create paths for trailing their animals. The woods, forest inspector H. D. Langille observed, "were looked upon as nobody's property for which no one was responsible."[55]

As settlers moved into the forests to mine, log, and mill, the frequency of forest fires increased. Machine-driven industrial logging and milling ignited fires, while the litter that was a by-product of regional logging practices increased fuel buildup and the likelihood that a burn would occur.[56] Moreover, fires in logged-off areas often proved deleterious to reforestation. They tended not only to destroy the seedlings necessary for forest regeneration, but also to remove the humus (thereby lessening the soil's ability to retain moisture) that was essential for sustaining a species like Douglas fir.[57]

Americans sometimes set fires for their own amusement. One of the most notable instances occurred at a Fourth of July celebration in the 1850s.

James Swan recounted how he and some acquaintances started a bonfire in an old cedar stump at Willapa Bay, Washington: "It made the best bonfire I ever saw; and after burning all night and part of the next day, finally set fire to the forest, which continued to burn for several months, till the winter rains finally extinguished it."[58] Swan's reminiscence reflects little regret over the forest fire the celebration had unleashed. If it had occurred in a settled prairie area it is very possible that Swan would have been more deeply concerned. Swan expressed a common attitude toward the forests. Woodlots near a homestead were good, but forests themselves were a barrier to settlement. Conceivably, the forest fire that Swan described was more than entertainment; it was also a good way to open a forest area for settlement. Besides, with so much forest, burning part of it hardly seemed wasteful or destructive.

Where there was fire, there must also be smoke. With the growing number of fires in the Northwest, smoke became a problem. Throughout the nineteenth and into the early twentieth centuries, smoke was everywhere but was worse in some seasons than in others. The smoke from the extensive fires in 1857 became so bad that the *Oregonian* warned of smoke-induced respiratory problems. More harrowing were the 1868 fall fires that raged from southern Oregon to British Columbia, with smoke blocking out the sun in some places. Navigation along the Columbia River came to a standstill, and limited visibility on the Willamette River led to the suggestion that a lighthouse be established to guide steamers.[59] A newspaper account details the situation at Olympia, Washington:

> All yesterday ashes from the fiery forests to windward were falling in this city, and the smoke was so dense lamps were used until 10 A.M., and were relighted at 4 P.M. Every thing looked gloomy as death. The gas jets were blue as a sulphur flame and the sun when visible at all, seemed merely like a red disk suspended in the Heavens. . . . Such a day has not been seen for many years if there ever was such a one before. . . . No one but would thank the Fates for a shower to quench the terrible fires that oppress us. . . . Whirlwinds and floods would be better than what we now endure.[60]

Smoke from the conflagration drifted south to engulf San Francisco.[61]

Yearly fires continued to plague the region, but no great fire year again threatened the Northwest until the summer and fall of 1902, when forest fires claimed the greatest amount of life and farm property recorded to that time. As in 1868, land clearing and campers' fires ignited flames that high winds fanned and swept along a corridor from southern Oregon to Puget Sound.[62]

Although Americans suppressed valley fires, forest fires increased during the settler and early industrial period. Nevertheless, the total amount of burned forestland at the turn of the twentieth century remained proportionately small. In Oregon's Cascade Forest Reserve, stretching from the California boundary to the Columbia River, only 8 percent was burned. The Olympic Forest Reserve showed only a 5 percent burn (177 square miles), owing no doubt to the rugged terrain that limited human intrusion and to its bountiful rainfall. In the more frequented Rainier Forest, 15.5 percent had been burned.[63]

There is little question that by the turn of the century the presence of settlers had increased the prevalence of forest fires in the region. Although some people became increasingly concerned about intentionally or accidentally started fires, older attitudes and actions did not die easily. Restricted human occupancy and limited logging did as much to minimize regional forest fires as American concerns and practices. Moreover, that same combination of increased forest fires and limited human intrusion meant that natural reproduction followed the fires, ensuring the regeneration of a subclimax Douglas-fir forest.[64] Only with the rise of a powerful lumber industry, the increasing commercial value attached to forests, the private ownership of forestland, and the conservation movement did attitudes towards forest fire begin to change.

As forestlands grew in value and passed into private ownership during the late nineteenth century, the movement to suppress wild fires grew. The desire to safeguard and protect property investment stood at the heart of the movement. According to fire historian Stephen Pyne, American fire policy was based on a belief that every fire could be controlled by preventing ignition, modifying potential fire environments, and suppressing fires quickly when they occurred so that they remained small. Part of the Progressive movement's general conservation ethos for order and scientific management, industrial society's fire system achieved neither control nor security.[65] Like other conservation policy measures, fire control had its ironic twists. In this case, fire suppression not only made forests vulnerable to insects and disease but also disallowed fire's regenerative role. By reducing the frequency of low-intensity fires a fuel buildup occurred, ensuring that once a fire began, a catastrophic crown conflagration would result.[66]

Like the use of fire, transportation choices highlighted similarities and differences between Anglo American and Native American culture. Both Indians and whites used waterways and the land as ways to transport themselves and their material goods, although water provided the dominant means for regional transport until the end of the settler period in the 1880s. While oceangoing cargo ships entered Northwest waters during the period of the fur trade, most goods and people were transported by canoes and scows until steamboats began plying regional waters in the 1850s.[67]

Transportation on land was achieved by foot, horse, and, occasionally, a form of animal-drawn vehicle where a road had been cleared. The initial land-based public transportation system began in 1846 with an ox-drawn stage operating between Oregon City and the Tualatin Plains. Permanent stagecoach service in the Willamette Valley, however, was not offered until 1849, and passenger service out of Olympia only came five years after that. Subsequent common carriers followed, with the California Stage Company establishing a line between Sacramento and Portland in 1860. A limited number of military wagon roads, constructed during the 1860s, provided an additional means of transport. Despite the innovations, overland transportation was limited. Most farmers avoided shipping their produce any distance by wagon before the 1890s. Unimproved roads with ruts and holes were dusty in summer and muddy quagmires in winter, and bridges were subject to washouts.[68]

Railroads were relatively unimportant until the mid-1860s, and for nearly twenty years afterward the region's track mileage remained limited. No rail line directly connected the Northwest to any outside area. Not until the 1880s was the region's isolation broken. The Northwest received its first transcontinental connection when Henry Villard's Northern Pacific Railroad linked Duluth, Minnesota, to Tacoma in 1883. Other interregional railroads soon followed. The Union Pacific connected Oregon to the Midwest in 1884. In 1887, the Southern Pacific joined Portland to Sacramento, not only tying Oregon to California but also giving Oregon an indirect continental tie-in to the east. In 1893, the Great Northern reached Seattle, linking that northwestern metropolis to Saint Paul, and the Chicago, Milwaukee, and St. Paul Railroad joined Seattle to the Midwest in 1909.[69]

Rail lines in the Pacific Northwest often paralleled nature's waterways, but that apparent conformity to the natural landscape was simply done to service the existing population centers along the rivers. The railroad's great magic was that it created its own geography and, in the process, altered the region's cultural and physical geography. Railroads seemingly abrogated time and space, linking the region more closely with the nation and the regional hinterlands with cosmopolitan centers of power. Little wonder that the coming of railroads to the Northwest became a symbol of the changes that would transform the landscape and peoples' lives, while signaling the movement from settler to industrial society. People, capital, natural resources, and processed goods traveled those rails. Increased population, access to natural resources, and markets all came with the railroads. Between 1880 and 1890, Oregon's population increased almost 80 percent and Washington's by a spectacular 365 percent. Newcomers to the Northwest had many different heritages and backgrounds. The emigrants from the Midwest increased the region's heterogeneity, particularly in sparsely settled Washington. Oregon's ethnic composition also grew, but its cultural homogeneity remained intact. Oregon's established communities attracted like-minded migrants and in numbers that did not overwhelm that state's chartering group culture. Capital investment in manufacturing, farm acreage, and agricultural production similarly exploded upwards but followed patterns established during the settler era: an increased but still small industrial base, a dependency on an extractive economy, and in Washington a continued reliance on outside capital investment while in Oregon, the region held to its more home-owned enterprises, which were capitalized internally.[70]

Railroads also connected interior places to regional trade centers such as Portland, Olympia, and Seattle. Town and countryside had never been distinct or mutually exclusive places, but the links between them became increasingly symbiotic and unequal. With the arrival of the railroads, urban power increased at the expense of rural areas. The border state–New England divisions that had marked the Northwest's country-town landscape from the beginning of settlement widened as concentrations of population and wealth were urbanized. Resentment toward those urban power centers became increasingly apparent. Wallis Nash spoke for many in the hinterland when he noted that should Portland's hegemonic grip ever loosen, "not one single sigh will escape these [Willamette] valley counties, which Portland has levied tribute on, and done her best to keep in bondage till the end of time."[71] Regional centers of power were in turn tied to larger transregional metropolitan areas, forming concentric lines of power that radiated outward. As railroads linked the Northwest to California and other areas of the country during the 1880s, power lines between metropolitan centers and local hinterlands became ever more prevalent and tightly drawn, interregionally and intraregionally.

Population growth, capital investment, technological improvements, and greater market access placed increased pressures on the land. The integrated corridors of trade transformed the region's culture and ecology as it realigned the human power structure. Paradoxically, that integration also meant disintegration of local communities and ecosystems. The segmented assembly line of industrial production provided an apt metaphor for the integration and disorganization that was taking place in all aspects of American life during industrialization.

The segmentation of people's lives proceeded hand-in-hand with an environmental segmentation that destabilized human and ecologicial communities alike. No longer were the demands that people placed on an ecosystem restricted to local residents. Railroads linked the region's ecology with the desires of people who lived outside the region. Distant capital and markets amassed greater power over the regional ecosystem by increasing the amount of resources that were extracted. Moreover, the extraction, production, and consumption of wood had itself become segmented. The process of converting a tree into lumber not only separated producers from users but also obscured from consumers the fact that the ultimate producer was the ecosystem. Obfuscation had profound ecological consequences. Early on, when local extraction and use were the dominant pattern, local control and ecological consequences were one and the same. But with translocal transportation, more than a decline in local control ensued. The people outside the Northwest who materially benefited from exploiting the region's resources never had to see or endure the social or environmental consequences of their actions. Burdens were experienced locally and borne by the least powerful members of society and by an ecosystem that had no standing at all.

On the surface, non-Indian and Native American society appeared to share numerous similarities. But although both peoples employed fire as a land-use tool and used water and pathways for transportation, the cultural systems that directed fire and transportation differed significantly. Out of those profound cultural dissimilarities emerged differing fire and transportation patterns that transformed not only regional social systems but also ecological structures.

CHAPTER SIX

Settler Society

The displacement of Native Americans by Euroamericans changed much more than the region's human ecology; it altered the entire ecology of the land. Whites lived in permanent settlements on privately owned, circumscribed plots of land. White farmers raised a variety of crops and animals not native to the region. Settlers sought to re-create homes not by adjusting to the environment but by making the new landscape adapt to imported familiar patterns of land use. Home meant achieving security in a domesticated and ordered landscape. It also meant that settlers relied on familiar foods, and in the process of importing grains, vegetables, and livestock, settlers unwittingly displaced indigenous species.

The region's physical environment aided settlers' transformation of the land. A mild climate with little snow or freezing weather, abundant moisture, fertile soil, year-round vegetation, and plentiful forests made settlement easier. Unlike other places, settlers in the Douglas-fir region did not have to build protective winter shelters or provide forage for animals. Winter rains were more a blessing than an annoyance, ensuring moisture for people, crops, and livestock. As Peter Burnett explained in an 1844 letter, Northwest rain was warm rather than cold and "fell in very gentle showers."[1]

There were occasionally harsh winters, but typically the climatic conditions for animals and crops was more favorable in the Northwest than in the places from which settlers came.[2] Charles Stevens, even during a particularly cold winter, thought Oregon's weather "the finest, the nicest, and the plesentest weather that I ever knew for the time of year. . . . If this wether should continue . . . we shall all fall in love with the country." Fall in love they did; Charles declared that no member "of the family . . . would go back to Illinois and live for the best fortune in the state."[3] Silas Plimpton called Oregon's climate "delightfull," noting that, unlike citizens of Massachusetts, people in Oregon were "not troubled at all with the heat." Indeed, "it is always necessary to sleep under two blankets" during summer nights. "Were I to make a climate to suit myself," Plimpton concluded, "I could not make any alteration that would suit me any better."[4] Emigrant Thomas Smith recalled: "Coming, as I did, from Northern Indiana [in 1847] where the mercury often went to 32 degrees below zero. I became a great admirer of the Pacific coast and have remained so ever since."[5]

Other environmental factors also made the Northwest attractive. Plentiful forests provided ample materials for houses, barns, fuel, and fences. Streams offered power for milling and manufacturing establishments. Settlers gathered seasonal fruit, including the Oregon grape, crab apples, and a variety of blackberries, raspberries, cranberries, and strawberries. The abundance was remarkable. Visiting Shoalwater Bay in 1855, Michael Luark recorded seeing "the greatest strawberry field that I ever saw, covering perhaps 1000 acres of ground." Emigrant George Riddle remembered how "white horses or cattle were changed to a strawberry color by rolling on the ripe fruit."[6] Deer, elk, fowl, salmon, and clams were also found in abundance and were free for the taking.[7] The Northwest allowed "the necessities of life" to be met "with less labor than . . . in any other country."[8] A December 1865 description of settlement along the Coquille River captures the environment and the pattern of life adopted by most early settlers—one that persisted well into the twentieth century, particularly among back-country hill people:

> They are a healthy and contented people, and make their living easily by rearing stock, hunting and cultivating a few acres of ground, which they have cleared with fire and ax. Their hogs do well upon the unfailing myrtle mast, while their horses and cattle range back on the bald mountain tops, formed by the timber being burned off generations ago by the Indians, the remains decaying, till now the wavy grass has taken the place of the "Titans of the Wood," presenting as beautifully diversified mountain, forest and prairie scenery as man ever gazed upon.[9]

This is not to say that settlers to the Northwest were not interested in advancing their well-being; indeed, they looked toward technology and markets to achieve that goal. Machinery promised to ease backbreaking work and increase productivity, enriching people's lives with more goods and free time for "mental improvement," while liberating people from a dependency on nature. By the 1880s, horse-pulled mowers and reapers had largely displaced the scythe. Wealthy farmers might even own a thrashing machine and a self-binding harvester.[10] Money was needed to buy machinery, however, and those farmers who aimed to accumulate wealth risked failure. Buffeted by periodic depressions through the last third of the nineteenth century and burdened with the capital costs involved in buying machinery, market-directed farmers enjoyed little free time. Technology increased productivity but did little to lighten the time and effort agriculturalists devoted to work. The availability of machinery encouraged farmers to manage fields more closely, intensifying land use and imposing a work-time discipline on the labor force. In the end, technology did not free people from nature.

At the time, however, settlers hailed technology as liberating. Markets, like machinery, seemed an expression of freedom and the means for an improved life. Nonetheless, few settlers produced solely for cash exchange. Most raised crops and animals for household consumption and exchanged surpluses at local markets, with wheat being the most marketable crop throughout the settler period.[11]

To some degree a fully developed market economy was a result of labor scarcity, geographical distance, and transportation limitations. Religious cooperative movement leader William Keil (who eventually established Bethel Colony in Aurora, Oregon) explained the role those factors played in the Willapa Valley, Washington:

> The land itself cannot be excelled anywhere in the world in fertility and productivity, for everything one plants grows luxuriantly and abundantly. But nobody knows what to do with the things he produces. In the first place, there is no market for the things produced; in the second place, there is no prospect for the development of such market; in the third place, everything that one needs is too far away and too expensive, and there is no way by which one can earn his livelihood. . . . If the few existing prairies in Willapa Valley should be fenced in, the wheat grown on them could be ground by me in a week, and the mill would stand idle the rest of the year. To the right and left there is no good farm land and can never be. One might put the mill wherever he might, only the few inhabitants of this valley could come to it, and then only with great difficulty.[12]

Households located near urban centers or transportation points of exchange raised crops, animals, and produced items like butter for market sale.[13] Such locations were few, however, urban populations were small, and transportation facilities were restricted, limiting intraregional and export trade.

Even settlers who were able to overcome these limitations and find an external market saw no end to their problems. Those who directed farm production toward export sale depended not only on nature but also on forces outside local control. As a result, they often saw their "produce destroyed for want of consumers." Northwest potatoes that brought high returns at San Francisco in 1853, for example, were thrown away two years later when the market collapsed: "One company here [Rainier, Oregon] got ten thousand bushel upon their wharf ready for shipment calculating to send them to San Francisco but there being no market for them at that place they were thrown into the [Columbia] river."[14]

Most settlers, however, did not face problems of market dependency. Beyond geographical distance, "the want of mills and labor-saving machines, and the price of labor, [that] discourage[d] . . . [crop] cultivation as articles of export" restricted production for external markets throughout the nineteenth century.[15] But these limitations do not fully explain the situation. Settler culture played a crucial role. Settlers approached markets cautiously, for although farmers wanted outlets for their surpluses, few were unlimited marketers merely awaiting the structures that would make profit maximization possible. Settlers farmed according to the "Oregon fashion," which sought to take advantage of market exchange while minimizing market risk. They accomplished their goal through raising a variety of crops and animals designed to meet household needs first and marketing only the surpluses. Regional abundance permitted the strategy, as this description of Tillamook County, Oregon, in 1885 makes clear: "Agriculture has made but little progress, owing chiefly to a lack of transportation, but partly to the fact that with a few cattle, a fishing rod and a gun, the settler can live in royal style without the labor that accompanies grain farming."[16] If the commingling of nature's abundance and landholding patterns framed the possibility for a safety-first agricultural strategy, settler culture prescribed the goal.

Emigrants entering the Douglas-fir region from the 1840s to the 1880s, particularly south of the Columbia River, were families in search of health and abundant land upon which they could establish permanent homes. Oregonians clearly recognized these goals as an important feature of their society and a significant element in framing a distinctive self-identity. L. F. Grover, in an 1853 Fourth of July speech, contrasted Oregon's steady progress with California's fluctuating periods of rapid growth and declines. For Grover, Oregon's superiority clearly rested with its "permanent population, characterized by intelligence, industry and wealth." Or, as Oregon Superintendent of Indian Affairs Anson Dart proudly noted, Oregon proved a poor country for "doctors, lawyers, clerks, speculators and gamblers."[17]

The new populace arrived imbued with notions of yeoman independence, republicanism, and family values that stressed freedom and security.[18] They sought independence by acquiring legal title to the land and by physically dominating it. The land's fertility and large parcel size allowed for personal well-being and provided sufficient property so children could be settled around their parents, ensuring the next generation's independence and a social security system for aging parents. Numerous settlers gave testimony to that desire. Andrew Wigle recalled coming in 1852 because "father wanted to go to Oregon that his children might secure homes and all settle near him." "Come to Oregon," Roselle Putnam wrote to her Indiana in-laws. In Oregon people could acquire tracts enough to meet current needs and "insure" for their heirs "an inheritance."[19] William Shaw noted a similar inducement for his coming to Oregon in 1846: "My family was a family of boys and they were getting to be men, and I was not able to settle them in

Missouri. Land began to get up, and it was hard to get, and I thought by moving to a new country my boys could shift for themselves."[20]

Freedom and security rested on owning and improving the land. Settlers' ideas, values, and material needs reinforced one another. When settlers spoke about their goals and beliefs they employed a republican idiom of civic virtue, independence, and a producer ideology. Oregon's image in the popular imagination was Edenic, and its settlers came with expectations of creating a society that would avoid the mistakes of the past. Oregon settlers wanted to create an exclusive country of white, settled families sharing republican values. This goal predicated a stable economic order based on a familial republican sociopolitical structure that welcomed industrious producers but excluded speculators. Oregon appealed for emigrants who desired "a sufficiency," who possessed "a reasonable ambition for wealth," and who wanted "secure homes, comfort and competence for themselves and their children." Those qualities informed the majority of persons drawn to Oregon. Joseph Henry Brown, who came overland to Oregon in 1847, recalled: "The condition of the country previous to the discovery of gold in California was that the people never expected to make fortunes here but simply to live peaceful and pastrol lives."[21]

That quest for independence and security and the preference for republican imagery were maintained well into the late nineteenth century, as the settlers who came to Oregon between 1840 and 1855 established cultural hegemony over the state.[22] "Large families . . . were able to call whole townships their own" by taking up adjoining land parcels under the Donation Land Law.[23] Historian David Johnson described how that control was produced and reproduced: "By virtue of ownership they collectively controlled others' access to the land, and by doing so necessarily molded—by deciding to whom they would sell, rent, or otherwise grant (in the form, for example, of inheritance bequests) their land—the makeup of Oregon's population and the shape of its agricultural economy."[24]

Even Oregon's more market-oriented settlers like Silas Plimpton or Charles Stevens, who moved between farm and town constantly looking to maximize their economic benefits, were rather conservative. Similarly, Oregon's urban capitalists were a more cautious and less speculative breed than their counterparts in other areas of the Far West.[25]

The few settlers who migrated north of the Columbia during the 1840s also included entire families with motives similar to those who settled to the south. Northern settlement, however, was limited by geopolitical uncertainty before 1846 and by physical geography. The vast extent of the Willamette Valley and Oregon's other good-sized interior valleys simply attracted more people. Those groups served as a magnet to draw still more like-minded settlers, further increasing the attraction and cultural homogeneity of those areas.

What gave Washington its defining characteristic was not its agricultural settlers but its lumbermen. Following the California gold rush, Washington's forests drew lumbermen based in New England and San Francisco, whose capital brought an influx of people and markets. Logging and lumbering became Washington's commercial linchpin and culturally defining structure. Timber enterprises were the hub for towns; supplied farmers with markets; gave Washington a more male, single, and diverse population than Oregon; and made it a place receptive to unbridled opportunism. It also meant, however, that Washington's development was more closely dependent on outside investment capital and externally driven market forces. Industrialization only furthered the trend and increased Washington's heterogeneity.[26]

Social relationships among settlers reflected a reluctance to surrender fully to market imperatives. Although cash had become the medium of exchange in towns by the 1850s, exchange in kind remained common among settlers well into the second half of the nineteenth century. A shortage of currency limited exchange, but a preference for preserving mutuality, familiarity, and kinship also curtailed the commodification of social relations.

Settler Michael Luark occasionally worked at mills around Olympia for wages, but he and his neighbors exchanged labor, tools, and goods as much as cash. Luark exchanged wheat and carpentry work for cattle. He received onions for repairing a neighbor's clock, and when he married a couple he received 200 pounds of flour as payment. On other occasions he exchanged labor. Luark helped a friend bind wheat, and the friend reciprocated by helping Luark stack hay. Mutuality also expressed itself in "logrolling" or a "chopping bee" to construct a woodhouse. Settlers kept accounts, calculated in dollars and cents, but interest did not figure into the exchange.[27] Not that hard bargaining for material advantage did not exist. Even in towns where cash nexus values found more expression, however, community restrictions were evident. Charles Stevens, while noting that mercantile business opportunities in Oregon were good, still cautioned that "loaning money at fifty pr cent I think would not shine very well."[28] Markets were present, but values of independence, face-to-face interactions, and competency continued to dominate social relationships in settler society.

Oregonians were especially reluctant to cede control to external markets. People accepted internal market development and the need to import goods not locally produced, but they wanted to avoid depending too much on outside markets. Most settlers had lived through the 1837 depression and had no desire for a repeat performance. The regional economy was to be the household writ large, producing primarily to meet internal needs and exporting surpluses. When urged to increase production for markets, then, northwesterners did so in the name of creating home markets and regional independence.[29] Residents knew that "no country can thrive which is not its own principal producer."[30] Failure, the *Oregon Statesman* acknowledged, brought dependence: "In most articles we have failed to supply the home demand, and in consequence our State has been drained of money in order to supply us with the necessaries of life." The *Statesman* added: "If we do not develop our own resources, and produce for home consumption every article adapted to our soil and climate all the gold and silver in our rich mines never will free us from a dependent position."[31] That same theme had been remarked upon a month earlier:

> We hold that no country is so prosperous as the one which is able to live within itself, or the one which does not depend upon foreign imports for the various articles in common use, and that therefore whoever aids home manufacture, or succeeds in the production of any article that otherwise would have to be imported, benefits not only himself, but gives material aid to the section in which he lives.[32]

Independence and prosperity required that production and profit be kept within the area of resource extraction. Otherwise, as one regional magazine phrased it, "Oregon is like a great warehouse feeding the capitalists, but never receiving anything in return."[33] Most settlers preferred a society of small producers, devoid of market social relations, where households of equals exchanged goods in a market they could control. Control, however, proved slippery, and settlers never understood that the market economy did not exist apart from the social relationships of the marketplace.

A producer ideology and concern for independence and security also influenced the way settlers viewed investors. Although settlers regarded nonproducers, including merchants, as "vampires" who lived off others' wealth, they made no blanket denunciation of finance capitalists. Newspapers continually called for capital investment in the region. The line of demarcation was largely drawn between internal and external investors. Resident capitalists were embraced, but migrant capitalists were another story: they not only accumulated wealth they did nothing to produce but also sought only to advance their own self-interest. Willing to move wherever investment promised the highest rate of return, foreign capitalists had no loyalty to the local community.[34] Transient capital threatened rather than sustained the order and stability of communities, settlers believed. Northwesterners, particularly Oregonians, would hold to that opinion well beyond the era of settler society, continuing to view themselves as a fiercely independent people.

Those attitudes also made settlers ambivalent toward railroads, because they were foreign owned and operated. Residents had long dreamed that railroads would bring to the area "such a flood of immigration, manufactures and commerce as the imagination of the wildest enthusiast can now scarcely anticipate."[35] But there was ambivalence, too, lest people be run over by locomotives they could not control:

> It is a rule that the pioneer seldom reaps the harvest for which he has sown the seed. The reasons are obvious: first, the habits and experience of frontier life have not qualified him to compete, in business pursuits, with those who are fresh from the struggles of civilization; and second, that civilization, with its fresh and skilled enterprise, also brings capital, a still more formidable competitor.[36]

Caution and ambivalence, however, stood little chance to block the engine of progress driven by those who desired expansion into the hinterlands.

From the 1840s to 1880s, settlers looked for security in permanent residency, local capital, and cultivated nature. They also raised a number of domestic species, believing monoculture agriculture to be a recipe for disaster. As the *Columbian* phrased it: "The prosperity of a country should never depend upon one staple commodity."[37] Even with the onset of industrial society, earlier warnings echoed. In an address at the third annual Lewis County, Washington, Agricultural Association fair, Joseph S. Allen told the assembled crowd: "The man who places his sole dependance in wheat or in any other single crop is like a man who patronizes the lottery."[38] Yet the attraction of more consumer articles and a belief that dependency could be avoided in this land of abundance, equality, and opportunity deflected the warnings.[39]

Geography, technology, external events, and settler attitudes landscaped the region, but the public expression of attitudes and power in government actions also shaped the cultural and ecological landscape. The federal government sponsored numerous exploratory expeditions that mapped the West and provided the public with detailed knowledge about the Douglas-fir region. Through treaties with Great Britain in 1846 and with native peoples during the 1850s, the national government secured American land claims to the Northwest. Military and civilian officeholders representing the U.S. government also played a role, particularly by providing legal and military shields of protection. In addition, the national government paid employees and purchased supplies for the military.[40] Nowhere, though, did the federal government play a more important role in framing the Northwest than through land-grant policies. As whites systematized the landscape, land laws did almost as much as technology and nature to alter the region's ecology.

Virginia senator John Floyd had introduced a bill in January 1821 that called for free land to induce Northwest settlement. Floyd's initial proposal, along with subsequent proposals throughout the 1820s and 1840s, met with defeat.[41] Congressional inaction, however, did not dissuade Americans from moving west. Westering Americans neither waited for treaties to acquire land from Indians nor for surveyors to prepare the land for sale. Settlers in the Douglas-fir region merely seized land parcels in anticipation of American sovereignty. Left without federal protection and seeking to secure property against other interlopers, Americans joined with a few French Canadians in the spring of 1843 to organize an independent provisional government in Oregon. The new government's lack of formal legal standing did not keep the settlers from adopting an organic code of laws that included four landownership articles. Two articles dealt with claim procedures and entitlement. Another, reflecting settlers' animus against speculation and monopoly, provided that no one could monopolize a townsite, water privileges, or other facilities necessary for conducting business if it harmed the general community. The land proviso limited individuals to 640 acres. Minor changes were made in the landownership articles in 1844 and 1845, but the original provisions remained intact until Oregon became a territory in 1848.[42]

Although the national government did not directly shape regional land law before 1850, it had established political boundaries with the 1846 treaty and had made Oregon a territory two years later. By midcentury, the federal government assumed formal control of Northwest land policy. With passage of the Oregon Donation Land Act in 1850, Congress granted 320 acres to white or "half-breed" males over eighteen who were citizens or had declared an intention to become citizens provided they had settled in the territory before December 1, 1850. If they married before December 1, 1851, another 320 acres could be claimed. Title was perfected by occupation and cultivation of the land for four continuous years. Later amendments provided that white male citizens twenty-one years and older who settled in the territory between December 1, 1850, and December 1, 1853, were eligible for 160 acres; their wives could claim an equal amount. An amendment in February 1853 extended the expiration date to December 1, 1855, and allowed the claimant to purchase the land for $1.25 per acre after living on the land for two years. The act's generous land-holding provisions meant that most arable land in the Willamette Valley had been removed from the public domain by the early 1850s.[43]

Following the expiration of the Donation Act on December 1, 1855, settlers could take up unoccupied federal land under terms of the 1841 Preemption Act or, after 1862, the Homestead Act. Generous special-purpose land grants also became a way to obtain land. The federal government gave Oregon and Washington the sixteenth and thirty-sixth sections in each township and allowed the states to then sell them to support public education. In addition, the national government extended lucrative land grants to private parties as inducements to construct transportation systems. Oregon became the only state outside the Mississippi Valley that received land for the promotion of wagon roads, and the sale of those lands by rail and wagon companies gave settlers yet another means for acquiring land. Special land-grant measures, however, carried important restrictions: they required immediate payment and actual settlement and restricted the acreage that could be conveyed to any one purchaser.[44] Like subsequent land laws, such as the Timber and Stone Act, the measures became embroiled in fraud as buyers and sellers circumvented restrictions. Finally, land could simply be bought from the current owner.

At the heart of American land policy was the nation's vision of itself, and land laws therefore reflected republican ideals about freedom and liberty. The public domain was an instrument for structuring the social and economic fabric of American society so it would maintain its republican nature. Laws to discourage large-scale land holding and speculation sought the socioeconomic ends of material prosperity, social mobility, and independence, particularly in the Northwest. The Donation Land Act marked the first time in American history that government made an outright gift of the public domain to settlers. The ideal was moderate-sized farms owned by American farmers who ordered the wilderness into a productive garden. In touch with nature and nature's god, the yeoman producer eschewed luxury and the evils of overcivilization. Balanced between chaos and corruption, savagery and overcivilization, settlers would re-create republican America as they systematized the landscape.[45]

Native Americans also influenced the settlement process. Because Northwest Indians were not a well-mounted, aggressive, and warlike people, isolated settlement by white Americans on large land holdings was possible. Security did not require that settlers create concentrated population areas. Moreover, the decimation of the Indian population by introduced diseases had created an ecological niche into which the pioneering Americans settled. Finally, the valley landscapes that settlers so admired, prized, and chose to settle were the result of Indian burning practices. Whether intentional or not, even in decline, native people acted to shape the dominant invaders.

Early land laws may have expressed a political-economic vision, but this cultural geography was uninformed by the geography of place. Private land holdings seldom conformed to the natural geography of the landscape. Instead, they reflected a geometric grid that imposed an ordered design on the land, asserting in one more way settlers desire to dominate, order, and control the land.[46]

Spearheaded by southern congressmen John Floyd, Lewis Linn, and Thomas Hart Benton, early settler land grants emulated a southern patterning rather than the physical landscape of the Douglas-fir region. Large land-holding parcels adopted by the Oregon provisional government and the Donation Land Act might have made sense in the South, with its tradition of extensive open-range livestock grazing, but it did not conform to the environmental realities of the Northwest. The imported old once more sought to shape the new, with little understanding or reference to the land itself.

Land laws created to secure an egalitarian, independent yeoman, republican social order carried unintended environmental consequences. The size of the land grants exceeded both what a settler could readily clear and what he needed to farm in the region's most fertile areas. According to *West Shore*, 40 to 80 acres was all one family could profitably cultivate or needed to live comfortably, even by the 1880s.[47] The environmental consequences of extensive land parcels were mixed. The practice lowered the impact of a concentrated population on the land by limiting settler density, but it extended human intrusion over a larger area.[48]

The social and economic results of those generous land policies did not please all northwesterners, nor did their fellow settlers' less than arduous efforts at land improvement and agricultural productivity.[49] One settler attempted to place a positive interpretation on the large land-holding parcels by noting that it imposed "a respectable distance" so that "there is no quarreling about neighbors *hens here*."[50] But to many newcomers, particularly New Englanders, so much land holding threatened the New England town ideal and the good order it represented. In 1853, Whig-appointed postmaster Nathaniel Coe explained: "Mile square farms are too large for schools and meetings."[51]

It was not, however, the mere size and spacing of farms that offended some northwesterners, but the kind of life those large fertile tracts made possible. Settlers with modernizing ideas, like Jesse Applegate, while not attacking regional land laws directly, did critique many of their fellow residents' work habits. Applegate charged that too many settlers were content with satisfying basic needs rather than aspiring to increase productivity or to improve their economic and social standing. He sharply criticized settlers who failed "to avail themselves of the natural advantages of the country, or to turn their attention exclusively to those branches of agriculture that markets and means of transportation make most profitable."[52] Frances Fuller Victor echoed these sentiments, noting "the general air of neglect and improvidence" that marked too much of the Willamette Valley. She was even more specific than the sage of Yoncalla about the cause:

In the first place, the farming community of the country was derived originally from the border States, as they were thirty years ago. They had never been *good* farmers in the States of Missouri, Illinois, or Kentucky. Upon immigrating to Oregon they received a large body of land—too large to cultivate properly—with no adequate market for its productions, if they could or would work it. They consequently fell into the habit of raising a little grain indifferently well, of raising stock in the same manner, without caring to improve it materially; of living on what they could buy with the money obtained for what they had to sell—instead of producing—a hundred things which the careful and thrifty farmer supplies himself with. . . .

Some of the most beautiful portions of Western Oregon are under this curse of bad stewardship.[53]

The "natural advantages" Applegate noted seemed to confirm an early and continuous refrain, that the region's abundance might create a society of lazy and contented people. Neil Howison remarked that the region's cultivated land in 1845 was "not a handsbreadth compared to the whole body claimed and held in idleness." Decades later that evaluation could still be heard. The *Oregon Statesman* praised Oregon's economic growth for 1865 but noted that only 140,000 acres of land were under agricultural production, and even that acreage existed in a state of "very careless cultivation." Just over ten years later, Oregon's farms were still said to be "imperfectly tilled." Moreover, much of the land remained "unimproved." Willamette Valley's unimproved land stood at 52.6 percent for 1860; in 1870, at 48.9 percent; in 1880, at 45.6 percent; and in 1890, at 49.5 percent. Michael Luark looked at the unimproved land, worm fences, and staid religious practices around Stayton and said it spoke volumes about "the character & energy of the people." Worse yet, according to Luark, "is that it is impossible to convince them of their need of a new life."[54]

While modernizing northwesterners seemed offended by the self-satisfied way that many of their countrymen went about their work, bourgeois outsiders were downright appalled. *Harper's* magazine reported that much of the best land in the Willamette Valley had been taken up early by "unenterprising" border state settlers. It was a group of "loungers," who possessed "thriftless habits" and generally constituted "an extremely poor class of vagabond farmers." Thankfully, the article concluded, the Oregon landscape had started to resemble Ohio and New York, with frame homes, schools, churches, and fine farms averaging more than one hundred acres. Those "old Oregonians" seemed at last to be giving way to "their betters" so that "thrift and neatness" was beginning to replace waste and carelessness.[55]

Whether or not *Harper's* accurately portrayed the character of Oregon's settlers, the magazine did identify social and economic changes that had begun to alter the region during the 1880s. Smaller land holdings, more rationally and intensely used, were occurring in older, more settled valleys. The big farms in early settled Washington County in Oregon were being broken up into smaller tracts through inheritance or sale.[56] A California visitor took note of the changed landscape: "There are no large landed estates in Oregon, so far as we know; at all events the country through which we passed is divided into small holdings, and the farms look as though they were occupied and tilled by the men and women who owned them. The houses are mostly cottages, the fields are usually small, well fenced, and well tilled."[57] Statistics support that observation. The number of Willamette Valley farms increased while the average acreage held declined. Valley farms increased from 4,592 in 1870, to 8,971 in 1880, and to 11,536 in 1890, while the average size of a farm declined during those same decades from 324 to 256 to 212 acres.[58] Yet Oregon did not abandon its character as an older settler society. Even though the land was becoming more intensely cultivated, agribusiness was still not the dominant ethos, and much of the land remained "unimproved." The homogeneity, self-governance, isolation, and early settler spirit maintained itself long after settler society gave way to a more urban, industrial Oregon. As geographer Jack Blok noted: "To a large extent the hesitancy for changing agricultural strategies was based upon the sense of values of the agrarian society. The ownership of a self-sufficing farm remained a primary goal throughout the first agricultural growth stage [1840–1900] and it persisted well into the second growth stage [1900–1950]."[59] Consequently, even in areas where settlers increased their production for outside markets, mixed farming continued to dominate.[60] Settlers' lives were changing, and in ways that also altered the land, but the extent of those changes was limited. Environmental intrusion during the settler period was profound when contrasted to the presettlement era but mild compared to the twentieth century, thanks to a mixed agricultural economy, an American vision of a republican sociopolitical order, and land policies that supported that vision.

As the forces of industrialization grew after the 1880s, traditional practices and attitudes appeared increasingly to be anachronistic impediments to modernization. Some observers felt that a spirit of independence, made possible in part by environmental abundance and an aversion to the rationalized, labor discipline of capitalism, actually endangered regional progress and the new industrial order. This anti-modernist bent of Oregonians threatened the state's "progress," critics said. Thus *Oregonian* editor Harvey Scott explained in 1899 that Oregon failed to progress because Oregonians were averse to adopting the new ways of modern industrial life. Similarly, H. S. Lyman noted Oregon's failure to match Washington's growth in population and wealth, because Oregonians lacked the "versatility and progressiveness" of Washington's people and remained "content with old-fashioned ways and the conservatism of age."[61] The railroads that lessened Oregon's isolation and increased the state's population did not fundamentally change the cultural ethos of the place. Communities absorbed the new arrivals into existing structures and values, altering only slightly the prevailing cultural patterns.[62]

To Scott, Oregonians were "an undisciplined people" whose "intense individualism" prevented them from submitting "to the steady grind of systematic industry."[63] During the twentieth century, a growth in technology, transportation systems, population, capital, bureaucracy, and markets did increasingly systematize the cultural and ecological landscape. But change did not come without resistance: "Habits planted at the beginning still rule the land. A thousand influences have intruded themselves, but they have bent to the conditions which existed before them. . . . The Oregon of today is the true child of the earlier Oregon, with the family likeness strong, with the family traits predominating. . . . This is the pioneer's land, and his spirit rules it."[64] Some commentators such as Judge John Breckenridge Waldo, a well-educated, prominent native Oregonian, were grateful for that continued spirit. Reacting to the rationalizing forces of industrialization, nature-preservationist Waldo saw in contented settlers the perseverance of republicanism against the unencumbered materialism of modern times: "Remote, unlettered, unambitious, slow, the dwellers in their retired houses lived their lives away; the feverish life of cities unfelt, unheard. Here is nurtured the blood to fill their degenerate vices."[65]

Because of its historical development, Washington exhibited fewer antimodernist impulses than Oregon. During the settler era, the area north of the Columbia River had lagged behind its southern neighbor. Developed by outside capital and dependent on a lumber industry geared to exportation, Washington's population was also more mobile. With the completion of the transcontinental railroad during the 1880s, however, Washington outstripped Oregon industrially and demographically.[66] As H. S. Lyman observed: "Eastern capital and eastern people saw opportunities open in the undeveloped resources of Washington which they could not so easily find in the older and slower Oregon. They have brought the latest methods, abundance of money, and the daring of youth."[67]

The Klondike gold rush in the 1890s only furthered Washington's growth in capital, trade, and population.[68] But industrial changes in Washington followed established lines of foreign capital investment and dependency on an extractive economy, centered on the timber industry. Investment capital now migrated from the Midwest rather than from San Francisco, but it largely retraced a well-worn course of external capitalization and a willingness to embrace unbridled opportunism.

Industrial society transformed the region, but much of the change followed paths blazed during the settler era. Driven by common processes of change, the region shared similar cultural and ecological changes. Yet Washington and Oregon also reacted somewhat differently, creating a slightly different landscape north and south of the Columbia River. Oregon continued to house a rather homogenous population, held to its conservative social imprinting, and maintained its long-standing pattern of a largely "home-owned" economy with resident capitalists and mixed agricultural farms. Washington showed continuity, as well, by holding to its more expansive, free-enterprise vision. Less exclusive than Oregon in its desire to attract people and capital, Washington continued to be more pluralistic and development- and growth-oriented. To a modernizer like Harvey Scott, Washingtonians were a "people who knew how to do things. They knew how to take hold of new resources, to go into the lumber business, to hunt for coal and to apply new methods to agriculture." Conversely, Scott could only conclude that "to a great part of the people of Oregon, long settled here, the methods of these new movements were all unknown." But Scott and other boosters overlooked the costs of being a colonial area subject to "foreign-owned" and controlled capital, costs that led one old-time settler to lament in 1899 that a Fourth of July celebration "of a free nation" was a "Mockery . . . with about 50,000,000 White Slaves to Monopoly."[69]

Cultural attitudes, external events, government actions, and the land itself influenced the shape of the regional landscape, but only by framing possibilities. An understanding of how those factors interacted to redesign one another requires a look at how American settler and industrial societies actually lived on the land.

CHAPTER SEVEN

Living on the Land

Settlers in the Douglas-fir region came with preconceptions about how to structure society and use the land, but expectation and reality did not always converge. As settlers tried to impose their cultural map on the landscape, they encountered unforeseen and intractable problems and consequences. When they encountered environmental limitations, correctives seldom proved ecologically sustainable, for settlers sought "solutions" within the cultural practices and understandings that had given rise to the problems in the first place.

Like the Indians, whites extracted from nature the basis for their material life, but they defined their needs differently from the indigenous people. Settlers satisfied their needs by raising a diversity of crops and animals on privately owned, circumscribed plots of land. Attempting to re-create a familiar landscape, they introduced recognizable food sources. Farmers fenced their fields and planted imported crops, such as wheat, barley, rye, and oats. They planted gardens with squash, pumpkins, tomatoes, potatoes, turnips, cabbage, cucumbers, carrots, beets, peas, onions, and assorted other vegetables. Only corn, because of cool summer nights, was not easily grown in the region.[1]

Except in the Puyallup River Valley and the Nisqually Plains, agriculture north of the Columbia River developed more slowly than in the Willamette Valley until the 1890s.[2] Still, farmers north and south of the Columbia raised specialized commercial crops as market opportunities expanded and contracted. Fruit was grown for market in the Willamette Valley, and hops had become a market crop by the 1870s in Oregon's Umpqua Valley and in Washington's Puyallup and White River valleys.[3] Labor efforts and the environment determined hop yields, but like much of the region's extractive commodities, distant markets also shaped hop production. Market prices fluctuated widely, and northwesterners found that crop conditions in New York State and Kent, England, influenced the local economy and, in turn, land-use patterns. Regional growers discovered to their chagrin that they could not control nature any better than they could control the market. Hop lice came, in Ezra Meeker's words, "like a clap of thunder." Throughout the valleys of western Oregon and Washington, hop cultivation was in decline by the mid-1890s.[4]

While hops, oats, and fruit orchards all dotted the rural landscape and found market outlets, wheat was the common settler staple and the region's dominant crop. The average farmer in Oregon harvested 20 to 25 bushels of wheat per acre, although a few settlers recorded yields of 50 to 65 bushels.[5] During the cash-poor decade of the 1840s, wheat had served as currency as well as food. Stimulated by a need to feed miners in the gold towns that dotted the West between 1848 and the 1860s, wheat was clearly the region's dominant crop by 1870. In the Willamette Valley, wheat production stood at 199,558 bushels in 1850, rose to 660,081 bushels in 1860, and then jumped to 2,086,826 bushels by 1870.[6] Above all, however, the burgeoning wheat demand of the 1870s, fueled by the Liverpool, England, market, brought a new intensity to wheat production. Willamette Valley farmers in particular began to manage their land for wheat exports, raising their wheat production to 5,365,117 bushels by 1880. In Marion and Polk counties, acreage grew by 320 percent and production increased 252 percent from 1870 to 1880. Wallis Nash concluded that the "temptation to grow wheat" was "very strong" for a number of reasons. Besides markets, he continued, wheat crops involved a minimal "amount of trouble and anxiety." Settlers had "a clear understanding of what it costs to plant, harvest, and warehouse," and wheat "hardly ever fails in quality."[7] Those who intensified their acreage output realized more than profits from their labors.

In the poorly drained floodplain areas of the Willamette Valley, continuous cultivation and the removal of organic material increased soil compaction and aggravated drainage problems. Failure to rotate crops or fallow fields, along with intensified and continuous cropping, depleted soils. Oregonian David Newsom wrote in December 1871: "A large amount of our lands is much exhausted by being run so much of the time, in wheat and oats. We do not vary the crops here or rotate as we should do." Frances Fuller Victor concurred: "Twenty years of grain-raising, without manuring, has been wearing out the oldest land instead of improving it." In an 1888 address before the Lewis County, Washington, Agricultural Association, Joseph S. Allen warned that unless area farmers undertook corrective measures they would suffer the same "baneful effects" that overuse had wrought on Willamette Valley lands.[8]

Not long thereafter, settlers began shifting away from their dependence on wheat. Remediation, however, had more to do with rust (which had first appeared in 1879), the wheat market crash of 1893, and competition from wheat growers in eastern Oregon and Washington than with an awareness that land practices had run up against environmental limitations.[9] Willamette Valley wheatlands were abandoned or converted to pasture, since no other readily marketable crop seemed suited to the heavy prairie soils. The soil thus had an opportunity to recover until new markets opened and the lands were once again farmed intensely.[10]

Settlers responded to commercial opportunities, but they did not produce strictly for markets nor did they practice monoculture agriculture. Instead, farmers employed a market-use, mixed-farming strategy where a variety of crops and animals were grown both for sale and to meet the basic needs of the household.[11] Oregonian Isaac Smith was typical. He grew wheat and oats, while raising hogs, chickens, fifteen horses, fifty-three cattle, and sixty-seven sheep. As Smith noted: "I have got a great deal [of stock] like most persons in Oregon, but nevertheless I have plenty."[12] It was a way of farming that may have been rooted in republican sociopolitical understandings about diversity, competency, and yeoman independence, but it carried important environmental consequences as well.

Market shifts, combined with a lack of intense and prolonged monoculture on extensive individual valley land-holding parcels, restricted environmental degradation. Settlers grew wheat, oats, and hay and raised domestic animals for food and clothing. Native people had collected wild camas, wapato, and tarweed and relied on fish, deer, elk, and bear for food. Those changes held direct and indirect consequences for the land and its occupants. The "extreme alteration" that settler agriculture brought to the Willamette Valley accelerated exponentially with industrial society's increasingly rationalized markets and means of production.[13]

While crops certainly modified the landscape, and the plow changed the land in more profound ways than Indian collecting practices ever had, the introduction of livestock initiated far more dramatic changes. Mild climate and abundant vegetation permitted livestock to forage on open land in a relatively unattended range management system. Cattle and hogs, particularly, who were able to defend themselves against predators, were favorites for open-range grazing.[14] Ecologically, the introduction of domestic animals placed more grazers on the land, but their presence in small patches of sparsely settled prairie woodland probably did not overburden the land's carrying capacity, especially since an increase in domestic stock paralleled a decline in native grazing and browsing animals.[15] In more heavily settled areas, however, a more damaging story unfolded. Oregon settler Absolom Harden remarked in 1848 on the damage done on the Tualatin Plains because of overgrazing: "The cattle has got poore down there for the grass is cheat and there has bin so many large bands of cattle runing on them plains for several year and the plains is small."[16]

Over a decade later, the environmental destruction had extended to other areas in the Willamette Valley. An Olympia, Washington, newspaper observed: "The natural grasses are destroyed by being tramped for years. See the bare hills and valley now! Stock can just get grass enough to keep alive."[17] This description was more than the mere hyperbole of a promotional tract to induce settlement from Oregon to Washington. Oregonians, too, noted the grassland destruction. The *Oregon Statesman* reported in 1862:

It is a fact of great importance to the settlers, twenty years ago and subsequently, that the wild grass then in its freshness, afforded subsistence for the winter to the stock, brought in by the immigrants; but that state of things is now gone. The grass is eaten up and mostly rooted out. The cattle, horses and sheep are, or have been, altogether too abundant in every locality to subsist on the product of the wild grass.[18]

Frances Fuller Victor agreed, noting how "indiscriminate pasturing [had] injured the grasses."[19]

Many farmers made raising livestock their primary activity in response to mining markets in such places as California's Sierra Nevadas, Yreka, the Jacksonville area of southern Oregon, the Fort Colville area on the upper Columbia, and the John Day River in eastern Oregon between 1848 and 1855; the 1858 Fraser River strike; and southwestern Idaho discoveries in 1861.[20] According to Isaac Smith, "The country is getting so over-stocked that we will have to raise some feed for hard spells in winter." By 1860, western Oregon and Washington farmers owned over 100,000 head of cattle, and the region's natural vegetation took a beating. The rich bunchgrass that had originally covered valley land "was killed out by over grazing, [and] trampling."[21]

Some settlers were aware of the problem and looked for a solution. Isaac Smith believed that much of the trouble stemmed from the existence of a commons. In 1857, he wrote to his brother and sisters that Oregonians had begun taking corrective measures: "The country is becoming over-stocked, and those who want grass will have to fence their land, and most every person who can is at it. The grass here is a great portion of the wealth of the country and without it we would be as hard up as the people of Ireland without potatoes."[22] But exclusive ownership provided only a partial solution when market prices tempted settlers to carry as much stock on their land as possible. The power of science proved to be the remedy that Americans persistently sought in dealing with environmental limitations or destruction. From the settlers' perspective, the problem lay not with too many animals but with inferior grasses (this despite previous testimony to the wonderful quality of the native grasses).[23] Human engineering, they believed, could overcome nature's limitations. According to the November 17, 1860, *Washington Standard*:

There can be no mistake in regard to the true policy in this case. . . . Most of the soils of the Willamette Valley are peculiarly adapted to the growth of the cultivated grasses. An acre of cultivated grass will produce more food for stock than ten acres of the natural grasses.

It is folly to suppose that we can go on increasing our stock in this valley, without cultivating the exotic grasses. . . . There is "gold in the

cultivated grasses." There is loss, disappointment and poverty, in relying upon the grasses for the raising of stock.[24]

In a land of abundance, limitations seemed ludicrous. Imported familiar legumes like timothy, red-top, and clover, and English and Kentucky
bluegrasses fed growing numbers of domesticated livestock.[25] Native
grasses were ill equipped to compete with the new grasses, and by the
early twentieth century over half of the grasses found in the Salem, Oregon, area were exogenous. In 1846, Oregon's natural flora had been rich
and extensive, with few importations. One hundred years later, Oregon
was home to about 325 exotic plants.[26]

While imported grasses changed the landscape, the exotics did not
resolve the problems of environmental damage caused by livestock. The
abundance that had made "the country . . . very hard to spoil" had more
to do with mitigating the environmental intrusion than did settler understandings or policies.[27] A collapse in mining markets, competition from
ranchers east of the Cascades, and a growing demand for wheat at seemingly dependable market prices conjoined to limit livestock production in
the region by 1870.[28] But if raising beef for markets became less important
in areas like the Willamette Valley, dairying increased in importance so that
valley livestock numbers actually rose from 45,692 to 73,970 between 1870
and 1880.[29] Market strategies may have shifted, but land-use practices and
attitudes remained in place.

Adding insult to injury, not all of the flora that settler society had carried west was desirable. Inadvertent imports such as weeds, scotch broom,
tansy ragwort, and thistles also made the journey to the Northwest, often
carried to the region in the hoofs of animals, in dung, in ships or wagons,
and in sacks containing desired grass seeds. One Willamette Valley settler
recalled that in the mid-1870s "farmers began to grow flax, and with the
flax came a great many weeds."[30] Canadian thistles thrived so much that
legislation became necessary to combat their spread. According to a Washington statute, "Any person or persons owning, possessing or having care
or charge of any land or lands . . . in this territory, shall knowingly, will-
fully, or willingly permit or suffer any Chinese or Canada thistles to grow
up thereon and suffer the same to stand until its seeds get ripe, such person or persons shall be guilty of a misdemeanor."[31] Oregon approved a
similar act February 25, 1889, and extended it to include Russian and Chinese thistles ten years later.[32] The weed "wild lettuce" invaded Columbia
County, Oregon, and ruined grain harvests.[33] In an attempt to provide
familiar food "greens," dandelions were brought to the region, the consequences of which led one commentator to state: "The memory of that pioneer at the present time is far from being blessed."[34]

Other grazing practices sometimes rebounded to the consternation of settlers as well. Settlers' open-range management system, for example, meant that stock occasionally went wild.[35] James Clyman noted on December 4, 1844: "I noticed that Horses and cattle do not appear as gentle as in the States owing no doubt to the want of being handled sufficiently but animals have the inclination to go wild in a climate whare there is no winter and are not dependent on their owners for forage but seek their own living at all times & all seasons."[36] That inclination necessitated hunting stock like any other "wild" animal or having roundups and branding. Sometimes, however, the beasts were not so easily corralled. In a Frankenstein scenario, hogs that some farmers had imported to enhance their well being and security went wild and preyed on settlers' lambs. Other unfenced domestically owned stock also did damage, sometimes to neighbors' property: "Fords hogs have committed some depredations on my wheat last night and today—which is horrible," wrote Michael Luark in 1855.[37]

Other management efforts also led to mixed results. Attempts to increase the area's freshwater fish population, for example, often resulted in eliminating highly prized indigenous fish. The introduction into Washington of largemouth bass, white crappie, and yellow perch in 1891 soon crowded out more desirable rainbow trout from lowland lakes. By the turn of the century, Washington State Fish Commissioner A. C. Little concluded: "The evil results of the lack of information in regard to the proper kinds of fish that should be introduced into our streams are becoming apparent to all."[38] An even more egregious example of unintended consequences occurred when carp was introduced to the Northwest during the 1880s. Regional publications touted its importation, even telling farmers to raise carp as a cash crop. Once again, desire for markets and profit outran knowledge. Carp did flourish as advertised, but they grew at the expense of more highly valued indigenous fish. Within two decades, the change was lamented and decried.[39] Nevertheless, carp, weeds, the loss of natural vegetation, and the destruction of wildlife habitat all seemed a tolerable price to pay for progress. In one of the rare instances when the decline of native flora received an acknowledgement, a November 1888 *Oregonian* called for a catalogue of indigenous plants before they disappeared so that a natural history could be written.[40]

The introduction of livestock, however, did much more than stress the land's carrying capacity and change the floral makeup of the region. It placed domestic stock in direct competition with indigenous animals and, in some instances, with native peoples like the Kalapuyans. Pigs, for example, liked eating camas and acorns, important parts of the Kalapuyans' diet. In some areas, foraging by hogs not only restricted this native food base but destroyed the root plants as well.[41]

Even when fenced in, domestic animals affected native species, for domestic pastures reduced the amount of land available to wild animals.

More and more fences enclosed the Willamette Valley, and by the 1880s open-range livestock persisted only in the bordering hill lands.[42] With fencing, competition for forage between domestic and wild animals was less direct but nonetheless real. Sheep, cattle, pigs, and horses polluted creeks and rivers directly through urination and defecation or indirectly through groundwater run-off and agricultural drainage ditches.[43] By 1888, animal and human refuse had made the Willamette River, in the words of one Oregon state senator, "the great sewer of this great Willamette valley." The *Oregonian* reported on January 16, 1889: "Willamette water will do for irrigation, and is all the better for this purpose from the fact that it carries so large an amount of fertilizing material: but it is not really fit to drink."[44]

Western Oregon stockmen, as well as the more numerous eastside ones, brought their herds, principally sheep, onto the western slopes of the Cascade Mountains for summer forage, reshaping that environment as well. To promote travel and ensure rich pastures, sheepherders burned mountain areas. In bringing sheep to the Cascades, herders reduced indigenous animals' habitat, directly through competition and indirectly by hazing.[45] Visiting the Oregon Cascades in 1886, John Breckenridge Waldo observed:

> At Crane Prairie once more; quite well but my fine Summer Resort has been discovered and turned to base uses—nearly four thousand sheep have dispossessed us and the deer and bear from a great part of our possessions—driven us into the nooks and corners of its wide expanse, still undisturbed, but with such occupation of a part, the charm of the whole is gone.[46]

Sheep and cattle polluted mountain streams and so destroyed vegetation that John Muir's characterization of sheep as "hoofed locus" seems fitting.[47] Finding 2,000 head of sheep at Diamond Lake in 1896, John Waldo reported that "sheep trails" now "traversed" the southern and middle Cascades of Oregon, leaving "the grassy meadows along the [North] Umpqua [River] look[ing] like they had been struck by a cyclone—the sheep having laid all the grass flat to the ground that they have not eaten."[48] Government agents made similar judgments. In 1903, Fred Plummer wrote: "Large tracts have been sheeped to such an extent that the wild forage grasses are almost exterminated, and the thin soil has been furrowed till it looks like sidehill plowing."[49] And Arthur Dodwell and Theodore Rixon observed:

> One band of sheep brought from Roseburg & pastured along the divide by Quartz Mountain & Black Rock ate up everything in sight, destroyed all the young growth, and where there would have been grass were they driven out of the reserve in September they left not

even a green blade in these tracts, and doubtless killed by tramping down in the snow any grass that might have escaped them.[50]

As settlers drew property lines, erected fences, and constructed buildings, a look of permanence extended over the landscape. The American vision of a systematized garden seemed to become a reality. But the achievement did not come easily or without costs. The reduction of habitat for native animals proved to be almost as lethal as direct killing, as settlers drained swamps and marshes, placed new domestic animals on the land, eliminated protective cover, and hazed nesting sites. Native species that were useful and conducive to domestication could be incorporated into the garden, but those plants that threatened the garden had to be weeded out. Whether desired or despised, however, most native species faced reductions in habitat and population. The native animals were shot for food and sport, in the name of scientific inquiry or because they threatened the garden's domestic species, and they declined rapidly in areas of densest human occupancy.

Killing nearly or completely eliminated the bald eagle, California condor, trumpeter swan, and whooping crane from the Douglas-fir region.[51] By the late 1840s, the availability of deer and elk as a food source became increasingly scarce. Echoing Peter Burnett's complaint about the lack of wild game on the Tualatin Plains, Lieutenant Neil Howison reported similar conditions throughout the Willamette Valley in 1846:

> I was surprised to find so great a scarcity of game in this country. I lugged a heavy gun more than a hundred and fifty miles through the Willammette [sic] valley, and in all that ride saw but three deer. . . . Elk are still numerous, but very wild, living in the depths of the forests, or near those openings which the white man has not yet approached. An Indian hunter often brought elk meat to us at Astoria, which he had killed in the unexplored forests between Clatsop plains and Young's river.[52]

As Howison observed, the settler landscape was not always lethal to selected species. Just as the most removed Indians suffered least from initial Euroamerican contact, plants and animals most distanced from settler occupancy felt the consequences least. Elk and black-tailed deer that lived in forests survived better than the Columbian white-tailed deer. Few people settled in southwestern Oregon or the Olympic peninsula, so some areas of the Coast Range and the Olympic mountains still carried heavy deer populations and herds, although even in those locations reductions were apparent by the late nineteenth century.[53]

Many species of bird faced other trade-offs as settlement increased. Draining and diking lands restricted bird habitat, but fields planted with grain made up for some of the loss. As Neil Howison observed: "The wild geese move over the country in clouds, and do great injury to the wheat fields upon which they determine to alight." Still, not all of the costs were borne by the settlers. Birds too, paid, sometimes with their lives, for consuming privately owned crops. Similarly, predators initially experienced the new domestic occupants less as competitors for habitat and more as a hoofed banquet, especially as deer and elk populations were killed and hazed out.[54] Phoebe Goodell Judson of Washington Territory complained that it sometimes seemed her husband "fattened as many bears with hogs as he did hogs with the grain."[55] John Minto remembered: "Enemies to the successful keeping of domestic fowls, sheep, pigs, calves or colts were so numerous that when we got a start of sheep in 1849, my wife, spinning wool on our cabin porch, kept the loaded rifle within her reach—in the use of which I had given her lessons on the day succeeding our marriage."[56]

For settlers, more was involved in the incursions of predators than the loss of food. Crops and livestock were private property, and they were being stolen by wolves, cougars, bears, and fowl who deserved death.[57] Even when legislation restricted hunting to certain seasons, property protection clauses allowed farmers to kill game animals at any time in defense of their crops. "An Act for the Protection of Fish and Game," for example, was passed on November 27, 1883. It limited the hunting season, extended the number of counties that prohibited deer hunting with dogs, and restricted the market sale of deer in Washington. The act also allowed people to kill deer and ducks, any time, on their own premises in order to protect crops.[58] In the defense of property, settlers used poison and radically recast the purpose of hunting. They hunted not just to fill the larder but also to eradicate "varmints" that destroyed their property. John Minto, for example, wrote that coyotes took such a heavy toll on his sheep flocks that he and other hunters used a team of eleven hounds to track and kill eight small wolves and a lynx.[59]

When the movement to organize a provisional government arose in Oregon, it derived, in part, from a concern to protect property. Under the guise of protecting stock from predators, settlers held a number of organizational meetings. At the March 6, 1843, "wolf meeting," the gathering created a committee to organize a government. It also adopted a committee report that called for "a defensive and destructive war" against predators that proved "destructive to the useful animals owned by the settlers of this colony." Scalp bounties were affixed to bears, wolves, and cougars and would continue to be offered throughout the nineteenth and most of the twentieth century.[60]

Not surprisingly, debate and passage of the first bounty law reflected settlers' desire for social order. To collect scalp money a person had to have paid a subscription fee of five dollars. It also helped to be white. The original proposal had suggested limiting payment to whites only, but economic considerations triumphed over racism. It was finally decided that Native Americans could collect a bounty, but they were to receive only half as much as whites.[61]

Extermination efforts against predators were successful. In 1878, settler Daniel Waldo recalled that he had "not heard a big wolf howl in 20 years" around his farm in the Waldo Hills east of Salem.[62] In time, wolves and grizzly bears were exterminated throughout western Oregon. The numbers of black bears and cougars declined due to bounty hunting and habitat reduction as they were increasingly forced into remote mountainous areas. As settlers, particularly sheep owners, began using the Cascade Mountains as summer rangeland, even mountainous areas provided little escape for wild animals.[63]

Sport hunting also added to the decline, especially of predators as hunters shot animals for amusement or as trophies.[64] But to "sportsmen," hunting involved much more than an amusing pastime. It brought excitement, improved a person's health with fresh air, and honed skills that would be helpful during war. Hunting seemed essential to testing oneself and preserving the martial spirit. Many believed it constituted an important part of what it meant to be male. An Oregon coastal farmer who called himself "O" expresses those sentiments:

> Man loves excitement and a certain amount he must have, and next to the field of battle the chase in a measure must supply that intense condition that cannot be experienced anywhere else. . . . There are a great many admirable qualities that can be cultivated in the chase which could be turned to account in the field of battle—the use of firearms, coolness and quickness of judgment and the study of expedients—all things that comes under the head of "presence of mind" are here learned. . . . You cultivate the mind [knowledge of wildlife behavior that makes for a successful hunt], the eye is trained and your health will be improved. The love of nature will be gratified, and in the solitudes of the mountains you will gain evidence of the "survival of the fittest" quite as convincing as could be obtained in America's or England's greatest cities.[65]

Native wildlife was no match for settlers' technology and numbers.[66]

A more important agent was at work in this process of species reduction and biological simplification. Like agriculture, dairying, and livestock raising, hunting became commercialized. Birds, deer, elk, and bear found themselves being hunted not for food or as threats to property but as market commodities. Hides, horns, and meat from elk and deer, as well as bird

feathers for plumage, found ready markets during the last half of the nineteenth century.

The abundant waterfowl on the lower Columbia that had kept William
Clark awake at night in 1805 was still plentiful in 1870, but by the early
twentieth century it had been drastically reduced, mainly because of commercial hunting.[67] In a private letter to his close friend and nature enthusiast John Gill, John Minto reflected on the precipitous decline of animal
life within and on the lower Columbia River since 1844:

> The salmon, seal, and water fowl, seen in a canoe trip from the present
> position of Portland to the west side of youngs bay were so much
> more then than they now are. That an honest estimate of the difference
> will read to people who have only seen present conditions like a leaf
> from Munchasens [Munchasen's] stories. . . . [W]est across Shallow
> Bay from Cathalamette point below Clifton the eye could could [sic]
> not cover the extent of feeding ground nor the variety [of] water fowl
> feeding on the . . . seeds of the tide flats. The abundance of life in and
> on the waters of Oregon in 1844 will never exist again.[68]

Deer and elk also suffered dramatic losses in population. J. R. Metzger
remembered that "wild game was very plentiful" around his Salem, Oregon, farm in the mid-1860s:

> Elk, Black-tailed Deer and White-tailed Deer were numerous. The
> White-tailed deer, which are now almost extinct, where natives of the
> Willamette Valley. . . . Most all the oak grub lands was full of White-
> tailed deer in those days.
>   It was not uncommon to see 25 or more elk in a band, almost as
> tame as the cattle. Of course, the elk were found in the foothills and
> mountains, but not as far back as you find them today if you find them
> at all.[69]

By the early twentieth century, sportsmen and commercial hunters had
taken a heavy toll. Metzger lamented in 1915:

> Where is all of our game today? It has been wasted by men not as
> thoughtful as the Indian, for the Indian killed only what he wanted for
> food. . . . I have seen on the North Fork of the South Santiam River
> great numbers of deer carcasses. The deer had been killed by hunters,
> their hides and the hams taken and the balance thrown in the
> creeks. . . . A great many hunters killed more than they could use sim-
> ply for the "sport" of shooting them. . . . Is it any wonder that we have
> very few of these noble animals left?[70]

By the 1860s, commercial hunting provided income to a growing number of northwesterners such as James Huddleston and his brother and Abraham Peck, who killed 415 deer along the McKenzie River over a two-month period. During the summer of 1888, Glendale, Oregon, resident T. A. Ireland killed 300 deer for market sale near his Douglas County home. Fellow Douglas County resident William Murray boasted that during the fifteen years of his hunting career in the late nineteenth century, he had killed 1,500 deer, 250 bears, hundreds of elk, and 50 cougars. John Murphy reported that he and four other hunters killed 40 deer in less than four days during one southern Oregon outing. On another hunting excursion with seven others, this time to western Washington, Murphy's party killed 60 deer in one week.[71]

Other contemporaries reported similarly high body counts. Benjamin F. Shields claimed that during the 1880s ten professional hunters in southern Oregon annually averaged "1,000 to 2,000 deer apiece." Another source claimed that "a pelter averaged ten deer per day when hunting."[72] Like those who had shot buffalo on the Great Plains, hunters left large amounts of meat to rot. Meat seemed abundant and it was difficult to transport, so commercial hunters often contented themselves with hides and took only the best portions of the carcass.[73]

As in the fur trade era, here were a new form of "furs" to be extracted from a Northwest "commons." The destruction of animals for market showed continuity with an earlier period of species exploitation for the market and with settler attitudes. Unencumbered by legal restrictions or animal ownership, commercial hunters found little reason to conserve unowned and unregulated animals. Conservation seemed ridiculous to Northwest settlers in light of the region's abundant wildlife and the farmers' goal of a simplified, systematized gardenlike landscape. Reducing the number of wild animals made sense. Hunting freed up necessary habitat for a simplified number of domesticated animals, eliminated predatory threats to these garden species, and allowed hunters to earn money.

Condemnations and restrictions came only with the rise of the conservation movement in the late nineteenth century, particularly as market-directed hunting got in the way of upper-class sportsmen who worried about the wildlife population. Once more, a situation existed in which each person's use of a resource could subtract from others' welfare and their use of that resource. Laws that prohibited market hunting, set hunting seasons, and required a licensing fee to hunt were easier to pass than to enforce, however, and indeed, hunting restrictions remained unenforced by common practice, a lack of enforcement personnel, and most of all by the laws' form and conceptual framework.[74]

Americans viewed the taking of wildlife as a right. Limitations on hunting still carried the aristocratic mantle of European exclusion. European hunting preserves were restricted to the upper-class, and class distinctions and monopolistic practices did not sit well with a people who saw themselves as democratic and egalitarian. Accustomed to wildlife being a commons free for the taking, many settlers considered restrictions and arguments that the state owned the commons as an infringement on individual rights. As a result, most farmers and ranchers resisted the law, especially those who raised grain and who saw little reason to conserve waterfowl that damaged their crops. In 1908, U.S. Forest Inspector F. E. Ames labeled attempts by game wardens to enforce the law as "flat failures." Seven years earlier, Washington State Fish Commissioner and ex officio game warden A. C. Little had reported: "We have on our statutes laws the equal of any state in the Union, but under the present conditions they amount to absolutely nothing. No attempt is made on the part of any of the county officials of the state to enforce the game laws, and nothing is done." U.S. Forest Service Deputy Supervisor P. T. Harris claimed that "there is a strong tendency toward violation [of the game laws] and the State officers are not very active in this locality [the Rainier National Forest]." County public officials were reluctant to enforce game laws that seemed a creation of "outsiders" and ran counter to local practices. Game warden Roy Dickson of Gold Beach, Oregon, identified yet another problem: most of the justices that adjudicated the cases "are game violators themselves." Even Forest Service personnel, who for a time doubled as game law enforcement officers, were reluctant to prosecute hunting violators. Vigorous policing would lead, one forest officer feared, to hunters taking their revenge by burning up the forests.[75]

Limited funding further hampered the enforcement of hunting statutes. In Oregon there was no one to enforce fish and game laws until the State Board of Fish Commissioners was established in 1887. Even then, enforcement was delayed because the legislature provided no funds for the hiring of game wardens. Not until 1893, when Governor Sylvestor Pennoyer made Hollister McGuire fish and game commissioner and gave him a budget of $500, did Oregon have its first enforcement official. Funding restrictions continued to limit the effectiveness of the fish and game commissioner, and changing the title to game and forestry warden in 1899 did little to alter enforcement. Not until the State Board of Fish and Game Commissioners was created in 1911 was the power and status of wildlife conservation seriously upgraded. With the new board and the appointment of conservationist William L. Finley as state game warden in the same year, an era of wildlife conservation began.[76]

Paralleling the new conservation policies was a growing conservationist sentiment among the populace at large. By the second decade of the twentieth century, support for licensing and game protection laws had gained ground among both nonhunters and hunters, including many back-

woods settlers.[77] Local rod and gun clubs and conservation organizations
such as the Audubon Society, even paid for game wardens out of their own
coffers. Business interests, who saw the presence of wildlife as a way to
draw visitors to the region, with hunters and tourists contributing to the
local economy, were especially supportive of conservation measures. By
1907, Chief Deputy Game Warden R. C. Beebe of Washington reported that
out of forty-nine arrests for game law violations, he had secured forty-seven
convictions.[78] Nonetheless, guilty verdicts could still prove difficult to
obtain, especially in isolated communities who disliked "outsiders" threatening their freedom and local customs. There were also setbacks when game
wardens appeared to enforce the laws unfairly.[79] Game warden W. G.
Emery of Newport, Oregon, reported one such case:

> Two deputies visited the home of F. O. Johnson on the Yachats [Lin-
> coln County], representing that they were Portland sportsmen who
> wanted to be put on a stand and have a deer run by them. Johnson
> spotted them as game wardens, so piloted them to a thick jungle sev-
> eral miles away, left them there and returned home and resumed his
> daily work. Late that night the wardens came into camp, sore because
> of the trick that had been played on them, and the next morning
> arrested a boy neighbor for cleaning a trout on the creek bank and
> throwing the entrails into the stream. Ten miles below at Waldport,
> two canneries empty all the offal into the river from the daily catch
> that is turned in to them.
>
> The boy pled guilty and his father paid his fine. The law was vin-
> dicated but game protection and preservation in the Yachats district
> took a long step backward.[80]

Still, increased protection helped some "game" species increase in population. Elk, for example, had recovered to the point in 1938 that an open
hunting season was possible.[81]

Conservation had seemingly restored abundance. But this testimony
to human engineering and nature's resiliency should not be overstated.
Restriction certainly played a part in the recovery, but other factors were
also involved. Extermination programs had limited the predators who
preyed on elk, such as wolves and coyotes. The restricted number of large
urban markets within Oregon and the state's remoteness from large metropolitan centers also limited commercial hunting within Oregon.[82] More
important, much of the forested habitat had not yet been disrupted or
destroyed through logging, human occupancy, or roads.

Restrictions and enforcement represented the managed environment
of a systematized landscape. And whereas conservation may have promoted an increase in selected game species—those valued for economic,

sporting, or aesthetic reasons—the policies themselves were self-limiting. Indeed, management created a new set of problems that often proved painful, even for the "preferred" species. A good example is the protection of deer and elk through hunting restrictions and predator reduction, conservation measures that were supposed to create a hunters' paradise. The result, however, was the destruction of vegetation and large deer and elk die-offs because of an imbalance between habitat and animal population. The most famous incident took place at the Kaibab National Forest in Arizona during the 1920s, where hunting restrictions and predator destruction had left deer herds unculled. The deer population soared, and overgrazing resulted. Because of habitat destruction, overpopulation, and a severe winter in 1924–1925, starvation hit the herd until the deer population came into balance with the land's carrying capacity. Less well known but similar incidents occurred in the Douglas-fir region among Roosevelt elk in the Olympic National Park during the winter of 1916–1917 and again in 1945.[83] Privileged species and "varmints" alike became victims to a society that did not see interconnected relationships. According to the cultural script by which Americans mapped the world, the systematization of nature appeared rational. For them, the simplification of the Douglas-fir landscape represented an improved landscape. The garden must be cultivated, managed, guarded, and thoroughly weeded.

Settlers made little attempt to understand how the culturally valued and the culturally valueless interacted to support the whole. The Oregon legislature underscored this point on February 2, 1899, when it created the position of state biologist: "The duties of such officer shall be scientific investigations as regards the animal resources of the state of Oregon, and, as far as possible, the development of all such resources which have an economic value."[84] In nature, the whole is more than the sum of its parts; nature's economy is not related to cultural values of the marketplace. Animals with little commercial value are often vital to the sustainability of culturally valued life forms. Thus, while technology and increased capital investment led to limited conservation measures, it did not always lead to habitat conservation or ecological health.

In organizing the land to create a landscape of ordered farms and towns, Euroamerican society also reduced the region's biodiversity. By the early twentieth century, the extent of those changes had profoundly altered the pre-1840 landscape, particularly for selected species. Yet nature's resiliency, limited technology, population size, land-holding patterns, laws, and a mixed agricultural economy had at least moderated the changes. All of the pieces were nonetheless in place for an accelerated assault on the region's ecological system. Referring to the dramatic biotic changes that would take place in Washington State between 1853 and 1953, one researcher wrote that only nature's "sudden catastrophes . . . can compare with the changes wrought by white men in so short a time."[85] The same could be said for most of the region. Firmly in place were attitudes of domination, commodification, and a belief in technological salvation. Northwesterners also were convinced that a rationalized, managed landscape of selected species geared to an expanding market could lead to a sustainable social and ecological order. Ultimately, neither the human nor the nonhuman community was well served by those attitudes and practices.

CHAPTER EIGHT

Settler Society and the Forests

Landscaping valley and tide-flat areas constituted only part of the settler enterprise in land transformation. The forests that blanketed the region remained the greatest challenge to subjugation. To emigrants the forests were a barrier to be torn down in order that the land could be redeemed and properly landscaped. As industrial society began to emerge and trees became increasingly valued, a utilitarian, commodified attitude beheld opportunity. Forests still needed to be landscaped, but their value as a market resource began to outweigh a careless policy of "wasteful" landscaping with fire and axe.

By the eighteenth century, Euroamericans shared a common, well-established aesthetic bias against evergreens.[1] Whether American or British, a consensual language labeled the Northwest's dense and extensive forests as monotonous, interminable, gloomy, somber, dark, wild, and savage.[2] When Euroamericans wrote about trees, it was in terms of their utility for construction or sale. Variations in that largely shared view arose from individual preferences, experiential differences, the reasons that drew emigrants to the Northwest, and what they expected to find. But whether they saw forests as a barrier to settlement, a material necessary to settlement, or a marketable resource, Euroamericans saw timber rather than trees.[3]

Early coastal fur traders used northwestern trees to repair their ships, to supply fuel, and even to make "spruce beer." When the sea otter trade began to decline in the early nineteenth century, traders started to supplement fur cargoes with planks and spars for markets in Hawaii. Still, timber exports were small until the mid-nineteenth century because of distance, the absence of markets, the scarcity of labor, and better investment opportunities elsewhere.[4] Land-based fur traders used the forests even more intensively than did oceangoing traders. This pattern became especially pronounced once the Hudson's Bay Company turned to agricultural production. Although the company selected agricultural sites that required only a modicum of forest clearing, fur establishments still required trees for building and fuel. Also, when circumstances made lumber exports profitable, the company cut and milled trees for their commercial value on the international market.

Most Hudson's Bay Company farms produced enough food to meet local post needs, but they did not create adequate surpluses to sustain a viable export trade in foodstuffs. Moreover, the seasonal nature of agriculture and the fur trade meant that the company's labor force was not being fully used, thereby lowering profits. But profitability depended not merely on cheap, available laborers; it also required access to an easily exploited natural resource that could be converted into a saleable product. Chief Factor John McLoughlin found that resource in the seemingly limitless Douglas-fir forests.[5]

Recognizing the potential profits in lumber, McLoughlin had a water-powered sawmill built a few miles from Fort Vancouver in 1828. Company officers realized their plans with the first shipment and sale of lumber to Hawaii in 1829. Lumber from the Fort Vancouver mill began to enter California markets by 1831. Governor George Simpson even suggested moving the mill to the Willamette River Falls, where superior water power and plentiful forests offered increased lumber production and profits, but the move never took place. Throughout the 1830s, the Fort Vancouver mill, worked by an Hawaiian sawmill crew of twenty-five to thirty workers, produced about 2,000 to 2,500 feet of lumber per day. Accidents, breakdowns, and inexperienced workmen interrupted production, but profits continued to outweigh costs.[6]

Despite Fort Vancouver's pioneering efforts, fur remained the company's dominant concern. During the next twenty years lumbering in the Northwest grew slowly. The first American mill, built by Methodists at their Willamette Valley mission in 1838, was typical of regional lumbering: small, water-powered enterprises that grew up in proximity to a settlement area to meet local building needs. By the 1840s, Absolom Harden noted, Oregon had "plenty of good saw mills" to supply settlers with lumber at prices commensurate with that found "in the States."[7]

Towns were particularly attractive places in which to locate a sawmill. Not surprisingly, Oregon City, the Northwest's preeminent town, had two sawmills by 1844. Using the Willamette Falls, Oregon City mills produced for the local market, selling lumber at $2 per hundred board feet. The Cowlitz settlement also had a sawmill to meet local building needs by 1846, and Portland had its first sawmill in 1849.[8] As the population increased, so did the number of mills.

Occasionally, mills like the first one built along the lower Columbia River by Henry H. Hunt in 1844 produced not only for local sale but for the export market as well. Hunt, who had emigrated from Smithfield, Indiana, smelled adventure and profit in the Far West. Rather than a sickle and scythe, he had carried sawmill equipment overland in 1843, with the express intention of producing lumber for export. Soon after he arrived, Hunt built his mill along the Columbia River thirty miles east of Astoria. The site Henry Hunt selected was adjacent to the two resources timbermen needed: trees and water. Waterways offered lumbermen not only access to timber and the water required to power mill saws but the transportation system necessary for carrying the lumber to market. Hunt built his mill on a bluff next to a 70-foot waterfall where the cascading water turned an overshot wheel that powered a sash saw. The sawed lumber was then shipped along the Columbia River to waiting markets. On a good day, the sixteen-member logging and milling crew produced 2,000 to 3,000 board feet that sold at about $12 per thousand feet.[9]

There were too few markets and too little capital, however, for many settlers to establish sawmills. Outside investors had little incentive to invest money in such enterprises, given the paucity of labor, geographic distance from markets, and problems navigating over the Columbia River bar.[10] Generally, eastern capitalists found more lucrative markets closer at hand than the distant Pacific Coast. But whether designed for export or local use, most regional sawmills were located to the south throughout the 1840s, simply because that's where most people lived.[11]

Northwest forests not only provided Americans with timber for sale and building materials but served them in other ways as well. In the cash-poor 1840s, both lumber and wheat were mediums of exchange.[12] In addition, the conversion of trees into timber provided employment for newly arrived settlers. The late-summer, early-fall arrival of overland emigrants was not well timed for the immediate establishment of a farm, and most settlers wanted to look over the landscape before settling on a homestead. The problem was to keep themselves and their families fed and housed in the interim. Although the region's kin-culture pattern of settlement lightened this burden for many, it did not completely eliminate the need for work.

In a predominantly subsistence economy, where few markets and even less currency existed, wage-labor jobs were not abundant. Yet tasks remained plentiful, and most depended on the omnipresent forests: cutting down trees, splitting wood, milling lumber, and constructing fences and buildings. John Minto's and Thomas Smith's initial labors in Oregon were to make fence rails and log walls for claim-holding cabins. Clement Bradbury found employment as a tree faller at Hunt's mill in 1847. When Daniel Knight Warren, his brother, and two other young men came to Oregon in September 1852, they found their first work in an Astoria sawmill.[13]

A few farsighted town residents saw in the forests a commercial future and a means to regional prosperity. In a revealing statement, the *Oregon Spectator* wrote on April 20, 1848, that "Oregon lumber is shipped to California and Sandwich Islands—and its value for shipment controls its price at home."[14] A dependent Northwest region that relied on an extractive economy and was tied to world markets seemed to be an unlikely future. Instead, some northwesterners dreamed of the demand for the region's lumber. In what would become a Northwest booster refrain, Peter Burnett wrote in 1844: "South America, the Sandwich Islands, and California, must depend upon us for their lumber. Already large quantities of shingles and plank are sent to the Islands. We shall always have a fine market for all our surplus."[15] Fledgling urban promoters dreamed about and touted the region's commercial future. "The day is not far distant," the *Oregon Spectator* boasted in 1848, "when people residing upon the Atlantic coast, will be engaged in the fishing and lumbering business upon the Pacific. Lumber is fast disappearing on the Atlantic."[16]

While the decline in eastern timber supplies did not occur until the latter part of the century, the growth of the Northwest lumber industry came much quicker than even the *Spectator* envisioned. Once again, an event that occurred beyond regional borders altered the Northwest landscape forever. Four months after the *Oregon Spectator*'s prognostication came word that gold had been discovered at John Sutter's California mill on January 24, 1848. The impact of the California gold rush on the Douglas-fir region had both short- and long-term consequences. During the fall, a majority of male northwesterners swarmed south in search of a new El Dorado. Businesses like Hunt's mill were abandoned, and nascent towns such as Salem stood deserted. Settlers even left their farms, resulting in lowered yields of wheat and creating general agricultural stagnation throughout the region for two years.[17]

As people from all over the world swept into California, however, some northwesterners realized that gold lay not only in mining but also in servicing the miners' needs. Oregonians sent vegetables, meat, flour, butter, eggs, and other produce south, garnering high returns on the California market and raising local prices as well. Butter went from twenty-five cents to a dollar a pound from 1848 to 1852. Wheat, the region's principal crop, was also a staple export. Matthew Deady recounted how "a good deal" was "raised for the California market" between 1850 and 1855. Wheat that had gone for a dollar a bushel now went for as high as seven dollars. Potatoes selling for five dollars a bushel in July 1853 had sold for as much as ten dollars. Generally high prices for other Oregon farm products also followed in wake of the gold rush.[18]

Oregon's initial population drain abated by midcentury, and the booming California export business brought back many Oregon country settlers who had ventured south for gold. It also attracted into Oregon the young merchants who were to become Oregon's business elite. Moreover, the Oregon Donation Land Act of 1850 acted like a magnet to draw former residents back and new emigrants to the Northwest, particularly those who came in pursuit of the yeoman ideal. Subsequent gold discoveries at Yreka, California, in the winter of 1850–1851 and in the southern Oregon area of Jacksonville in 1851 created new markets for Willamette Valley products. Currency began to appear in the region. More and more people, goods, and coin began to make their way to the Northwest.[19]

In a pattern often repeated over the next half-century, mining served to accelerate the commercial logging of northwestern forests. Increasingly, loggers cut trees in regional forests and shipped sawed lumber products south to California markets. In 1851, Captain Lewis Love, who had just taken up a farm at the Columbia Slough, rafted about 300,000 feet of logs to Portland for shipment south. Love remarked that "there was quite a number of other fools in the same business. Logging was carried on all along the Slough." According to Oregonian Matthew Deady, Oregon lumber prices between 1849 and 1850 were "fabulous." Lumber brought $60 a thousand foot by early 1851, and $75 to $100 per thousand feet the following year, and eventually reaching $150. Investment alchemists were not slow to convert the region's "green gold," in Patricia Marchak's apt words, into yellow gold.[20]

One such alchemist was Isom Cranfill. A carpenter and an ordained regular Baptist minister, Cranfill brought his family overland to Oregon in 1847. Settling in Oregon City, Cranfill preached monthly to a small congregation while working as a carpenter to support his family. Then came the gold rush. Sensing opportunity, Cranfill, in partnership with Benjamin Simpson, purchased the Cutting sawmill on the Clackamas River. Cranfill's bid for economic security seemed to be paying off, and for several months the partners made over $300 a day. But if milling carried high profits it also brought risks. Some of those risks extended beyond fluctuating markets to changes in nature, and it was the latter that undid the Reverend Cranfill's bid for financial security. Heavy snow and rain in December 1849 created flooding conditions that destroyed many Willamette Valley mills. The January 10, 1850, *Oregon Spectator* reported "that nearly all the mills in the Territory have been swept away, or seriously injured." Cranfill's was one of those mills, with nearly $4,000 worth of lumber lost and sawmill damages that totaled $1,600. Nonetheless, given the substantial profits he had made in his initial venture, Cranfill decided to go into the milling business again. With a new partner, W. T. Matlock, he built a new sawmill and a substantial mill dam on the Clackamas River in the spring of 1850. Unfortunately for Cranfill, a spring freshet came raging down the river and washed his investment away.[21]

Cranfill was only one of many early mill owners in the Northwest who depended on an environment they could not yet control. In addition to the dangers of raging streams, logs being transported to a mill or lumber rafted to markets were lost to storms or rocks.[22] Sawmills also proved particularly vulnerable to fire, and owners already short of capital could not always afford to rebuild once a mill was destroyed.[23] Such occurrences undoubtedly promoted the exploitation of the forests. Tomorrow might bring profit, but it also held out the possibility of loss. Besides, the forests were vast. There was little incentive for loggers to concern themselves with forest conservation.

As demand for lumber climbed and prices rose, the number of sawmills increased. Eighteen small, water-powered sawmills operated on the Willamette and lower Columbia rivers in the spring of 1848, and fewer than a quarter of that number north of the Columbia River.[24] The number of Oregon mills had increased to about thirty by February 1849, and three years later, Superintendent of Indian Affairs Anson Dart reported that Oregon possessed about one hundred mills. Theodore Winthrop caught the beginnings of the change in 1853, when he wrote in a poetic letter to his mother that along the Columbia River "numberless sawmills are fast opening little breathing-holes in the sunless forest." Washington underwent a similar growth. Largely devoid of settlers and mills before the gold rush, Puget Sound had an estimated fourteen sawmills by 1853. In early 1855, twenty-four mills were reportedly operating, and two years later James Swan listed thirty-seven sawmills for Washington Territory.[25] By 1920, when Washington ranked first and Oregon ranked second in national lumber production, Theodore Winthrop's "little breathing-holes" were becoming gaping maws.

The lumber industry brought an influx of non-Indian people and capital to the region, accelerating urban growth, creating new markets for farmers, and augmenting a barter exchange economy with species payment. Lumbering, as one regional paper phrased it, became "the principal of our domestic instrumentalities, not only in bringing in a large amount of money, but also of distributing that money among the people." In short order, the lumber industry became the Northwest's commercial linchpin.[26]

The profitability of the timber industry attracted more than mere capital to the Northwest; it also lured people with knowledge about the industry. Technological advances were the most noticeable changes the new lumbermen brought with them. New Hampshire native Cyrus Reed, in partnership with William Penn Abrams, established the Northwest's first steam sawmill at Portland in 1850. Henry Yesler constructed the initial steam sawmill north of the Columbia River at Seattle in 1853. Other steam-powered sawmills soon followed. A water-powered mill like Henry Hunt's had turned out 2,000 to 3,000 thousand feet of lumber a day in the 1840s. By 1857, the large Pope and Talbot steam mill at Port Gamble, Washington, could manufacture 30,000 feet of lumber a day, while providing jobs for 160 to 180 loggers and sawyers. Twenty-one years later, Pope and Talbot's Port Gamble mill produced 200,000 feet daily and employed about 300 mill workers, with a similar number working at logging camps and on company steamers.[27]

Steam sawmills and lumber production continued to grow throughout the region during the 1860s, with lumbermen always mindful to locate their mills near navigable streams with easy access to timber.[28] Expansion continued, though at a modest rate, during the 1870s, with Washington Territory manufacturing and exporting an estimated 200 million board feet of lumber in 1876. Three years later, Washington's total lumber production stood at 160 million feet.[29] The introduction of electric lights in the early 1880s further boosted productivity by allowing mills to work around-the-clock. By 1883, when the transcontinental railroad reached its Northwest terminus on Commencement Bay in Tacoma, Washington, eight large Puget Sound sawmills were producing nearly 100,000 feet of lumber daily.[30] Settler society was giving way to an industrial society.

During the 1850s, distinctive patterns emerged in Washington and Oregon that would differentiate the two states in the twentieth century. With 126 mills, Oregon possessed four times more sawmills than Washington by 1860, but western Washington's larger, more heavily capitalized export-directed mills produced far more lumber.[31] Although those different conditions reflected and helped configure the socioeconomic and political landscape of Oregon and Washington, physical geography framed those divergent cultural patterns.

Buffeted by high winds and rough seas throughout the year and with stretches of low sea cliffs and basaltic headlands, the Northwest coastline offered few deep-water harbors with easy access to the Pacific. Coos Bay on the southern Oregon coast was one of those harbors, and it had a thriving lumber economy by the 1850s. The other major Oregon harbor was farther north at Tillamook Bay, drained by the Nestachee, Trask, and Nestucca rivers. The drawback at Tillamook, however, was "the want of safe anchorage for ships of size." Not until the settler era had passed did the Tillamook area become a major lumber-producing location. Although a few other coastal harbors had small-producing mills, Coos Bay remained the only place along the Northwest coast where mills clustered until 1880.[32]

The Columbia River offered a navigable waterway, but the shifting sandbars at the mouth of the river made it a graveyard for ships. Delays also were a problem. It was not unknown for ships to have to wait months for the necessary winds and tides that would allow them to cross the bar safely. The difficulty was not easily overcome and was another reason why ships and investors looked farther north.[33] There were also few streams in Oregon large enough to transport timber. Even the Columbia and the Willamette rivers made transportation difficult. Cascade Locks on the Columbia, approximately thirty miles east of Portland, and Willamette Falls, about twenty miles up the Willamette at Oregon City, inhibited easy river passage. North of the Columbia, the sheltered waterways at Willapa Bay and Grays Harbor provided harbors for seagoing ships, but mudflats, sloughs, and shifting channels made those locations problematic as well. Moreover, the less desirable spruce and hemlock dominated the tidewater areas, while the more valuable Douglas fir grew in less accessible inland locations.[34]

By proceeding to Cape Flattery and passing into the Straits of Juan de Fuca, however, ships could enter Puget Sound. Known for its accessibility and safety, Puget Sound was an important reason why American boundary negotiators insisted on a more northerly line of demarcation between British and American territory.[35] Called the "Mediterranean of the North-West" by boosters, the sound was a lumberman's paradise. Placid, deep waters allowed oceangoing ships to easily traverse the sound, while numerous inlets provided safe harbors.[36] More important for lumbermen, the forests were abundant and readily accessible. The location and physical makeup of those forests, along with the convenient harbors and streams, framed the development of the Northwest lumber industry. That same geography of the market that had located a fitting physical geography played an important role in shaping the historical similarities and differences of two states sharing a common forest bioregion.

The extensive valleys that made western Oregon an attractive place of settlement were also relatively free of forests. The bulk of Oregon's forests were in the Coast and Cascade ranges, not in easily accessible lowlands. The inaccessibility of timber combined with limitations in technology and transportation to restrict logging and lumbering during the settlement era in Oregon. The state's few export lumber mills were concentrated along the lower Columbia River and at Coos Bay, where they produced principally for the San Francisco market.[37] Most of Oregon's sawmills were small, internally capitalized establishments with production geared toward local needs. There was substantial capital investment in lumbering during the settler period, but most outside investors looked towards Washington rather than Oregon. Less populated by a culturally fixed and exclusive rural society, Washington offered a more attractive milieu to the entrepreneurial, liberal economic lumberman. A letter written in Olympia typified those sentiments: "A man that is not willing to take the risk of a small investment, with all these advantages [around Grays Harbor], a little in advance of an *actual demand* for lumber, will never make a rapid fortune."[38]

Evergreen forests along the easily navigable waterway of Puget Sound literally came to the water's edge. No steep mountains or canyons had to be surmounted. The technological limitations and a separation of logging, milling, and shipping points that restricted inland harvesting proved to be no problem along the sound. Trees were chopped down, moved a short distance, milled, and loaded, all operations within close proximity to one another.[39] Resource, market, capital, and transportation conjoined along the sound to create the core of a timber industry that would dominate the Pacific Northwest economy for over a century. That extractive economic base along with dependency on external markets and outside capital investment were critical factors in defining the region's history, particularly in

Washington. It also provided one of the shaping themes of Northwest and western history in general: the American West as "plundered province."

Washington residents were clearly mindful of the important role the timber industry played in their lives. In 1871, the *Washington Standard* observed that although western Washington's agricultural lands met "home demands," for "the agriculturalist . . . this country is far from attractive." The Olympia newspaper continued that Washington's "wealth and population must depend almost entirely upon the improvement of its unrivalled commercial and manufacturing advantages." And nature made "timber . . . the chief source of our future wealth."[40]

The lumber industry was Washington's leading manufacturing enterprise and economic centerpiece by the late 1850s. The abundant and apparently "inexhaustible forests of fir, . . . spruce and . . . cedar," seemed to assure Washington's people of a secure, prosperous future. Through the nineteenth century and into the twentieth, those sentiments became a common refrain.[41] A typical settler era publication read:

> Lumber, as has been the case, will for years hence continue to be the great staple of the country, and its production will be of greater benefit, by affording steady employment to a greater number of persons, than any other enterprise which can ever obtain a foothold in the Territory. As an unfailing source of supply for this product, we have, as before stated, a dense forest of gigantic firs and cedars covering the table lands on either side of the Sound and reaching thence to the summits of the mountains, which nearly enclose this great basin of untold natural wealth; and for its rapid production there are a dozen extensive steam mills in constant operation, which manufacture and export about 200,000,000 feet of lumber.[42]

The industrial period saw little change in attitude. The September 1, 1901, *Seattle Post-Intelligencer* trumpeted: "The future of the Puget Sound country; the commercial interest of the state of Washington; the prosperity of the city of Seattle—its past, present and future—all center around the wonderful timber lands of the state."[43]

While the growth of sawmills was a mark of progress and a point of pride for Oregonians, Washington residents felt particularly proud. The "progressive" sawmills along Puget Sound dominated the region's lumber production. Few in number but with a concentration of economic and technical power, the mills represented the modern industrial age. By 1871, for example, approximately 90 percent of Washington Territory's lumber production came from twelve mills.[44] A concentration of power, however, meant much more than how many board feet were produced.

Little capital was required to enter the lumber business with water-powered mills. Larger, technologically sophisticated mills, however, required investment capital that few northwesterners possessed. If Washington's lumber business was to grow, it needed money from somewhere else. Experienced eastern lumbermen, particularly from Maine, saw an opportunity to supply lumber to the burgeoning California population and the Pacific Rim market. What the Hudson's Bay Company had first seen dimly in the 1820s and 1830s, these eastern-backed, San Francisco–based investors saw clearly.[45]

Fixed capital costs, inadequate transportation systems, and limited regional markets meant that venture capitalists were interested in the potential of market opportunities outside the region. Linked to the wider world by water, those mill owners hitched their fortunes to the cargo trade. With San Francisco supplying the region's financial capital and California offering the primary market, the ride was often anything but smooth. Tied to the vicissitudes of Californian and international market forces, the region rode a boom-and-bust economic roller-coaster, especially the less economically diverse and more heavily lumber-dependent area of Washington. Thomas Cox, one of the most knowledgeable historians about those processes, has concluded: "Washington, possessing a narrow economic base and dependent on markets susceptible to extremes of fluctuations, experienced the vagaries of the nation's financial cycles to an even more pronounced degree than the country as a whole."[46]

After several years of heavy demand for lumber following the California gold rush, there was a dip in the lumber market. A demand for wood to rebuild Sacramento following a major fire in 1852 temporarily revived timber prices, but dependency on the San Francisco cargo trade plunged Washington's lumber industry once again in the doldrums during 1854 and 1855.[47] The owners' answer to the economic downturn was an extension of the thinking that had helped create the problem in the first place: dependency on market exports of timber. This time, the call was to create markets throughout the Pacific Rim. To "have the boundless Pacific for a market" could be Washington's "manifest destiny," trumpeted the *Pioneer and Democrat* on November 18, 1854: "We were born to command it." Destiny appeared to be following its chartered course, as the lumber trade picked up in late 1856. The Pacific Coast largely escaped the 1857 depression that struck the East, partly because of geographical distance but also because of Pacific Rim markets. But in 1860, boom turned to bust one more time. On July 27, Olympia's *Pioneer and Democrat* lamented both the state of the economy and the endemic problems attached to heavy dependency on a single resource: "With a dull market for lumber—the main, and, we might say, about the only commodity of commerce from which we could hope to secure a return of the cash which is so regularly and constantly leaving the Territory, in payment for goods and wares consumed by our people."[48]

What occurred in the 1850s was emblematic of the economy throughout the settler era and beyond. Eldridge Morse recorded the effects of a depressed lumber economy from 1877 to 1880 for timber-dependent Snohomish City, Washington: "Nearly every business man on the river became bankrupt or suspended his business. Real estate could not be sold at any price."[49] Driven by forces external to the region, investors showed little interest in maintaining community stability or a local forest resource base. It was a situation where a "geography of capital," to use historian William Cronon's phrase, created an unstable geography of place. No particular place remained essential. Resources could be liquidated and capital invested in the next place that offered abundant forests and ready profit.[50]

Moreover, because cargo mills produced mostly for export rather than home consumption, those sawmills created their own dependent communities. Washington's settlement structure, unlike much of Oregon's, reflected the lumber industry's pervasive influence by the 1880s. The lumber industry framed both the location of settlements along Puget Sound and controlled their economic well being through their dependency on sawmill or logging operations. Even in scattered lowlands farmers relied on lumber industry markets for the sale of their foodstuffs. The largest mill sites existed as company towns and exemplified one more form that concentrated power took.[51] Caroline Leighton may not have detailed the dark side of company mill towns in 1865, but she did outline their coercive power:

> It seems . . . as if we might be living in feudal times, these great mill-owners have such authority in the settlements. Some of them possess very large tracts of land, have hundreds of men in their employ, own steamboats and hotels, and have very large stores of general merchandise, in connection with their mill-business. They sometimes provide amusements for the men,—little dramatic entertainments, etc.,—to keep them from resorting to drink; and encourage them to send for their families, and to make gardens around their houses.[52]

The largest companies also created satellite logging camps. Those towns and the nearby farmers prospered, but only as long as the trees held out. Once the forests were denuded, the company moved its cash and personnel to re-create a cut-and-run scenario in yet another place. Although most mill sites did not grow beyond the confines of the company town, a few eventually became major urban centers, such as Bellingham, Seattle, and Tacoma.

Oregon's mills were also important to the state's economy. To use the *Oregonian*'s metaphor, Oregon's timber industry by the 1880s was "the wheel which sets all other wheels in motion."[53] Still, most Oregon lumbermen geared production around internal needs and markets. Small mills with a 15,000-board-foot daily capacity, labeled the "Oregontype," were the norm south of the Columbia River. Changes in technology, transportation, and markets; dwindling forests in other areas; and increased investments in Oregon timberland gradually shifted the mix between domestic and export production towards external markets by 1890. But throughout the settler period, smaller enterprises that were less reliant on foreign market sales dominated lumber production south of the Columbia. While six or seven large merchant mills on the lower Columbia aggregated 75 million to 100 million board feet of lumber each year in foreign trade, most Oregon mills sawed primarily for local markets. Except for Coos Bay, Oregon's largest mills could not match the output of those on Puget Sound. At no time during the nineteenth century could it be said of Oregon lumber markets, as it was of Puget Sound markets, that they "are entirely foreign, being South America, Australia, Central America and the Pacific ocean islands."[54]

The Douglas-fir region was being colonialized as well as colonized. Washington producers in particular lived in the shadow of both the Cascade Mountains and the city of San Francisco; it had become a resource hinterland to the metropolitan City by the Bay.[55] Believing that they benefited from external capital investment and markets, Washingtonians overlooked the attendant loss of control and costs of dependency. Only occasionally were cautionary voices raised about the need for greater economic self-sufficiency. James G. Swan's view that Washington's extractive lumber trade was more indicative of a colonial status than a sign of independence was rare:

The oyster trade [at Bruceport on Shoalwater Bay], like the lumber trade on the Sound, does not do much for the Territory. Like the Chinese in California, they take away all that is of value, spending only just so much as it costs to place on board vessels for transportation the products of our forests and our waters and adding the wealth derived from this Territory to the wealth of other places. If our lumber, our coal, and our fishing interests could be made to benefit this Territory as the lumber of Maine, the coal of Pennsylvania, the fisheries of Massachusetts, and the oysters of Virginia have benefitted those States, Washington Territory, long before this, would have been, from the development of its own resources, one of the best States on the Pacific Coast. It is to be hoped that when we have a railroad from the Sound to the Columbia which will open up the means of emigration, that our mill owners may find it to their interest to invest some of their capital for the benefit and growth of the Territory which enriches them.[56]

When concerns did arise, there was a call to rely less on imports and one dominant export and to diversify domestic agriculture and manufacturing. The *Washington Pioneer*, for example, asked in 1853 whether the state's economic dependence on lumber exports did not mean being "controlled by irresponsible SHARPERS AND SPECULATORS, resident in Sacramento, San Francisco and elsewhere along the coast?" To that question the newspaper responded with a resounding yes, that the situation did make "us subservient to the interests of the people of another State—make us 'hewers of wood and drawers of water,' with but an uncertain, and at all events with but a very inadequate reward." The remedy, suggested the *Pioneer*, lay with Washington lumbermen controlling their own business.[57]

Immediate benefits, however, seemed more real and tangible than a distant future. Gains seemingly outweighed the costs, at least until the bill had to be paid. Only when the costs could not be avoided did critics decry colonialism and corporate greed. Then the colonial innocents loudly bemoaned their dependent status and looked to scapegoats rather than themselves for an explanation. At times, blame was fixed on the central government. Because Washington did not gain statehood until 1889, residents felt particularly impotent to construct laws to protect themselves. Most often, however, invective centered on concerns about how "the profits arising . . . from Washington have gone to enrich other cities than her own." The finger of guilt was pointed at monopolists from San Francisco who controlled the price of lumber and drained Washington of its resources and profits.[58]

Despite occasional outbursts, most northwesterners held to a belief in the region's destiny, the world demand for its lumber, a natural market economy of supply and demand, and the ability to find new markets. Setbacks were considered unnatural and temporary. When the market slumped, there was a general belief that the natural law of supply and demand had been violated, whether through government policies, attempts at price-fixing, businesses' attempts to go beyond a "reasonable profit," or overproduction.[59] Whatever the cause, correction seemed assured and the future open. Destiny and a natural law of supply and demand left little room for believers in limited growth. The June 26, 1896, *Washington Standard* crystallized that belief:

> Again, when but a few decades ago it was found that the great sperm whale was fast becoming extinct on account of its wholesale slaughter in the northern seas; when it was a common thing for whaling ships to seek the home port in ballast after a fruitless three years' cruise, and the price of the best oil went up to five dollars a gallon, while for the purposes of public illumination tallow candles were a mockery, and gas was beyond the reach of the millions, then the voice of Providence was

heard again, by the people of Western Pennsylvania, "Up; bestir your-
selves, pierce the solid ground with your drills and pump up the oil I
have stored in the great tanks that honeycomb the bowels of the earth."
And now, as if all this were not enough, electricity comes flashing and
scattering into outer darkness all its predecessors.[60]

The dominant perspective was that capital investment in any part of
the economy aided all sectors and all people. In an address that modern
adherents to an export-base theory of economic development could
endorse, Washington laywer, acting governor during the Civil War, and
speaker of the house in the 1870s Elwood Evans observed: "Heavy capitalists are necessary in just such a country, and for the benefits, they bring
to our Territorial development, we may tolerate a tyranny which capital
extorts."[61] Increased capital investment, agricultural expansion, and diver-
sified commercial and manufacturing ventures seemed bound to follow a
growing timber industry. Despite persistent calls for economic diversity
and increased manufacturing to supply local needs and bolster exports, the
region developed only a minimal manufacturing sector until the First
World War. For better or worse, it remained dependent on a boom-and-
bust, resource-based economy.[62]

Throughout the settler period, the white population in the Douglas-fir
region believed their destiny was progress. Blessed with an abundant physical environment, the Northwest awaited only the transforming hand of an
industrious people. Regional limitations to development seemed a temporary situation that human ingenuity would soon surmount. It was widely
believed that technological improvement, the elimination of careless practices, increased population, and more capital would complete the region's
manifest destiny, though Oregonians were generally specific that the population they wanted was "industrious farmers" while Washingtonians
seemed more interested in capital. Few people during the settlement era
thought of resources as finite and as a factor that might limit the region's
economic growth. People believed that lumbering "must increase for years
to come, the capacity of the Sound for its production being such that its
only limitation must be in the demand, giving employment to thousands
of hands."[63] Nature's abundance would guarantee greatness, just as soon
as the limitations could be eradicated.

As the settler society gave way to the industrial era, human and regional limitations appeared to have been surmounted. By 1880, eastern
forests had been largely cut over, and Great Lakes timberlands were declining rapidly. Timber capitalists began to look for new areas to exploit. Some
investors turned to the yellow pine forests of the South, but even more
looked westward. The new transcontinental railroads brought more and
more people and capital to the Northwest. Although new to the region,

these emigrants were a constitutive part of an old migratory pattern of capital colonization of a natural resource, the exploitive extraction and depletion of that resource, and the migration of capital to some other place where the boom-bust cycle of dependency could be acted out again. In Washington, capital investment changes meant that external control had merely shifted from San Francisco to the Midwest; in Oregon, outside capital investment was less pervasive.

For industrial society, as for the earlier fur and settler societies, the Far West seemed the land of opportunity. Earlier booster predictions about the Pacific Slope seemed to be coming true. Nature's dictates concerning "Westward the course of Empire" were finding fulfillment. The most far-reaching and symbolic example of the processes working to transform the region came in 1900 when Minnesota lumber magnate Frederick Weyerhaeuser and his associates acquired 900,000 acres of Washington forestland for $5.4 million from the Northern Pacific Railroad. With that transaction "Washington's forest economy was instantly transformed."[64] Sawmill size and productivity rose exponentially. With the completion in 1914 of the Weyerhaeuser sawmill at Everett, Washington, the Northwest could claim title to the world's most productive lumber operation. Between 1898 and 1914, Oregon tripled its lumber production, and, in 1905, Washington became the nation's leading timber-producing state.[65]

Local boosters took pride in the growth of the Northwest as the region moved from isolation to a fully integrated member of the nation's industrial economy. From the Jefferson administration through the 1840s, the Northwest had been a focus of western expansionists, a centerpiece in congressional debate, and a prominent feature in the American imagination. But geography had kept the Northwest isolated. During the late nineteenth and early twentieth centuries, however, the Douglas-fir region no longer seemed a peripheral land of hopeful dreams but an emerging central place filled with promise. As the center of the lumber industry began to shift westward, few northwesterners gave any critical thought to the ways that this new geography of capital would seriously reshape the region's ecology of place. To be sure, industrial society would transform the region's cultural and physical landscape, but those changes would represent not so much a change in direction as an acceleration of earlier patterns.

CHAPTER NINE

Transforming the Forests

The acceleration of settlement timber production patterns, during the industrial period, however, requires a closer look at the earlier era and the processes that gave rise to the new age. Despite accelerated productivity, regional lumber output was limited until the 1880s.[1] Several factors kept the total acreage of cut-over forests during the settlement period small. Settlers seldom entered the forests to create homesteads, and the region lacked the technology to cut and mill the largest of the Northwest's coniferous trees. Other limitations included a physical geography that inhibited logging and transporting lumber, as well as the fact that forests still existed in other parts of the country. In addition, the lumbermen's unfamiliarity with many of the region's species made those trees a risky investment.

Little technological change occurred during the settlement period to alter the tribulations that Alexander Ross and the Astorians had faced in 1811 in felling the Northwest's giant evergreens. Cutting down trees took up to an hour with the single-bitted axe, and the axe and crosscut saw for bucking remained the fallers' principal tools until the early 1880s.[2] Moreover, only trees from 5 to 6 feet in diameter could be cut because sawmills could not handle larger diameter logs. Since mature evergreens were large and abundant, and the base pitchy, cutting was generally done 10 or more feet above the tree butt.[3] Theodore Winthrop described how the giant trees continued to stand against the axe: "These giants with their rough plate-armor were masters here; one of human stature was unmeaning and incapable. With an axe, a man of muscle might succeed in smiting off a flake or a chip; but his slight fibers seemed naught to battle, with any chance of victory, with the time-hardened sinews of these Goliaths."[4]

A restricted transportation system also limited timber harvests and inhibited access to markets. Because animal power dominated yarding operations until the 1880s, logging was necessarily a slow and localized enterprise, its range kept to a radius of a mile or two, the average distance being one-half to three-quarters of a mile. Hitching downed trees to horse teams or, more commonly, yoked oxen, logs were generally dragged over skid roads constructed from small-diameter trees. Skidding was used during the 1850s, and within two decades was a fully developed operation. Trimmed and cut into 9-foot lengths, the logs were laid at right angles to the direction of skidding in 7- to 8-foot intervals. Hot animal fat or fish oil was then poured on the skid roads to facilitate movement and reduce friction. By the late 1870s, according to one observer, a crew of eight oxen and ten men could haul approximately 100,000 feet per week over a mile-long road.[5]

Inadequate roads and an absence of railroads during the settler era also meant that logging and milling operations were heavily dependent on water. Hauling logs to a mill along skid roads restricted logging to on-site milling or to riverine areas where navigable streams allowed river drives or where splash dams could be constructed until spring freshets carried the logs downriver to mill sites.[6] Where logging and milling occurred in close proximity but shipping facilities were a mile or two away, lumbermen sometimes constructed flumes to connect the two sites.[7] Once milled, lumber had to reach markets. Regional waterways may have been adequate for overland travel, but few streams were deep enough to allow cargo ships safe passage. Even streams with sufficient depth were often encumbered by snags, log jams, and waterfalls. In addition, with the Northwest Coast having few safe harbors, only a small number of mills clustered along the Northwest coast line, except at Coos Bay, until the 1880s. Only on Puget Sound was an adequate water system available for carrying lumber to a wide number of markets.

The production of timber from forests in the Midwest also kept interest away from Northwest forests, though unfamiliarity with the region played a role as well. Most Americans had not only never seen trees of such size, except for northern California's sequoias and redwoods, but they also lacked knowledge about the properties of Northwest trees. The cultural values Americans brought to the Northwest had not prepared them for a region without traditionally known and highly valued hardwoods, such as hickory, walnut, or locust. The ash and oak that did grow in the Northwest seemed deficient in quantity and quality, and the region's prairie oak appeared to be "very Low and scrubby" compared to "that in the States." Visitors like Lieutenant Neil Howison concluded that Oregon's trees in "quality and usefulness are in nowise comparable to that produced in the United States."[8] Once again, preconceptions had framed understandings about a place where the observer did not live.

As emigrants became residents, however, transported understandings gave way to the experience of place. Settlers found that hazelwood, maple, and ash were adequate substitutes for hickory, and that the region's cedars and Douglas fir provided a superior wood. Absolom Harden wrote that "you can generaly git from 8 to 13 Rail cuts from one tree and they split well as any timber in the wourld." Settlers used alder to make furniture, and cedar became a valued finishing wood.[9] Nonetheless, old attitudes died hard, particularly among those who lived outside the Northwest. While the region's Douglas fir and cedar gained a worldwide reputation, other species languished. The Oregon yew was ignored, and spruce and hemlock were thought to be like their eastern counterparts and consequently of little value. The regional press, to boost timber sales, waged a battle to convince others outside the region that Northwest spruce and hemlock were a different species that provided straight-grained and durable lumber.[10]

Because logging was concentrated in areas easily accessible to settler communities and water courses, land with steep inclines and remote locations was relatively untouched. Even though areas like the Puget Sound shoreline were shorn of their timber, logged-off lands constituted only a small proportion of the region's forests. As Congregational minister George Atkinson told his Portland audience during a public lecture in 1871: "By labor and skill the forests of Puget Sound yield 200,000,000 feet of lumber per year, and yet they have hardly been touched a mile from the shore." A similar judgment was made in an 1882 article about the Willamette Valley, which observed that only "forests easily accessible have been despoiled of all likely trees."[11]

But if environmental, technological, and market factors determined the lumber industry's size, few restrictions encumbered access to the forests. To early timbermen, the region's forests were a "commons," free for everyone to use.[12] Reflecting on this era late in his life, former Chief Forester William B. Greeley remarked: "The forest story of America begins with the tradition of free land. Free timber was part of the tradition. . . . It is not surprising that venturesome spirits on the frontier took the trees as they took the beaver pelts or panned gold nuggets from the rivers."[13]

Pacific Northwest farmers wanted cleared land, merchants wanted more business, and lumbermen wanted access to cheap timber. But Americans had framed their land laws to promote the yeomen's republic, not the lumber business. The government provided no way for lumbermen to buy timber on the public domain without purchasing the land itself. Moreover, land purchased for its timber ran up against laws that limited the acreage that could be bought and requirements that governed residency and cultivation. The result, as the December 2, 1865, Olympia's *Washington Standard* readily admitted, was that Puget Sound lumbermen obtained most of their logs illegally from the public domain. Even if the law provided for the lumbermen's needs, however, there seems little reason to believe timber theft would have diminished. The resource itself seemed to be inexhaustible, its "free" availability increased profits, and forest exploitation was a way to increase the region's population and wealth. In addition, before Puget Sound became settled, timber thieves found that it was simple to escape detection from government agents.[14] Given those conditions, public officials made few efforts to halt the theft, and individuals who attempted to do so met with little success. When John J. McGilvra arrived in the Northwest in 1861 to take up his post as U.S. District Attorney for Washington

Territory, he found timber theft a common and openly accepted practice. In a report to the solicitor of the treasury, McGilvra wrote that approximately fifteen sawmills on Puget Sound that cut from 5,000 to 40,000 feet of lumber daily were "almost wholly supplied with logs from the government land." Part of his job, as McGilvra saw it, was to prosecute such theft under a March 2, 1831, federal law that had made it illegal to "wantonly" destroy "timber standing, growing, or being on any lands of the United States." Yet he was not unmindful of the economic role that lumbering played in the Washington economy. In an August 31, 1861, letter, McGilvra explicitly stated that a strict policy of prosecution would stop the mills and "injure the prosperity and prospects of the Territory very much." McGilvra took the compromise position that prosecution was not intended to persecute, but to work out a modus vivendi in light of actual practices and laws that did not reflect the lumbermen's needs. Unable to patrol all of the logging camps with government agents and knowing that virtually all of the logs milled were cut from federal land, McGilvra simply charged the mills a fixed stumpage fee based on the amount of lumber produced. The arrangement allowed McGilvra to uphold the law, deflect hostility away from a federal government already involved in the Civil War, and yet sustain a sound lumbering economy. Besides, it was difficult to get convictions against mill owners. Federal officials were outsiders whose actions received a warm welcome when they supported local economic growth and outcries of protest when they restricted economic expansion. Historian Frederick Yonce summarized the situation: "Juries were composed of men equally guilty; logging was the principal business of the country, and outside of a few towns, nine-tenths of the men were directly or indirectly engaged in it."[15]

Although stumpage fees varied, collecting money for trees cut from the public land became a standard procedure. McGilvra may have reached the best possible solution under the circumstances, but the low fees amounted to a policy of subsidies for lumbermen. Andrew Pope paid $325 for cutting 2,510,000 feet, while Marshall Blinn cut 5,500,000 feet and was charged $825.[16] When stumpage fees in Washington threatened a rise to $2.50 per thousand feet in 1865, cries came not just from lumbermen but from newspapers that recognized how important the lumber industry was to the territory's economy:

The system of "stumpage" has been acquiesced in by the lumber makers very patriotically, as a burden they would cordially bear toward sustaining the Government, but when two dollars and fifty cents is suggested, instead of the fifteen cents per thousand, heretofore paid, it becomes a prohibition to further enterprise. For the Government to pursue a policy of this character, is to cripple not only the enterprise of this Territory, but to depopulate it.[17]

When a similar fee was proposed in 1868, Washington congressional delegate Alavan Flanders interceded with the General Land Office to allow judges in Washington to fix stumpage "at an equitable figure."[18]

A more stringent policy of arrests, fines, and stumpage fees began in 1870 as the commercial value of Northwest forests increased and as a nascent concern for conservation began to take shape among a small group of well-educated scientists.[19] In 1870, General Land Office Special Agent B. B. Tuttle took the first of many actions against mill owners when he seized the logs of Spencer Kellogg. Tuttle confiscated a number of log booms in 1871 for having cut off government land. The culprits were allowed to keep the logs, but only after paying a stumpage fee of forty cents per thousand foot. Sometimes, however, the district court made the thieves forfeit the stolen logs in addition to paying fines and court costs. The government then sold the stolen timber to a local sawmill. Not surprisingly, lumbermen considered the government's actions to be unjust, especially when they heard rumors that agents would overlook illegally obtained logs for a price. They rebelled by finding ways to avoid detection or by sabotaging seized log booms.[20]

The more stringent policy against lumbermen arose from a growing awareness about the increased dollar value of the forest, conflicting private interests, and a short-lived government policy of forest reform. The Northern Pacific Railroad land grant of 1870 included a great deal of western Washington forestland, stretching from the Columbia River to British Columbia. Unable to distinguish Northern Pacific forest holdings from public forests, lumbermen trespassed on Northern Pacific land. Concerned for their own profits and not easily swayed by public opinion or local politics, the Northern Pacific pressured the government to arrest trespassers and then hired its own agents to stop the theft. More illegal logs were confiscated, but enforcement did not end timber theft. Stumpage settlement payments and sales of seized logs simply did not equal the value of stolen timber.[21]

The theft continued even after the General Land Office—as part of a forest reform program under Secretary of the Interior Carl Schurz—appointed special timber agents as enforcement personnel in 1877. The extent of the forested land and a limited budget that restricted manpower combined to hamper suppression. Moreover, once Henry Teller succeeded Schurz as secretary of the interior, forest reform measures stopped altogether. The Timber Trespass law of 1880 tacitly admitted that suppression had failed and attempted to recover at least some revenue from the stolen timber. The law granted amnesty to anyone who had stolen timber from the public domain before March 1, 1879, provided they paid $1.25 per acre for the logs taken.[22] Lumbermen nevertheless continued to steal logs from the public lands. In 1886, the secretary of agriculture's annual report observed:

The cutting of timber from public land for sale and speculation has been permitted to continue for such a length of time without notice or with but feeble interference by the Government that in some sections of country the mill-men and speculators have come to regard the public timber as theirs by tacit right, and come to consider any attempt of the Government to now restrict their cutting and disposing of the same to the express terms of the law as an unwarranted interference. So prevalent is this feeling that the most flagrant and persistent violators of the law adduce in their defense the practice in their localities for years under the authority and permission secured from a former lax administration of the law.[23]

Timber depredation continued because local residents did not believe the practice was harmful. They would not condemn the practice until timber theft threatened the lumber industry and the Northwest economy, particularly in Washington. Even then, the blame was directed at a particular group of thieves whom locals regarded as outsiders, not at all lumbermen who trespassed on government land. In 1879, when timber theft was blamed for weakening the lumber economy through overproduction, gyppo-type loggers were targeted as the culprits. Former laborers who now fancied themselves "bosses" were charged with stealing trees that amounted to millions of board feet from public land, which they then sold at $3.50 to $4.00 per thousand foot.[24] By contrast, well-capitalized lumbermen who engaged in similar practices were not held responsible for the economic slump. In other words, it was all right for heavily capitalized lumbermen to cut timber from public lands, but not a lower class of loggers who could not be controlled and who threatened stable lumber prices.

Outsiders who took from the local resource treasury without benefiting local communities were also condemned for stealing timber. These loggers were not only physically outside the community, they were also beyond the pale of community control. Timber theft by "foreigners" was a long-standing complaint in the Northwest. Americans railed against British thievery when the British ship, *Albion,* was caught with spars cut from Oregon forests in 1850.[25] When a convention gathered at Cowlitz, Washington, in late August 1851 to consider organizing Washington as a separate territory, timber trespass was an issue. The delegates requested aid from the national government because "ships and foreigners are in the habit of coming into our seaboard and cutting timber off the unsettled lands, and shipping the timber away for commerce to foreign ports, to the great detriment of future settlements of the country."[26]

When the U.S. District Court for Oregon convicted "foreigner" Ned Tichenor for cutting timber on public lands during the summer of 1864, the eventual outcome did not please the *Oregon Statesman:*

That H. H. Luse, a hard-working Oregonian and mill owner of Coos Bay, was convicted of the same offence for a small amount of timber cut with his own hands. He paid his fine, about $600, as we remember, and we have never heard any whining or grumbling over his case. But here is a rich California speculator who has hired timber cut to the value of $20,000 in gold a year from the public lands in Oregon, for over ten years, and when at last he is convicted and fined by an Oregon jury and fined $18,000 in greenbacks by an Oregon court, California politicians and Judges beseech the President for a pardon, and upon one-sided representations obtained it.[27]

Even loggers who did not openly cut trees from a Northwest commons often treated the regional forests in much the same way. Lumbermen took up settlement land claims, not with any intention of living on the land, but to cut the marketable timber and move on. The Olympia *Columbian* reported on December 25, 1852:

One of the "ABUSES" of the land law—palpable, and highly discreditable to persons who avail themselves of the discrepancy of its provisions, is the practice, of too frequent occurrence, of persons taking valuable timbered claims along the Sound, and after securing, converting into piles, square timber, etc., all the most desirable portion for foreign use, ABANDON them, for some *new* localities for the same object—without improvement, and greatly detracting from their value when finally occupied by permanent settlers. In this way, the whole country along the Sound might be culled over, without being in any way advantageous to the country, but on the contrary prove highly detrimental to its future interests. This is a species of speculation, too, connected with the public lands, against which, congress should assert a prompt interference, and by suitable modifications in the land law, the better adapt it to the onward progress of our country.[28]

To curb abuses, the commissioner general of the land office prohibited homesteaders from cutting timber for market sale until they had gained full title to the land.[29] Prohibition was one thing, of course, and enforcement was quite another.

Smaller sawmills were able to find plenty of timber in the common forests. Limited capital costs, production capacity, and markets meant that it took a number of years before these small mills would cut-over adjacent forests. Larger milling operations, however, had a problem. With high levels of production, the mills logged surrounding forests at a much faster pace than smaller operations. Because large mills had higher capital investments, they could not move their milling operations as easily as small-scale operators could once the readily available forests had been logged off. They found two partial solutions. First, mill owners contracted with independent loggers rather than operate their own company logging camps.[30] Second, they began to buy forestlands.

Sawmill owners discovered a real advantage in using independent loggers. They could cut from a forest commons and leave sawmill owners free from any possible conviction for timber theft. But this made the vertical integration of the extractive and production processes by sawmill owners impossible. Besides, convictions for timber theft proved problematic and did little to deal with the increased costs lumbermen faced once the forests immediately adjacent to mills had been cut. The second solution—buying forestland—appeared more satisfactory, but it too had problems.

The biggest problem was finding the means to purchase the amount of forestland needed to sustain a well-capitalized sawmill. Government land policy, whose purpose was to create and maintain a yeoman republic, made it difficult to purchase large tracts of land. Unsurveyed land could not be purchased at all, and surveyors were slow to map out forested lands in the Northwest due to limited funding, weather, and difficult terrain. Even if lumbermen had not faced those restrictions, they still confronted another important problem. No federal legislation expressly provided for the sale of government-owned timberland until the Timber and Stone Act was passed in 1878. The act allowed an individual to purchase 160 acres of timberland for personal use at a minimum price of $2.50 an acre. More importantly, for the first time forestland "valuable chiefly for timber, but unfit for cultivation" was recognized as a land type. Nonetheless, the act was a particularly inappropriate piece of legislation. It had little value to farmers who had no desire for land that was unsuitable for agriculture. For lumbermen, the legislation was no more appropriate given the small size of the tracts that could be taken up.[31]

Although neither federal nor state land laws were specifically directed toward transferring the public domain into the hands of lumbermen until the 1870s, timber companies still managed to acquire local forestland during the early 1860s. The federal government had reserved some territorial land that would become state lands for the support of universities. Normally those lands did not become available for purchase until statehood, but Washington did not wait for that formality. A special territorial commission began selling 41,000 acres of land that had been set aside for the University of Washington in 1861. At $1.50 an acre, the largest lumber firms stepped forward to purchase substantial amounts of the timberland.[32]

The federal government then put up for sale almost 3 million acres of Washington land during the summer of 1863, evidently responding to local pressures and the Union's need for revenue to prosecute the Civil War. Territorial boosters hoped the availability of land would attract more immigrants and lead to economic prosperity. In the initial auction, however, only 2,765 acres were sold, and the remaining parcels became available for purchase in unlimited blocks at a minimum of $1.25 an acre. Once again, lumber companies took advantage of the opportunity and bought up thousands of acres. An independent logger warned of the monopoly holdings this encouraged, but the dominant view was that the presidential proclamation was necessary to benefit lumber interests.[33]

> It is believed that this policy will operate favorably upon the lumber interest, which constitutes the great trade of the Sound. The building of mills necessarily involves the outlay of a large capital, which will be the more readily invested now that there will be no difficulty in acquiring absolute titles to whatever lands may be wanted for lumber, etc. Heretofore a mill could acquire no more land than it was permitted to hold under the pre-emption or donation law. Those who now embark in the business may readily become the absolute owners of timber sufficient to last them for many years to come, without the risk taken by such as built mills on unsurveyed lands, to find, perhaps, after spending large sums of money upon their property, the best timbered tracts adjoining them, taken by others under the donation or pre-emption laws, on account of the enhanced value given to them by the mills.[34]

Besides, abundant forests and access to them seemed to check most people's fears about the danger of monopoly ownership.

Lumbermen also used clearly fraudulent methods to acquire ownership of timberlands. They paid dummy entrymen, for example, to claim land through preemption, the 1862 Homestead Act, and the 1873 Timber Culture Act. After registry, the claimant would turn the land title over to the lumbermen. The Timber and Stone Act itself was an invitation to fraud and became a means for speculators and lumbermen to increase their landholdings by hiring false entrymen and witnesses. "It is," reported Olympia's *Washington Standard* in 1883, "a notorious fact that 'timber rights,' have been sold in this community as openly as was Esau's birth-right."[35] A few years later, in 1888, the *Oregonian* vividly described what was taking place in the region:

> In Columbia and Clatsop, as well as every other county . . . timber land getting has been carried on by the wholesale. Nearly all loggers and millmen have been concerned in transactions which, if capable of being proved, would send them to state's prison instanter. . . . Go where you will among the woods you will see, if you look closely enough, a few rails laid together to simulate a cabin; or a bark hut

built, perhaps big enough to shelter a weary dog. This is the house that some paid and perjured wretch has sworn on the bible to be his castle, erected as a permanent residence, although he knows that it is not big enough to accommodate Tom Thumb, and that he built it in an hour, never expecting it to serve as any other than a frame to stretch his blasphemous lies upon. The . . . mill owner, stands outside the land office door waiting to pay Mr. Bone-and-sinew about $65 as the price of all his remancing.

In this way, various enterprising gentlemen, many of whom would scorn to steal coppers from dead men's eyes, have come to own various sized tracts of timber land of as good quality as ever the sun shone on. . . . No very large transactions . . . have been known in Oregon, the business being small and unimportant beside the enormous grab of the Puget Sound Lumber Company near Seattle, an association who emulate the great robber barons of medieval Europe in their hoggish propensities.[36]

Economic, social, and political changes had begun to make forest landownership increasingly desirable. Both the legal and extralegal means that lumbermen used to acquire timber during the settler period carried over into the industrial era, where an increasing amount of the public forest land accrued to large, private timber companies. Forestland ownership by those powerful businessmen undoubtedly limited the "tragedy of the commons," but it did little to restrict environmental change.

Although timber harvesting is intrusive in any forest ecosystem, some logging practices are more disruptive than others. Except along shoreline areas, early operators practiced selective tree cutting because it was practical. Markets limited harvests to a few merchantable species of optimum size, which allowed for the natural reseeding and regeneration of the forests.[37] But not all preindustrial logging was benign. Streamside forests and riverine areas used for yarding were dramatically altered. Large logs dumped into streams broke down embankments. When logs held behind splash dams were released and driven downstream, they created havoc to riverine environments. Torrents of water unleashed by the dams swept away gravel spawning grounds and destroyed salmon embryos as rushing water cut away embankments and covered the eggs with sedimentation. In some instances, splash dams actually drove salmon entirely out of streams.[38] The Washington State fish commissioner's report in 1898 expressed serious concern: "Large dams have been built for the purpose of splashing the streams in order to drive the logs to tidewater, and even had these dams, which they have not, proper fishways for the ascent of the fish, the flooding of the streams during the period when the salmon spawn, in its most critical stage, must inevitably drive the fish entirely from the river."[39]

Milling also altered landscapes. Owners built their mills next to rivers and constructed dams to store saw logs. The dams prevented the flow of logs downstream, but they also restricted the movement of fish upstream. Few splash or holding dams had fish ladders or provided other means for fish passage, despite laws that required them to do so. The result "materially depleted the run of fish that reach[ed] the spawning grounds." Not until the early twentieth century were tentative steps taken to correct the situation, and even then the practice of damming did not end.[40]

The actual milling of logs caused further disruption. Mills were equipped with saws that not only limited the dimensions into which boards could be cut but also created vast amounts of wood waste. That meant much of the log was debris collected into "great heaps of bright yellow sawdust" that required disposal. Some of the sawdust, bark, and slabs became landfill. At a few mills, wood by-products were burned in refuse burners, filling the atmosphere with smoke, cinder, and ash.[41] But a much more cost-effective means of disposal was simply to dump the wood refuse directly into streams and lakes. Companies could reap profits and pass the environmental costs on to the community.

Mill refuse in Northwest waters was obvious as early as the 1850s. Journeying up the lower Columbia River in 1852, James Swan observed "great quantities of drift-logs, boards, chips, and saw-dust, with which the whole water around us was covered."[42] As population and mills along the lower Columbia multiplied, operators discharged more and more mill by-products into riverine systems. At the same time, the increasingly important salmon industry experienced a decline in the river's fish populations. Growing concerns about declining commercial fish runs led Oregon and Washington to pass protective legislation during the early 1870s. Included in these conservation statutes were provisions against dumping sawdust into streams. Those conservation measures were based on the conclusion that declining fish populations harmed "the interests of trade and commerce."[43] The laws focused even more on regulating what was perceived as a chaotic fishing industry where the exploitation of the commons knew no bounds. In trying to order and preserve the industry from unlimited entry and overproduction, statutes concentrated on regulating fishing seasons and fishing techniques rather than sawmill disposal.

Some northwesterners were aware of the detrimental impact that sawdust dumping had on fish. The region's most powerful newspaper, the *Oregonian*, made an explicit link between flushing sawdust into streams and the decline of anadramous fish runs in 1888. The paper was politically astute enough to cite abuses from eastern Washington rather than Oregon.[44] No one would take responsibility for declining fish runs. Mill owners denied that sawdust and other lumber waste had a negative effect on fish, claiming that responsibility for the decline in salmon rested with fishermen.[45] For their part, fishermen blamed the sawdust that mill owners continually dumped into the water. The argument continued, and mills refused to change their practices. Eventually, the tie between sawdust dumping and declining numbers of fish became harder for lumbermen to deny. Washington's first fish commissioner, James Crawford, provided evidence in his 1890 report that buttressed the position of regional fishermen: "On one of my visits this summer to Chinook Beach, I saw a fine salmon that would have weighed twenty-five or thirty pounds, gasping upon the beach; and upon examining its gills found them clogged with sawdust, and the irritation produced from that foreign substance had caused a festering sore that had eaten away a large portion of the gills."[46]

The *Washington Standard* made a similar assessment in December 1890: "It has been proven without a doubt that the promiscuous dumping of sawdust into the rivers is very detrimental to the salmon. . . . In examining fish that have been killed by sawdust, it is found that the fine particles of wood that have been swallowed in the water lodge in the gullet and abdominal cavities and clog them up, soon killing the fish."[47]

Legal statutes against sawdust dumping, however, were difficult to enforce because of community indifference and a general lack of adequate enforcement personnel.[48] Communities were reluctant to interfere with a manufacturing enterprise that generated local jobs. Not until mill pollution threatened other local property interests was a community likely to act against the dumping. In Olympia, for example, the Richardson shingle mill had disposed of its debris in the bay adjacent to Olympia for years, scattering the shoreline with shingle litter and sawdust until pollution harmed other powerful property holders. Olympia's leading newspaper observed:

> This matter has often been called to the attention of the *Standard*, but it has forbore comment simply by a desire to afford all the encouragement possible to an "infant industry," even though it be at some public and personal sacrifice. The assurance is not, however, afforded that the shingle business is sufficiently lucrative to afford the cost of the appliances used elsewhere to prevent the refuse from becoming a nuisance as it has to all who have property on the eastern arm of the bay.[49]

The power of the timber industry explains the weak enforcement. A public agency like the state fish commission was caught in a web of necessity, political expediency, and cultural values about unlimited opportunity and abundant resources. As a result, building fish hatcheries rather than restricting human abuse seemed the wisest course to pursue. Acknowledging that political realities limited enforcement, personnel, and funding, Washington State Fish Commissioner A. C. Little considered the establishment and maintenance of fish hatcheries as his agency's most important work.[50] In his 1907 report, Fish Commissioner John Riseland agreed: "Our lakes and streams are being depleted and the natural spawning grounds along the mountain creeks are being occupied by the lumber and shingle mills and are being used for the purpose of floating timber products of the forest to market. These conditions will necessarily continue until the forests are removed. The solution of this important problem is the trout hatchery."[51]

Consequently, state agencies aggressively addressed mill pollution only as sawdust dumping interfered with other powerful interest groups. Although the Washington State fish commissioner was aware by 1901 that saw and shingle mill refuse in Puget Sound interfered with navigation, he took no action until six years later, when the federal government threatened to withhold harbor appropriations unless the situation was remedied. Once again, money talked and people listened. Faced with the threat of losing federal money, Washington's attorney general instructed the state fish commissioner to inform sawmill owners that they must "put in burners to dispose of their refuse, instead of sending it adrift in the waters of streams, lakes or the bay, where it is known to endanger fish life." Faced with litigation, mills in the Willapa Harbor and Grays Harbor areas constructed burners between 1915 and 1917; the Point Defiance Mill Company in Tacoma built bulkheads to keep sawdust out of local waters. Still, the dumping of sawdust into waterways persisted into the 1920s.[52]

During this same period of industrialization, other momentous changes were underway. Improved mechanization changed the lumber industry, which was itself reshaping the Northwest landscape during the 1880s. Advances in technology increased productivity and improved access to markets. The long-handled, double-bitted axe and the crosscut saw accelerated timber falling in the last quarter of the nineteenth century. The invention of the steam donkey by John Dolbeer in 1881 and the building of logging railroads during the 1880s began to displace animal power, making it possible to cut large trees and to extend logging into previously inaccessible forests.[53] The steam donkey alone dramatically changed logging practices, as Grays Harbor, Washington, lumberman George Emerson noted: "When one considers [that steam donkeys] . . . require no stable and no feed, that all expense stops when the whistle blows, no oxen killed and no teams to winter, no ground too wet, no hill too steep, it is easy to see they are a revolution in logging."[54] The donkey engine was revolutionary. It altered where and when logging could occur and changed cutting practices. Although selective cutting continued to dominate logging through the nineteenth century, the donkey engine made clearcutting the efficient way to log, further increasing wood waste and environmental disruption.[55]

Logging had always been a wasteful enterprise. During the bull-team era, loggers took only the finest grained, most marketable species. Timber fallers usually cut the tree ten or more feet above the ground with the use of platform springboards to avoid the fir's thick and pitchy base. As the tree fell, it struck adjacent trees, breaking off limbs and bark and knocking smaller trees to the ground. Loggers added to the waste by cutting off branches and great lengths of wood toward the crown of the downed trees and leaving the rest as slash. Low stumpage costs (often attributed to glutted markets or distance from markets) and seemingly inexhaustible forests provided little incentive for lumbermen to use more of the tree. By the end of the nineteenth century, waste seemed endemic to regional lumbering practices.[56]

As stumpage costs, market prices, and the variety of marketable species increased during the industrial era, loggers began to be a little more circumspect in their cutting practices.[57] Nevertheless, the technology that made it possible to log the largest trees also led to the destruction of trees that had no economic value. Ironically, the market that began to decrease the waste of valued species conversely accelerated the destruction of nonmarketable trees.

As early as the 1880s, newspapers pointed to the folly of laying waste to trees without apparent commercial value. Logging mimicked careless practices in the eastern United States, newspapers warned, and pointed out that easterners had destroyed black walnut, regarding it as a worthless species, only to find out later that the tree had a commercial value.[58] The warnings generally fell on deaf ears.

The use of a steam donkey made clearcutting both technologically necessary and rational from a market perspective. Because it pulled logs along the ground, the land had to be as free of obstacles as possible. Therefore, both commercial and noncommercial trees had to be cut: noncommercial trees hindered the cutting of the marketable species, and commercial trees had cash value.[59]

The new technology was faster but far more intrusive. The land itself was torn up as steam donkeys, according to a 1902 description, drew logs "up through the forest, threshing and beating and groaning, tearing up small trees and plowing great furrows in the earth." Young-growth and lesser-valued trees that would have been left under older logging methods were destroyed, reducing the potential for natural reseeding in cut-over areas.[60] Clearcutting not only destroyed "worthless" species but furthered ecological disruption by opening adjacent forest stands to windthrow and facilitating nitrogen and phosphorous losses from the soil. The increasing amount of slash and debris left on the ground recycled nutrients back into the soil, protected soil, and aided wildlife habitat, but it also fueled an increase in frequency and intensity of fires. Those fires then changed the species makeup of the forest and adversely affected smaller animals.[61] Short-term profits brought long-term consequences. Soil erosion from cut-over areas silted streams and affected fish and aquatic life. Without the deep root systems of trees, streamside embankments were particularly subject to undercutting. Moreover, without the protective cover of streamside trees, water temperatures rose, harming the fish population.[62]

Cutting riparian trees destabilized fish habitat in other ways as well. Once riparian vegetation was stripped away, litter no longer added nutrients to the water. Significant, too, was the fact that the structure of rivers and creeks changed. Debris and fallen logs had provided streams with a structurally diverse habitat of riffles, deep pools, and cover. Removing the trees altered that complex environment into a simplified habitat, reducing fish regeneration and species diversity. Loggers had only to remove the marketable conifers to have a deleterious effect, for the shallow root systems of deciduous trees offer much less protection against bank erosion than do evergreens.[63]

Between 1864 and 1866, George Perkins Marsh, Frederick Starr, and Andrew Fuller warned about a future timber famine, and those warnings found an increased number of spokesmen and national adherents in the 1870s. Northwest newspapers kept their readership informed about the national discussion, as well as the flooding and climatic changes that forest destruction had apparently wrought in Europe and parts of the eastern and midwestern United States.[64]

In the 1880s, local writers criticized settlers who treated trees as "a mere incumbrance and obstruction." Farmers were reminded that forests in the Midwest, like those in the Douglas-fir region, seemed endless until they were cut to clear the land for agriculture. George Atkinson told readers of the *West Shore* that forestland clearing for farming had denuded much of the country and that if it were not halted in the Douglas-fir region "it will prove a dire calamity to all the settlements of the interior, and a waste of our surest source of income."[65] Other observers echoed Atkinson's sentiments. Carlos Shane issued a typical warning:

"A willful waste brings a woful want," is an old adage, but still true as when first spoken. Choice logging timber is fast disappearing, and the distance from mills on the rapid increase. We will soon be called to go to still more remote forests for our best quality of lumber or to ship it from abroad. Let us preserve all our best and only destroy, if we must cut and burn, the poorest. . . . Till well and carefully a small parcel of land—leave the rest for grass and forest.[66]

Regional sermons against wasteful tree cutting included timber industry practices as well.[67]

While the yeoman ideal and the desire to clear forests to make way for farms did not disappear with these warnings, the commercial worth of forests did at least begin to receive increased attention. Occasionally, writers even acknowledged the ecological value of forests: "A mass of irrefutable evidence has demonstrated that trees play a part in the economy of nature for which no equal substitute can be found. . . . Some natural processes are at once so beneficent and so complex that for man not to avail himself of them as they are is to sacrifice irretrievably the most manifest advantage."[68] Regional newspapers and magazines printed the results of scientific studies of forest influences on climate and water flow during the 1870s and 1880s, as well as information on forest destruction and preservation measures in Europe.[69] Criticism of the timber industry could gain a hearing because its practices had threatened other economic interests, and the print media were careful to frame their critiques in terms of economic responsibility.

As those sentiments gained ground, a movement for forest preservation, spearheaded by a small scientific elite, took form in the United States. A committee of the American Association for the Advancement of Science petitioned Congress in 1873 to protect the nation's disappearing forests. Three years later, Congress responded by setting aside $2,000 for the commissioner of agriculture to undertake a wide-ranging study of America's forests. The investigation was to determine timber consumption, import-export volumes, future timber supply, means for preservation and renewal, and forests' influence on climate. Although the meager appropriation indicated how much farther congressional commitment to forest protection had to go, the investigation and its four-volume report was significant in shaping subsequent forest policy. The report also seemed to have an institutional effect, for a Division of Forestry was created within the Department of Agriculture in 1881. The report's author, Franklin B. Hough, was made its first chief.[70]

Events also moved Americans to reconsider their forest practices. By the late 1870s, floods in the eastern states renewed discussion of forest destruction and flooding. In 1879, when Harvard Professor of Arboriculture Charles Sprague Sargent called for the federal government to preserve forestland from settlement, Northwest publications reprinted portions of his address. The *Washington Standard* agreed with Sargent: "The evils to which we have alluded are not so glaringly apparent, perhaps, in Oregon and Washington Territory as in California, but it is only a question of time, along this part of the coast, in view of the present elements at work [by this the article meant the axe, accidental and purposely set fires, and herds of browsing animals killing seedling trees]."[71] When the federal government held a "land conference" in Washington, D.C., in May 1879, Olympia's *Washington Standard* reported the meeting as a positive step away from wasteful destruction and toward timber preservation.[72] Federal agencies, along with national and state land laws, began to reflect a growing awareness about the value of trees and a concern to ensure the future of the forests.[73]

A few northwesterners were part of the forest conservation movement, but most people in the region believed the area could never be deforested. Residents continued to think and write about their region in terms of "inexhaustible" forests, although latent fears that the possibility might exist did begin to surface. A few citizens began to call on lawmakers to regulate forest use and reseed trees before history repeated itself. If wasteful practices threatened seemingly inexhaustible forests, then regulating the cut ought to avert the threat.[74]

Growing concern about forests, then, did not mean a shift away from cultural values that viewed nature as a resource to be managed and used. Forest protection grew from utilitarian fears about a timber famine, climate changes, streamflow, and the need to safeguard urban watersheds. Watershed protection was central in creating the Forest Reserve Act of 1891, and two of Oregon's earliest forest reserves, Bull Run (1892) and Ashland (1893), were created for that purpose.[75]

The goal of ensuring abundance by eliminating waste stood at the center of forest preservation concerns. The ethics of a capitalist market economy dictated decisions about land use. Waste, after all, detracted from future profits. Moreover, leaders of the lumber industry believed that expanding markets would be theirs when demands for wood products increased and forest supplies declined in other regions of the country. "We have here the largest body of valuable timber now remaining in the United States," the *Oregonian* observed on November 10, 1887. "Instead of wasting it we ought to preserve it for the market that surely awaits it in the near future." Fourteen years later the *Seattle Post-Intelligencer* wrote similarly about the region's holding "the last great supply of standing timber" and the need to eliminate "wasteful destruction" so that the region's forests might provide "a perpetual fountain of industry and wealth." In this view, forest destruction elsewhere provided opportunity at home; perpetuating abundant regional forests meant economic prosperity.[76]

It was in this larger context that federal and state legislatures during the 1870s and 1880s began considering bills to protect forests, with some of the measures proposing the creation of state or national forest reserves. On January 14, 1889, John Breckenridge Waldo introduced a memorial in the Oregon House of Representatives asking the federal government to create a forest reserve in the Cascade Mountains. Waldo was one of the few northwesterners whose sympathies actually ran toward a modern, preservationist understanding. His memorial passed the House but failed to garner the necessary Senate votes. Sheep owners, who feared that the reserve would eliminate their free and unrestricted use of the Cascades for summer grazing, were the major opponents.[77]

The defeat was short-lived. Included in the omnibus General Revision Act passed by Congress in March 1891 was a little-debated section that gave the president the power to withdraw from public entry any federally owned forestland. On September 28, 1893, President Grover Cleveland created the Cascade Range Forest Reserve, the first of many forest reserves in western Oregon and Washington.[78]

The creation of forest reservations was part of the development of a larger conservation ethic in the United States during the late nineteenth century. Two large tributary streams of preservationism and utilitarianism fed into this conservation river and expressed the ambivalence Americans were experiencing as they moved toward an urban, industrial, bureaucratic society. They sought progress but felt uneasy about changes related to their modern world. Large-scale business holdings, rising numbers of eastern and southern European immigrants, increasing urbanization with concomitant problems of poverty and crime, conflicts between labor and capital, political boss rule, land monopolization, and a growing selfishness seemed to be undermining Americans' opportunities, self-reliance, and sense of mission.[79] As people rushed into a new and rapidly changing future, much of what had given Americans their sense of uniqueness and historical primacy seemed to be passing away as well. The nation stood positioned between an older world being transformed and an unformed new order. Americans felt both fear and optimism, anxiety and hope. They wanted development but desired to maintain the known past through which they knew and understood themselves.

Especially important in this regard was the land, particularly in the West. For people who accepted the dominant cultural myth, the West represented the way Americans understood themselves, their uniqueness, and their mission. The western lands were a repository for national identity, and if they were filled up, the West would no longer be the West, and the republic would decline. Thus, a sense of national identity also played a role in creating a movement to preserve at least some of the land in the West. Preservationists and utilitarians in the conservation movement both took pride in their nation's development but also felt ambiguous about progress—fearful that middle-landscape republicanism, situated between nature and civilization, might also be giving way. Both camps looked for reform from the activist, bureaucratic state that had been growing since the Civil War, yet preservationists and utilitarians held different opinions on some issues.

In general, the preservation wing of the conservation movement held a more antimodernist ethos than the utilitarians did. Most preservationists expressed a therapeutic quest for meaning, freedom, and harmony that seemed increasingly threatened by industrialization, bureaucracy, and a spirit of individualistic materialism. Preservationists believed that contact with primitive, pure nature offered a tonic and a promise of self-fulfillment. The monotonous, gloomy, silent forests began to be venerated. Yet even those antimodern believers desired progress and sought through nature a means to revitalize American culture and to accommodate themselves to the new industrial order.[80] The preservationist call to personally experience nature was also compatible with an individualistic ethos and an emerging consumer culture. Tourism could be packaged and sold back to Americans as a nature experience. C. B. Watson, in an address before the Oregon Development League Convention in 1906, talked about the potential market value of selling pristine nature to tourists:

> The millions upon millions of dollars that are annually carried out of our own country by the sight-seeing pilgrims to foreign land are no less purchasers of the products of such lands than those who buy of their manufactured articles or the fruits of their soil.
>
> No country is richer in these great natural wonders than our own. If such sights and scenes are resources of great value there, why ought not we, with many as great, and some greater, not class them also upon the utilitarian side in that which they bring to us from the coffers of the sight-seeing, while at the same time our aesthetic sense is charmed and strengthened?[81]

Moreover, contact with nature was generally meant to enliven personal feelings of empowerment rather than to generate a change in the power structures that framed personal relationships.

Advocates of the utilitarian approach also sought revitalization through confronting nature. No less than the preservationists, utilitarian conservationists were deeply concerned about threats to American institutions and character. Competition, individualism, industriousness, and the martial spirit appeared to be giving way to greed, selfishness, moral decay, and physical laxity. Conservation seemed to offer an antidote. Expressing moral outrage, progressive-era conservationists, like their counterparts in politics, may have proposed modern statist solutions, but they also spoke in terms of an older republican idiom. Theirs was a democratic protest, conservationists claimed, against selfish monopolists who threatened to destroy American opportunity and the common good. But utilitarian conservationists' desire to conserve nature had a less aesthetic and romantic bent than the approach taken by preservationists. Utilitarians desired a nature against which they could test themselves. In contesting nature and imposing human will on the wild, they could experience virility, autonomy, mastery, and progress.[82] Utilitarianism promised to revitalize old goals of individualism and opportunity through modern structures, ironically betraying the very ends it sought to revive. Wise, rational, scientific management for sustained use was to replace waste. Disinterested professionals would now represent the public, diminishing citizens' need for involvement while ensuring the common good.

The dominant conservationist ethic found expression in the creation of forest reserves. To ensure that the forest reserves were not to be locked up, they were renamed national forests in 1907.[83] Reserves suggested English game preserves or, more troubling, "the Indian reservation, and helped to fix in the minds of settlers the troublesome idea that the national forest was a sort of 'state within a state' a thing segregated and set apart from ordinary, normal, helpful use—a species of foreign substance in the body economic and politic."[84]

The utilitarian ends that governed forest reservations were clear from the beginning. Reserves would serve as game preserves and aesthetic wonderlands, but its two primary purposes were to be a source of timber supply and to influence climate, erosion, and streams. As Edward Bowers, secretary of the American Forestry Association, explained in 1904, forest reserves existed "for the *use* of their forests and for the regulation of the streams." That is, forest reserves ought to be primarily "woodlots and natural reservoirs."[85]

Utilitarians also sought conservation methods that would protect investments and thereby preserve abundance—most notably through suppressing fires and restructuring logging practices. The desire to protect both property and scenic landscapes led to a broad-based movement of government, business, and the general public to protect forests from fires. Americans had used fire for decades to clear land. The fires were sometimes hard to control, but escaped burns generated little protest as long as they occurred outside private land holdings and did not endanger American lives or property. By the 1860s, Washington legislators had enacted laws against the deliberate setting of fires to lands other than their own and, in 1877, passed the territory's first law specifically designed to protect forests from fire.[86] A few public officials even began to voice a concern over forest fires, particularly because of the economic loss that resulted. Washington Territorial Governor E. S. Salomon told the legislature in 1871: "Although our supply of lumber seems almost inexhaustible, it becomes necessary to devise some effective means to check the destruction of the most valuable parts of our forests by fire. The damage done during the last three or four summers is alarming, and some law ought to be passed and rigidly executed to protect this most important branch of our industry."[87] Gradually, the popular press started to advocate fire suppression. Not until the rise of the conservation movement and the destructive fires of 1902, however, were organizational efforts to regulate forest fires seriously undertaken.[88]

Fire represented chaos to predominantly middle- and upper-class conservationists, who were concerned with physical and social order. Bernard

Fernow and Gifford Pinchot labeled those who started forest fires as immoral and lawless; their actions were an assault on property rights.[89] Fire also wasted good timber, some complained, especially as more forestland became privately owned and was increasingly valuable both for its merchantable lumber and for its contribution to agricultural production and urban drinking water. Finally, with warnings of a timber famine being reported in local newspapers, fire prevention seemed an appropriate measure.[90]

Washington governor John McGraw, in his last message to the state legislature in 1897, called for a law to create a forest preservation patrol whose duties would include the prevention of forest fires. Even though incoming governor John R. Rogers did not take up his predecessor's concern for forests in his inaugural message, more and more people began urging forest protection. Buttressed by studies indicating that fire destroyed far more forests than the axe, fire suppression seemed economically sound, politically wise, and culturally consonant. Fires, after all, wasted timber. J. B. Montgomery of Portland wrote: "It is perfectly awful to go through the forests of Oregon and Washington and see the waste caused by needless fires." In Chenowith, Washington, timber cruiser R. F. Cox warned: "If nothing is done to save this great wealth of forest at once, it will soon be too late."[91]

Abundance could be sustained and accomplished without threatening economic interests. Toward that end, the Pacific Northwest led the way in forest protection. The Washington legislature made the state land commissioners ex officio fire wardens in 1903, and the first arrest received notice and approval: "We heartily commend the zeal and watchfulness of Fire Warden Rief in this matter, and we are sure that he will have the unanimous support of all the citizens of this commonwealth in the enforcement of this law." The following year. the Booth-Kelly Lumber Company initiated a cooperative fire patrol in Lane County, Oregon. Washington timberland owners established the Washington Forest Fire Association in 1908 to supplement the state's efforts to defend forest land holdings. In 1909, a consortium of private timber owners from the Northwest and California formed the Western Forestry and Conservation Association, one of the first systematic fire protection programs. In 1912, the association launched a media campaign in schools with "Keep Them Green" pamphlets, posters, and essays; it reached the wider public through magazines, periodicals, newspapers, granges, and clubs.[92]

The region's fire protection system was built on a foundation of fire control rather than fire use and on the belief that fire can and should be controlled. A threefold strategy was developed: to prevent ignition; to modify the fire environment, especially fuels, so that fires would burn with less intensity; and to suppress fires while they were small. The policy, however, was not accepted without opposition. Some northwesterners knew about the Indians' light burning practices and pressed for adopting that method, though without success. As the foremost historian of fire has concluded: "The history of modern fire protection is basically the story of how one fire regime, that of frontier economies, was replaced by another, that of an industrial state."[93]

The fire-suppression movement solidified a program of cooperative forestry between government agencies and large timber owners. It also reduced wild fires. Still, like many other conservation measures, fire policy had its ironic twists. Increased protection and fire suppression allowed fuel to build up so that once a fire started a wild-fire conflagration was ensured. Moreover, with the advent of industrial logging practices and the creation of even-aged tree stands, the forest that had been protected from fire became a prime target of fire as well as of wind and insects.[94]

Scientific forestry advocates also pushed for a reform of logging practices that would encourage loggers to adopt policies of clearcutting, slash burning, removal of fire-scarred timber, and cutting of trees over two hundred years old. Conservationists regarded mature trees as waste; Douglas fir more than two hundred years old, in their view, had passed its maximum wood-producing stage and stood as an overripe crop in need of harvesting. Moreover, scientists at the turn of the century feared that the marketable wood of century-old trees would be susceptible to disease and rot. Only rarely did a voice like C. Frederick Schwarz offer an alternative vision. Schwarz argued that old-growth areas in forest reserves should be preserved and studied for scientific and aesthetic reasons.[95] Not many people agreed.

To the new forestry experts, fire suppression and reformed logging practices were conservation at its waste-eliminating best. Scientific forestry meant that waste gave way to rationalized management, producing a fully utilized forest environment capable of sustaining abundance and future growth. The chairman of the Oregon Conservation Commission, Joseph Nathan Teal, explained in 1909: "Conservation is the antithesis of waste. It does not mean non-use. It means a wise use." The goal was a stable timber industry with secure profits. "Forestry . . . is not forests at all," said E. T. Allen, forester for the Western Forestry and Conservation Association in 1914, it is the "forest industry, that we seek to perpetuate."[96] Lumbermen applauded Allen's sentiments, along with his remarks before the National Conservation Congress:

> And there is entirely too much forgetting that forests are useless unless used; that not forests, but forest industry, is what we really seek to perpetuate. Except from their protection of streamflow and game, the community has little to gain from forest preservation unless it also preserves, on a profitable and permanent footing, the industry that makes

forests usable and worth preserving, that employs labor, affords markets for crops and services, pays taxes, and manufactures and distributes an indispensable commodity. Forest wealth is community wealth, but not without forest industry to coin it.[97]

For the lumber industry, Allen said, forest conservation meant "protecting forests, growing new ones, and economical use." These aims were to be accomplished through "fire prevention, just taxation, and business encouragement." Although conservation could also embrace game, scenery, health, pleasure, and morals, the chief local interest in the Pacific Northwest lay in "maintaining a primary industry." Few disagreed "that wherever the public is unfriendly to lumbering it injures its own welfare." This view was particularly widespread in Washington, where almost two-thirds of the state's wage earners depended on the lumber industry for their livelihood by 1910.[98]

Forest conservation altered the Northwest's political, economic, and physical landscape. Reserves ensured that the federal government would be a permanent and increasingly influential fixture in the region and legitimated the growth of bureaucratic power and the nation-state. But those political changes also affected forest practices. Increasingly, Forest Service silvicultural techniques were adopted by "progressive" lumbermen. Timber was now defined as a crop. The administrative transfer of federal forest reserves from the Department of Interior to the Department of Agriculture in 1905 testified to this change.[99]

When environmental limitations or human actions threatened abundance, changes were made. Yet all of those adaptations remained securely within the dominant Anglo-American cultural paradigm, where market imperatives governed biological considerations and where scientific, technological, and political decision making followed suit. The commodity value of nature was to be preserved in order to assure its continued abundance. In that sense, nature's economy could be socially engineered. Natural limitations could be surmounted, "waste" eliminated, and growth assured.

In the quest to assure a permanent supply of timber, politics and science were handmaidens to economics. Government and corporate bureaucracies found a common landscape of opportunity in the West to advance their power. Sometimes the two came into conflict, but most often they located a middle ground of similar interests and values by which they could support one another while claiming to protect and serve the public good. Although each entity had to accommodate to the local environment, federal and corporate bureaucracies possessed ultimate power.[100] Profit and progress dominated a conservationism that furthered the drive toward modern, centralized, large-scale organizational structures of power, and the carelessness that impaired America's progress and abundance would be replaced by a rationalized environmental and economic landscape. The progressive wing of the lumber industry supported conservationist ideals of forest management as big business and federal government bureaucracy allied in pursuit of stabilized markets.[101] All of these policymakers and their supporters, however, did not consider that animals, plants, and trees with little commercial value are vital to the sustainability of culturally valued species. Alders do not have the commercial value of Douglas fir, but they make possible the nitrogen-rich soil that nurtures the more marketable Douglas fir. Although technology and increased capital investment stimulated conservation measures, they did not always lead to the conservation of habitat or to ecological health. The practice of valorizing some trees, no less than negating the value of others, disrupted forests. As the December 5, 1884, *Washington Standard* rightly noted: "Since it [timber] has been admitted to be commercially of value, its fortune has been almost worse. The population has regarded its forests as a mine of which the proper destiny was to be straightway severed from the soil."[102]

Governed by market economy rather than nature's economy, biological considerations could not stand, in the short term, against economic determinants. Besides, scientific principles administered by trained professionals promised to ensure American progress without threatening power structures, cultural myths, and practices that sustained those systems of control.[103] To a growing culture of consumption and a far-western region that still wanted to believe in infinite opportunity those professionals carried welcome news. Northwesterners could continue to believe that the future was theirs.

Still, Pacific northwesterners were not oblivious to the fact that the cultural script they followed brought consequences they neither desired or envisioned. Cultural imperatives might delay but could not surmount the natural world. Nature had its own way of intruding into cultural realities. To recognize a problem, however, is not to find a solution, and settler and industrial society generally lacked the cultural and economic information to generate another model of behavior. They sought answers within the parameters that had created the problem in the first place. The result was a culturally and ecologically altered landscape that recast life for everyone in the Pacific Northwest.

EPILOGUE

The Pacific Northwest has undergone tremendous changes during the twentieth century, particularly since the Second World War. Nonethethess, the region today still bears a family resemblance to its settlement and early industrial era history. The Pacific Northwest remains a largely economic colony. Increasingly urban and with a greater industrial base, the region's economy is still closely tied to its forest, fishing, agricultural, and tourist industries.[1] Metropolitan and hinterland divisions, very much linked to the land and its use, continue to characterize the region. Urbanites often see nature as a recreational and spiritual escape, while those in the hinterlands view the environment as a natural resource to be exploited if their lives and communities are to survive.

Although the region displays commonalities, Oregon and Washington are distinctively different. Oregon remains a more conservative, homogeneous place that seeks to preserve its Edenic image and protect its insular cultural ideals; although it embraced political reformism during the progressive era, it surrendered to nativism in the 1920s. During the 1970s, the "unwelcome" campaign to "outsiders" took hold, launched by Governor Tom McCall's famous remark before the Junior Chamber of Commerce convention in Portland in 1971. McCall encouraged visitors to the state, but then added "for heaven's sake, don't move here to live." The 1971 bottle bill made Oregon the first state in the nation to outlaw pull-tab cans and nonreturnable bottles as well as to require consumers to pay cash deposits on beer and soft-drink containers. In 1973, the Land Conservation and Development Commission was created to direct land-use planning. All of these policies and actions were part and parcel of a nineteenth-century cultural legacy. Washington persists in its tradition, too, as a more open, cosmopolitan, heterogenous place wedded to outside capital investment and a military-industrial complex. It is not surprising that Seattle has a space needle and calls its professional basketball team the Supersonics, while Portland has no such symbol and has named its ball club the Trailblazers. The larger forces that molded the two states during the nineteenth and early twentieth centuries continue to shape the region.

Native Americans as a people and as a distinct culture also remain visible reminders of the region's past and are shapers of its present and future. The Indian population has grown since the devastation tribes experienced in the nineteenth century, and native peoples have continued the process of cultural adjustment and preservation. Numerical growth and cultural identity, however, have not always translated into political or economic power. Yet Native Americans are exercising an increasing influence over their own lives and that of the region. Ironically, the source of that power is often the rights granted in nineteenth-century treaties, especially fishing rights.

The presence of the federal government still carries important economic and environmental consequences for the region. Government-created sites such as the military-related plants in the Puget Sound area or the Hanford Nuclear Plant site near Richland, Washington, generated jobs and population growth, but they also meant increased federal dependency. The federal government also supplied the money and expertise to construct the massive Bonneville and Grand Coulee dams that gave the region a cheap source of hydroelectric power. As private timberlands were cut over, the national forests became an increasing source of timber. That development, too, translated into increased dependency on the national government and on decision makers outside the region. The consequences of these collective changes meant that the national government would not escape being a key player in regional conflicts, particularly in issues related to the environment—not surprisingly, since the environment is at the heart of the region's economy, politics, art, and identity.

The environment has largely defined the Pacific Northwest. Natural resource extractive industries, such as timber, agriculture, and fishing, continue to be important components in the regional economy, along with a significant tourist industry. Numerous political controversies center on issues related to land use. Nature and peoples' response to the environment are dominant themes in the region's literature, and the regional landscape continues to be a significant fact of how Northwesterners understand themselves. As Portland author Robin Cody recently noted, "Nature still lies at the heart of what it means to live here [the Pacific Northwest]."[2] Historian Carlos Schwantes sums up the phenomenon well:

> In the Pacific Northwest, as in few parts of the United States, regional identity is almost wholly linked to natural setting. The Pacific Northwest without its mountains, its rugged coastline, its Puget Sound fogs . . . is as unthinkable as New England without a Puritan heritage, the South without the Lost Cause, the Midwest without its agricultural cornucopia, or California without its gold rush mentality.[3]

It is perhaps no surprise that the environmental problems that troubled northwesterners during the late nineteenth and early twentieth centuries are still around today. Exotic plants such as thistles and scotch broom still infest many areas. Animal imports, such as the possum, inhabit even urban areas, as roadkill along Portland's streets testify each morning. Besides the newer forms of pollutants, such as dioxins, PCBs, pesticides, and car emissions, older environmental problems persist. The much-heralded Willamette River clean-up during the McCall governorship (1967–1975) did a lot to reduce the degradation that the *Oregonian* had written about in the 1880s, but raw sewage still finds its way into the Willamette during rainstorms and agricultural run-off continues to pollute the river.[4] Smoke pollution from fires, now created by Willamette Valley grass-seed farmers, and debates surrounding forest fire suppression and controlled burns are still part of the regional scene.

Declines in fish populations, most notably the salmon, have created familiar crisis. The older technological solution of increasing fish stocks through hatcheries has not been able to sustain the population. Indeed, the traditional hatchery practice of flooding streams with hatchery fish has actually weakened wild runs, not to mention causing problems in the genetic makeup of hatchery-stocked fish. While hydroelectric dams are certainly an important factor in the salmon's decline, older forms of environmental intrusion also play a role. The draining and development of estuaries, agricultural practices, and logging continue to alter and destroy needed habitat. Commercial and sport fishing has taken a toll as well. Just as in the earlier debate between the fishing and lumbering industries about fish declines, conflicting interest groups blame one another. Chris West of the Northwest Forestry Association believes that "ocean conditions and hatchery practices have had the biggest impact." Those in the fishing industry, such as Garibaldi, Oregon, charter skipper John Laws, targets "logging, grazing and development along streams."[5] Regardless of who is most responsible for the decline, the net result has been a radical drop in anadromous fish runs and the regional loss of more than 60,000 jobs in the past twenty years.[6] The boom-bust of an economy dependent on resource extraction, the problem of the commons and market determinants, and the close association between the exploitation of nonhuman species and people as well as the relationship between the stable biotic and human communities remain an ongoing story.

Important as the fish controversy is for what it reveals about the region's past and present, it is the heated debate surrounding the timber industry that most clearly demonstrates the relationships between environmental and human exploitation, between stable biotic and human communities. This debate also highlights the federal government's continuing role in the region's history and older issues of local versus national control and private property against community regulation. Current conflicts involve issues of how to manage public forests, while echoes from the earlier conservation movement reverberate in public forestry discussions. The U.S. Forest Service's switch to prescribed burns rather than complete fire suppression renewed an old debate and unearthed a persistent belief that trees are "wasted" if not harvested. The debate takes a variety of forms, including whether salvage logging should be allowed in burned forest areas. One side opposes such harvesting as harmful to sound biology, while another side sees it as wasting a natural resource and throwing money away. A spokesman for the Northwest Forestry Association, Ross Mickey, commented on the opposition to logging the 9,000-acre Warner Creek, Oregon, burn: "What are the American people buying by leaving $30 million just rotting on the ground?"[7]

Current discussions also involve old conflicts over state or federal control of lands, with battles sounding earlier themes of the creation of national forests. Some factions are demanding the sale or gift of federal lands to counties or states. In extreme cases, individuals have staked out claims on the public domain, declaring that the federal government illegally owns and manages the land.[8] This situation certainly relates to present political, economic, and cultural issues, but it also exists because of the turn-of-the-century conservation movement. The conservation movement helped create the federal lands and agencies that are now so disputed but did not solve fundamental issues about access and use of those lands. Some disputants are angry that the agencies place restrictions on their use of the public lands. Others object that the government allowed a utilitarian ethic and economic decision making to govern land-management decisions, with the result of conflict and instability for ecological and human communities.

Pursued in the media, the political arena, and courtrooms, largely discussed in economic and ecological terms and falsely bifurcated as a fight between jobs or the environment, the struggles are, in fact, battles about power structures and the myths that sustain them. It remains to be seen whether another story will displace the old myths that western writer William Kittredge calls "a horseshit excuse for bad conduct and the pursuit of greed."[9] In place of a mythology of abundance, it may be necessary to substitute a recognition of the limits of technology and science to surmount nature's limitations. Perhaps economics cannot determine political decisions regarding the environment. To envision a new future, triumphal narratives of conquest and domination need to be interpreted jointly with stories that detail environmental costs and cultural values of restraint.

That new understanding will not emerge without a thorough understanding of the region's history, for the past is never past. Unless the people of the Northwest envision a historically informed future, they face the prospect of losing the environment that has so fundamentally shaped what it has meant to be a Pacific northwesterner. The environment and its people thus stand at an interesting crossroads as Congress looks to limit federal environmental regulations through law and by cutting the budgets for agencies such as the Environmental Protection Agency, the National Park

Service, the U.S. Forest Service, and the U.S. Fish and Wildlife Service. The wrong turn risks the same judgment of history that an anonymous Oregonian in 1888 said would be lodged against his generation if it ignored its responsibility toward the land and its inhabitants:

> The same destructive spirit which has robbed us of the buffalo, which is fast extirpating the elk and threatens to make the salmon extinct, works its wanton will with our forests. When at last we are without wild game, large or small, when our valuable food fish are exterminated, we shall all then by the rivers of Oregon sit down and weep in vain. And when our descendants are told what forests we had here and how we wasted them, they will wonder whether they ought to revere the wisdom of their fathers.[10]

To ignore the actions of those who have lived and shaped the past of the Pacific Northwest is to sweep aside a rich legacy that can and should inform and educate. If the current generation does not broaden current understandings, it will have failed to honor that pioneer legacy, even though it may have been a legacy of conquest. Where better to reinvent ourselves and the myths that frame our understandings than in the West, that mythic Eden first envisioned by a pioneering generation?

NOTES

INTRODUCTION

1. Donald Worster, *Dust Bowl: The Southern Plains in the 1930s* (New York: Oxford University Press, 1979), 5–8.
2. Charles L. Rosenfeld, "Landforms and Geology," in A. Jon Kimerling and Philip L. Jackson, eds., *Atlas of the Pacific Northwest* (Corvallis: Oregon State University Press, 1985), 41.
3. The Pacific Northwest and the Douglas-fir region are not synonymous, although I often equate the two for purposes of style.
4. Perry Miller, *Nature's Nation* (Cambridge, Mass.: Harvard University Press, 1967).
5. William H. McNeill, *The Great Frontier: Freedom and Hierarchy in Modern Times* (Princeton: Princeton University Press, 1983).

CHAPTER ONE: THE NATIVE AMERICAN LANDSCAPE

1. Chris Maser, *Forest Primeval: The Natural History of an Ancient Forest* (San Francisco: Sierra Club Books, 1989), 3.
2. Roy L. Carlson, "Cultural Antecedents," in Wayne Suttles, ed., *Northwest Coast*, vol. 7 in *Handbook of North American Indians*, ed. William C. Sturtevant (Washington, D.C.: Smithsonian Institution, 1990), 68.
3. See Richard L. Bryant, Leslie Conton, Robert E. Hurlbett, and John R. Nelson, *Cultural Resource Overview of the Mt. Hood National Forest, Oregon*, vol. 1 (Eugene, Ore.: Pro-Lysts, Inc., for the U.S. Forest Service, Region 6, 1978), 31–36.
4. Robert T. Boyd, "Demographic History, 1774–1874," in *Handbook of North American Indians*, 7:135.
5. Gary E. Moulton, ed., *The Journals of the Lewis & Clark Expedition, November 2, 1805–March 22, 1806*, vol. 6 (Lincoln: University of Nebraska Press, 1990), 410. Wayne Suttles, "Environment," in *Handbook of North American Indians*, 7:26. James G. Swan, *The Northwest Coast; Or, Three Years' Residence in Washington Territory* (1857; reprint, Fairfield, Wash.: Ye Galleon Press, 1989), 83–85.
6. Yvonne Hajda, "Southwestern Coast Salish," in *Handbook of North American Indians*, 7:507; James V. Powell, "Quileute," in ibid., 7:431; Ann M. Renker and Erna Gunther, "Makah," in ibid., 7:423.
7. Swan, *The Northwest Coast*, 26, 59–60, 82, 85–86.
8. Gabriel Franchere, *A Voyage to the Northwest Coast of America*, ed. Milo Milton Quaife (New York: Citadel Press, 1968), 185–86.
9. Moulton, ed., *The Journals of the Lewis & Clark Expedition*, 6:9, 22–23, 208, 210; Swan, *The Northwest Coast*, 29, 92–95; John Ball, "Oregon Trip—Troy Lectures, Second Lecture Given, 1835," typescript, John Ball Papers, Oregon Historical Society, Portland, Mss 195, 20.

10. Pierre-Jean De Smet, S.J., *Oregon Missions and Travels over the Rocky Mountains in 1845–46* (1847; reprint, Fairfield, Wash.: Ye Galleon Press, 1978), 109.

11. Moulton, ed., *The Journals of the Lewis & Clark Expedition*, 6:342–44; Alexander Ross, *Adventures of the First Settlers on the Oregon or Columbia River, 1810–1813* (Lincoln: University of Nebraska Press, 1986), 108.

12. Frederick Merk, ed., *Fur Trade and Empire: George Simpson's Journal* (Cambridge, Mass.: Harvard University Press, 1931), 102–3; Swan, *The Northwest Coast*, 38–41, 104–7, 264; Charles Wilkes, *Narrative of the United States Exploring Expedition During the Years 1838, 1839, 1840, 1841, 1842*, vols. 4 and 5 (Philadelphia: Lea and Blanchard, 1845), 4:344–46, 373–74, 418; Theodore Winthrop, *The Canoe and the Saddle*, ed. John H. Williams (Tacoma: Franklin-Ward Company, 1913), 27–30.

13. Fred H. Everest, Neil B. Armantrout, Steven M. Keller, William D. Parante, James R. Sedell, Thomas E. Nickelson, James M. Johnston, and Gordon N. Haugen, "Salmonids," in E. Reade Brown, ed., *Management of Wildlife and Fish Habitats in Forests of Western Oregon and Washington*, Part 1, Chapter Narratives (Portland, Ore.: U.S. Department of Agriculture, Forest Service, Pacific Northwest Region, June 1985), 204, 214, 216, 219–21.

14. James R. Sedell, Peter A. Bisson, Frederick J. Swanson, and Stanley V. Gregory, "What We Know About Large Trees That Fall into Streams and Rivers," in Chris Maser, Robert F. Tarrant, James M. Trappe, and Jerry F. Franklin, eds., *From the Forest to the Sea: A Story of Fallen Trees*, General Technical Report PNW-GTR-229 (Portland, Ore.: U.S. Department of Agriculture, Forest Service, and U.S. Department of Interior, Bureau of Land Management, Pacific Northwest Research Station, September 1988), 55, 59, 68, 70, 72, 73, 75.

15. Patricia Benner, "Historical Reconstruction of the Coquille River and Surrounding Landscape" (draft copy, n.d.), 3.2-28, 48, 61–63; 3.2-55, 63; 3.3-18–19.

16. Sedell et al., "What We Know About Large Trees That Fall into Streams and Rivers," 64, 65, 79.

17. H. H. Norton, E. S. Hunn, C. S. Martinsen, and P. B. Keely, "Vegetable Food Products of the Foraging Economies of the Pacific Northwest," *Ecology of Food and Nutrition* 14 (1984): 223–25.

18. Moulton, ed., *The Journals of the Lewis & Clark Expedition*, 6:224, 228, 229, 230–31, 303; Swan, *The Northwest Coast*, 87–89.

19. Moulton, ed., *The Journals of the Lewis & Clark Expedition*, 6:17, 74; Swan, *The Northwest Coast*, 89–91.

20. Stephen Dow Beckham, *Cultural Resource Overview of the Siskiyou National Forest, Western Oregon*, vol. 1 (Portland, Ore.: U.S. Department of Agriculture, Forest Service, Pacific Northwest Region, Siskiyou National Forest, 1978), 17.

21. Elliott A. Norse, *Ancient Forests of the Pacific Northwest* (Washington, D.C.: Island Press, 1990), 95–96; Suttles, "Environment," 7:26.

22. Gary W. Witmer, Mike Wisdom, Edmund P. Harshman, Robert J. Anderson, Christopher Carey, Mike P. Kuttel, Ira D. Luman, James A. Rochelle. Raymond W. Scharpf, and Doug Smithey, "Deer and Elk," in Brown, ed., *Management of Wildlife and Fish Habitats*, 234, 236, 242.

23. Moulton, ed., *The Journals of the Lewis & Clark Expedition*, 6:76, 206, 208–10, 347–48.

24. Kenneth C. Hansen, "Samish," in *Inventory of Native American Religious Use, Practices, Localities, and Resources* (Seattle: Institute of Cooperative Research, 1981), 194–95; Moulton, ed., *The Journals of the Lewis & Clark Expedition*, 6:74, 215, 218–19, 249, 434–35; Albert B. Reagan, "Uses of Plants by West Coast Indians," *Washington Historical Quarterly* 25:2 (April 1934): 133; Wilkes, *Exploring Expedition*, 4:317.

25. David Lavender, ed., *The Oregon Journals of David Douglas; of His Travels and Adventures Among the Traders and Indians in the Columbia, Willamette, and Snake Regions During the Years 1825, 1826, and 1824*, 2 vols. (Ashland: Oregon Book Society, 1972), 1:69; John B. Leiberg, "Cascade Range and Ashland Forest Reserves and Adjacent Regions," in U.S. Department of the Interior, *Twenty-First Annual Report of the United States Geological Survey to the Secretary of the Interior 1899–1900*, Part 5, Forest Reserves (Washington, D.C.: Government Printing Office, 1900), 290–91; Swan, *The Northwest Coast*, 104, 110–11, 180, 267; Franchere, *A Voyage to the Northwest Coast of America*, 186–88; D. Michael Pavel, Gerald B. Miller, and Mary J. Pavel, "Too Long, Too Silent: The Threat to Cedar and the Sacred Ways of the Skokomish," *American Indian Culture and Research Journal* 17:3 (1993): 57–61, 75–79.

26. Susan Kent, "Tulalip Tribes," in *Inventory of Native American Religious Use, Practices, Localities, and Resources*, 313.

27. By this I mean that the region's people did not cultivate, plant, or tend plants in the commonly accepted notion of agriculture. The one possible exception may have been tobacco, but even its cultivation was apparently restricted. See Wilkes, *Exploring Expedition*, 4:299.

28. James Douglas, March 5, 1835, Journal 1835, transcript, University of Washington Manuscripts and Archives Division, Seattle, vertical file folder 305C (Mss D74j), 3; Franchere, *A Voyage to the Northwest Coast of America*, 180; Wilkes, *Exploring Expedition*, 4:344–46.

29. Rick Minor, "Prehistoric Background," in Rick Minor with Paul W. Baxter, Stephen Dow Beckham, and Kathryn Anne Toepel, *Cultural Resource Overview of the Willamette National Forest: A 10-Tear Update*, Report no. 60 (Eugene, Ore.: Heritage Research Associates, 1987), 57; O. B. Sperlin, ed., "Our First Official Horticulturist," *Washington Historical Quarterly* 21:4 (October 1930): 303–4. Lieut. R. S. Williamson, assisted by Lieut. Henry L. Abbot, "Report of Lieut. Henry L. Abbot, Upon Explorations for a Railroad Route, from the Sacramento Valley to the Columbia River," in *Reports of Explorations and Surveys to Ascertain the Most Practicable and Economical Route for a Railroad from the Mississippi River to the Pacific Ocean, 1854–5*, vol. 6, pt. 1 (Washington, D.C.: Beverley Tucker, 1857), 30; "John Work's Journey from Fort Vancouver to Umpqua River, and Return, in 1834," *Oregon Historical Quarterly* 24:3 (September 1923): 265; Bryant et al., *Cultural Resource Overview of the Mt. Hood National Forest, Oregon*, 1:48, 69.

30. Charles L. Camp, ed., *James Clyman, Frontiersman* (Portland, Ore.: Champoeg Press, 1960), 153; Wilkes, *Exploring Expedition*, 4:318–19.

31. Jerry V. Jermann and Roger D. Mason, *A Cultural Resource Overview of the Gifford Pinchot National Forest, South-Central Washington*, Reconnaissance Reports no. 7 (Seattle: University of Washington Office of Public Archaeology, Institute for Environmental Studies, March 1976), 78, 79.

32. F. Ann McKinney, "Kalapuyan Subsistence: Reexamining the Willamette Falls Salmon Barrier," *Northwest Anthropological Research Notes* 18:1 (Spring 1984): 23–33. Rick Minor, Stephen Dow Beckham, Phyliss E. Lancefield-Steeves, and Kathryn Anne Toepel, *Cultural Overview of the BLM Salem District*, University of Oregon Anthropological Papers no. 20 (Portland, Ore., 1980), 16, 28, 43, 58.

33. Joseph E. Taylor, "'Steelhead's Mother Was His Father, Salmon: Development and Declension of Aboriginal Conservation in the Oregon Country Salmon Fishery" (M.A. thesis, University of Oregon, 1992), 59, 63–64.

34. Erhard Rostlund, "Freshwater Fish and Fishing in Native North America," in *University of California Publications in Geography*, vol. 9 (Berkeley: University of California Press, 1952), 17.

35. Randall F. Schalk, "Estimating Salmon and Steelhead Usage in the Colum-

bia Basin Before 1850: The Anthropological Perspective," *Northwest Environmental Journal* 2:2 (Summer 1986): 21.

36. Ibid., 54, 58, 73.

37. I am indebted to historian Donald Wolf for this insight. Letter from Don Wolf to the author, August 19, 1994.

38. Lavender, ed., *The Oregon Journals of David Douglas*, 2:129, 132; September 8, 1828, "Alex R. McLeod's Journal Southern Expedition," in Maurice S. Sullivan, ed., *The Travels of Jedediah Smith* (Santa Ana, Calif.: Fine Arts Press, 1934), 113; O. B. Sperlin, ed., "Our First Horticulturist—Brackenridge's Journal of the Willamette Route to California, 1841," *Washington Historical Quarterly* 22:3 (July 1931): 216, 218.

39. S. A. Clarke, *Pioneer Days of Oregon History*, 2 vols. (Cleveland: Arthur H. Clark Company, 1905), 1:91; Wilkes, *Exploring Expedition*, 5:229, 231, 237.

40. Joseph Henry Brown, "Settlement of Willammette [*sic*] Valley," Salem, Oregon, interview, June 12, 1878, Bancroft Library, University of California, Berkeley, P-A 10, 2; Leiberg, "Cascade Range and Ashland Forest Reserves," 278.

41. Clarke, *Pioneer Days of Oregon History*, 1:90–91.

42. Lavender, ed., *The Oregon Journals of David Douglas*, 2:145; John Kirk Townsend, *Across the Rockies to the Columbia* (Lincoln: University of Nebraska Press, 1978), 226.

43. Robert Boyd, "Strategies of Indian Burning in the Willamette Valley," *Canadian Journal of Anthropology* 5 (Fall 1986): 80; George M. Savage, Reminiscences, box 1, University of Washington Manuscripts and Archives Division, Seattle, V0243f, 90.

44. William E. Lawrence interview with E. C. Roberts, July 18, 1918, William E. Lawrence, "Field Book #3" (Unpublished paper, Herbarium, Oregon State University, n.d.), 63; Wilkes, *Exploring Expedition*, 5:222; George W. Riddle, *History of Early Days in Oregon* (Riddle, Ore.: reprinted from the *Riddle Enterprise*, 1920), 45–46; Jesse Applegate, *A Day with the Cow Column in 1843: Recollections of My Boyhood*, ed. Joseph Schafer (Chicago: Caxton Club, 1934), 136–37.

45. Boyd, "Strategies of Indian Burning in the Willamette Valley," 76–79; John Minto, "From Youth to Age as an American," *Oregon Historical Quarterly* 9:2 (June 1908): 152; Wilkes, *Exploring Expedition*, 5:232; Lavender, ed., *The Oregon Journals of David Douglas*, 2:130; Beckham, *Cultural Resource Overview of the Siskiyou National Forest*, 1:31.

46. Peter Dominic Adrian Teensma, "Fire History and Fire Regimes of the Central Western Cascades of Oregon" (Ph.D. dissertation, University of Oregon, 1987), 90–91.

47. Fred G. Plummer, "Mount Rainier Forest Reserve, Washington," in U.S. Department of the Interior, *Twenty-First Annual Report of the United States Geological Survey to the Secretary of Interior 1899–1900*, 135; Bob Zybach, "The Great Fires of the Oregon Coast Range: 1770–1933" (Unpublished paper, May 1, 1988), 31; Teensma, "Fire History and Fire Regimes," 88, 90, 92, 97; Stephen J. Pyne, *Fire in America: A Cultural History of Wildland and Rural Fire* (Princeton: Princeton University Press, 1982), 335.

48. Pyne, *Fire in America*, 26, 334; Teensma, "Fire History and Fire Regimes," 23, 25; Zybach, "The Great Fires of the Oregon Coast Range: 1770–1933," 100, 106.

49. Thomas A. Spies and Jerry F. Franklin, "Old Growth and Forest Dynamics in the Douglas-Fir Region of Western Oregon and Washington," *Natural Areas Journal* 8:3 (July 1988): 198.

50. Ibid., 193, 198.

51. James A. Baenen, "Stillaguamish, Snohomish, Snoqualmie & Duwamish," in *Inventory of Native American Religious Use, Practices, Localities, and Resources*, 418.

52. By communal culture, I mean that the individual is subordinate to the common good. This overlaps with an organic view that similarly subordinates the individual to the group, stresses the interdependence of parts to the whole, and sees all creation is alive.

53. Wayne Suttles, "Introduction," in *Handbook of North American Indians*, 7:4.

54. Franchere, *A Voyage to the Northwest Coast of America*, 186; Wilkes, *Exploring Expedition*, 4:300.

55. Wayne Suttles and Aldona C. Jonaitis, "History of Research in Ethnology," in *Handbook of North American Indians*, 7:87.

56. Moulton, ed., *The Journals of the Lewis & Clark Expedition*, 6:222; Wilkes, *Exploring Expedition*, 4:311; Merk, ed., *Fur Trade and Empire*, 97.

57. Eugene S. Hunn, *Nch'i-Wana, "The Big River": Mid-Columbia Indians and Their Land* (Seattle: University of Washington Press, 1990), 139, 209, 219–25.

58. Suttles and Jonaitis, "History of Research in Ethnology," 7:84, 85.

59. Daniel Lee and Joseph H. Frost, *Ten Years in Oregon* (1844; reprint, New York: Arno Press, 1973), 314; Taylor, "Steelhead's Mother Was His Father," 102–5.

60. Robert T. Boyd and Yvonne P. Hajda, "Seasonal Population Movement Along the Lower Columbia River: The Social and Ecological Context," *American Ethologist* 14:2 (May 1987): 310; Paul Tennant, *Aboriginal Peoples and Politics: The Indians Land Question in British Columbia, 1849–1989* (Vancouver: University of British Columbia Press, 1990), 12; Hunn, *Nch'i-Wana*, 153; Madhav Gadgil, "Diversity: Cultural and Biological," *Trends in Ecology and Evolution* 2:12 (December 1987): 371, 372; and David Feeny, Fikret Berkes, Bonnie J. McCay, and James M. Acheson, "The Tragedy of the Commons: Twenty-Two Years Later," *Human Ecology* 18:1 (March 1990): 4.

61. Hunn, *Nch'i-Wana*, 230.

62. Baenen, "Stillaguamish, Snohomish, Snoqualmie & Duwamish," 407–8, 451–52; Kent, "Tulalip Tribes," 371, 385; Kurt Russo, "Lummi and Nooksack," in *Inventory of Native American Religious Use, Practices, Localities, and Resources*, 135–37; Sally Snyder, "Swinomish, Upper Skagit, & Sauk-Suiattle," in ibid., 228–36, 292.

63. Baenen, "Stillaguamish, Snohomish, Snoqualmie & Duwamish," 446.

64. Ross, *Adventures of the First Settlers*, 111.

65. William Fraser Tolmie, *The Journals of William Fraser Tolmie, Physician and Fur Trader* (Vancouver: Mitchell Press, 1963), 167.

66. "Report of Lieutenant Neil M. Howison on Oregon, 1846," *Oregon Historical Quarterly* 14:1 (March 1913): 47–48.

67. Ross, *Adventures of the First Settlers*, 103.

CHAPTER TWO: FUR TRADE SOCIETY

1. Carlos A. Schwantes, *The Pacific Northwest: An Interpretive History* (Lincoln: University of Nebraska Press, 1989), 39–41.

2. Gordon B. Dodds, *Oregon: A Bicentennial History* (New York: W. W. Norton, 1977), 13.

3. James R. Gibson, *Otter Skins, Boston Ships, and China Goods: The Maritime Fur Trade of the Northwest Coast, 1785–1841* (Seattle: University of Washington Press, 1992), 22–23.

4. Robert E. Ficken, *Forested Land: A History of Lumbering in Western Washington* (Seattle: University of Washington Press, 1987), 8.

5. Dodds, *Oregon*, 13, 16, 20–25.

6. James R. Gibson, "The Maritime Trade of the North Pacific Coast," in

Wilcomb E. Washburn, ed., *History of Indian-White Relations*, vol. 4 of *Handbook of North American Indians*, ed. William C. Sturtevant (Washington, D.C.: Smithsonian Institution, 1988), 380–81.

7. Robert E. Ficken and Charles P. LeWarne, *Washington: A Centennial History* (Seattle: University of Washington Press, 1988), 10–11.

8. James P. Ronda, "Essay Review. 'The Writingest Explorers': The Lewis and Clark Expedition in American Historical Literature," *Pennsylvania Magazine of History and Biography* 112:4 (October 1988): 607–30; Ronda, "Calculating Ouragon," *Oregon Historical Quarterly* 94:2–3 (Summer–Fall 1993): 120–40.

9. James Douglas to the governor, deputy governor, and committee of the Hudsons Bay Company, October 18, 1838, in E. E. Rich, ed., *The Letters of John McLoughlin from Fort Vancouver to the Governor and Committee. First Series, 1825–38* (London: Champlain Society for the Hudson's Bay Record Society, 1941), 261.

10. Alexander Ross, *Adventures of the First Settlers on the Oregon or Columbia River, 1810–1813* (Lincoln: University of Nebraska Press, 1986), 114.

11. Gabriel Franchere, *A Voyage to the Northwest Coast of America*, ed. Milo Milton Quaife (New York: Citadel Press, 1968), 74, 76; "Report of Lieuts. Warre and Vavasour, Dated 26 October, 1845, Directed to 'the Rt. Hon. the Secretary of State for the Colonies,'" in Joseph Schafer, ed., "Documents Relative to Warre and Vavasour's Military Reconnoissance in Oregon, 1845–6," *Oregon Historical Quarterly* 10:1 (March 1909): 76; "John Work's Journey from Fort Vancouver to Umpqua River, and Return, in 1834," *Oregon Historical Quarterly* 24:3 (September 1923): 241–42.

12. Douglas to the governor, etc., October 18, 1838, in Rich, ed., *Letters of John McLoughlin*, 241.

13. Ross, *Adventures of the First Settlers*, 90–92.

14. "Report of Lieutenant Neil M. Howison on Oregon, 1846," *Oregon Historical Society* 14:1 (March 1913): 51; Eldridge Morse, Notes of the History and Resources of Washington Territory, Book 22, The River Valleys, Bancroft Library, University of California, Berkeley, P-B 51, 3–8.

15. Douglas, April 29, 1835, Journal 1835, transcript, University of Washington Manuscripts and Archives Division, Seattle, vertical file folder 305C (Mss D74j), 14; C. F. Newcombe, ed., *Menzies' Journal of Vancouver's Voyage: April to October, 1792* (Victoria: William H. Cullin, 1923), 112.

16. William Fraser Tolmie, *The Journals of William Fraser Tolmie, Physician and Fur Trader* (Vancouver: Mitchell Press, 1963), 166–67.

17. George M. Savage, "Life and Adventures of George Savage," Reminiscences, box 1, University of Washington Manuscripts and Archives Division, Seattle, V0243f, 35–36.

18. Frederick Merk, ed., *Fur Trade and Empire: George Simpson's Journal* (Cambridge, Mass.: Harvard University Press, 1931), 62, 261.

19. Gibson, *Otter Skins, Boston Ships, and China Goods*, 25, 35, 61, 62, 73–74, 82.

20. Charles Wilkes, *Narrative of the United States Exploring Expedition During the Years 1838, 1839, 1840, 1841, 1842*, vols. 4 and 5 (Philadelphia: Lea and Blanchard, 1845), 5:227.

21. Gibson, "The Maritime Trade of the North Pacific Coast," 375–76; William R. Swagerty, "Indian Trade in the Trans-Mississippi West to 1870," in *Handbook of North American Indians*, 4:353.

22. Robin Fisher, *Contact and Conflict: Indian-European Relations in British Columbia, 1774–1890* (Vancouver: University of British Columbia Press, 1977), 10–11; Gibson, *Otter Skins, Boston Ships, and China Goods*, 116–17; Gibson, "The Maritime Trade of the North Pacific Coast," 4:386–88.

23. Gibson, *Otter Skins, Boston Ships, and China Goods*, 125, 134–35.

24. John McLoughlin to the governor, deputy governor, and committee of the Hudsons Bay Company, October 31, 1837; McLoughlin to George Simpson, March 16, 1831; and Douglas to Simpson, March 18, 1838, all in Rich, ed., *Letters of John McLoughlin*, 212, 228, 281.

25. Richard White, *The Middle Ground: Indians, Empires, and Republics in the Great Lakes Region, 1650–1815* (Cambridge: Cambridge University Press, 1991), x.

26. Dell Hymes, "Languages and Their Uses," in Carolyn M. Buan and Richard Lewis, eds., *The First Oregonians* (Portland: Oregon Council for the Humanities, 1991), 28.

27. Douglas to Simpson, March 18, 1838, in Rich, ed., *Letters of John McLoughlin*, 280.

28. Ross, *Adventures of the First Settlers*, 230–31.

29. "Slacum's Report on Oregon, 1836–7," *Oregon Historical Quarterly* 13:2 (June 1912): 200.

30. Douglas to the governor, etc., in Rich, ed., *Letters of John McLoughlin*, 262.

31. Paul Tennant, *Aboriginal Peoples and Politics: The Indians Land Question in British Columbia, 1849–1989* (Vancouver: University of British Columbia Press, 1990), 17; Wilkes, *Exploring Expedition*, 4:299.

32. John Ball, first lecture in Troy, New York, 1835, typed copy, John Ball Papers, Oregon Historical Society, Portland, Mss 195, 8–9.

33. Robert T. Boyd, "Demographic History, 1774–1874," in Wayne Suttles, ed., *Northwest Coast*, vol. 7 of *Handbook of North American Indians*, ed. William C. Sturtevant (Washington, D.C.: Smithsonian Institution, 1990), 137; Robert H. Ruby and John A. Brown, *The Chinook Indians: Traders of the Lower Columbia River* (Norman: University of Oklahoma Press, 1988), 81.

34. Alfred W. Crosby, Jr., *The Columbian Exchange: Biological and Cultural Consequences of 1492* (Westport, Conn.: Greenwood Press, 1972), 30–31, 35–58.

35. Boyd, "Demographic History, 1774–1874," 7:137–38; Gary E. Moulton, ed., *The Journals of the Lewis & Clark Expedition, November 2, 1805–March 22, 1806*, vol. 6 (Lincoln: University of Nebraska Press, 1990), 81, 286–87, 286 n.5.

36. John Ball, "Oregon Trip—Troy Lectures, Second Lecture Given, 1835," typescript, John Ball Papers, 19; Boyd, "Demographic History, 1774–1874," 7:139; McLoughlin to the governor, etc., October 11, 1830; October 20, 1831; October 28, 1832; October 31, 1837, all in Rich, ed., *Letters of John McLoughlin*, 88, 233, 104, 205; Tolmie, *Physician and Fur Trader*, 183; "Slacum's Report on Oregon, 1836–7," 200.

37. John Kirk Townsend, *Across the Rockies to the Columbia* (Lincoln: University of Nebraska Press, 1978), 223.

38. Boyd, "Demographic History, 1774–1874," 7:139; Pierre-Jean De Smet, S.J., *Oregon Missions and Travels over the Rocky Mountains in 1845–46* (1847; reprint, Fairfield, Wash.: Ye Galleon Press, 1978), 22–23; James Douglas, April 24, 1840, Journal, 1840–1841, transcription, University of Washington Manuscripts and Archives Division, Seattle, vertical file folder 305 D (Mss D74j), 3–4; Carl Landerholm, trans., *Notices and Voyages of the Famed Quebec Mission to the Pacific Northwest* (Portland, Ore.: Champoeg Press, 1956), 18; Wilkes, *Exploring Expedition*, 4:417.

39. Jerry V. Jermann and Roger D. Mason, *A Cultural Resource Overview of the Gifford Pinchot National Forest, South-Central Washington*, Reconnaissance Reports no. 7 (Seattle: University of Washington Office of Public Archaeology, Institute for Environmental Studies, March 1976), 60–66.

40. Ibid., 66; S. A. Clarke, *Pioneer Days of Oregon History*, 2 vols. (Cleveland: Arthur H. Clark Company, 1905), 1:320–22; George Gibbs, "Tribes of Western Wash-

ington and Northwestern Oregon," in U.S. Geographical and Geological Survey of the Rocky Mountain Region, *Contributions to North American Ethnology*, vol. 1, pt. 2 (Washington, D.C.: Government Printing Office, 1877), 170.

41. This letter is quoted in the "Introduction" by W. Kaye Lamb of Rich, ed., *Letters of John McLoughlin*, lxviii.

42. The governor and committee (of the Hudson's Bay Company) to the Chief Factors Columbia Department, July 27, 1825, and the governor and committee to Governor Simpson, March 12, 1827, in Merk, ed., *Fur Trade and Empire*, 252, 286; McLoughlin to the governor, etc., September 1, 1826, in Rich, ed., *Letters of John McLoughlin*, 36.

43. Douglas to Simpson, March 18, 1838, in Rich, ed., *Letters of John McLoughlin*, 279; David Lavender, ed., *The Oregon Journals of David Douglas; of His Travels and Adventures Among the Traders and Indians in the Columbia, Willamette, and Snake Regions During the Years 1825, 1826, and 1827*, 2 vols. (Ashland: Oregon Book Society, 1972), 1:45–46; Moulton, ed., *The Journals of the Lewis & Clark Expedition*, 6:161; Ross, *Adventures of the First Settlers*, 130.

44. Part of dispatch from George Simpson Esqr., governor of Ruperts Land, to the governor and committee of the Hudson's Bay Company, March 1, 1829, in E. E. Rich, ed., *Simpson's 1828 Journey to the Columbia* (London: Champlain Society for the Hudson's Bay Record Society, 1947), 67–70; Tolmie, *Physician and Fur Trader*, 179.

45. Gibson, *Otter Skins, Boston Ships, and China Goods*, 242–43, 251–67; Lorne Hammond, "Marketing Wildlife: The Hudson's Bay Company and the Pacific Northwest, 1821–49," *Forest and Conservation History* 37:1 (January 1993): 14–25.

46. "Slacum's Report on Oregon, 1836–7," 191; Charles Wilkes, "Report on the Territory of Oregon," *Oregon Historical Quarterly* 12:3 (September 1911): 287.

47. Georgiana Ball, "The Monopoly System of Wildlife Management of the Indians and the Hudson's Bay Company in the Early History of British Columbia," *BC Studies* 66 (Summer 1985): 37–58.

48. Garrett Hardin, "The Tragedy of the Commons," *Science* 162:3849 (December 13, 1968): 1243–48.

49. Colin W. Clark, "The Economics of Overexploitation," *Science* 181:4100 (August 17, 1973): 630–34; David Feeny, Fikret Berkes, Bonnie J. McCay, and James M. Acheson, "The Tragedy of the Commons: Twenty-Two Years Later," *Human Ecology* 18:1 (March 1990): 6–12; Arthur F. McEvoy, *The Fisherman's Problem: Ecology and Law in the California Fisheries, 1850–1980* (Cambridge: Cambridge University Press, 1986), 95–100, 110; M. Patricia Marchak, "What Happens When Common Property Becomes Uncommon?" *BC Studies* 80 (Winter 1988–1989): 3–23.

50. Hammond, "Marketing Wildlife," 19–20.

51. Gibson, "The Maritime Trade of the North Pacific Coast," 4:390; Gibson, *Otter Skins, Boston Ships, and China Goods*, 110, 270–77.

CHAPTER THREE: NATURE'S SOCIETY

1. Oregon typifies Wilbur Zelinsky's "Doctrine of First Effective Settlement": "Whenever an empty territory undergoes settlement, or the earlier population is dislodged by invaders, the specific characteristics of the first group able to effect a viable, self-perpetuating society are of crucial significance for the later social and cultural geography of the area, no matter how tiny the initial band of settlers may have been" (*The Cultural Geography of the United States* [Englewood Cliffs, N.J.: Prentice-Hall, 1973], 13).

2. Leo Marx, *The Machine in the Garden: Technology and the Pastoral Ideal in America* (New York: Oxford University Press, 1964).

3. Stephen Dow Beckham, *Land of the Umpqua: A History of Douglas County, Oregon* (Roseburg, Ore.: Douglas County Commissioners, 1986), 53–56, 91; T. C. Elliott, ed., "British Values in Oregon, 1847," *Oregon Historical Quarterly* 32:1 (March 1931): 30, 41.

4. James R. Gibson, *Farming the Frontier: The Agricultural Opening of the Oregon Country, 1786–1846* (Seattle: University of Washington Press, 1985), 50–51.

5. John McLoughlin to the governor, deputy governor, and committee of the Hudsons Bay Company, November 16, 1836, in E. E. Rich, ed., *The Letters of John McLoughlin from Fort Vancouver to the Governor and Committee. First Series, 1825–38* (London: Champlain Society for the Hudson's Bay Record Society, 1941), 173; the governor and committee to John McLoughlin Esqr. or the officer in charge of Fort Vancouver, September 27, 1843, in E. E. Rich, ed., *The Letters of John McLoughlin from Fort Vancouver to the Governor and Committee. Second Series, 1839–44* (London: Champlain Society for the Hudson's Bay Record Society, 1943), 313; Willard H. Rees, "Annual Address," in *Transactions of the Seventh Annual Re-Union of the Oregon Pioneer Association* (Salem, Ore.: E. M. Waite, 1880), 20–23.

6. William Fraser Tolmie, *The Journals of William Fraser Tolmie, Physician and Fur Trader* (Vancouver: Mitchell Press, 1963), 178–79.

7. James R. Gibson, *Otter Skins, Boston Ships, and China Goods: The Maritime Fur Trade of the Northwest Coast, 1785–1841* (Seattle: University of Washington Press, 1992), 258–60.

8. James Douglas to George Simpson, March 18, 1838, in Rich, ed., *Letters of John McLoughlin, 1825–38*, 285.

9. Jean Barman, *The West Beyond the West: A History of British Columbia* (Toronto: University of Toronto Press, 1991), 42–43.

10. James Douglas, April 29, 1840, Journal, 1840–1841, transcript, University of Washington Manuscripts and Archives Division, Seattle, vertical file folder 305 D (Mss D74j), 6; Charles Wilkes, *Narrative of the United States Exploring Expedition During the Years 1838, 1839, 1840, 1841, 1842*, vols. 4 and 5 (Philadelphia: Lea and Blanchard, 1845), 4:315; Joseph Schafer, ed., "Documents Relative to Warre and Vavasour's Military Reconnoissance in Oregon, 1845–6," *Oregon Historical Quarterly* 10:1 (March 1909): 56; Eldridge Morse, Notes of the History and Resources of Washington Territory, Book 1, Settlement, Bancroft Library, University of California, Berkeley, P-B 30, 41; Michael Leon Olsen, "The Beginnings of Agriculture in Western Oregon and Western Washington" (Ph.D. dissertation, University of Washington, 1970), 44; Charles Wilkes, "Report on the Territory of Oregon," *Oregon Historical Quarterly* 12:3 (September 1911): 284.

11. J. G. Cooper, "Report on the Botany of the Route," in *Reports of Explorations and Surveys to Ascertain the Most Practicable and Economical Route for a Railroad from the Mississippi River to the Pacific Ocean, 1853–5*, vol. 12, bk. 2, pt. 2, Botanical Report (Washington, D.C.: Thomas H. Ford, 1860), 21–22; Gibson, *Farming the Frontier*, 60–61; Douglas, April 29, 1840, Journal, 1840–1841, 6–7; McLoughlin to the governor, etc., November 20, 1840, in Rich, ed., *Letters of John McLoughlin, 1839–44*, 17; Olsen, "The Beginnings of Agriculture in Western Oregon and Western Washington," 47; Carlos A. Schwantes, *The Pacific Northwest: An Interpretive History* (Lincoln: University of Nebraska Press, 1989), 63; George B. Roberts to Mrs. Francis Fuller Victor, May 23, 1879, in "Letters to Mrs. F. F. Victor, 1878–83," *Oregon Historical Quarterly* 63:2–3 (June–September 1962): 211.

12. W. Kaye Lamb, "Introduction," in Rich, ed., *Letters of John McLoughlin*,

1825–38, lvi; part of dispatch from George Simpson Esqr. governor of Ruperts Land to the governor and committee of the Hudson's Bay Company London, March 1, 1829, in ibid., 68.

13. McLoughlin to the governor, etc., October 31, 1837, and James Douglas to George Simpson, March 18, 1838, in Rich, ed., *Letters of John McLoughlin, 1825–38,* 205, 207, 208, 284–85. Wilkes, *Exploring Expedition,* 4:334–35; John Work to Edward Ermatinger, February 24, 1834, transcription, John Work Papers, 1823–1862, box 1, University of Washington Manuscripts and Archives Division, Seattle, V0249C, 2.

14. Samuel B. Crockett to Mrs. Mary Crockett, July 4, 1846, typescript, Edmond S. Meany Papers, box 72, folder 7, University of Washington Manuscripts and Archives Division, Seattle, 106-70-12, 2; Olsen, "The Beginnings of Agriculture in Western Oregon and Western Washington," 23, 48; Joel Palmer, *Journal of Travels over the Rocky Mountains* (1847; reprint, Fairfield, Wash.: Ye Galleon Press, 1983), 103–4.

15. Schwantes, *The Pacific Northwest,* 66, 79, 80, 84.

16. John Minto, "Antecedents of the Oregon Pioneers and the Light These Throw on Their Motives," *Oregon Historical Quarterly* 5:1 (March 1904): 42.

17. John Ball, "Oregon Trip—Troy Lectures, Second Lecture Given, 1835," typescript, John Ball Papers, Oregon Historical Society, Portland, Mss 195; Fred Wilbur Powell, "Hall Jackson Kelley—Prophet of Oregon," *Oregon Historical Quarterly* 18:1 (March 1917): 1–54, 18:2 (June 1917): 93–139, 18:3 (September 1917): 167–223; George W. Riddle, *History of Early Days in Oregon* (Riddle, Ore.: reprinted from the *Riddle Enterprise,* 1920), 4; William Shaw, "Mississippi & Columbia River Valley Pioneer Life Compared" (1878), Bancroft Library, University of California, Berkeley, P-A 64, 7.

18. Peter H. Burnett, "Letters of Peter H. Burnett," *Oregon Historical Quarterly* 3:4 (December 1902): 421–26; Burnett, "Documents," *Oregon Historical Quarterly* 4:2 (June 1903): 180–83; Phoebe Goodell Judson, *A Pioneer's Search for an Ideal Home,* ed. John M. McClelland, Jr. (Tacoma: Washington State Historical Society, 1966), 7; Michael Luark Diary, Microfilm Roll 2, University of Washington Manuscripts and Archives Division, Seattle, October 27, 1855; Minto, "Antecedents of the Oregon Pioneers," 40–43, 48.

19. William A. Bowen, *The Willamette Valley: Migration and Settlement on the Oregon Frontier* (Seattle: University of Washington Press, 1978), 11–13; Schafer, ed., "Documents Relative to Warre and Vavasour's Military Reconnoissance in Oregon, 1845–6," 48–49, 53.

20. Bowen, *The Willamette Valley,* 24–58, 95.

21. Silas Bullard Plimpton to Nathaniel and Judith Wright, June 2, 1853, in Helen Betsy Abbott, ed., "Life on the Lower Columbia, 1853–1866," *Oregon Historical Quarterly* 83:3 (Fall 1982): 253; *Oregon Statesman,* November 6, 1865, p. 1, c. 5; Morse, Notes of the History and Resources of Washington Territory, Book 1, Settlement, 15–16, 21; *Washington Standard,* February 16, 1861, p. 2, c. 4.

22. Ralph C. Geer, "Occasional Address," in *Transactions of the Seventh Annual Re-Union of the Oregon Pioneer Association* (Salem, Ore.: E. M. Waite, 1880), 32.

23. James Ronald Warren, "A Study of the Congressional Debates Concerning the Oregon Question" (Ph.D. dissertation, University of Washington, 1962), 19–25, 100–121; Mary Hayden, *Pioneer Days* (1915; reprint, Fairfield, Wash.: Ye Galleon Press, 1979), 38; Minto, "Antecedents of the Oregon Pioneers," 39; Shaw, "Mississippi & Columbia River Valley Pioneer Life Compared," 7.

24. Wilson Blain to John B. Dales, April 1, 1851, typescript, Wilson Blain folder, Letters, 1848–1852, Oregon Historical Society, Portland, Mss 1035, 54; Roselle Put-

nam to father and mother (in-laws), January 25, 1852, in Sheba Hargreaves, "The Letters of Roselle Putnam," *Oregon Historical Quarterly* 29:3 (September 1928): 254; "Letter to Isaac M. Nash, Ballston Spa, Saratoga County, NY from Tallmadge B. Wood, Clatsop, Clatsop County, Oregon Territory, February 19, 1846," in Tallmadge B. Wood, Letters, *Oregon Historical Quarterly* 4:1 (March 1903): 81.

25. Isaac N. Ebey to brother, April 25, 1851, typescript, Edmond S. Meany Papers, box 72, folder 43, 4; Judson, *A Pioneer's Search for an Ideal Home*, 2. Competency that defined work's purpose from the end of feudalism to industrial capitalism for most white Americans meant a "comfortable independence" through "the possession of sufficient property to absorb the labors of a given family while providing it with something more than a mere subsistence" (Daniel Vickers, "Competency and Competition: Economic Culture in Early America," *William and Mary Quarterly*, 3d ser., 47:1 [January 1990]: 3). Fred Lockley, "Interview with H. C. Thompson," Edmond S. Meany Papers, box 74, folder 45, 2; John Minto, "From Youth to Age as an American," *Oregon Historical Quarterly* 9:2 (June 1908): 144.

26. Peter H. Burnett, *Recollections and Opinions of an Old Pioneer* (New York: D. Appleton and Company, 1880), 192; Daniel Waldo, "Critiques" (1878), Bancroft Library, University of California, Berkeley, P-A 74, 13.

27. Plimpton to Nathaniel and Judith Wright, June 2, 1853, in Abbott, ed., "Life on the Lower Columbia, 1853–1866," 251; Walter Crockett to Samuel B. Crockett, March 29, 1845, Edmond S. Meany Papers, box 72, folder 7, 1; Absolom B. Harden to his brothers and sisters, March 25, 1848, Absolom B. Harden folder, Letters, 1848, Oregon Historical Society, Portland, Mss 11, 20; Mrs. Mary F. Sheppard, personal reminiscences, March 11, 1912, Meany Papers, box 74, folder 6; Isaac Smith to brother and sister, August 6, 1854, typescript, Butler-Smith Family Papers, Oregon Historical Society, Portland, Mss 2623, 1.

28. Joseph P. Eagon and Sarah Eagon to his brother, July 16, 1853, Joseph Eagon Papers, Oregon Historical Society, Portland, Mss 2516, 2.

29. Ball, "Oregon Trip—Troy Lectures," 22; Minto, "Antecedents of the Oregon Pioneers," 38–39.

30. Isaac Pettijohn Diary, April 18, 1847, Bancroft Library, University of California, Berkeley, P-A 336; *Pioneer and Democrat*, July 18, 1856, p. 1, c. 4.

31. Cooper, "Report on the Botany of the Route," 38; Theodore Winthrop, *The Canoe and the Saddle*, ed. John H. Williams (Tacoma: Franklin-Ward Company, 1913), 210.

32. *West Shore* 3 (May 1878): p. 129, c. 1.

33. *Washington Standard*, January 8, 1888, p. 1, c. 5.

34. Schwantes, *The Pacific Northwest*, 2.

35. Harden to his brothers and sisters, March 25, 1848, Absolom B. Harden, Letters, 1848, 11, 14.

36. Plimpton to Solomon Nickerson and Dexter Wright, July 20, 1855, in Abbott, ed., "Life on the Lower Columbia, 1853–1866," 261; John Ball to father (Nathaniel) and mother, February 23, 1833, John Ball Papers, 1.

37. Roselle Putnam to Mr. Francis Putnam (brother-in-law), June 8, 1851, in Hargreaves, "The Letters of Roselle Putnam," 250–51.

38. Wilkes, "Report on the Territory of Oregon," 285.

39. Burnett, "Documents," 426; "Letter to Isaac M. Nash, Ballston Spa," 81.

40. *Oregonian*, January 5, 1888, p. 2, c. 1; *Washington Standard*, April 8, 1904, p. 1, c. 4–5.

41. Burnett, "Documents," 425.

42. Ball, "Oregon Trip—Troy Lectures," 19.

43. *Oregon Statesman*, September 18, 1852, p. 2, c. 2–3.

44. Ibid., June 8, 1852, p. 2, c. 1; November 14, 1864, p. 1, c. 3; January 29, 1866, p. 3, c. 2; March 19, 1866, p. 3, c. 1.

45. Luark Diary, Microfilm Roll 4, July 27, 1879.

46. *Pioneer and Democrat*, September 3, 1858, p. 1, c. 5.

47. Judson, *A Pioneer's Search for an Ideal Home*, 188; Harvey W. Scott, "The Pioneer Character of Oregon Progress," *Oregon Historical Quarterly* 18:4 (December 1917): 261; *Oregonian*, December 20, 1887, p. 2, c. 1; *Washington Standard*, October 17, 1890, p. 2, c. 4.

48. David Lowenthal, "The Pioneer Landscape: An American Dream," *Great Plains Quarterly* 2:1 (Winter 1982): 7; Robin W. Winks, *The Relevance of Canadian History: U.S. and Imperial Perspectives* (Toronto: Macmillan Company, 1979), 34–35.

49. Judson, *A Pioneer's Search for an Ideal Home*, 97, 188; *Columbian*, September 24, 1853, p. 2, c. 3.

50. *Washington Standard*, September 18, 1869, p. 1, c. 4.

51. *Pioneer and Democrat*, September 7, 1860, p. 3, c. 1.

52. Ibid., March 3, 1866, p. 1, c. 1.

53. *Oregon Statesman*, October 29, 1866, p. 2, c. 2. *Washington Standard*, September 9, 1865, p. 2, c. 1.

54. Luark Diary, Microfilm Roll 3, December 31, 1866; Winthrop, *Canoe and Saddle*, 37, 63; Tolmie, *Physician and Fur Trader*, 189, 192.

55. Judson, *A Pioneer's Search for an Ideal Home*, 97; Alexander Ross, *Adventures of the First Settlers on the Oregon or Columbia River, 1810–1813* (Lincoln: University of Nebraska Press, 1986), 120; Winthrop, *Canoe and Saddle*, 180.

56. Caroline C. Leighton, *Life at Puget Sound with Sketches of Travel in Washington Territory, British Columbia, Oregon, and California, 1865–1881* (Boston: Lee and Shepard, 1884), 135–36.

57. Judson, *A Pioneer's Search for an Ideal Home*, 97.

58. John Kirk Townsend, *Across the Rockies to the Columbia* (Lincoln: University of Nebraska Press, 1978), 196; *Pioneer and Democrat*, January 11, 1861, p. 1, c. 1; *Washington Standard*, December 12, 1868, p. 2, c. 1; May 9, 1879, p. 1, c. 3; *West Shore* 7 (October 1881): p. 246, c. 2.

59. *Pioneer and Democrat*, October 20, 1860, p. 1, c. 6.

60. *Oregon Statesman*, September 18, 1852, p. 2, c. 2; *Pioneer and Democrat*, July 13, 1855, p. 1, c. 4–5.

61. Judson, *A Pioneer's Search for an Ideal Home*, 64–65.

62. Cooper, "Report on the Botany of the Route," 22, 28; Luark Diary, Microfilm Roll 2, October 7, 1853.

63. Martha A. Minto, "Female Pioneering in Oregon" (1878), Bancroft Library, University of California, Berkeley, P-A 51, 14.

64. Cooper, "Report on the Botany of the Route," 39.

65. Wilkes, *Exploring Expedition*, 4:312.

66. James Douglas to the governor, etc., October 18, 1838, in Rich, ed., *Letters of John McLoughlin, 1825–38*, 241.

67. Judson, *A Pioneer's Search for an Ideal Home*, 65–66; Henry Coonse, Diary, transcript, January 10, 1852, January 16, 1852, March 11, 1852, June 20, 1852, Henry Coonse, Diary, 1851–1854, University of Washington Manuscripts and Archives Division, Seattle, vertical file 286; Luark Diary, Microfilm Roll 2, May 3, 1854, and May 13, 1855; Leighton, *Life at Puget Sound*, 138.

68. Rev. Gustavus Hines, *Life on the Plains of the Pacific. Oregon* (New York: C. M. Saxton, 1859), 322; Winthrop, *Canoe and Saddle*, 39, 41; A. B. Guthrie, Jr., "Our

Lordly Mountains," in David Peterson, ed., *Big Sky, Fair Land: The Environmental Essays of A. B. Guthrie, Jr.* (Flagstaff, Ariz.: Northland Press, 1988), 95.

69. Harden to his brothers and sisters, March 25, 1848, Harden folder, Letters, 1848, 7; Tolmie, *Physician and Fur Trader,* 171.

70. *Oregon Statesman,* June 8, 1852, p. 2, c. 1.

71. *Washington Standard,* October 17, 1890, p. 1, c. 4.

72. *Oregon Spectator,* December 19, 1850, p. 2, c. 5.

CHAPTER FOUR: SETTLER SOCIETY AND NATIVE AMERICANS

1. Peter H. Burnett, *Recollections and Opinions of an Old Pioneer* (New York: D. Appleton and Company, 1880), 148, 149–50.

2. *Columbian,* September 25, 1852, p. 1, c. 1.

3. Harvey W. Scott, "The Pioneer Character of Oregon Progress," *Oregon Historical Quarterly* 18:4 (December 1917): 248.

4. *Transactions of the Twenty-First Annual Reunion of the Oregon Pioneer Association for 1893* (Portland, Ore.: Geo. H. Himes and Company, 1894), 65.

5. *Washington Standard,* February 19, 1870, p. 1, c. 6.

6. James G. Swan, *The Northwest Coast; Or, Three Years' Residence in Washington Territory* (1857; reprint, Fairfield, Wash.: Ye Galleon Press, 1989), 166.

7. *West Shore* 8 (January 1882): p. 1, c. 1.

8. *Columbian,* September 11, 1852, p. 4, c. 3.

9. Ibid., February 12, 1853, p. 1, c. 2; *Pioneer and Democrat,* October 1, 1858, p. 2, c. 3.

10. Intensive development favors planned economic growth that is orderly and stable, ensures vested property rights, and involves a minimum of structural change. Extensive development is more open, dynamic, entrepreneurial, less structured, but also less ordered and stable.

11. *Columbian,* September 18, 1852, p. 4, c. 3; *Pioneer and Democrat,* September 14, 1860, p. 1, c. 4; *Oregonian,* January 2, 1888, p. 13, c. 4; *Washington Standard,* August 4, 1893, p. 2, c. 1.

12. "Free security" and its egalitarianism come from C. Vann Woodward, "The Age of Reinterpretation," *American Historical Review* 66:1 (October 1960): 2–8, and William H. McNeill, *The Great Frontier: Freedom and Hierarchy in Modern Times* (Princeton: Princeton University Press, 1983), 26–27.

13. *Pioneer and Democrat,* July 13, 1855, p. 1, c. 3, 5.

14. Ibid., October 1, 1858, p. 2, c. 3.

15. *Columbian,* May 14, 1853, p. 2, c. 1.

16. *Pioneer and Democrat,* October 1, 1858, p. 2, c. 2.

17. Theodore Winthrop, *The Canoe and the Saddle,* ed. John H. Williams (Tacoma: Franklin-Ward Company, 1913), 11, 28; Rev. Gustavus Hines, *Life on the Plains of the Pacific. Oregon* (New York: C. M. Saxton, 1859), 236; Roselle Putnam to father and mother (in-laws), January 25, 1852, in Sheba Hargreaves, "The Letters of Roselle Putnam," *Oregon Historical Quarterly* 29:3 (September 1928): 254; J. G. Cooper, "Report on the Botany of the Route," *Reports of Explorations and Surveys to Ascertain the Most Practicable and Economical Route for a Railroad from the Mississippi River to the Pacific Ocean, 1853–5,* vol. 12, bk. 2, pt. 2, Botanical Report (Washington, D.C.: Thomas H. Ford, 1860), 21.

18. Arthur D. Howden Smith, ed., *The Narrative of Samuel Hancock, 1845–1860* (New York: Robert M. McBride and Company, 1927), 182.

19. Robert T. Boyd, "Demographic History, 1774–1874," in Wayne Suttles, ed., *Northwest Coast*, vol. 7 of *Handbook of North American Indians*, ed. William C. Sturtevant (Washington, D.C.: Smithsonian Institution, 1990), 141–42; George B. Roberts, "The Cowlitz Farm Journal, 1847–51," *Oregon Historical Quarterly* 63:2–3 (June–September 1962): 138–41, 145; "Tallmadge B. Wood to Isaac Nash and sister, December 23, 1847," in Tallmadge B. Wood, Letters, *Oregon Historical Quarterly* 4:1 (March 1903): 85; John Work to Edward Ermatinger, November 9, 1848, transcription, John Work Papers, 1823–1862, box 1, University of Washington Manuscripts and Archives Division, Seattle, V0249C, 1; George Gibbs, "Tribes of Western Washington and Northwestern Oregon," in U.S. Geographical and Geological Survey of the Rocky Mountain Region, *Contributions to North American Ethnology*, vol. 1, pt. 2 (Washington, D.C.: Government Printing Office, 1877), 173.

20. Absolom B. Harden to his brothers and sisters, March 25, 1848, Absolom B. Harden folder, Letters, 1848, Oregon Historical Society, Portland, Mss 11, 4.

21. Boyd, "Demographic History, 1774–1874," 7:135.

22. Stephen Dow Beckham, *The Indians of Western Oregon: This Land Was Theirs* (Portland, Ore.: Glass-Dahlstron, 1977), 155; Charles Wilkes, *Narrative of the United States Exploring Expedition During the Years 1838, 1839, 1840, 1841, 1842*, vols. 4 and 5 (Philadelphia: Lea and Blanchard, 1845), 4:417.

23. Michael T. Simmons to James W. Nesmith, June 30, 1858, in U.S. Senate, *Message of the President of the United States*, 35th Congress, 2d sess., 1858, S. Ex. Doc. 1, Part 1, Serial 974, 581; George M. Savage, Reminiscences, box 1, University of Washington Manuscripts and Archives Division, Seattle, V0243f, 93–99.

24. John Ball, "Oregon Trip—Troy Lectures, Second Lecture Given, 1835," typed copy, John Ball Papers, Oregon Historical Society, Portland, Mss 195, 21–22.

25. Sunday, February 8, 1852, transcript, Henry Coonse Diary, 1851–1854, University of Washington Manuscripts and Archives Division, Seattle, vertical file 286; Tallmadge B. Wood, "Letter," *Oregon Historical Quarterly* 3:4 (December 1902): 397.

26. Eighteen inhabitants on Applegate Creek to Joel Palmer, November 20, 1854, Joel Palmer Papers, box 1, folder 7, Letters, November–December, 1854, Special Collections, Knight Library, University of Oregon, Eugene, Ax 57; Savage, Reminiscences, 82–83.

27. Stephen Dow Beckham, "History of Western Oregon Since 1846," in *Handbook of North American Indians*, 7:187.

28. Phoebe Goodell Judson, *A Pioneer's Search for an Ideal Home*, ed. John M. McClelland, Jr. (Tacoma: Washington State Historical Society, 1966), 67; Wilkes, *Exploring Expedition*, 4:313–14.

29. Hines, *Life on the Plains of the Pacific. Oregon*, 117–18.

30. *Columbian*, May 14, 1853, p. 2, c. 3.

31. Silas Plimpton to George Lowell Plympton, November 8, 1855, in Helen Betsy Abbott, ed., "Life on the Lower Columbia, 1853–1866," *Oregon Historical Quarterly* 83:3 (Fall 1982): 262; *Pioneer and Democrat*, October 21, 1854, p. 2, c. 4.

32. Wilson Blain to David R. Kerr, March 15, 1854, Wilson Blain folder, Letter, 1853–1855, Oregon Historical Society, Portland, Mss 1035, 3–4.

33. Beckham, *The Indians of Western Oregon*, 132–33, 137.

34. Judson, *A Pioneer's Search for an Ideal Home*, 71. Although women generally were more sympathetic than men toward Indians, not all women were empathetic; see Putnam to father and mother, January 25, 1852, in Hargreaves, "The Letters of Roselle Putnam," 253; Martha A. Minto, "Female Pioneering in Oregon" (1878), Bancroft Library, University of California, Berkeley, P-A 51, 9.

35. George W. Riddle, *History of Early Days in Oregon* (Riddle, Ore.: reprinted from the *Riddle Enterprise*, 1920), 36, 55, 57.

36. *Washington Standard*, August 17, 1867, p. 2, c. 3; January 18, 1879, p. 1, c. 2; April 1, 1887, p. 1, c. 4.

37. E. Ingersoll, "In the Wahlamet Valley of Oregon," *Harper's New Monthly Magazine* 65:389 (October 1882): 770.

38. *Washington Standard*, June 13, 1890, p. 1, c. 2–3; Lee Clark Mitchell, *Witnesses to a Vanishing America: The Nineteenth-Century Response* (Princeton: Princeton University Press, 1981), 77–91.

39. *Washington Standard*, January 8, 1892, p. 1, c. 2.

40. Ibid., August 12, 1871, p. 1, c. 5.

41. S. A. Clarke, *Pioneer Days of Oregon History*, 2 vols. (Cleveland: Arthur H. Clark Company, 1905), 1:88.

42. Caroline C. Leighton, *Life at Puget Sound with Sketches of Travel in Washington Territory, British Columbia, Oregon and California, 1865–1881* (Boston: Lee and Shepard, 1884), 36, 39, 141, 142.

43. Ibid., 174.

44. Ibid., 162.

45. Robert Hull to Joel Palmer, November 17, 1853; E. P. Stone to Joel Palmer, November 17, 1853, box 1, folder 3, Letters, 1853; Eighteen citizens of Pleasant Valley to Joel Palmer, April 1854, box 1, folder 5, Letters, April–June 1854; Eighteen inhabitants on Applegate Creek to Joel Palmer, November 20, 1854, box 1, folder 7, Letters, November–December 1854; George P. Wrenn to Joel Palmer, May 20, 1855, box 1, folder 8, Letters, January–May 1855; Settlers of the Coquille Valley to Joel Palmer, June 4, 1855, box 1, folder 9, Letters, June–September 1855, Palmer Papers.

46. *Oregon Statesman*, November 6, 1852, p. 2, c. 2–3.

47. Ibid., May 28, 1853, p. 2, c. 4.

48. Beckham, "History of Western Oregon Since 1846," 7:180–82; Terrence O'Donnell, *An Arrow in the Earth: General Joel Palmer and the Indians of Oregon* (Portland: Oregon Historical Society, 1991): 153–54, 166–68, 172, 182–83; Cesare Marino, "History of Western Washington Since 1846," in *Handbook of North American Indians*, 7:169–71.

49. O'Donnell, *An Arrow in the Earth*, 215–16; Riddle, *History of Early Days in Oregon*, 36, 54, 56–57, 59; Beckham, "History of Western Oregon Since 1846," 182; Marino, "History of Western Washington Since 1846," 7:171–72.

50. Stevens to his brother and sister, November 9, 1855, in E. Ruth Rockwood, ed., "Letters of Charles Stevens," *Oregon Historical Quarterly* 38:2 (June 1937): 168. Eldridge Morse, Notes of the History and Resources of Washington Territory, Book 1, Settlement, P-B 30, 17–18, and Book 14, End of Indian War 1855 and 1856, P-B 43, 53–59, Bancroft Library, University of California, Berkeley; Kent D. Richards, *Isaac I. Stevens: Young Man in a Hurry* (Provo: Brigham Young University Press, 1979), 255–72. Some places did benefit from the hostilities. Portland apparently experienced an upturn in its economy during the war, and one historian has even suggested that southern Oregon businessmen actually precipitated hostilities in order to spur a dull economy by selling goods to the government at inflated prices (Arthur L. Throckmorton, *Oregon Argonauts: Merchant Adventurers on the Western Frontier* [Portland: Oregon Historical Society, 1961], 185–87, 189).

51. Plimpton to Plympton, November 8, 1855, in Abbott, "Life on the Lower Columbia, 1853–1866," 263.

52. Harry Hobucket, "Quillayute Indian Tradition," *Washington Historical Quarterly* 15:1 (January 1934): 57–59; Eldridge Morse, Notes of the History and Resources of Washington Territory, Book 21, History of the River Valleys, Bancroft Library, University of California, Berkeley, P-B 50, 32–34.

53. *Pioneer and Democrat*, February 27, 1857, p. 2, c. 2.

54. Beckham, *The Indians of Western Oregon*, 135.

55. Richards, *Isaac I. Stevens*, 200–202.

56. C. A. Huntington to E. P. Smith, August 25, 1875, in U.S. House of Representatives, *Report of the Secretary of the Interior*, 44th Congress, 1st sess., 1875, H. Ex. Doc. 1, pt. 5, Serial 1680, 866.

57. Ben Wright to Joel Palmer, February 5, 1855, Palmer Papers, box 1, folder 8, Letters, January–May 1855, 57.

58. Joseph Jeffers to Joel Palmer, June 26, 1856, Palmer Papers, box 2, folder 2, Letters, April–June 1856.

59. Elliott Bowman to Joel Palmer, June 27, 1856, Palmer Papers, box 2, folder 2, Letters, April–June 1856; Captain William Tichenor, "Among the Oregon Indians," Bancroft Library, University of California, Berkeley, P-A 84, 122–23; L. P. Day to Joel Palmer, July 28, 1856, Palmer Papers, box 2, folder 3, Letters, July 1856; E. A. Schwartz, "Blood Money: The Rogue River Indian War and Its Aftermath, 1850–1986" (Ph.D. dissertation, University of Missouri, Columbia, 1991), 347; Beckham, *The Indians of Western Oregon*, 145; Marino, "History of Western Washington Since 1846," 7:172, 178.

60. J. Ross Browne to the Secretary of the Interior, November 17, 1857, in U.S. House of Representatives, *Indian Affairs in the Territories of Oregon and Washington*, 35th Congress, 1st sess., 1858, H. Ex. Doc. 39, Serial 955, 45.

61. Royal A. Bensell, *All Quiet on the Yamhill: The Civil War in Oregon*, ed. Gunter Barth (Eugene: University of Oregon Books, 1959), 47, 129–30, 132–33, 137, 144–48.

62. Wallis Nash, *Two Years in Oregon* (New York: D. Appleton and Company, 1882), 141; E. P. Drew to Joel Palmer, July 3, 1856, Palmer Papers, box 2, folder 3, Letters, July 1856, and C. M. Walker to Joel Palmer, August 2, 1856, August 5, 1856, Palmer Papers, box 2, folder 4, Letters, August–October 1856.

63. Bensell, *All Quiet on the Yamhill*, 135, 138, 183–84; O'Donnell, *An Arrow in the Earth*, 280, 285–92; R. [Robert] C. Fay to M. T. Simmons, June 30, 1858, in U.S. Senate, *Message of the President of the United States*, 592. Sidney S. Ford to Simmons, June 30, 1858, 602; John F. Miller to James W. Nesmith, July 28, 1858, 612, 614; Simmons to Nesmith, June 30, 1858, 581, all in U.S. Senate, *Message of the President of the United States;* E. C. Chirouse to E. P. Smith, September 21, 1875, 869, and Henry to Smith, September 1, 1875, 867, in U.S. House of Representatives, *Report of the Secretary of the Interior.*

64. Browne to the Secretary of the Interior, November 17, 1857, in U.S. House, *Indian Affairs in the Territories of Oregon and Washington*, 27.

65. Ibid.; Metcalfe to Nesmith, July 27, 1858, in U.S. Senate, *Message of the President of the United States*, 603; Philip H. Sheridan, *Personal Memoirs*, vol. 1 (New York: Charles L. Webster and Company, 1888), 99.

66. Walker to Palmer, August 5, 1856, and Walker to Palmer, August 9, 1856, Palmer Papers, box 2, folder 4, Letters, August–October 1856; Fay to Simmons, June 30, 1858, 592; Ford to Simmons, June 30, 1858, 602; Metcalfe to Nesmith, July 27, 1858, 605; Paige to Simmons, July 1, 1858, 599, all in U.S. Senate, *Message of the President of the United States.*

67. Browne to the Secretary of the Interior, November 17, 1857, in U.S. House, *Indian Affairs in the Territories of Oregon and Washington*, 27, 45.

68. J. H. Fairchild to Smith, September 1, 1875, in U.S. House, *Report of the Secretary of the Interior*, 852.

69. Stephen Dow Beckham, Kathryn Anne Toepel, and Rick Minor, *Cultural Resource Overview of the Siuslaw National Forest, Western Oregon*, vol. 1 (Portland, Ore., 1982), 225.

70. Quoted from Dorothy and Jack Sutton, eds., *Indian Wars of the Rogue River* (Grants Pass, Ore.: Josephine County Historical Society, 1969), 262.

71. Browne to the Secretary of the Interior, November 17, 1857, in U.S. House, *Indian Affairs in the Territories of Oregon and Washington*, 25; Metcalfe to Nesmith, July 27, 1858, 603; Miller to Nesmith, July 28, 1858, 612; Nesmith to Charles E. Mix, August 20, 1858, 569, all in U.S. Senate, *Message of the President of the United States*.

72. *Oregon Statesman*, February 20, 1865, p. 1, c. 3; Nesmith to Mix, August 20, 1858, in U.S. Senate, *Message of the President of the United States*, 569.

73. *Oregon Statesman*, November 28, 1864, p. 1, c. 2.

74. Ibid., February 13, 1865, p. 2, c. 5, February 20, 1865, p. 1, c. 3, 4.

75. *Oregonian*, August 15, 1888, p. 4, c. 3; Beckham, *The Indians of Western Oregon*, 167.

76. William A. Newell, *Message of William A. Newell, Governor of Washington Territory, to the Legislative Assembly, Session of 1881* (Olympia, Wash.: C. B. Bagley, 1881), 16.

77. *Washington Standard*, August 29, 1884, p. 2, c. 2.

78. William A. Newell, *Message of William A. Newell, Governor of Washington Territory, to the Legislative Assembly, Session of 1883* (Olympia, Wash.: C. B. Bagley, 1883), 22.

79. *Washington Standard*, February 4, 1887, p. 1, c. 7–8.

80. Ibid., December 26, 1890, p. 1, c. 5.

81. Beckham, "History of Western Oregon Since 1846," 7:184–85; Marino, "History of Western Washington Since 1846," 7:175–76.

82. Marino, "History of Western Washington Since 1846," 7:173; William T. Hagan, "United States Indian Policies, 1860–1900," in Wilcomb E. Washburn, ed., *History of Indian-White Relations*, vol. 4 of *Handbook of North American Indians*, ed. William C. Sturtevant (Washington, D.C.: Smithsonian Institution, 1988), 53; Chirouse to Smith, September 21, 1875, 868–89, and Henry to Smith, September 1, 1875, 867, in U.S. House, *Report of the Secretary of the Interior*.

83. Eldridge Morse, Notes on the History and Resources of Washington Territory, Book 24, Bancroft Library, University of California, Berkeley, P-B 53, 17.

84. John Beeson to Joel Palmer, April 24, 1857, Palmer Papers, box 2, folder 6, Letters, 1857; Marino, "History of Western Washington Since 1846," 7:173–74; Beckham, "History of Western Oregon Since 1846," 7:183.

85. *Washington Standard*, April 1, 1887, p. 1, c. 2, 3.

86. Nash, *Two Years in Oregon*, 137–39.

87. David Hamer, *New Towns in the New World: Images and Perceptions of the Nineteenth-Century Urban Frontier* (New York: Columbia University Press, 1990), 213, 218–19.

88. Leighton, *Life at Puget Sound*, 23, 35–36; Nash, *Two Years in Oregon*, 141–42; Sheridan, *Personal Memoirs*, 1:106–9, 119; Marino, "History of Western Washington Since 1846," 7:176.

89. Bensell, *All Quiet on the Yamhill*, 123–25, 131, 136, 140, 174; Luark Diary, Microfilm Roll 2, April 28, 1854; Luark Diary, Microfilm Roll 3, March 6, 11, 1863, August 12, September 29, 1864, October 17, 1865, University of Washington Manuscripts and Archives Division, Seattle; Morse, Notes of the History and Resources of Washington Territory, Book 1, Settlement, 24–33, Book 14, End of Indian War 1855 and 1856, 59–60, Book 24, 4; Frances Fuller Victor, *All over Oregon and Washington* (San Francisco: John H. Carmany and Company, 1872), 353.

90. *Washington Standard*, August 12, 1871, p. 1, c. 2–3.

91. Marino, "History of Western Washington Since 1846," 7:172.

92. Quoted in Michael Leon Olsen, "The Beginnings of Agriculture in Western Oregon and Western Washington" (Ph.D. dissertation, University of Washington, 1970), 194.

93. Beckham, "History of Western Oregon Since 1846," 7:183; Pamela T. Amoss, "The Indian Shaker Church," in *Handbook of North American Indians*, 7:633–69; Marino, "History of Western Washington Since 1846," 7:174.

94. Kurt Russo, "Lummi and Nooksack," *Inventory of Native American Religious Use, Practices, Localities, and Resources* (Seattle: Institute of Cooperative Research, 1981), 143.

CHAPTER FIVE: SETTLEMENT

1. An ecological revolution represents a paradigmatic shift in how the natural and cultural landscape is structured and the ways that nature and human ecologies relate with one another (Carolyn Merchant, *Ecological Revolutions: Nature, Gender, and Science in New England* [Chapel Hill: University of North Carolina Press, 1989], 2–3).

2. Charles L. Camp, ed., *James Clyman, Frontiersman* (Portland, Ore.: Champoeg Press, 1960), 154.

3. *Pioneer and Democrat*, July 18, 1856, p. 2, c. 1.

4. Theodore Winthrop, *The Canoe and the Saddle*, ed. John H. Williams (Tacoma: Franklin-Ward Company, 1913), 104; J. A. Hussey, *Champoeg: Place of Transition* (Portland: Oregon Historical Society, 1967), 43–118.

5. Matthew P. Deady, "History & Progress of Oregon After 1845" (1878), Bancroft Library, University of California, Berkeley, P-A 24, 69; Parke D. Snavely, Jr., and Norman S. MacLeod, "The Willamette Valley," in Paul E. Heilman, Harry W. Anderson, and David M. Baumgartner, eds., *Forest Soils of the Douglas-Fir Region* (Pullman: Washington State University, 1979), 19.

6. Rev. Gustavus Hines, *Life on the Plains of the Pacific. Oregon* (New York: C. M. Saxton, 1859), 341; Lieut. R. S. Williamson, assisted by Lieut. Henry L. Abbot, "Report of Lieut. Henry L. Abbot, Upon Explorations for a Railroad Route, from the Sacramento Valley to the Columbia River," in *Reports of Explorations and Surveys to Ascertain the Most Practicable and Economical Route for a Railroad from the Mississippi River to the Pacific Ocean, 1854–5*, vol. 6, pt. 1 (Washington, D.C.: Beverley Tucker, 1857), 34; *Oregon Statesman*, November 6, 1865, p. 1, c. 4; *Oregonian*, January 2, 1888, p. 13, c. 2.

7. James R. Habeck, "The Original Vegetation of the Mid-Willamette Valley, Oregon," *Northwest Science* 35:2 (May 1961): 69, 72–76; Jerry F. Franklin and C. T. Dyrness, *Natural Vegetation of Oregon and Washington* (Corvallis: Oregon State University Press, 1988), 111–13, 116, 121; Robert E. Frenkel and Eric F. Heintz, "Composition and Structure of Oregon Ash *(Fraxinus latifolia)* Forest in William L. Finley National Wildlife Refuge, Oregon," *Northwest Science* 61:4 (1987): 203–4, 208; J. E. Kirkwood, "The Vegetation of Northwestern Oregon," *Torreya* 2:9 (September 1902): 130–31; John F. Thilenius, "The *Quercus Garryana* Forests of the Willamette Valley, Oregon," *Ecology* 49:6 (Autumn 1968): 1125–30.

8. Franklin and Dyrness, *Natural Vegetation of Oregon and Washington*, 124–26; Habeck, "The Original Vegetation of the Mid-Willamette Valley," 74–75; James R. Sedell and Judith L. Froggatt, "Importance of Streamside Forests to Large Rivers: The Isolation of the Willamette River, Oregon, U.S.A., from Its Floodplain by Snagging and Streamside Forest Removal," *Verhandlungen: Internationale Vereinigung für*

theorelitche und angewandte Limnologie [International Association of Theoretical and Applied Limnology] 22 (December 1984): 1830.

9. Edward R. Alverson, "Use of a County Soil Survey to Locate Remnants of Native Grassland in the Willamette Valley, Oregon," in *Ecosystem Management: Rare Species and Significant Habitats*, Bulletin no. 471 (New York: New York State Museum, 1990), 107; Deady, "History & Progress of Oregon After 1845," 70; Dale C. Darris and Scott M. Lambert, "Improving Native Cool Season Grasses for Conservation Use in the Pacific Northwest" (Unpublished paper, February 11, 1990), 24, 26, 30–32; Anne Sutherlin Waite, "Pioneer Life of Fendel Sutherlin," *Oregon Historical Quarterly* 31 (December 1930): 375. Edward R. Alverson, who is preparing a study on native Willamette Valley grasses, provided the acreage estimate in a telephone conversation, March 29, 1993.

10. E. Ingersoll, "In the Wahlamet Valley of Oregon," *Harper's New Monthly Magazine* 65:389 (October 1882): 766.

11. Charles Wilkes, "Report on the Territory of Oregon," *Oregon Historical Quarterly* 12:3 (September 1911): 283; Sedell and Froggatt, "Importance of Streamside Forests to Large Rivers," 1830; Walter Crockett to Samuel B. Crockett, March 29, 1845, box 72, folder 7, 1; and interview with N. A. King, Fred Lockley folder, box 74, folder 45, 1–2, Edmond S. Meany Papers, University of Washington Manuscripts and Archives Division, Seattle, 106-70-12.

12. Hines, *Life on the Plains of the Pacific*, 140.

13. Ibid., 141.

14. *Oregon Spectator*, January 10, 1850, p. 2, c. 3; Isaac and Margaret Smith to sister, December 29, 1861, typescript, Butler-Smith Family Papers, Oregon Historical Society, Portland, Mss 2623, 1; *Washington Standard*, December 14, 1861, p. 2, c. 3.

15. Harlow Head's study of Donation Act land claims clearly demonstrates that pattern (Harlow Zinser Head, "The Oregon Donation Claims and Their Patterns" [Ph.D. dissertation, University of Oregon, 1971], 35–39, 98, 106–8, 112–15, 132–33, 146–47); William A. Bowen, *The Willamette Valley: Migration and Settlement on the Oregon Frontier* (Seattle: University of Washington Press, 1978), 61; Wilson Blain to David R. Kerr, December 30, 1853, typescript, Wilson Blain folder, Letters, 1853–1855, Oregon Historical Society, Portland, Mss 1035, 102; *West Shore* 9 (June 1883): p. 128, c. 1–2.

16. *Washington Standard*, February 16, 1861, p. 2, c. 5; *Oregonian*, January 2, 1888, p. 3, c. 3; J. Ross Browne to the Secretary of the Interior, November 17, 1857, in U.S. House of Representatives, *Indian Affairs in the Territories of Oregon and Washington*, 35th Congress, 1st sess., 1858, H. Ex. Doc. 39, Serial 955, 13.

17. *Washington Standard*, August 12, 1871, p. 2, c. 1.

18. Horace Holden, "Oregon Pioneering" (1878), Bancroft Library, University of California, Berkeley, P-A 40, 2; *Oregon Statesman*, September 4, 1865, p. 3, c. 1.

19. Bowen, *The Willamette Valley*, 62; Charles Stevens to his sister and brother Levi, June 27, 1853, in E. Ruth Rockwood, ed., "Letters of Charles Stevens," *Oregon Historical Quarterly* 37:4 (December 1936): 335; *Washington Standard*, March 16, 1861, p. 2, c. 6.

20. William Keil to his dear brothers and sisters in Christ, October 13, 1855, transcript, William Keil, Letters, 1855–1870, University of Washington Manuscripts and Archives Division, Seattle, vertical file 34, 23–24.

21. Delos Waterman to George A. Waterman, July 5, 1885, Delos Waterman Letters, 1862–1896, University of Washington Manuscripts and Archives Division, Seattle, vertical file 416, 2; George P. Wheeler, "On the Lower Columbia," *West Shore* 5 (March 1879): p. 94, c. 1–2.

22. Eldridge Morse, Notes of the History and Resources of Washington Territory, Book 1, Settlement, Bancroft Library, University of California, Berkeley, P-B 30, 16–17, 52–53; "Report of Lieutenant Neil M. Howison on Oregon, 1846," *Oregon Historical Society* 14:1 (March 1913): 20.

23. Steven G. Archie, "Surficial Geology of the Puget Sound Lowlands," in Heilman, Anderson, and Baumgartner, eds., *Forest Soils of the Douglas-Fir Region,* 48–49; Arthur R. Kruckeberg, *The Natural History of Puget Sound Country* (Seattle: University of Washington Press, 1991), 30–32, 438.

24. J. G. Cooper, "Report on the Botany of the Route," in *Reports of Explorations and Surveys to Ascertain the Most Practicable and Economical Route for a Railroad from the Mississippi River to the Pacific Ocean, 1853–5,* vol. 12, bk. 2, pt. 2, Botanical Report (Washington, D.C.: Thomas H. Ford, 1860), 19, 22; Phoebe Goodell Judson, *A Pioneer's Search for an Ideal Home,* ed. John M. McClelland, Jr. (Tacoma: Washington State Historical Society, 1966), 57, 64, 87–88, 90; Luark Diary, Microfilm Roll 2, May 2, 1854, University of Washington Manuscripts and Archives Division, Seattle.

25. *Washington Standard,* December 14, 1867, p. 1, c. 2; August 15, 1868, p. 2, c. 2.

26. Ibid., December 14, 1867, p. 1, c. 2, and May 9, 1879, p. 1, c. 3; Morse, Notes of the History and Resources of Washington, Book 1, Settlement, 19–27; Book 21, History of the River Valleys, P-B 50, 13; Book 2, Settlement, P-B 31, 69; Book 22, The River Valleys, P-B 51, 9–10.

27. Joseph A. Dugan, "Memories of Yesteryears" (1962), typescript, Diaries and Reminiscences—Misc., Dugan, Joseph A., Oregon Historical Society, Portland, Mss 1509, 1; *Washington Standard,* September 24, 1870, p. 2, c. 1; October 4, 1889, p. 1, c. 5.

28. Cooper, "Report on the Botany of the Route," 20; Patricia Benner, "Historical Reconstruction of the Coquille River and Surrounding Landscape" (draft copy, n.d.), 3.2–28, 48, 55, 61–63; 3.3–19.

29. Morse, Notes of the History and Resources of Washington Territory, Book 21, History of the River Valleys, 41–42; Michael Leon Olsen, "The Beginnings of Agriculture in Western Oregon and Western Washington" (Ph.D. dissertation, University of Washington, 1970), 200; Morse, Notes of the History and Resources of Washington Territory, Book 22, The River Valleys, 33–34, 35; *West Shore* 15 (February 1889): 72; Duncan W. Thomas, *Changes in Columbia River Estuary Habitat Types over the Past Century* (Astoria, Ore.: Columbia River Estuary Study Taskforce, July 1983), 33; H. S. Lyman, "David Knight Warren Reminiscences," *Oregon Historical Quarterly* 3:3 (September 1902): 307; Peter G. Boag, *Environment and Experience: Settlement Culture in Nineteenth-Century Oregon* (Berkeley: University of California Press, 1992), 122–23; *West Shore* 9 (June 1883): p. 128, c. 1, and (March 1889): p. 148, c. 2.

30. John Minto, "From Youth to Age as an American," *Oregon Historical Quarterly* 9:2 (June 1908): 142.

31. A recent study concluded that estuary diking projects to increase agricultural land accounted for 90 percent of Oregon and Washington's habitat loss from settlement society to the 1930s (Marc E. Boule and Kenneth F. Bierly, "History of Estuarine Wetland Development and Alteration: What Have We Wrought?" *Northwest Environmental Journal* 3:1 [Winter 1987]: 55–56, 59–60); Eldridge Morse, Notes on the History and Resources of Washington Territory, Book 24, Bancroft Library, University of California, Berkeley, P-B 53, 40.

32. Thomas E. Dahl, *Wetland Losses in the United States 1780's to 1980's* (Washington, D.C.: U.S. Department of the Interior, Fish and Wildlife Service, 1990), 6; David D. Shively, "Landscape Change in the Tualatin Basin" (Unpublished paper, Department of Geosciences, Oregon State University, 1993), 15; Marc E. Boule, Nancy Olmsted, and Tina Miller, *Inventory of Wetland Resources and Evaluation of*

Wetland Management in Western Washington (Olympia: Washington State Department of Ecology, June 1983), 27, 29–33; Thomas, *Changes in Columbia River Estuary Habitat Types over the Past Century*, 10, 11, 22, 23–25, 33–35.

33. Morse, Notes of the History and Resources of Washington Territory, Book 22, The River Valleys, 13–15, 21–23, 26–28, 31; Olsen, "The Beginnings of Agriculture in Western Oregon and Western Washington," 199, 203–6.

34. Minto, "From Youth to Age as an American," 152.

35. Ibid., 131–32.

36. William G. Morris, "Forest Fires in Western Oregon and Western Washington," *Oregon Historical Quarterly* 35:4 (December 1934): 314; Peter Dominic Adrian Teensma, "Fire History and Fire Regimes of the Central Western Cascades of Oregon" (Ph.D. dissertation, University of Oregon, 1987), 45; Bob Zybach, "The Great Fires of the Oregon Coast Range: 1770–1933" (Unpublished paper, May 1, 1988), 1.

37. Jesse A. Applegate, *A Day with the Cow Column in 1843: Recollections of My Boyhood*, ed. Joseph Schafer (Chicago: Caxton Club, 1934), 137–38.

38. Joseph Henry Brown, "Settlement of Willammette [*sic*] Valley" (1878), Bancroft Library, University of California, Berkeley, P-A 10, 1–2; Deady, "History & Progress of Oregon After 1845," 70.

39. Jerry C. Towle, "Changing Geography of Willamette Valley Woodlands," *Oregon Historical Quarterly* 83:1 (Spring 1982): 71, 83–84; Carl L. Johannessen, William A. Davenport, Artimus Millet, and Steven McWilliams, "The Vegetation of the Willamette Valley," *Annals of the Association of American Geographers* 61:2 (June 1971): 296; Deady, "History & Progress of Oregon After 1845," 70.

40. Brown, "Settlement of Willammette [*sic*] Valley," 1–2.

41. David Lavender, ed., *The Oregon Journals of David Douglas; of His Travels and Adventures Among the Traders and Indians in the Columbia, Willamette, and Snake Regions During the Years 1825, 1826, and 1827*, 2 vols. (Ashland: Oregon Book Society, 1972), 2:130; "Letter to Dear Brother [H. G. Bristow] from E. L. Bristow, Pleasant Hill, Land Co, OT March 15th 1857," and "Letter to James J. Rogers from E. L. Bristow, Pleasant Hill, Lane Co OT May 4th 1857," in Elijah Lafayette Bristow, "The Letters of Elijah Lafayette Bristow Oregon Pioneer of 1848," typescript, Lane County Pioneer-Historical Society, Eugene, Ore., March 1961.

42. Interview with Jaspar N. Miller, who lived near Dallas, Oregon, by William E. Lawrence, August 2, 1918, William E. Lawrence, "Field Book #3" (Unpublished paper, Herbarium, Oregon State University, n.d.), 106; Wallis Nash, *Two Years in Oregon* (New York: D. Appleton and Company, 1882), 44; Isaac Smith to his brother and sisters, October 22, 1854, Butler-Smith Family Papers.

43. Luark Diary, Microfilm Roll 3, August 1, 1865.

44. *Oregonian*, April 8, 1888, p. 2, c. 3.

45. Luark Diary, Microfilm Roll 3, August 21, 1863; April 27, 1864; and May 28, 29, 1866; Stevens to his brother Levi, July 3, 1853, in Rockwood, ed., "Letters of Charles Stevens," 337.

46. Judson, *A Pioneer's Search for an Ideal Home*, 188.

47. Luark Diary, Microfilm Roll 3, February 3, July 27, 1864; *Oregonian*, February 2, 1888, p. 3, c. 1.

48. Luark Diary, Microfilm Roll 2, August 2, 1855; Luark Diary, Microfilm Roll 3, August 3, 1865, and June 27, 1866.

49. Frances Fuller Victor, *All over Oregon and Washington* (San Francisco: John H. Carmany and Company, 1872), 292, 57.

50. Camp, ed., *James Clyman, Frontiersman*, 115, 120; *West Shore* 9 (February 1882): p. 35, c. 2; 11 (April 1885): p. 106, c. 2, p. 113, c. 2.

51. Absolom B. Harden to his brothers and sisters, March 25, 1848, Absolom B. Harden folder, Letters, 1848, Oregon Historical Society, Portland, Mss 11, 7.

52. Reminiscences of Thomas Pier Hastie in Washington Territory, recorded at Mount Vernon, Washington, July 25, 1914, Meany Papers, box 73, folder 43, 8.

53. John B. Leiberg, "Cascade Range and Ashland Forest Reserves and Adjacent Regions," in U.S. Department of the Interior, *Twenty-First Annual Report of the United States Geological Survey to the Secretary of the Interior 1899–1900*, Part 5, Forest Reserves (Washington, D.C.: Government Printing Office, 1900), 279; O. B. Sperlin, ed., "Our First Official Horticulturist—Brackenridge's Journal of the Willamette Route to California, 1831," *Washington Historical Quarterly* 21:4 (October 1930): 300.

54. Zybach, "The Great Fires of the Oregon Coast Range: 1770–1933," 110; S. A. Clarke, *Pioneer Days of Oregon History*, 2 vols. (Cleveland: Arthur H. Clark Company, 1905), 1:92.

55. Overton Dowell, Jr., "Notes on Some of Our Vanishing Fur Animals," *Oregon Sportsman* 5 (January 1917): 15–16; H. D. Langille, "Northern Portion of Cascade Range Forest Reserve," in H. D. Langille, Fred G. Plummer, Arthur Dodwell, Theodore F. Rixon, and John B. Leiberg, *Forest Conditions in the Cascade Range Forest Reserve Oregon*, Professional Paper no. 9 (Washington, D.C.: Government Printing Office, 1903), 40; Fred G. Plummer, "Mount Rainier Forest Reserve, Washington," in U.S. Department of the Interior, *Twenty-First Annual Report of the United States Geological Survey to the Secretary of the Interior 1899–1900*, 134, 135, 141.

56. Fred G. Plummer, "Central Portion of Cascade Range Forest Reserve," in Langille et al., *Forest Conditions in the Cascade Range Forest Reserve Oregon*, 93; Stephen J. Pyne, *Fire in America: A Cultural History of Wildland and Rural Fire* (Princeton: Princeton University Press, 1982; paper 1988), 56, 334.

57. Richard White, *Land Use, Environment, and Social Change: The Shaping of Island County, Washington* (Seattle: University of Washington Press, 1980), 108.

58. Israel Cook Russell, "Glaciers of Mount Rainier," in U.S. Department of the Interior, *Eighteenth Annual Report of the United States Geological Survey to the Secretary of the Interior 1896–97*, Part 2, Papers Chiefly of a Theoretic Nature (Washington, D.C.: Government Printing Office, 1898), 411; James G. Swan, *The Northwest Coast; Or, Three Years' Residence in Washington Territory* (1857; reprint, Fairfield, Wash.: Ye Galleon Press, 1989), 134.

59. Morris, "Forest Fires in Western Oregon and Western Washington," 326–27, 330; Pyne, *Fire in America*, 335–36.

60. *Washington Standard*, September 26, 1868, p. 2, c. 2.

61. Ibid.

62. Morris, "Forest Fires in Western Oregon and Western Washington," 332–33.

63. Henry Gannett, "Introduction," in Langille et al., *Forest Conditions in the Cascade Range Forest Reserve Oregon*, 24; Arthur Dodwell and Theodore F. Rixon, "Forest Conditions in Olympic Forest Reserve, Washington," in Dodwell and Rixon, *Forest Conditions in the Olympic Forest Reserve, Washington*, Professional Paper no. 7 (Washington, D.C.: Government Printing Office, 1902), 14, 17; Plummer, "Mount Rainier Forest Reserve, Washington," 133.

64. Gannett, "Introduction," 24; Dodwell and Rixon, *Forest Conditions in the Olympic Forest Reserve, Washington*, 14; Langille, "Northern Portion of Cascade Range Forest Reserve," 35–36; Leiberg, "Cascade Range and Ashland Forest Reserves and Adjacent Regions," 284; Plummer, "Mount Rainier Forest Reserve, Washington," 134, 136.

65. Pyne, *Fire in America*, xiv, 27.

66. Larry D. Harris, *The Fragmented Forest: Island Biogeography Theory and the Preservation of Biotic Diversity* (Chicago: University of Chicago Press, 1984), 32.

67. Oscar Osburn Winther, *The Old Oregon Country: A History of Frontier Trade, Transportation, and Travel* (Lincoln: University of Nebraska Press, 1969), 157–70.

68. Carlos A. Schwantes, *The Pacific Northwest: An Interpretive History* (Lincoln: University of Nebraska Press, 1989), 150–51; Jerry A. O'Callaghan, *The Disposition of the Public Domain in Oregon* (Washington, D.C.: Government Printing Office, 1960), 50–59; Deady, "History & Progress of Oregon After 1845," 18; Winther, *The Old Oregon Country*, 123–34, 139–41, 146–48.

69. Gordon B. Dodds, *The American Northwest: A History of Oregon and Washington* (Arlington Heights, Ill.: Forum Press, 1986), 137–40; Winther, *The Old Oregon Country*, 293–300.

70. Dodds, *The American Northwest*, 114–18, 121–34, 141–42, 148–49; Schwantes, *The Pacific Northwest*, 185–91.

71. Schwantes, *The Pacific Northwest*, 191–99; Nash, *Two Years in Oregon*, 263.

CHAPTER SIX: SETTLER SOCIETY

1. Absolom B. Harden to his brothers and sisters, March 25, 1848, Absolom B. Harden folder, Letters, 1848, Oregon Historical Society, Portland, Mss 11, 7, 14; J. Orin Oliphant, ed., "Thomas S. Kendall's Letter on Oregon Agriculture, 1852," *Agricultural History* 9:4 (October 1935): 189; *David Newsom: The Western Observer 1805–1882* (Portland, Ore.: Glass–Dahlstrom Printers, 1972): 46, 182–83; Peter H. Burnett, "Documents," *Oregon Historical Quarterly* 3:4 (December 1902): 424–25.

2. Jesse Applegate, "Umpqua Agriculture, 1851," *Oregon Historical Quarterly* 32:2 (June 1931): 140; E. L. Bristow to his brother (Henry G. Bristow), March 18, 1862, in Elijah Lafayette Bristow, "The Letters of Elijah Lafayette Bristow, Oregon Pioneer of 1848," typescript, Lane County Pioneer-Historical Society, Eugene, Ore., March 1961, 1–2; Isaac Smith to his brother and sister, March 2, 1857, typescript, Butler-Smith Family Papers, Oregon Historical Society, Portland, Mss 2623, 1.

3. Charles Stevens to his brother Levi, January 24, 1853, in E. Ruth Rockwood, ed., "Letters of Charles Stevens," *Oregon Historical Quarterly* 37:3 (September 1936): 241; Charles Stevens to his sister Emma, June 10, 1853, in ibid., 259.

4. Silas Plimpton to Dexter Cummings Wright, July 24, 1853, in Helen Betsy Abbott, ed., "Life on the Lower Columbia, 1853–1866," *Oregon Historical Quarterly* 83:3 (Fall 1982): 255.

5. An undated letter (written sometime during the first decade of the twentieth century) to the editor of an unidentified newspaper by Judge Thomas Smith, in "Diary of Thomas Smith, 1870–1871," typed copy, Douglas County Museum of History and Natural History, Roseburg, Oregon, 808.883 Smi, 3.

6. Stevens to his brother Levi, January 24, 1853, 241; letter from Charles Stevens, December 3, 1854, in E. Ruth Rockwood, ed., "Letters of Charles Stevens," *Oregon Historical Quarterly* 38:1 (March 1937): 88; Luark Diary, Microfilm Roll 2, January 25, 1855, University of Washington Manuscripts and Archives Division, Seattle; George W. Riddle, *History of Early Days in Oregon* (Riddle, Ore.: reprinted from the *Riddle Enterprise*, 1920), 40.

7. Margaret Post to her dear sister (Mary Barlow), February 8, 1857, and Ezra Post to his dear friends (John L. and Mary Barlow), November 20, 1859, John L. Barlow Letters, Special Collections, Knight Library, University of Oregon, Eugene, A 265; letter from Charles Stevens, October 15, 1854, in Rockwood, ed., "Letters of Charles Stevens," 87.

8. Roselle Putnam to Mr. Francis Putnam, June 8, 1851, in Sheba Hargreaves, "Letters of Roselle Putnam," *Oregon Historical Quarterly* 29:3 (September 1928): 250–51.

9. *Oregon Statesman,* January 29, 1866, p. 3, c. 2.

10. *Pioneer and Democrat,* January 11, 1861, p. 1, c. 1; *Washington Standard,* October 21, 1865, p. 2, c. 3; Wallis Nash, *Two Years in Oregon* (New York: D. Appleton and Company, 1882), 63, 68.

11. Ezra Post to her old friend Dock (John L. Barlow), July 10, 1857, Barlow Letters; Luark Diary, Microfilm Roll 2, August 25, 1855; *West Shore* 11 (April 1885): p. 104, c. 2.

12. William Keil to his dear brothers and sisters in Christ, October 13, 1855, transcript, William Keil, Letters, 1855–1870, University of Washington Manuscripts and Archives Division, Seattle, vertical file 34, 24.

13. Mary Hayden, *Pioneer Days* (1915; reprint, Fairfield, Wash.: Ye Galleon Press, 1979), 38, 41; Charles Stevens to his dear brother and sister, May 28, 1853, in Rockwood, ed., "Letters of Charles Stevens," 255.

14. Silas Plimpton to Solomon Nickerson and Dexter Wright, July 20, 1855, in Abbott, ed., "Life on the Lower Columbia, 1853–1866," 259, 260.

15. Applegate, "Umpqua Agriculture, 1851," 140, 143–44.

16. Nash, *Two Years in Oregon,* 72; *West Shore* 11 (April 1885), p. 113, c. 1.

17. *Oregon Statesman,* July 26, 1853, p. 1, c. 3; July 3, 1852, p. 2, c. 7.

18. David A. Johnson, "Migration, Settlement, and the Political Culture of Oregon, 1840–1880" (Paper delivered at the Western Historical Association meeting, September 10, 1990), 1, 4–5, 14–19.

19. Rev. A. J. Wigle, "Overland Journey Account, 1852," typescript, Reminiscences (1898), Oregon Historical Society, Portland, Mss 587, 5; Roselle Putnam to her father and mother (in-laws), January 25, 1852, in Sheba Hargreaves, "The Letters of Roselle Putnam," *Oregon Historical Quarterly* 29:3 (September 1928): 254.

20. William Shaw, "Mississippi & Columbia River Valley Pioneer Life Compared" (1878), Bancroft Library, University of California, Berkeley, P-A 64, 6–7.

21. Isaac N. Ebey to his brother, April 25, 1851, transcription, Edmond S. Meany Papers, box 72, folder 43, University of Washington Manuscripts and Archives Division, Seattle, 106-70-12, 2–4; David Alan Johnson, *Founding the Far West: California, Oregon, and Nevada, 1840–1890* (Berkeley: University of California Press, 1992), 9, 139–40, 159–61, 174–75, 182–85; William L. Lang, "An Eden of Expectations: Oregon Settlers and the Environment They Created," *Oregon Humanities* (Winter 1992): 26, 28; *Oregon Statesman,* September 18, 1852, p. 2, c. 2; Joseph Henry Brown, "Settlement of Willammette [*sic*] Valley" (1878), Bancroft Library, University of California, Berkeley, P-A 10, 4.

22. Fred Lockley, "Oregon, My Oregon," *Pacific Monthly* 19 (June 1908): 678–79; *West Shore* 7 (August 1881): p. 220, c. 1.

23. Frances Fuller Victor, *All over Oregon and Washington* (San Francisco: John H. Carmany and Company, 1872), 185.

24. Johnson, "Migration, Settlement, and the Political Culture of Oregon, 1840–1880," 18.

25. Helen Betsy Abbott, ed., "Life on the Lower Columbia, 1853–1866, *Oregon Historical Quarterly* 83:3 (Fall 1982): 248–87; E. Ruth Rockwood, ed., "Letters of Charles Stevens," *Oregon Historical Quarterly* 37:3 (September 1936): 241–61; 37:4 (December 1936), 334–53; 38:1 (March 1937): 63–91; 38:2 (June 1937): 164–92; 38:3 (September 1937): 328–54; Jack H. Blok, "The Evolution of Agricultural Resource Use Strategies in the Willamette Valley" (Ph.D. dissertation, Oregon State University, 1973), 6–7, 11, 32, 70, 86, 192.

26. Eldridge Morse, Notes of the History and Resources of Washington Territory, Book 1, Settlement, Bancroft Library, University of California, Berkeley, P-B 30, 17, 20, 34–36; Carlos A. Schwantes, *The Pacific Northwest: An Interpretive History* (Lincoln: University of Nebraska Press, 1989), 185–91.

27. Luark Diary, Microfilm Roll 2, August 31 and September 6, 1855; Microfilm Roll 3, May 29, June 13, July 9, July 25, 1862; January 8, February 23, June 3, August 17, 22, 28, 1863; October 20, 1864; January 22, October 17, 1865; April 12, 1866; June 14, 1868.

28. Charles Stevens to his brother Levi and sister Emma, May 13, 1853, in Rockwood, ed., "Letters of Charles Stevens," 254.

29. *Oregon Statesman,* April 11, 1864, p. 2, c. 4; *Washington Pioneer,* December 10, 1853, p. 2, c. 1–2; *Pioneer and Democrat,* July 27, 1860, 2, c. 2; November 9, 1860, 2, c. 1.

30. *Columbian,* February 19, 1853, p. 1, c. 4.

31. *Oregon Statesman,* May 2, 1864, p. 2, c. 4.

32. Ibid., April 11, 1864, p. 2, c. 4.

33. Ibid., January 4, 1864, p. 2, c. 2; *West Shore* 1 (March 1876): p. 8, c. 2.

34. *Columbian,* February 19, 1853, p. 1, c. 4; *Washington Standard,* March 4, 1865, p. 2. c. 2; May 30, 1868, p. 2, c. 1; February 26, 1870, p. 1, c. 4; *Pioneer and Democrat,* October 3, 1856, p. 2, c. 3.

35. *Washington Standard,* September 24, 1870: p. 2, c. 2.

36. Ibid., January 20, 1872, p. 2, c. 1.

37. *Columbian,* February 19, 1853, p. 1, c. 4.

38. *Washington Standard,* September 17, 1880, p. 1, c. 5.

39. Ibid., January 2, 1885, p. 2, c. 1; *West Shore* 11 (April 1885): p. 104, c. 2.

40. H. S. Lyman, "David Knight Warren Reminiscences," *Oregon Historical Quarterly* 3:3 (September 1902): 307; Michael Leon Olsen, "The Beginnings of Agriculture in Western Oregon and Western Washington" (Ph.D. dissertation, University of Washington, 1970), 54.

41. The fullest discussion of the bills is in James Ronald Warren, "A Study of the Congressional Debates Concerning the Oregon Question" (Ph.D. dissertation, University of Washington, 1962).

42. William A. Bowen, *The Willamette Valley: Migration and Settlement on the Oregon Frontier* (Seattle: University of Washington Press, 1978), 69–71.

43. Harlow Zinser Head, "The Oregon Donation Claims and Their Patterns" (Ph.D. dissertation, University of Oregon, 1971), 19–26; Jerry A. O'Callaghan, *The Disposition of the Public Domain in Oregon* (Washington, D.C.: Government Printing Office, 1960), 32, 34.

44. O'Callaghan, *The Disposition of the Public Domain in Oregon,* 32, 37–41, 49, 61, 63, 66–67, 97.

45. Ibid., 33.

46. Peter Boag notes that settler land claims in the Calapooia Valley between 1846 and the Oregon Donation Land Act used natural markers before the latter imposed cadastral survey lines. Boag uses this fact to support his general argument that early Calapooia Valley settlers lived in intimacy and understanding with the land (Peter G. Boag, *Environment and Experience: Settlement Culture in Nineteenth Century Oregon* [Berkeley: University of California Press, 1992], 52–56, 116–20).

47. *Oregon Statesman,* March 19, 1866, p. 3, c. 1; *West Shore* 15 (February 1889): 73.

48. Harden to his brothers and sisters, March 25, 1848, Harden folder, 12; Victor, *All over Oregon and Washington,* 184–85.

49. Smith to his brother and sisters, October 22, 1854, typescript, Butler-Smith Family Papers, 1.

50. Lydia Plimpton to Nathaniel and Judith Wright, August 24, 1853, in Abbott, "Life on the Lower Columbia, 1853–1866," 257.

51. Victor, *All over Oregon and Washington,* 185–86; "Letter to S. P. Williams [Samuel Porter Williams of Lima, Indiana] from Dr. Thomas White, Butteville, Marion County O.T. April 19th 1853," in Oscar O. Winter and Gayle Thornbrough, eds., *To Oregon in 1852: Letter of Dr. Thomas White La Grange County, Indiana, Emigrant* (Indianapolis: Indiana Historical Society, 1964), 24; Nathaniel Coe to N. H. Fordyce, August 7, 1853, transcription, Coe Family Papers, box 1, folder 5, Oregon Historical Society, Portland, Mss 431, 2.

52. Applegate, "Umpqua Agriculture, 1851," 138.

53. Victor, *All over Oregon and Washington,* 195, 196.

54. "Report of Lieutenant Neil M. Howison on Oregon, 1846," *Oregon Historical Quarterly* 14:1 (March 1913): 51; *Oregon Statesman,* March 19, 1866, p. 3, c. 1; *West Shore* 2 (January 1877): p. 84, c. 1–2; Boag, *Environment and Experience,* 121; Luark Diary, Microfilm Roll 5, December 31, 1890.

55. E. Ingersoll, "In the Wahlamet Valley Oregon," *Harper's New Monthly Magazine* 65:389 (October 1882): 766.

56. Blok, "The Evolution of Agricultural Resource Use Strategies in the Willamette Valley," 76, 78; *Oregonian,* January 2, 1888, p. 3, c. 3.

57. *Oregonian,* January 8, 1888, p. 1, c. 1.

58. Boag, *Environment and Experience,* 115.

59. Blok, "The Evolution of Agricultural Resource Use Strategies in the Willamette Valley," 192.

60. *West Shore* 6 (December 1880): p. 314, c. 2; 11 (April 1885): pp. 104–5.

61. H. S. Lyman, "An Oregon Literature," *Oregon Historical Quarterly* 2:4 (December 1901): 402.

62. Johnson, *Founding the Far West,* 350; Lancaster Pollard, "The Pacific Northwest," in Merrill Jensen, ed., *Regionalism in America* (Madison: University of Wisconsin Press, 1954), 196.

63. Harvey W. Scott, "The Pioneer Character of Oregon Progress," *Oregon Historical Quarterly* 18:4 (December 1917): 261–62.

64. Ibid., 261.

65. John Waldo, "Third Camp, Eagle Creek, Sunday Evening, July 26 [1891]," in Gerald W. Williams, ed., *Judge John Breckenridge Waldo: Diaries and Letters from the High Cascades of Oregon 1880–1907* (U.S. Department of Agriculture, Forest Service, Pacific Northwest Region, Umpqua National Forest, April 1989), 117.

66. While the population in Oregon increased nearly 80 percent (79.5 percent) between 1880 and 1890, growing from 174,768 to 313,767, Washington's population grew by almost 400 percent (365.1 percent), skyrocketing from 75,116 to 149,390 (Schwantes, *The Pacific Northwest,* 185).

67. Lyman, "An Oregon Literature," 402.

68. Robert E. Ficken and Charles P. LeWarne, *Washington: A Centennial History* (Seattle: University of Washington Press, 1988), 33.

69. Scott, "The Pioneer Character of Oregon Progress," 264; Luark Diary, Microfilm Roll 5, July 4, 1899.

CHAPTER SEVEN: LIVING ON THE LAND

1. Jesse Applegate, "Umpqua Agriculture, 1851," *Oregon Historical Quarterly* 32:2 (June 1931): 142; Absolom B. Harden to his brothers and sisters, March 25, 1848, Absolom B. Harden folder, Letters, 1848, Oregon Historical Society, Portland, Mss

11, 6, 7, 13; letter from Mrs. A. M. James, November 14, 1852, transcript, Edmond S. Meany Papers, box 74, folder 6, University of Washington Manuscripts and Archives Division, Seattle, 106-70-12, 2; J. Orin Oliphant, ed., "Thomas S. Kendall's Letter on Oregon Agriculture, 1852," *Agricultural History* 9:4 (October 1935): 193, 194.

2. Michael Leon Olsen, "The Beginnings of Agriculture in Western Oregon and Western Washington" (Ph.D. dissertation, University of Washington, 1970), 155.

3. Jack H. Blok, "The Evolution of Agricultural Resource Use Strategies in the Willamette Valley" (Ph.D. dissertation, Oregon State University, 1973), 67, 70, 72; Ezra Meeker, *The Busy Life of Eighty Years* (Seattle: Ezra Meeker, 1916), 225–26; Eldridge Morse, Notes of the History and Resources of Washington Territory, Book 22, The River Valleys, Bancroft Library, University of California, Berkeley, P-B 51, 36–37; *West Shore* 6 (December 1880): p. 314, c. 2; 11 (April 1885): p. 102, c. 2, p. 103, c. 1.

4. Stephen Dow Beckham, *Land of the Umpqua: A History of Douglas County, Oregon* (Roseburg, Ore.: Douglas County Commissioners, 1986), 212–13; Meeker, *The Busy Life of Eighty Years*, 227–28.

5. Harden to his brothers and sisters, March 25, 1848, Harden folder, 6, 13; Rev. Gustavus Hines, *Life on the Plains of the Pacific. Oregon* (New York: C. M. Saxton, 1859), 342.

6. Arthur L. Throckmorton, *Oregon Argonauts: Merchant Adventurers on the Western Frontier* (Portland: Oregon Historical Society, 1961), 94–95, 98, 123, 207, 256; Peter G. Boag, *Environment and Experience: Settlement Culture in Nineteenth-Century Oregon* (Berkeley: University of California Press, 1992), 115.

7. Boag, *Environment and Experience*, 115; Blok, "The Evolution of Agricultural Resource Use Strategies in the Willamette Valley," 75; Olsen, "The Beginnings of Agriculture in Western Oregon and Western Washington," 154–55; Wallis Nash, *Two Years in Oregon* (New York: D. Appleton and Company, 1882), 35.

8. John T. Whistler and John H. Lewis, *Rogue River Valley Project and Willamette Valley Investigations Irrigation and Drainage* (Washington, D.C.: Department of the Interior, U.S. Reclamation Service, February 1916), 19; Ira A. Williams, "The Drainage of Farm Lands in the Willamette and Tributary Valleys of Oregon," *Mineral Resources of Oregon* 1:4 (June 1914): 25–26; *David Newsom: The Western Observer, 1805–1882* (Portland, Ore.: Glass-Dahlstrom Printers, 1972), 169; Frances Fuller Victor, *All over Oregon and Washington* (San Francisco: John H. Carmany and Company, 1872), 204; *Washington Standard*, September 17, 1880, p. 1, c. 4.

9. Blok, "The Evolution of Agricultural Resource Use Strategies in the Willamette Valley," 81; Nash, *Two Years in Oregon*, 100–101.

10. Jerry Charles Towle, "Woodland in the Willamette Valley: An Historical Geography" (Ph.D. dissertation, University of Oregon, 1974), 100.

11. "Life in Douglas County in 1858," *Umpqua Trapper* 1:2 (Summer Hunt 1965): 17; Luark Diary, Microfilm Rolls 2 and 3, University of Washington Manuscripts and Archives Division, Seattle; "Diary of Thomas Smith, 1870–1871," typescript, Douglas County Museum of History and Natural History, Roseburg, Oregon, 808.883 Smi; "Diary of William Thiel of Oregon," *Umpqua Trapper* 12:4 (Winter Hunt 1976): 83–96; 13:1 (Spring Hunt 1977): 17–23; 13:2 (Summer Hunt 1977): 30–48.

12. Margaret B. Smith to her brother and sister, February 8, 1854, typescript, 1; Isaac Smith to his brother and sisters, October 22, 1854, typescript, 2; Smith to his brother and sister, September 8, 1858, typescript, 1, all in Butler-Smith Family Papers, Oregon Historical Society, Portland, Mss 2623.

13. James R. Habeck, "The Original Vegetation of the Mid-Willamette Valley, Oregon," *Northwest Science* 35:2 (May 1961): 66.

14. Luark Diary, Microfilm Roll 2, May 15 and June 29, 1855; Microfilm Roll 3, February 25, 1865; Harden to his brothers and sisters, March 25, 1848, Harden folder, 7; Daniel Waldo, "Critiques" (1878), Bancroft Library, University of California, Berkeley, P-A 74, 11.

15. Towle, "Woodland in the Willamette Valley," 88.

16. Harden to his brothers and sisters, March 25, 1848, Harden folder, 7.

17. *Washington Standard*, November 17, 1860, p. 4, c. 1.

18. *Oregon Statesman*, February 24, 1862, p. 2, c. 7.

19. Victor, *All over Oregon and Washington*, 184.

20. Matthew P. Deady, "History & Progress of Oregon After 1845" (1878), Bancroft Library, University of California, Berkeley, P-A 24, 5, 23–24, 38; Dorothy O. Johansen and Charles M. Gates, *Empire of the Columbia: A History of the Pacific Northwest* (New York: Harper and Row, 1957), 321–22; Olsen, "The Beginnings of Agriculture in Western Oregon and Western Washington," 117–18, 120–21.

21. Isaac Smith to his brother and sisters, March 28, 1858, typescript, Butler-Smith Family Papers, 1; Olsen, "The Beginnings of Agriculture in Western Oregon and Western Washington," 119; interview with E. C. Roberts of Albany, Oregon, by William E. Lawrence, July 18, 1918, in William E. Lawrence, "Field Book #3" (Unpublished paper, Herbarium, Oregon State University, n.d.), 64; Habeck, "The Original Vegetation of the Mid-Willamette Valley, Oregon," 66.

22. Isaac Smith to his brother and sisters, September 6, 1857, typescript, Butler-Smith Family Papers.

23. See Wilson Blain to David R. Kerr, Autumn, 1850, typescript, 2; Blain to Kerr, March 5, 1851, typescript, 47; Blain to Gray, July, 1851, typescript, 61, all in Wilson Blain folder, Letters, 1848–1852, Oregon Historical Society, Portland, Mss 1035; Charles L. Camp, ed., *James Clyman, Frontiersman* (Portland, Ore.: Champoeg Press, 1960), 143, 144, 152, 157, 158.

24. *Washington Standard*, November 17, 1860, p. 4, c. 1.

25. Smith to his brother and sisters, March 28, 1858, typescript, Butler-Smith Family Papers; *Washington Standard*, November 17, 1860, p. 4, c. 1.

26. Habeck, "The Original Vegetation of the Mid-Willamette Valley, Oregon," 76; Morton E. Peck, "Invasion of Exotic Plants and Their Economic Significance in Oregon," *Northwest Science* 22:3 (August 1948): 128.

27. Victor, *All over Oregon and Washington*, 196.

28. Olsen, "The Beginnings of Agriculture in Western Oregon and Western Washington," 119, 124–25, 164.

29. Blok, "The Evolution of Agricultural Resource Use Strategies in the Willamette Valley," 76; Boag, *Environment and Experience*, 109.

30. Helmut K. Buechner, "Some Biotic Changes in the State of Washington, Particularly During the Century 1853–1953," *Research Studies of the State College of Washington* 21:2 (June 1953): 170; Peck, "Invasion of Exotic Plants and Their Economic Significance in Oregon," 129; Lawrence interview with E. C. Roberts, July 18, 1918, in Lawrence, "Field Book #3," 66.

31. Washington (State), *Code*, chap. 163, sec. 2238 (1881), 386.

32. Oregon, *General Laws* (1899), 15–17.

33. *Washington Standard*, May 20, 1892, p. 1, c. 8.

34. *Oregonian*, May 4, 1888, p. 4, c. 2.

35. Terence Emmons, ed., "Documents: Hadley Hobson, Marion County Pioneer," *Oregon Historical Quarterly* 93:1 (Spring 1992): 67.

36. Camp, ed., *James Clyman, Frontiersman*, 123.

37. Ibid., 136–37; Luark Diary, Microfilm Roll 3, May 14, 1864; Anne Suther-

lin Waite, "Pioneer Life of Fendel Sutherlin," *Oregon Historical Quarterly* 31 (December 1930): 375–76; Luark Diary, Microfilm Roll 2, August 3, 1855.

38. Buechner, "Some Biotic Changes in the State of Washington," 185; A. C. Little, *State of Washington. Tenth and Eleventh Annual Reports of the State Fish Commissioner to the Governor of the State of Washington* (Olympia, Wash.: Gwin Hicks, State Printer, 1901), 18, 19.

39. *Washington Standard*, March 16, 1883, p. 2, c. 2; Little, *State of Washington. Tenth and Eleventh Annual Reports of the State Fish Commissioner*, 18.

40. *Oregonian*, November 1888, p. 4, c. 3.

41. George W. Riddle, *History of Early Days in Oregon* (Riddle, Ore.: reprinted from the *Riddle Enterprise*, 1920), 54; John Minto, "From Youth to Age as an American," *Oregon Historical Quarterly* 9:2 (June 1908): 152–53.

42. Towle, "Woodland in the Willamette Valley," 91.

43. David D. Shively, "Landscape Change in the Tualatin Basin" (Unpublished paper, Department of Geosciences, Oregon State University, 1993), 11; *Washington Standard*, January 4, 1862, p. 2, c. 2.

44. *Oregonian*, January 30, 1889, p. 1, c. 6, and January 16, 1889, p. 4, c. 1.

45. H. D. Langille, "Northern Portion of Cascade Range Forest Reserve," in H. D. Langille, Fred G. Plummer, Arthur Dodwell, Theodore F. Rixon, and John B. Leiberg, *Forest Conditions in the Cascade Range Forest Reserve Oregon*, Professional Paper no. 9 (Washington, D.C.: Government Printing Office, 1903), 38, 40; Fred G. Plummer, "Mount Rainier Forest Reserve, Washington," in U.S. Department of the Interior, *Twenty-First Annual Report of the United States Geological Survey to the Secretary of the Interior 1899–1900*, Part 5, Forest Reserves (Washington, D.C.: Government Printing Office, 1900), 135, 141.

46. John Waldo, "Crane Prairie, August 9, 1886," in Gerald W. Williams, ed., *Judge John Breckenridge Waldo: Diaries and Letters from the High Cascades of Oregon 1880–1907* (Roseburg, Ore.: U.S. Department of Agriculture, Forest Service, Pacific Northwest Region, Umpqua National Forest, April 1989), 51.

47. Langille, "Northern Portion of Cascade Range Forest Reserve," 39.

48. John Waldo, "Rigdon's Station, Sunday Afternoon, August 23, 1896," in Williams, ed., *Judge John Breckenridge Waldo*, 220–21.

49. Fred G. Plummer, "Central Portion of Cascade Range Forest Reserve," in Langille et al., *Forest Conditions*, 124.

50. Arthur Dodwell and Theodore F. Rixon, "Cascade Range Forest Reserve, Between Townships 18 and 29 South," in Langille et al., *Forest Conditions*, 155.

51. Buechner, "Some Biotic Changes in the State of Washington," 172–75.

52. "Report of Lieutenant Neil M. Howison on Oregon, 1846," *Oregon Historical Quarterly* 14:1 (March 1913): 49; Peter Burnett, *Recollections and Opinions of an Old Pioneer* (New York: D. Appleton and Company, 1880), 174–75.

53. Buechner, "Some Biotic Changes in the State of Washington," 180; Roselle Putnam to her father and mother (in-laws), January 25, 1852, in Sheba Hargreaves, "The Letters of Roselle Putnam," *Oregon Historical Quarterly* 29:3 (September 1928): 255; *West Shore* 2 (January 1877): p. 85, c. 1; 8 (January 1882): p. 2, c. 1; Larry Maring Rymon, "A Critical Analysis of Wildlife Conservation in Oregon" (Ph.D. dissertation, Oregon State University, 1969), 92–94; F. E. Ames, "Siskiyou National Forest Report, July 1908, Section IX—Protection," box 3, folder, Siskiyou National Forest 1908, Records of the Forest Service, Record Group 95, National Archives, Pacific Northwest Region, Seattle, Washington, 2; A. C. Little, *State of Washington. Ninth Annual Report of the State Fish Commissioner to the Governor of the State of Washington* (Olympia, Wash.: Gwin Hicks, State Printer, 1898), 80.

54. Nash, *Two Years in Oregon*, 32, 92–94; Buechner, "Some Biotic Changes in the State of Washington," 177; "Report of Lieutenant Neil M. Howison on Oregon, 1846," 49; A. H. Morgan to the Oregon Alpine Club, January 29, 1890, Associations, Institutions, etc. Misc., Oregon Alpine Club, Oregon Historical Society, Portland, Mss 1511, 1; Waite, "Pioneer Life of Fendel Sutherlin," 375.

55. Phoebe Goodell Judson, *A Pioneer's Search for an Ideal Home*, ed. John M. McClelland, Jr. (Tacoma: Washington State Historical Society, 1966), 91.

56. Minto, "From Youth to Age as an American," 133–34.

57. Luark Diary, Microfilm Roll 3, April 20, 21, July 31, 1864; April 13, 1866; William V. Wells, "Wild Life in Oregon," *Harper's New Monthly Magazine* 13:77 (October 1856): 602.

58. Washington (State), *General Laws* (1884), 100.

59. Minto, "From Youth to Age as an American," 150; Putnam to her father and mother (in-laws), January 25, 1852, in Hargreaves, "Letters of Roselle Putnam," 256; Daniel Waldo, "Critiques," 11.

60. T. T. Geer, "Incidents in the Organization of the Provisional Government," *Oregon Historical Quarterly* 2:4 (December 1901): 368; Washington, *General Laws* (1862), 494–95; (1871), 62; (1877), 325; (1879), 141–42; (1885–1886), 112; Jno. L. Riseland, *State of Washington. Sixteenth and Seventeenth Annual Reports of the State Fish Commissioner and Game Warden to the Governor of the State of Washington* (Olympia, Wash.: C. W. Corham, Public Printer, 1907), 70; *Oregon Sportsman* 1 (October 1913): 6; 2 (May 1914): 10.

61. Geer, "Incidents in the Organization of the Provisional Government," 369.

62. Daniel Waldo, "Critiques," 11.

63. Rymon, "A Critical Analysis of Wildlife Conservation in Oregon," 269–74.

64. Luark Diary, Microfilm Roll 3, April 12, July 31, 1864.

65. *Oregonian*, January 13, 1889, p. 1, c. 5.

66. Rymon, "A Critical Analysis of Wildlife Conservation in Oregon," 270–72, 273–74, 277–79, 283–85.

67. Ibid., 311–12.

68. John Minto to John Gill, October 26, 1910, John Minto, Papers, box 1, folder 3, Oregon Historical Society, Portland, Mss 752, 1.

69. J. R. Metzger, "Wild Game as It Used to Be," *Oregon Sportsman* 3 (October 1915): 188.

70. Ibid.

71. *Oregon Statesman*, February 26, 1866, p. 3, c. 1; *Oregonian*, October 20, 1888, p. 3, c. 4; Rymon, "A Critical Analysis of Wildlife Conservation in Oregon," 104; John Mortimer Murphy, *Sporting Adventures in the Far West* (London: Sampson Low, Marston, Searle, and Rivington, 1879), 277, 290.

72. George B. Abdill, "The Hide Hunters," *Umpqua Trapper* 4:1 (Spring Hunt 1968): 9.

73. John E. Bennett, "Hunting in Southern Oregon," *Overland Monthly* 30:176 (August 1897): 150.

74. *Oregon Statesman*, September 29, 1862, p. 2, c. 4; *Oregon Spectator*, December 18, 1865, p. 2, c. 5; Oregon, *General Laws* (1872), 25–28; *Washington Standard*, May 13, 1865, p. 1, c. 6, and March 22, 1873, p. 2, c. 4; *Oregonian*, January 13, 1889, p. 1, c. 5; F. Berkes, D. Feeny, B. J. McCay, and J. M. Acheson, "The Benefits of the Commons," *Nature* 340 (July 13, 1989): 91; Washington (State), *General Laws* (1884), 100; Rymon, "A Critical Analysis of Wildlife Conservation in Oregon," 114, 117, 122–23, 158; Oregon, *General Laws* (1905), chap. 204, 336–38.

75. Albert E. Cowdrey, *This Land, This South: An Environmental History* (Lexington: University of Kentucky Press, 1983), 50; Morgan Sherwood, *Big Game in*

Alaska: A History of Wildlife and People (New Haven: Yale University Press, 1981), 18–19; *Oregon Sportsman* 2 (September 1914): 1; Abdill, "The Hide Hunters,"12; Oregon, *Third and Fourth Annual Reports of the Game and Forestry Warden to the Governor of Oregon for the Years 1901 and 1902* (Salem, Ore.: J. R. Whitney, State Printer, 1903), 3; *Oregon Sportsman* 5 (July 1917): 229–30; Ames, "Siskiyou National Forest Report, July 1908," 2; Little, *State of Washington. Tenth and Eleventh Annual Reports of the State Fish Commissioner,* 116; Deputy Supervisor P. T. Harris, "Supervisor's Inspection Report, February 29, 1912," box 3, folder, Rainier National Forest, 1912, Records of the Forest Service, Record Group 95, National Archives, Pacific Northwest Region, Seattle, Washington, 2; Forest Inspector I. A. Macrum to Commissioner General of the Land Office, October 28, 1901, box 1, 1901 folder, Cascade Forest Reserve, Records of the Forest Service, Record Group 95, National Archives, Pacific Northwest Region, Seattle, Washington, 5.

76. Rymon, "A Critical Analysis of Wildlife Conservation in Oregon," 112–14, 125–26, 155.

77. Little, *State of Washington. Tenth and Eleventh Annual Reports of the State Fish Commissioner,* 123; Riseland, *State of Washington. Sixteenth and Seventeenth Annual Reports of the State Fish Commissioner,* 70; *Oregon Sportsman* 5 (April 1917): 104; 5 (July 1917): 230.

78. Rymon, "A Critical Analysis of Wildlife Conservation in Oregon," 115, 118, 125, 158–59; Little, *State of Washington. Tenth and Eleventh Annual Reports of the State Fish Commissioner,* 126; T. R. Kershaw, *State of Washington. Thirteenth Annual Report of the State Fish Commissioner to the Governor of the State of Washington* (Seattle: Metropolitan Press, 1902), 27–28; Riseland, *State of Washington. Sixteenth and Seventeenth Annual Reports of the State Fish Commissioner,* 74.

79. Jno. L. Riseland, *State of Washington. Twenty-Second and Twenty-Third Annual Reports of the State Fish Commissioner and Ex-Officio Game Warden to the Governor of the State of Washington* (Olympia, Wash.: Frank M. Lamborn, Public Printer, 1913), 120.

80. *Oregon Sportsman* 5 (July 1917): 230.

81. Rymon, "A Critical Analysis of Wildlife Conservation in Oregon," 254.

82. Ibid., 120.

83. Thomas R. Dunlap, *Saving America's Wildlife: Ecology and the American Mind, 1850–1990* (Princeton: Princeton University Press, 1988), 65–70; Buechner, "Some Biotic Changes in the State of Washington," 180–81.

84. Oregon, *General Laws* (1899), 1.

85. Buechner, "Some Biotic Changes in the State of Washington," 154.

CHAPTER EIGHT: SETTLER SOCIETY AND THE FORESTS

1. See Douglas Cole, "Early Artistic Perceptions of the British Columbia Forest," *Journal of Forest History* 18:4 (October 1974): 128–31.

2. J. G. Cooper, "Report on the Botany of the Route," in *Reports of Explorations and Surveys to Ascertain the Most Practicable and Economical Route for a Railroad from the Mississippi River to the Pacific Ocean, 1853–5,* vol. 12, bk. 2, pt. 2, Botanical Report (Washington, D.C.: Thomas H. Ford, 1860), 21, 23, 32, 39; William Fraser Tolmie, *The Journals of William Fraser Tolmie, Physician and Fur Trader* (Vancouver: Mitchell Press, 1963), 166–67, 169, 181, 193, 201.

3. Frederick Merk, ed., *Fur Trade and Empire: George Simpson's Journal* (Cambridge, Mass.: Harvard University Press, 1931), 62, 261; Roselle Putnam to Mr. Francis Putnam (brother-in-law), June 8, 1851, and Roselle Putnam to her mother and

sister (in-laws), February 9, 1852, in Sheba Hargreaves, "The Letters of Roselle Putnam," *Oregon Historical Quarterly* 29:3 (September 1928): 250, 259.

4. James R. Gibson, *Otter Skins, Boston Ships, and China Goods: The Maritime Fur Trade of the Northwest Coast, 1785–1841* (Seattle: University of Washington Press, 1992), 242; W. Kaye Lamb, "Early Lumbering on Vancouver Island: Part I, 1844–1855," *British Columbia Historical Quarterly* 2:1 (January 1938): 31–32.

5. John McLoughlin to the governor, deputy governor, and committee of the Hudsons Bay Company, October 31, 1837, in E. E. Rich, ed., *The Letters of John McLoughlin from Fort Vancouver to the Governor and Committee. First Series, 1825–38* (London: Champlain Society for the Hudson's Bay Record Society, 1941), 206.

6. Howard J. Burnham, "Hudson Bay Co. Sawmill," typescript, Oregon Historical Society, Portland, Mss 505, 1; James Douglas to the governor, deputy governor, and committee of the Hudsons Bay Company, October 18, 1838, 259–60; James Douglas to George Simpson, March 18, 1838, 285; John McLoughlin to George Simpson, March 16, 1831, 226, all in Rich, ed., *The Letters of John McLoughlin;* "Part of Dispatch from George Simpson Esqr. Governor of Ruperts Land to the Governor & Committee of the Hudson's Bay Company London, March 1, 1829," in E. E. Rich, ed., *Simpson's 1828 Journey to the Columbia* (London: Champlain Society for the Hudson's Bay Record Society, 1947), 84; "Slacum's Report on Oregon, 1836–7," *Oregon Historical Quarterly* 13:2 (June 1912): 185.

7. Kenneth A. Erickson, "The Morphology of Lumber Settlements in Western Oregon and Washington" (Ph.D. dissertation, University of California, Berkeley, 1965), 110–11; Absolom B. Harden to his brothers and sisters, March 25, 1848, Absolom B. Harden folder, Letters, 1848, Oregon Historical Society, Portland, Mss 11, 3.

8. Peter H. Burnett, "Documents," *Oregon Historical Quarterly* 3:4 (December 1902): 426; Mrs. Charlotte Moffett Cartwright, "Glimpses of Early Days in Oregon," *Oregon Historical Quarterly* 4:1 (March 1903): 60; James R. Gibson, *Farming the Frontier: The Agricultural Opening of the Oregon Country, 1786–1845* (Seattle: University of Washington Press, 1985), 93; Harold Karl Steen, "Forestry in Washington to 1925" (Ph.D. dissertation, University of Washington, 1969), 57.

9. Letter to George H. Himes from John Minto, Salem, Oregon, December 2, 1910, John Minto, Papers, box 1, folder 4, 1–3; John Minto, "Canoeing on the Columbia" (n.d.), John Minto, Papers, box 2, folder 6, Memoirs, Beginning Life in Oregon, 1–3; and John Minto, "Chapter II," John Minto, Papers, box 2, folder 8, Memoirs, Middle Life in Oregon, all in Oregon Historical Society, Portland, Mss 752.

10. "Report of Lieutenant Neil M. Howison on Oregon, 1846," *Oregon Historical Society* 14:1 (March 1913): 39.

11. Erickson, "The Morphology of Lumber Settlements in Western Oregon and Washington," 111.

12. *Oregon Spectator*, July 23, 1846, p. 2, c. 3.

13. H. S. Lyman, "David Knight Warren Reminiscences," *Oregon Historical Quarterly* 3:3 (September 1902): 302–3; Lyman, "Reminisances of Clement Adams Bradbury, 1846," *Oregon Historical Review* 2:3 (September 1901): 315–16; John Minto, "From Youth to Age as an American," *Oregon Historical Quarterly* 9:2 (June 1908): 127; "Thomas Smith," in *Transactions of the Eighteenth Annual Reunion of the Oregon Pioneer Association for 1890* (Portland, Ore.: A. Anderson and Company, 1892), 77–78.

14. *Oregon Spectator*, April 20, 1848, p. 2, c. 4.

15. Peter H. Burnett, "Documents," *Oregon Historical Quarterly* 3:4 (December 1902): 425.

16. *Oregon Spectator*, April 20, 1848, p. 2, c. 4.

17. Joseph Henry Brown, "Settlement of Willammette [*sic*] Valley" (1878), Ban-

croft Library, University of California, Berkeley, P-A 10, 9; Matthew P. Deady, "History & Progress of Oregon After 1845" (1878), Bancroft Library, University of California, Berkeley, P-A 24, 5; Arthur D. Howden Smith, ed., *The Narrative of Samuel Hancock, 1845–1860* (New York: Robert M. McBride and Company, 1927), 60; Lyman, "Reminisances of Clement Adams Bradbury, 1846," 316; John Minto to George H. Himes, December 2, 1910, John Minto, Papers, box 1, folder 4, 2.

18. Brown, "Settlement of Willammette [sic] Valley," 8–9; *Oregon Statesman,* July 3, 1852, p. 2, c. 7; Deady, "History & Progress of Oregon After 1845," 38; Harden to his brothers and sisters, March 25, 1848, Harden folder, 3; Silas Plimpton to Dexter Cummings Wright, July 24, 1853, in Helen Betsy Abbott, ed., "Life on the Lower Columbia, 1853–1866," *Oregon Historical Quarterly* 83:3 (Fall 1982): 254–55; Charles Stevens to his mother, November 9, 1852, in E. Ruth Rockwood, ed., "Letters of Charles Stevens," *Oregon Historical Quarterly* 37:2 (June 1936): 150; "Letter to S. P. Williams [Samuel Porter Williams of Lima, Indiana] from Dr. Thomas White, Butteville, Marion County O.T. April 19th 1853," in Oscar O. Winter and Gayle Thornbrough, eds., *To Oregon in 1852: Letter of Dr. Thomas White La Grange County, Indiana, Emigrant* (Indianapolis: Indiana Historical Society, 1964), 27.

19. Smith, ed., *The Narrative of Samuel Hancock, 1845–1860,* 92–93; Arthur L. Throckmorton, *Oregon Argonauts: Merchant Adventurers on the Western Frontier* (Portland: Oregon Historical Society, 1961), 85–180; Eban Weld to Martin Weld, February 20, 1852, photostatic copy, Martin Weld, Letters, 1850–1858, University of Washington Manuscripts and Archives Division, Seattle, vertical file 417, 2; A. J. Wigle, "Overland Journey Account, 1852," typescript, Reminiscences (1898), Oregon Historical Society, Portland, Mss 587, 5; Jesse Applegate, "Umpqua Agriculture, 1851," *Oregon Historical Quarterly* 32:2 (June 1931): 137; Deady, "History & Progress of Oregon After 1845," 5, 23–24; Eban Weld to Martin Weld, February 16, 1851, photostatic copy, Martin Weld, Letters, 4; Harvey W. Scott, "The Pioneer Character of Oregon Progress," *Oregon Historical Quarterly* 18:4 (December 1917): 248, 251.

20. *Oregon Spectator,* March 13, 1851, p. 2, c. 1; October 21, 1851, p. 2, c. 1; Captain Lewis Love's memoir, dictated in 1899, Lewis Love, Oregon Historical Society, Portland, Mss 1509, 1; Deady, "History & Progress of Oregon After 1845," 15; Patricia Marchak, *Green Gold: The Forest Industry in British Columbia* (Vancouver: University of British Columbia Press, 1983); Weld to Weld, February 16, 1851, photostatic copy, and Eban Weld to Martin Weld, December 2, 1852, photostatic copy, Martin Weld, Letters, 4, 3.

21. *Oregon Spectator,* December 27, 1849, p. 2, c. 2, and January 10, 1850, p. 2, c. 3; Isom Cranfill, Book, Oregon Historical Society, Portland, Mss 1416, 50–62; Fred Lockley folder, Edmond S. Meany Papers, box 74, folder 45, University of Washington Manuscripts and Archives Division, Seattle, 106-70-12.

22. *Oregon Spectator,* January 13, 1852, p. 2, c. 2; *Washington Standard,* November 9, 1878, p. 1, c. 4; *Puget Sound Weekly Courier,* January 23, 1880, p. 1, c. 3, 4.

23. Michael Luark Diary, Microfilm Roll 4, October 16, 1883, University of Washington Manuscripts and Archives Division, Seattle; Eldridge Morse, Notes on the History and Resources of Washington Territory, Book 23, Sawmills and Logging Camps on Puget Sound, Bancroft Library, University of California, Berkeley, P-B 52, 9, 14.

24. Erickson, "The Morphology of Lumber Settlements in Western Oregon and Washington," 111; *Oregon Spectator,* April 20, 1848, p. 2, c. 4.

25. *Oregon Spectator,* February 22, 1849, p. 1, c. 1; *Oregon Statesman,* July 3, 1852, p. 2, c. 7; Theodore Winthrop, *The Canoe and the Saddle,* ed., John H. Williams (Tacoma: Franklin-Ward Company, 1913), 242; James G. Swan, *The Northwest Coast; Or, Three Years' Residence in Washington Territory* (1857; reprint, Fairfield, Wash.: Ye

Galleon Press, 1989), 399; *Columbian*, March 26, 1853, p. 2, c. 2; *Pioneer and Democrat*, February 17, 1855, p. 2, c. 2.

26. *Oregon Spectator*, October 4, 1849, p. 2, c. 5; *Pioneer and Democrat*, February 17, 1855, p. 2, c. 2; *Oregon Spectator*, August 29, 1850, p. 2, c. 1; *Oregon Statesman*, July 3, 1852, p. 2, c. 7.

27. Cartwright, "Glimpses of Early Days in Oregon," 60; John R. Finger, "Seattle's First Sawmill, 1853–1869," *Forest History* 15 (January 1972): 25–26; *Pioneer and Democrat*, November 27, 1857, p. 2, c. 4; *Washington Standard*, March 16, 1861, p. 2, c. 6, p. 3, c. 1; June 15, 1878, p. 4, c. 2; November 16, 1878, p. 1, c. 4.

28. Erickson, "The Morphology of Lumber Settlements in Western Oregon and Washington," 114, 125–26.

29. *North-Pacific Rural* 1 (January 1877): p. 7, c. 3; Robert E. Ficken with William R. Sherrard, "The Port Blakely Mill Company, 1888–1903," *Journal of Forest History* 21:4 (October 1977): 204.

30. *West Shore* 8 (October 1882): p. 183, c. 2; Erickson, "The Morphology of Lumber Settlements in Western Oregon and Washington," 120.

31. Robert E. Ficken, *The Forested Land: A History of Lumbering in Western Washington* (Seattle: University of Washington Press, 1987), 38, 39; Throckmorton, *Oregon Argonauts*, 215.

32. Erickson, "The Morphology of Lumber Settlements in Western Oregon and Washington," 121–24, 125; *Oregonian*, February 2, 1888, p. 3, c. 2.

33. Alexander Ross, *Adventures of the First Settlers on the Oregon or Columbia River, 1810–1813* (Lincoln: University of Nebraska Press, 1986), 78, 85; Winthrop, *Canoe and Saddle*, 242; "Report of Lieutenant Neil M. Howison on Oregon, 1846," 13; Caroline C. Leighton, *Life at Puget Sound with Sketches of Travel in Washington Territory, British Columbia, Oregon, and California, 1865–1881* (Boston: Lee and Shepard, 1884), 45; Overton Johnson and William H. Winter, *Route Across the Rocky Mountains with a Description of Oregon and California* (Lafayette, Ind.: John B. Semans, 1846; reprinted in "Migration of 1843," *Oregon Historical Quarterly* 7:2 (June 1906): 177.

34. Thomas R. Cox, "Trade, Development, and Environmental Change," in Richard P. Tucker and J. F. Richards, eds., *Global Deforestation and the Nineteenth-Century World Economy* (Durham: Duke University Press, 1983), 22; Erickson, "The Morphology of Lumber Settlements in Western Oregon and Washington," 115, 122.

35. Gibson, *Farming the Frontier*, 191–92.

36. *Washington Standard*, September 9, 1865, p. 2. c. 1; July 20, 1888, p. 1, c. 3; Swan, *The Northwest Coast*, 119–20.

37. Erickson, "The Morphology of Lumber Settlements in Western Oregon and Washington," 113–25.

38. *Pioneer and Democrat*, August 5, 1859, p. 2, c. 4.

39. Samuel B. Crockett to his mother, Mrs. Mary Crockett, July 4, 1846, typescript, Meany Papers, box 72, folder 7, 2; *Pioneer and Democrat*, November 18, 1854, p. 2, c. 1.

40. *Washington Standard*, February 15, 1871, p. 2, c. 1–2.

41. *Pioneer and Democrat*, March 5, 1858, p. 2, c. 1; Delos Waterman to George A. Waterman, February 5, 1884, Delos Waterman Letters, 1862–1895, University of Washington Manuscripts and Archives Division, Seattle, vertical file 416, 3; *Washington Standard*, May 2, 1863, p. 2, c. 2; January 6, 1893, p. 1, c. 5; *Seattle Mail and Herald* 9 (January 20, 1906): p. 3, c. 1.

42. *North-Pacific Rural* 1 (January 1877): p. 7, c. 3.

43. *Seattle Post-Intelligencer*, September 1, 1901, p. 30, c. 1.

44. *Oregon Statesman,* March 19, 1866, p. 3, c. 1; *Washington Standard,* December 12, 1868, p. 2, c. 1; E. S. Salomon, *Biennial Message of Governor E. S. Salomon to the Legislative Assembly of the Territory of Washington, at Its Third Biennial Session,* Olympia, Monday, October 2, 1871 (Olympia, Wash.: Prosch and McElroy, 1871), 18.

45. Erickson, "The Morphology of Lumber Settlements in Western Oregon and Washington," 117–18.

46. Steen, "Forestry in Washington to 1925," 58; Ficken, *The Forested Land,* 36, 39; Thomas R. Cox, "Lower Columbia Lumber Industry, 1880–93," *Oregon Historical Quarterly* 67:2 (June 1966): 163.

47. Weld to Weld, December 2, 1852, photostatic copy, Martin Weld, Letters, 2; *Columbian,* March 26, 1853, p. 2, c. 2; Luark Diary, Microfilm Roll 2, August 31, 1853; September 22, 1854; August 11, September 5, 1855.

48. *Pioneer and Democrat,* February 17, 1855, p. 2, c. 2; March 3, 1855, p. 2, c. 1; November 18, 1854, p. 2, c. 3; December 26, 1856, p. 2, c. 1; Plimpton to Wright, December 7, 1857, and Silas Plimpton to Dexter Wright, May 1, 1858, in Abbott, ed., "Life on the Lower Columbia, 1853–1866," 270, 271; *Pioneer and Democrat,* July 27, 1860, p. 2, c. 2.

49. Eldridge Morse, Notes on the History and Resources of Washington Territory, Book 21, History of the River Valleys, Bancroft Library, University of California, Berkeley, P-B 50, 10–11.

50. William Cronon, *Nature's Metropolis: Chicago and the Great West* (New York: W. W. Norton, 1991), 83–84, 90, 180, 198, 200, 339–40; Capt. C. M. Scammon, "Lumbering in Washington Territory," *Overland Monthly* 5 (July 1870): 55.

51. Eldridge Morse, Notes on the History and Resources of Washington Territory, Book 17, The Islands of Puget Sound, Bancroft Library, University of California, Berkeley, P-B 46, 1–2; *West Shore* 6 (December 1880): p. 314, c. 2; 7 (November 1881): p. 280, c. 2; 8 (October 1882): p. 183, c. 2; 11 (March 1885): p. 81, c. 1; 15 (February 1889): p. 73, c. 1.

52. Leighton, *Life at Puget Sound,* 26.

53. *Oregonian,* January 2, 1888, p. 13, c. 5.

54. February 2, 1888, p. 3, c. 1; Cox, "Lower Columbia Lumber Industry, 1880–93," 161–62; *Washington Standard,* September 26, 1890, p. 1, c. 6.

55. Ficken, *The Forested Land,* 26, 28.

56. *Washington Standard,* August 1, 1868, p. 2, c. 3.

57. *Columbian,* February 19, 1853, p. 1, c. 4; *Washington Pioneer,* December 10, 1853, p. 2, c. 1–2.

58. *West Shore* 8 (October 1882): p. 183, c. 1.

59. Ibid.; *Oregonian,* January 2, 1888, p. 13, c. 5; *Washington Standard,* May 22, 1891, p. 2, c. 1; *Seattle Post-Intelligencer,* January 2, 1896, p. 3, c. 4; November 1, 1898, p. 6, c. 2–3; *Oregon Statesman,* November 6, 1852, p. 1, c. 2–3; *Washington Standard,* August 14, 1885, p. 1, c. 7; May 22, 1891, p. 2, c. 1.

60. *Washington Standard,* June 26, 1896, p. 2, c. 2.

61. Ibid., February 26, 1870, p. 1, c. 4.

62. Ibid., May 22, 1891, p. 2, c. 1; February 5, 1892, p. 2, c. 1; Carlos A. Schwantes, *The Pacific Northwest: An Interpretive History* (Lincoln: University of Nebraska Press, 1989), 181–83.

63. *Oregon Statesman,* March 19, 1866, p. 3, c. 1; *Washington Standard,* May 2, 1863, p. 2, c. 2; September 9, 1865, p. 2, c. 1; March 2, 1867, p. 2, c. 3.

64. Robert E. Ficken and Charles P. LeWarne, *Washington: A Centennial History* (Seattle: University of Washington Press, 1988), 30.

65. Schwantes, *The Pacific Northwest,* 180.

CHAPTER NINE: TRANSFORMING THE FORESTS

1. Kenneth A. Erickson, "The Morphology of Lumber Settlements in Western Oregon and Washington" (Ph.D. dissertation, University of California, Berkeley, 1965), 113–14, 117–18, 125.

2. Ibid., 23; *West Shore* 9 (July 1882): p. 136, c. 2.

3. Capt. C. M. Scammon, "Lumbering in Washington Territory," *Overland Monthly* 5 (July 1870): 56; *West Shore* (July 1882): p. 136, c. 2.

4. Theodore Winthrop, *The Canoe and the Saddle*, ed., John H. Williams (Tacoma: Franklin-Ward Company, 1913), 68.

5. Eldridge Morse, Notes on the History and Resources of Washington Territory, Book 24, Bancroft Library, University of California, Berkeley, P-B 53, 18–45; Erickson, "The Morphology of Lumber Settlements in Oregon and Washington," 27–28; Morse, Notes on the History and Resources of Washington Territory, Book 23, Sawmills and Logging Camps on Puget Sound, Bancroft Library, University of California, Berkeley, P-B 52, 24–27.

6. Erickson, "The Morphology of Lumber Settlements in Western Oregon and Washington," 35.

7. Joseph A. Dugan, "Memories of Yesteryears" (1962), typescript, Diaries and Reminiscences—Misc., Dugan, Joseph A., Oregon Historical Society, Portland, Mss 1509, 3–4; Morse, Notes on the History and Resources of Washington Territory, Book 24, 20, 23.

8. Absolom B. Harden to his brothers and sisters, March 25, 1848, Absolom B. Harden folder, Letters, 1848, Oregon Historical Society, Portland, Mss 11, 9, 10; Roselle Putnam to mother and sister (in-laws), February 9, 1852, in Sheba Hargreaves, "The Letters of Roselle Putnam," *Oregon Historical Quarterly* 29:3 (September 1928): 260; William Henry Mitchell to his father, April 2, 1855, William Henry Mitchell, Letters, 1854–1873, University of Washington Manuscripts and Archives Division, Seattle, vertical file 79, 2; "Report of Lieutenant Neil M. Howison on Oregon, 1846," *Oregon Historical Society* 14:1 (March 1913): 49.

9. Frances Fuller Victor, *All over Oregon and Washington* (San Francisco: John H. Carmany and Company, 1872), 281, 286, 291; Harden to his brothers and sisters, March 25, 1848, Harden folder, 10–11; Putnam to his mother and sister (in-laws), February 9, 1852, in Hargreaves, "The Letters of Roselle Putnam," 260.

10. Victor, *All over Oregon and Washington*, 280; *Washington Standard*, August 1, 1868, p. 2, c. 3.

11. *Washington Standard*, May 30, 1879, p. 4, c. 6; November 7, 1871, p. 2, c. 3; E. Ingersoll, "In the Wahlamet Valley of Oregon," *Harper's New Monthly Magazine* 65:389 (October 1882): 765.

12. John J. McGilvra to William F. Prosser, December 1, 1881, J. J. McGilvra Letters (Letterbook) January 1, 1880–November 25, 1882, box 2; John J. McGilvra, Papers, box 6, folders 14–15, "Reports as U.S. District Attorney," University of Washington Manuscripts Division, Seattle; Eldridge Morse, Notes of the History and Resources of Washington Territory, Book 2, Settlement, Bancroft Library, University of California, Berkeley, P-B 31, 60; Morse, Notes on the History and Resources of Washington Territory, Book 23, 28–29.

13. William B. Greeley, *Forests and Men* (New York: Doubleday and Company, 1951), 34–35.

14. Frederick J. Yonce, "Lumbering and the Public: The Era of Disposal," *Journal of Forest History* 22:1 (January 1978): 8, 13, 17; *Washington Standard*, December 2, 1865, p. 2, c. 1; May 30, 1879, p. 4, c. 6.

15. Ivan Clark Doig, "John J. McGilvra: The Life and Times of an Urban Frontiersman, 1827–1903" (Ph.D. dissertation, University of Washington, 1969), 50, 54–57, 59–60, 63–64; Yonce, "Lumbering and the Public," 12.

16. Doig, "John J. McGilvra," 60–63; McGilvra, Papers, box 6, folder 15, "Reports as U.S. District Attorney."

17. *Washington Standard,* December 2, 1865, p. 2, c. 1.

18. Ibid., February 20, 1869, p. 2, c. 3.

19. Harold Karl Steen, "Forestry in Washington to 1925" (Ph.D. dissertation, University of Washington, 1969), 5–6, 24–25, 39–40, 49–50; Michael Williams, *Americans and Their Forests: A Historical Geography* (Cambridge: Cambridge University Press, 1989), 370–71, 374–76, 382–87, 393–401, 405–7.

20. Morse, Notes on the History and Resources of Washington Territory, Book 23, 29–34; *Washington Standard,* April 1, 1871, p. 2, c. 3; November 4, 1881, p. 3, c. 2; May 6, 1871, p. 2, c. 3; Yonce, "Lumbering and the Public," 11.

21. Yonce, "Lumbering and the Public," 10–13.

22. Steen, "Forestry in Washington to 1925," 21, 36, 45.

23. Ibid., 46–47.

24. *Washington Standard,* May 30, 1879, p. 4, c. 6.

25. *Oregon Spectator,* October 10, 1850, p. 3, c. 2; October 17, 1850, p. 3, c. 3; October 24, 1850, p. 4, c. 4.

26. Ibid., September 23, 1851, p. 1, c. 5.

27. *Oregon Statesman,* February 27, 1865, p. 2, c. 1.

28. *Columbian,* December 25, 1852, p. 2, c. 2.

29. *Oregon Statesman,* February 15, 1864, p. 1, c. 6.

30. Morse, Notes on the History and Resources of Washington Territory, Book 23, 35–48; Morse, Notes on the History and Resources of Washington Territory, Book 24, 1–3.

31. Robert E. Ficken, *The Forested Land: A History of Lumbering in Western Washington* (Seattle: University of Washington Press, 1987), 41; Erickson, "The Morphology of Lumber Settlements in Western Oregon and Washington," 20.

32. Ficken, *The Forested Land,* 41.

33. Ibid., 42; *Washington Standard,* May 3, 1862, p. 2, c. 1–2; May 24, 1862, p. 1, c. 2; May 29, 1869, p. 2, c. 5.

34. *Washington Standard,* May 2, 1863, p. 2, c. 2.

35. Ficken, *The Forested Land,* 42, 49–52; Steen, "Forestry in Washington to 1925," 18–20, 41, 43–47; *Washington Standard,* November 17, 1882, p. 2, c. 1; December 28, 1883, p. 2, c. 3.

36. *Oregonian,* February 2, 1888, p. 3, c. 2–3. See also the *Washington Standard,* September 21, 1883, p. 2, c. 1; March 13, 1885, p. 3, c. 2.

37. *West Shore* 9 (July 1882): p. 136, c. 2.

38. *Washington Standard,* September 4, 1891, p. 1, c. 8; A. C. Little, *State of Washington. Tenth and Eleventh Annual Reports of the State Fish Commissioner to the Governor of the State of Washington* (Olympia, Wash.: Gwin Hicks, State Printer, 1901), 16–17.

39. A. C. Little, *State of Washington. Ninth Annual Report of the State Fish Commissioner to the Governor of the State of Washington* (Olympia, Wash.: Gwin Hicks, State Printer, 1898), 39.

40. "An Act to Prevent the Destruction of Fish in Any Fresh Water Streams, Creeks, or Lakes in Washington Territory" (approved November 22, 1871), in Washington, *General Laws* (1871), sec. 4, 94; "An Act for the Protection of Game and Fish" (approved October 17, 1872), in Oregon, *General Laws* (1872), sec. 9, 27; Little, *State*

of Washington. Ninth Annual Report of the State Fish Commissioner, 38–39; L. H. Darwin, *State of Washington. Twenty-Eighth and Twenty-Ninth Annual Reports of the State Fish Commissioner to the Governor of the State of Washington* (Olympia, Wash.: Frank M. Lamborn, Public Printer, 1920), 31; Jno. L. Riseland, *State of Washington. Sixteenth and Seventeenth Annual Reports of the State Fish Commissioner and Game Warden to the Governor of the State of Washington* (Olympia, Wash.: C. W. Corham, Public Printer, 1907), 74; Riseland, *State of Washington. Twenty-Second and Twenty-Third Annual Reports of the State Fish Commissioner and Ex-Officio Game Warden to the Governor of the State of Washington* (Olympia, Wash.: Frank M. Lamborn, Public Printer, 1913), 121; *Washington Standard*, January 30, 1920, p. 1, c. 1.

41. "In the Wahlamet Valley of Oregon," *Harper's*, 765; Fred Lockley, "Gray's Harbor: The Largest Lumber-Shipping Port in the World," *Pacific Monthly* 17:6 (June 1907): 729; Scammon, "Lumbering in Washington Territory," 59.

42. James G. Swan, *The Northwest Coast; Or, Three Years' Residence in Washington Territory* (1857; reprint, Fairfield, Wash.: Ye Galleon Press, 1989), 19.

43. The Anglo American fishing industry, started by the Hume brothers on the lower Columbia River in 1866, grew until by 1883 the tributaries and banks of the lower Columbia numbered over fifty canneries (Carlos A. Schwantes, *The Pacific Northwest: An Interpretive History* [Lincoln: University of Nebraska Press, 1989], 164); "An Act Regulating Salmon Fisheries on the Waters of the Columbia River" (approved November 8, 1877), in Washington (State), *General Laws* (1877), Preamble to the sections, 230.

44. James Crawford, *State of Washington. First Report of the State Fish Commissioner* (Olympia, Wash.: O. C. White, State Printer, 1890), 28; *Oregonian*, September 29, 1888, p. 3, c. 3.

45. Crawford, *State of Washington. First Report of the State Fish Commissioner*, 25.

46. Ibid., 28–29.

47. *Washington Standard*, December 19, 1890, p. 1, c. 4.

48. James Crawford, *State of Washington. Fifth Annual Report of the State Fish Commissioner* (Olympia, Wash.: O. C. White, State Printer, 1894), 19.

49. *Washington Standard*, March 23, 1900, p. 3, c. 3.

50. *West Shore* 11 (April 1885): p. 107, c. 2; Little, *State of Washington. Tenth and Eleventh Annual Reports of the State Fish Commissioner*, 18.

51. Riseland, *State of Washington. Sixteenth and Seventeenth Annual Reports of the State Fish Commissioner*, 68–69.

52. Little, *State of Washington. Tenth and Eleventh Annual Reports of the State Fish Commissioner*, 17; *Washington Standard*, November 8, 1907, p. 2, c. 5; L. H. Darwin, *State of Washington. Twenty-Sixth and Twenty-Seventh Annual Reports of the State Fish Commissioner to the Governor of the State of Washington* (Olympia, Wash.: Frank M. Lamborn, Public Printer, 1917), 33; T. L. Powell to Ralph Cowgill, May 14, 1928, Ralph P. Cowgill, "Report on Sprague River" (no date, but pictures included in the report are dated August 28, 1928); Ralph P. Cowgill, "Report on Mill City Dam North Santiam River" (April 16, 1929); Ralph P. Cowgill, "Report on South Santiam River" (April 30, 1929); Ralph P. Cowgill, "Pictorial Report: Miscellaneous Sawmill Pollution" (1929), all in Ralph Penniwell Cowgill Collection, Oregon Historical Society, Portland, Mss 2539.

53. Erickson, "The Morphology of Lumber Settlements in Western Oregon and Washington," 23; *West Shore* 10 (March 1884): p. 73, c. 1; *Washington Standard*, July 20, 1888, p. 1, c. 2; Richard H. Kennedy, "Logging Our Great Forests," *Pacific Monthly* 13 (January 1905): 30.

54. Quoted in William G. Robbins, "The 'Luxuriant Landscape': The Great Douglas Fir Bioregion," *Oregon Humanities* (Winter 1990): 4.

55. *Washington Standard,* December 20, 1895, p. 1, c. 2.

56. *West Shore* 10 (March 1884): p. 73, c. 2; 9 (July 1882): p. 136, c. 2; Fred G. Plummer, "Mount Rainier Forest Reserve, Washington," in U.S. Department of the Interior, *Twenty-First Annual Report of the United States Geological Survey to the Secretary of the Interior 1899–1900,* Part 5, Forest Reserves (Washington, D.C.: Government Printing Office, 1900), 110; *Pacific Monthly* 10 (November 1903): 313; 11 (April 1904): 282–83; Lockley, "Gray's Harbor: The Largest Lumber-Shipping Port in the World," 727–28; *Washington Standard,* December 20, 1895, p. 1, c. 3.

57. *West Shore* 7 (August 1881): p. 220, c. 2; 11 (March 1885): p. 81, c. 1; "Lumbering in Washington," *Overland Monthly* 20, 2d ser. (July–December 1892): pp. 26–27, c. 2–1.

58. *West Shore* 10 (May 1884): p. 137, c. 1.

59. *Washington Standard,* June 3, 1910, p. 2, c. 3.

60. Edgar L. Hampton, "A Day in Camp," *Seattle Mail and Herald* 5 (September 6, 1902): p. 11, c. 3–4; Thomas R. Cox, "Trade, Development, and Environmental Change," in Richard P. Tucker and J. F. Richards, eds., *Global Deforestation and the Nineteenth-Century World Economy* (Durham: Duke University Press, 1983), 20; Richard White, *Land Use, Environment, and Social Change: The Shaping of Island County, Washington* (Seattle: University of Washington Press, 1980), 108–9.

61. Thomas A. Spies and Jerry F. Franklin, "Old Growth and Forest Dynamics in the Douglas-Fir Region of Western Oregon and Washington," *Natural Areas Journal* 8:3 (July 1988): 194; White, *Land Use, Environment, and Social Change,* 109, 111.

62. Fred H. Everest, Neil B. Armantrout, Steven M. Keller, William D. Parante, James R. Sedell, Thomas E. Nickelson, James M. Johnston, and Gordon N. Haugen, "Salmonids," in E. Reade Brown, ed., *Management of Wildlife and Fish Habitats in Forests of Western Oregon and Washington,* Part 1, Chapter Narratives (Portland, Ore.: U.S. Department of Agriculture, Forest Service, Pacific Northwest Region, June 1985), 204, 216, 218, 219–21.

63. James R. Sedell, Peter A. Bisson, Frederick J. Swanson, and Stanley V. Gregory, "What We Know About Large Trees That Fall into Streams and Rivers," in Chris Maser, Robert F. Tarrant, James M. Trappe, and Jerry F. Franklin, *From the Forest to the Sea: A Story of Fallen Trees,* General Technical Report PNW-GTR-229 (Portland, Ore.: U.S. Department of Agriculture, Forest Service, and U.S. Department of Interior, Bureau of Land Management, Pacific Northwest Research Station, September 1988), 47, 55, 56, 64, 67, 68; Everest et al., "Salmonids," in Brown, ed., *Management of Wildlife and Fish Habitats,* 214, 215, 219, 222.

64. Steen, "Forestry in Washington to 1925," 13, 31–34, 49–50; Williams, *Americans and Their Forests,* 393–94; *Oregonian,* June 5, 1888, p. 6, c. 6; August 6, 1889, p. 4, c. 3; *Washington Standard,* December 5, 1884, p. 1, c. 1; September 19, 1890, p. 1, c. 5.

65. *Washington Standard,* December 5, 1884, p. 1, c. 1; *Oregonian,* February 12, 1889, p. 4, c. 2; Rev. G. H. Atkinson, "The Choice of a Home by Settlers in Oregon or Washington or Idaho," *West Shore* 16 (February 1880): p. 40, c. 1.

66. *West Shore* 10 (May 1884): p. 138, c. 1–2.

67. *Washington Standard,* October 1, 1880, p. 1, c. 6.

68. Ibid., December 5, 1884, p. 1, c. 1.

69. *Oregonian,* September 2, 1889, p. 4, c. 1.

70. Steen, "Forestry in Washington to 1925," 50–51; Harold K. Steen, *The U.S. Forest Service: A History* (Seattle: University of Washington Press, 1976), 17.

71. *Washington Standard,* June 6, 1879, p. 4, c. 5.

72. Ibid., July 4, 1879, p. 4, c. 3.

73. Samuel Trask Dana, *Forest and Range Policy: Its Development in the United*

States (New York: McGraw-Hill, 1956), 76–102; Williams, *Americans and Their Forests,* 375–411.

74. *Oregonian,* January 2, 1888, p. 13, c. 5; February 2, 1888, p. 3, c. 2; March 1, 1889, p. 4, c. 1; *Seattle Post-Intelligencer,* January 2, 1896, p. 3, c. 4; November 1, 1898, p. 6, c. 2–3; *Washington Standard,* December 23, 1887, p. 1, c. 5; July 20, 1888, p. 1, c. 3; September 26, 1890, p. 1, c. 6; September 15, 1899, p. 1, c. 4; *West Shore* 10 (March 1884): p. 90, c. 2.

75. *Oregonian,* June 5, 1888, p. 6, c. 6; January 10, 1889, p. 4, c. 4; August 6, 1889, p. 4, c. 3; John B. Leiberg, "Cascade Range and Ashland Forest Reserves and Adjacent Regions," in U.S. Department of the Interior, *Twenty-First Annual Report of the United States Geological Survey to the Secretary of the Interior 1899–1900,* Part 5, Forest Reserves (Washington, D.C.: Government Printing Office, 1900), 472; Harold K. Steen, *The Beginning of the National Forest System,* FS-488 (Portland, Ore.: U.S. Department of Agriculture, Forest Service, 1991), 23.

76. *Oregonian,* November 10, 1887, p. 4, c. 1; *Seattle Post-Intelligencer,* July 12, 1901, p. 4, c. 3; *Pacific Monthly* 10 (November 1903): 313–14.

77. Lawrence Rakestraw, "A History of Forest Conservation in the Pacific Northwest, 1891–1913" (Ph.D. dissertation, University of Washington, 1955), 31–34.

78. Ibid., 35–68.

79. Donald J. Pisani, "Forests and Conservation," *Journal of American History* 72 (September 1985), 340–59; *Washington Standard,* March 12, 1886, p. 2, c. 1; July 10, 1891, p. 1, c. 5.

80. The best treatment of antimodernism in this period is T. J. Jackson Lears, *No Place of Grace: Antimodernism and the Transformation of American Culture 1880–1920* (New York: Pantheon Books, 1981).

81. C. B. Watson, "Scenic America," *Chamber of Commerce Bulletin* 5 (October 1906): 11.

82. *Pacific Monthly* 22 (July 1909): 103; 22 (December 1909): 652c; 25 (March 1911): 333; *Washington Standard,* March 12, 1886, p. 2, c. 1; *Pacific Monthly* 13 (March 1905): 193. See also Samuel P. Hays, *Conservation and the Gospel of Efficiency: The Progressive Conservation Movement 1890–1920* (New York: Atheneum, 1969), 122–98; Roderick Nash, *Wilderness and the American Mind* (New Haven: Yale University Press, 1973), 129–30, 135–40.

83. Steen, *The U.S. Forest Service,* 74–75.

84. *Forestry and Irrigation* 13 (April 1907): 168.

85. "Report to the Commissioner of the General Land Office from Special Agent C. E. Bayard, January 30, 1893," Records of the General Land Office, Division R, National Forests, Ashland, box 4, Record Group 49, National Archives, Washington, D.C., 4; Henry Gannett, "The Forests of the United States," in U.S. Department of the Interior, *Nineteenth Annual Report of the United States Geological Survey to the Secretary of the Interior 1897–98,* Part 5, Forest Reserves (Washington, D.C.: Government Printing Office, 1899), 1; "Report to the Secretary of the Interior from Special Agent R. G. Savery of the General Land Office, July 23, 1892," Records of the General Land Office, Division R, National Forests, Willamette, box 177, Record Group 49, National Archives, Washington, D.C., 1, 3–4; Edward A. Bowers, "The Future of Federal Forest Reservations," *Forestry and Irrigation* 10 (March 1904): 131, 132; emphasis in original.

86. Washington (State), *General Laws,* Criminal Procedure (1862), 287, 293; *General Laws,* (1877), 300–301.

87. E. S. Salomon, *Biennial Message of Governor E. S. Salomon to the Legislative Assembly of the Territory of Washington, at Its Third Biennial Session* (Olympia, Wash.: Prosch and McElroy, 1871), 18.

88. William G. Morris, "Forest Fires in Western Oregon and Western Washington," *Oregon Historical Quarterly* 35:4 (December 1934): 332–34; *Seattle Post-Intelligencer,* April 24, 1896, p. 3, c. 1; *Washington Standard,* January 15, 1897, p. 3, c. 4.

89. Stephen J. Pyne, *Fire in America: A Cultural History of Wildland and Rural Fire* (Princeton: Princeton University Press, 1982), 163, 165.

90. *Seattle Post-Intelligencer,* April 24, 1896, p. 3, c. 1; *West Shore* 8 (January 1882): p. 2, c. 3, p. 3, c. 1; 11 (May 1885): p. 157, c. 1.

91. Gannett, "The Forests of the United States," in *Nineteenth Annual Report,* 40–41; Henry Gannett, "The Forests of the United States," in U.S. Department of the Interior, *Twentieth Annual Report of the United States Geological Survey to the Secretary of the Interior 1898–99,* Part 5, Forest Reserves (Washington, D.C.: Government Printing Office, 1900), 17; *Washington Standard,* January 15, 1897, p. 1–2, p. 3, c. 4; *Forester* 5 (July 1899): 164.

92. Pyne, *Fire in America,* 167, 328, 339; *Seattle Mail and Herald* 6 (July 25, 1903): p. 2, c. 2.

93. Gifford Pinchot, *Breaking New Ground* (New York: Harcourt, Brace and Company, 1947), 46; Warren E. Coman, "Did the Indian Protect the Forest?" *Pacific Monthly* 26 (September 1911): 301–2; Pyne, *Fire in America,* xiv, 27, 82.

94. Pyne, *Fire in America,* 328, 334; Peter Dominic Adrian Teensma, "Fire History and Fire Regimes of the Central Western Cascades of Oregon" (Ph.D. dissertation, University of Oregon, 1987), 45, 80–81.

95. "Report of Offices in District Office, District 6, Fiscal Year 1911," in U.S. Forest Service, Portland Regional Office, Regional Forester—National Forests 1904–1916, box 1, folder, District 6, Fy 1911, Records of the Forest Service, Report of Offices, Record Group 95, National Archives, Pacific Northwest Region, Seattle, Washington, 29–30; *Forestry and Irrigation* 11 (June 1905): 287–89; H. D. Langille, "Northern Portion of Cascade Range Forest Reserve," in H. D. Langille, Fred G. Plummer, Arthur Dodwell, Theodore F. Rixon, and John B. Leiberg, *Forest Conditions in the Cascade Range Forest Reserve Oregon,* Professional Paper no. 9 (Washington, D.C.: Government Printing Office, 1903), 33.

96. *Pacific Monthly* 23 (May 1910): 557; 24 (July 1910): 112; address of Mr. Joseph N. Teal, chairman Oregon State Conservation Commission, delivered at the University of Oregon on Commonwealth Day, "Oregon's Heritage of Natural Resources—Shall They be Conserved for the People?" (February 13, 1909), 10; E. T. Allen, "Forests, Lumber, and the Consumer," Chautauqua, New York, June 10, 1914, Western Forestry and Conservation Association, box 1, Western Forestry and Conservation Association Permanent Papers, vol. 2, Miscellaneous Addresses (1910–1916), Oregon Historical Society, Portland, Mss 1106, 4.

97. E. T. Allen, "Conservation (Forest) Redefined" (speech, probably at St. Paul, Minnesota, in 1911), Western Forestry and Conservation Association, 7–8.

98. E. T. Allen, "Forest Conservation," address before the National Education Association, San Francisco, California, July 12, 1911, Western Forestry and Conservation Association, 1; Allen, "Conservation (Forest) Redefined," 8; "National Influence of Pacific Coast Forest Organizations," March 7, 1914, Western Forestry and Conservation Association, 8; Charles M. Gates, "A Historical Sketch of the Economic Development of Washington Since Statehood," *Pacific Northwest Quarterly* 39:3 (July 1948): 216.

99. Gannett, "The Forests of the United States," in *Nineteenth Annual Report,* 1; Steen, *The U.S. Forest Service,* 74.

100. Richard White has most eloquently put forth this argument and made it a central theme in *It's Your Misfortune and None of My Own: A History of the American West* (Norman: University of Oklahoma Press, 1991).

101. *Pacific Monthly* 23 (May 1910): 557; 24 (July 1910): 112; *Seattle Post-Intelligencer,* July 28, 1907, p. 13, c. 1–4.

102. *Washington Standard,* December 5, 1884, p. 1, c. 1.

103. *Pacific Monthly* 22 (October 1909): 428.

EPILOGUE

1. Carlos A. Schwantes, *The Pacific Northwest: An Interpretive History* (Lincoln: University of Nebraska Press, 1989), 329, 340, 347–49.

2. *Oregonian,* July 2, 1995, p. E4, c. 4.

3. Schwantes, *The Pacific Northwest,* 368.

4. *Oregonian,* July 20, 1995, p. C7, c. 4; October 25, 1995, p. C1, c. 2, C4, c. 1.

5. Ibid., July 19, 1995, p. A6, c. 2, 3, 4.

6. Ibid., July 20, 1995, p. C10, c. 2.

7. Ibid., August 12, 1995, p. D3, c. 3.

8. Ibid., July 26, 1995, p. C2, c. 2–6; July 24, 1995, p. A1, c. 1–4, p. A6, c. 1–4.

9. William Kittredge, *Owning It All* (Saint Paul, Minn.: Graywolf Press, 1987), 160–61.

10. *Oregonian,* October 6, 1888 , p. 4.

BIBLIOGRAPHY

PRIMARY SOURCES

Manuscripts

Ball, John. Papers. Oregon Historical Society, Portland, Mss 195. Typed copies—originals in Grand Rapids, Michigan, Public Library.

Bancroft, A. L. "Diary of Journey to Oregon." 1862. Bancroft Library, University of California, Berkeley, C-E 133.

Barlow, John L. Letters. Special Collections, Knight Library, University of Oregon, Eugene, A 265.

Blain, Wilson. Letters, 1848–1852. Typescript. Oregon Historical Society, Portland, Mss 1035.

Bristow, Elijah Lafayette. "The Letters of Elijah Lafayette Bristow, Oregon Pioneer of 1848." Typescript. Lane County Pioneer-Historical Society, Eugene, Ore., March 1961.

Brown, Joseph Henry. "Settlement of Willammette [*sic*] Valley." Salem, Oregon, interview, June 12, 1878. Bancroft Library, University of California, Berkeley, P-A 10.

Burnham, Howard J. "Hudson Bay Co. Sawmill." Typescript. Oregon Historical Society, Portland, Mss 505.

Butler-Smith Family Papers. Typescript. Oregon Historical Society, Portland, Mss 2623.

Clarke, David Dexter. "Personal Experiences of a Surveyor and Civil Engineer in the States of Oregon and Washington 1864–1920." Manuscript. David Dexter Clarke Papers, Oregon Historical Society, Portland, Mss 1056.

Coe Family Papers. Transcription. Oregon Historical Society, Portland, Mss 431.

Coonse, Henry. Diary, 1851–1854. Transcript. University of Washington Manuscripts and Archives Division, Seattle, vertical file 286.

Cowgill, Ralph Penniwell. Collection. Oregon Historical Society, Portland, Mss 2539.

Cranfill, Isom. Book. Oregon Historical Society, Portland, Mss 1416.

Cranston, Susan Marsh. "Letters of Susan and Warren Cranston to Huldah [Susan's sister] and Reuben Fairchild." Typescript. Bancroft Library, University of California, Berkeley, P-A 303.

Deady, Matthew P. "History & Progress of Oregon After 1845." Portland, Oregon, interview, June 11, 1878. Bancroft Library, University of California, Berkeley, P-A 24.

Douglas, James. Journal 1835. Transcription of his journey from Fort Vancouver to York Factory and return, March to November 1835. University of Washington Manuscripts and Archives Division, Seattle, vertical file folder 305C (Mss D74j 1835).

———. Journal, 1840–1841. Transcription from a manuscript at Bancroft Library, University of Washington Manuscripts and Archives Division, Seattle, vertical file folder 305 D (Mss D74j).

Dugan, Joseph A. "Memories of Yesteryears." 1962. Typescript. Diaries and Reminiscences—Misc. Dugan, Joseph A., Oregon Historical Society, Portland, Mss 1509.

Eagon, Joseph. Papers. Oregon Historical Society, Portland, Mss 2516.

Finaley, Richard C. Documents and Correspondence, 1854–1890. Oregon Historical Society, Portland, Mss 725.

Freeland, Benjamin. Oregon Historical Society, Portland, Mss, 811.

Gardner, Ira. Letters from Oregon. Special Collections, Knight Library, University of Oregon, Eugene, A 256.

Gilbert, Wells Smith. Papers, box 1. Oregon Historical Society, Portland, Mss 1423.

Harden, Absolom B. Letters, 1848. Oregon Historical Society, Portland, Mss 11.

Holden, Horace. "Oregon Pioneering." Salem, Oregon, interview, June 14, 1878. Bancroft Library, University of California, Berkeley, P-A 40.

Love, Lewis. Captain Lewis Love's Memoir, Dictated in 1899. Oregon Historical Society, Portland, Mss 1509.

Luark, Michael. Diary. Microfilm Rolls 1–5. University of Washington Manuscripts and Archives Division, Seattle.

McGilvra, John J. Letterbook, box 2. University of Washington Manuscripts and Archives Division, Seattle.

———. "Reports as U.S. District Attorney." University of Washington Manuscripts and Archives Division, Seattle, Papers, box 6, folders 14 and 15.

Meany, Edmond S. Papers, box 72, folder 7, 43; box 73, folder 43; box 74, folder 6, 45; box 76, folder 74. University of Washington Manuscripts and Archives Division, Seattle, 106-70-12.

Minto, John. Papers, box 1, folder 3, 6; box 2, folder 6, 8. Oregon Historical Society, Portland, Mss 752.

Minto, Martha A. "Female Pioneering in Oregon." Salem, Oregon, interview, June 16, 1878. Bancroft Library, University of California, Berkeley, P-A 51.

Mitchell, William Henry. Letters, 1854–1873. University of Washington Manuscripts and Archives Division, Seattle, vertical file 79.

Morse, Eldridge. Notes of the History and Resources of Washington Territory. Book 1, Settlement, P-B 30; Book 2, Settlement, P-B 31; Book 14, End of Indian War 1855 and 1856, P-B 43; Book 17, The Islands of Puget Sound, P-B 46; Book 19, Olympic Mountains . . . Climate, Soil of the Sound, P-B 48; Book 21, History of the River Valleys, P-B 50; Book 22, The River Valleys, P-B 51; Book 23, Sawmills and Logging Camps on Puget Sound, P-B 52; Book 24, (no title), P-B 53. Bancroft Library, University of California, Berkeley.

Oregon Alpine Club. Associations, Institutions, etc. Oregon Historical Society, Portland, Mss 1511.

Palmer, Joel. Papers, boxes 1 and 2. Special Collections, Knight Library, University of Oregon, Eugene, Ax 57.

Rodgers, Andrew. Papers. Typescript. Oregon Historical Society, Portland, Mss 1208.

Records of the Forest Service. Record Group 95. Box 1, folder, Cascade Forest Reserve Oregon, Northern Division Report, 1904. National Archives, Pacific Northwest Region, Seattle, Washington.

———. Record Group 95. Box 1, folder, District Forester's Annual Report, 1911. National Archives, Pacific Northwest Region, Seattle, Washington.

———. Record Group 95. Box 1, folder, District 6 Report of Offices. National Archives, Pacific Northwest Region, Seattle, Washington.

———. Record Group 95. Box 2, folder, Columbia National Forest Inspection Report, 1909. National Archives, Pacific Northwest Region, Seattle, Washington.

———. Record Group 95. Box 3, folder, Mt. Rainier Inspection Report, 1905. National Archives, Pacific Northwest Region, Seattle, Washington.

_____. Record Group 95. Box 3, folder, Olympic, 1909. National Archives, Pacific Northwest Region, Seattle, Washington.

_____. Record Group 95. Box 3, folder, Rainier National Forest, 1907. National Archives, Pacific Northwest Region, Seattle, Washington.

_____. Record Group 95. Box 3, folder, Rainier National Forest, 1912. National Archives, Pacific Northwest Region, Seattle, Washington.

_____. Record Group 95. Box 3, folder, Siskiyou National Forest, 1908. National Archives, Pacific Northwest Region, Seattle, Washington.

_____. Record Group 95. Box 4, folder, Siuslaw National Forest, 1909. National Archives, Pacific Northwest Region, Seattle, Washington.

_____. Record Group 95. Box 4, folder, Snoqualmie, 1909. National Archives, Pacific Northwest Region, Seattle, Washington.

_____. Record Group 95. Box 4, folder, Umpqua, 1906. National Archives, Pacific Northwest Region, Seattle, Washington.

_____. Record Group 95. Box 5, folder, Washington National Forester Inspection, Part 1, 1907. National Archives, Pacific Northwest Region, Seattle, Washington.

Records of the General Land Office. Division R, National Forests. Record Group 49. Ashland, box 4. National Archives, Washington, D.C.

_____. Record Group 49. Olympic, boxes 111 and 112. National Archives, Washington, D.C.

_____. Record Group 49. Willamette, boxes 175, 176, and 177. National Archives, Washington, D.C.

Savage, George M. Reminiscences, box 1. University of Washington Manuscripts and Archives Division, Seattle, V0243f.

Shaw, William. "Mississippi & Columbia River Valley Pioneer Life Compared." Salem, Oregon, interview, June 1878. Bancroft Library, University of California, Berkeley, P-A 64.

Smith, Thomas. Diary, 1870–1871. Typescript. Douglas County Museum of History and Natural History, Roseburg, Oregon, 808.883 Smi.

Tichenor, Captain William. "Among the Oregon Indians." Bancroft Library, University of California, Berkeley, P-A 84.

Waldo, Daniel. "Critiques." Salem, Oregon, interview, June 16, 1878. Bancroft Library, University of California, Berkeley, P-A 74.

Waterman, Delos. Letters, 1862–1896. University of Washington Manuscripts and Archives Division, Seattle, Vertical file 416.

Weld, Martin. Letters, 1850–1858. Photostatic copies from the Minnesota Historical Society. University of Washington Manuscripts and Archives Division, Seattle, vertical file 417.

Western Forestry and Conservation Association. Permanent Papers, vol. 2. Box 1, Miscellaneous Addresses (1910–1916); box 16, folder, Statistics—General, 1914–1922. Oregon Historical Society, Portland, Mss 1106.

Wigle, A. J. "Overland Journey Account, 1852." Typescript. Reminiscences. 1898. Oregon Historical Society, Portland, Mss 587.

Work, John. Papers, 1823–1862, box 1. University of Washington Manuscripts and Archives Division, Seattle, V0249C.

Newspapers and Periodicals

Chamber of Commerce Bulletin
Columbian
Forestry and Irrigation
North-Pacific Rural

Oregonian
Oregon Spectator
Oregon Sportsman
Oregon Statesman
Pacific Monthly
Pioneer and Democrat
Puget Sound Weekly Courier
Seattle Mail and Herald
Seattle Post-Intelligencer
Washington Standard
West Shore

Books

Applegate, Jesse A. *A Day with the Cow Column in 1843: Recollections of My Boyhood.* Edited by Joseph Schafer. Chicago: Caxton Club, 1934.
Bensell, Royal A. *All Quiet on the Yamhill: The Civil War in Oregon.* Edited by Gunter Barth. Eugene: University of Oregon Books, 1959.
Burnett, Peter H. *Recollections and Opinions of an Old Pioneer.* New York: D. Appleton and Company, 1880.
Camp, Charles L., ed. *James Clyman, Frontiersman.* Portland, Ore.: Champoeg Press, 1960.
Clarke, S. A. *Pioneer Days of Oregon History.* 2 vols. Cleveland: Arthur H. Clark Company, 1905.
Cummins, Sarah J. *Autobiography and Reminiscences.* Freewater, Ore.: M. J. Allen, 1914.
David Newsom: The Western Observer 1805–1882. Portland, Ore.: Glass-Dahlstrom Printers, 1972.
de Mofras, Eugene Duflot. *Oregon.* Translated by Don Wilkins. W.P.A. Project no. 5605. Seattle: University of Washington, 1937.
De Smet, Pierre-Jean, S.J. *Oregon Missions and Travels over the Rocky Mountains in 1845–46.* New York: Edward Dunigan, 1847. Reprint, Fairfield, Wash.: Ye Galleon Press, 1978.
Franchere, Gabriel. *A Voyage to the Northwest Coast of America.* Edited by Milo Milton Quaife. New York: Citadel Press, 1968.
Greeley, William B. *Forests and Men.* New York: Doubleday and Company, 1951.
Hayden, Mary. *Pioneer Days.* San Jose: Murgotten Press, 1915. Reprint, Fairfield, Wash.: Ye Galleon Press, 1979.
Hines, Rev. Gustavus. *Life on the Plains of the Pacific. Oregon: Its History, Condition, and Prospects; Containing a Description of the Geography, Climate, and Productions, with Personal Adventures Among the Indians During a Residence of the Author on the Plains Bordering the Pacific While Connected with the Oregon Mission: Embracing Extended Notes of a Voyage Around the World.* New York: C. M. Saxton, 1859.
Johnson, Overton, and William H. Winter. *Route Across the Rocky Mountains with a Description of Oregon and California.* Lafayette, Ind.: John B. Semans, 1846. Reprinted in "Migration of 1843." *Oregon Historical Quarterly* 7:2 (March, 1906): 62–104, and 7:2 (June 1906): 163–210.
Judson, Phoebe Goodell. *A Pioneer's Search for an Ideal Home.* Edited by John M. McClelland, Jr. Tacoma: Washington State Historical Society, 1966.
Landerholm, Carl, trans. *Notices and Voyages of the Famed Quebec Mission to the Pacific Northwest.* Portland, Ore.: Champoeg Press, 1956.
Lavender, David, ed. *The Oregon Journals of David Douglas; of His Travels and Adven-*

tures Among the Traders and Indians in the Columbia, Willamette, and Snake Regions During the Years 1825, 1826, and 1827. 2 vols. Ashland: Oregon Book Society, 1972.

Lee, Daniel, and Joseph H. Frost. *Ten Years in Oregon.* New York: J. Collord, 1844. Reprint, New York: Arno Press, 1973.

Leighton, Caroline C. *Life at Puget Sound with Sketches of Travel in Washington Territory, British Columbia, Oregon, and California, 1865–1881.* Boston: Lee and Shepard, 1884.

Meeker, Ezra. *The Busy Life of Eighty Years.* Seattle: Ezra Meeker, 1916.

Merk, Frederick, ed. *Fur Trade and Empire: George Simpson's Journal.* Cambridge, Mass.: Harvard University Press, 1931.

Moulton, Gary E., ed. *The Journals of the Lewis & Clark Expedition, November 2, 1805–March 22, 1806.* Vol. 6. Lincoln: University of Nebraska Press, 1990.

Murphy, John Mortimer. *The Oregon Hand-Book and Emigrants' Guide.* Portland, Ore.: S. J. McCormick, 1873.

_____. *Sporting Adventures in the Far West.* London: Sampson Low, Marston, Searle, and Rivington, 1879.

Nash, Wallis. *Two Years in Oregon.* New York: D. Appleton and Company, 1882.

Newcombe, C. F., ed. *Menzies' Journal of Vancouver's Voyage: April to October, 1792.* Victoria: William H. Cullin, 1923.

Palmer, Joel. *Journal of Travels over the Rocky Mountains.* Cincinnati: J. A. and U. P. James, 1847. Reprint, Fairfield, Wash.: Ye Galleon Press, 1983.

Pinchot, Gifford. *Breaking New Ground.* New York: Harcourt, Brace and Company, 1947.

Rich, E. E., ed. *The Letters of John McLoughlin from Fort Vancouver to the Governor and Committee. First Series, 1825–38.* London: Champlain Society for the Hudson's Bay Record Society, 1941.

_____. *The Letters of John McLoughlin from Fort Vancouver to the Governor and Committee. Second Series, 1839–44.* London: Champlain Society for the Hudson's Bay Record Society, 1943.

_____. *Simpson's 1828 Journey to the Columbia.* London: Champlain Society for the Hudson's Bay Record Society, 1947.

Riddle, George W. *History of Early Days in Oregon.* Riddle, Ore.: reprinted from the *Riddle Enterprise,* 1920.

Rollins, Philip Ashton, ed. *The Discovery of the Oregon Trail: Robert Stuart's Narratives of His Overland Trip Eastward from Astoria in 1812–13.* New York: Edward Eberstadt and Sons, 1935.

Ross, Alexander. *Adventures of the First Settlers on the Oregon or Columbia River, 1810–1813.* Lincoln: University of Nebraska Press, 1986.

Sheridan, Philip. H. *Personal Memoirs.* Vol. 1. New York: Charles L. Webster and Company, 1888.

Smith, Arthur D. Howden, ed. *The Narrative of Samuel Hancock, 1845–1860.* New York: Robert M. McBride and Company, 1927.

Sullivan, Maurice S., ed. *The Travels of Jedediah Smith.* Santa Ana, Calif.: Fine Arts Press, 1934.

Swan, James G. *The Northwest Coast; Or, Three Years' Residence in Washington Territory.* New York: Harper and Brothers, 1857. Reprint, Fairfield, Wash.: Ye Galleon Press, 1989.

Tolmie, William Fraser. *The Journals of William Fraser Tolmie, Physician and Fur Trader.* Vancouver: Mitchell Press, 1963.

Townsend, John Kirk. *Across the Rockies to the Columbia.* Lincoln: University of Nebraska Press, 1978.

Transactions of the Twenty-First Annual Reunion of the Oregon Pioneer Association for 1893. Portland, Ore.: Geo. H. Himes and Company, 1894.

Victor, Frances Fuller. *All over Oregon and Washington*. San Francisco: John H. Carmany and Company, 1872.

Wilkes, Charles. *Narrative of the United States Exploring Expedition During the Years 1838, 1839, 1840, 1841, 1842*. Vols. 4 and 5. Philadelphia: Lea and Blanchard, 1845.

Winter, Oscar O., and Gayle Thornbrough, eds. *To Oregon in 1852: Letter of Dr. Thomas White La Grange County, Indiana, Emigrant*. Indianapolis: Indiana Historical Society, 1964.

Winthrop, Theodore. *The Canoe and the Saddle*. Edited by John H. Williams. Tacoma: Franklin-Ward Company, 1913.

Articles

Abbott, Helen Betsy, ed. "Life on the Lower Columbia, 1853–1866." *Oregon Historical Quarterly* 83:3 (Fall 1982): 248–87.

Applegate, Jesse. "Umpqua Agriculture, 1851." *Oregon Historical Quarterly* 32:2 (June 1931): 135–44.

Bagley, Clarence B., ed. "Journal of Occurrences at Nisqually House, 1833." *Washington Historical Quarterly* 6:3 (July 1915): 179–97.

Bennett, John E. "Hunting in Southern Oregon." *Overland Monthly* 30:176 (August 1897): 146–52.

Burnett, Peter H. "Documents." *Oregon Historical Quarterly* 4:2 (June 1903): 180–83.

———. "Letters of Peter H. Burnett." *Oregon Historical Quarterly* 3:4 (December 1902): 421–26.

Chase, A. W. "Timber Belts of the Pacific Coast." *Overland Monthly* 13:3 (September 1874): 242–49.

"Diary of William Thiel of Oregon." *Umpqua Trapper* 12:4 (Winter Hunt 1976): 83–96; 13:1 (Spring Hunt 1977): 17–23; 13:2 (Summer Hunt 1977): 30–48.

Elliott, T. C., ed. "British Values in Oregon, 1847." *Oregon Historical Quarterly* 32:1 (March 1931): 27–45.

Emmons, Terence, ed. "Documents: Hadley Hobson, Marion County Pioneer." *Oregon Historical Society* 93:1 (Spring 1992): 66–73.

Geer, Ralph C. "Occasional Address." In *Transactions of the Seventh Annual Re-Union of the Oregon Pioneer Association*, 32–42. Salem, Ore.: E. M. Waite, 1880.

Hargreaves, Sheba. "The Letters of Roselle Putnam." *Oregon Historical Quarterly* 29:3 (September 1928): 242–64.

Ingersoll, E. "In the Wahlamet Valley of Oregon." *Harper's New Monthly Magazine* 65:389 (October 1882): 764–71.

John Work's Journey from Fort Vancouver to Umpqua River, and Return, in 1834. *Oregon Historical Quarterly* 24:3 (September 1923): 238–68.

"Letters to Mrs. F. F. Victor, 1878–83." *Oregon Historical Quarterly* 63:2–3 (June–September 1962): 175–236.

"Life in Douglas County in 1858." Excerpts from a letter by John Franklin Sutherlin of Winchester, Douglas County, Oregon, to his brother, Owen Sutherlin of Greencastle, Indiana, April 9th, 1858. *Umpqua Trapper* 1:2 (Summer Hunt 1965): 17–18.

Lyman, H. S. "Daniel Knight Warren. Reminiscences." *Oregon Historical Quarterly* 3:3 (September 1902): 296–309.

———. "An Oregon Literature." *Oregon Historical Quarterly* 2:4 (December 1901): 402–9.

———. "Reminisances of Clement Adams Bradbury, 1846." *Oregon Historical Review* 2:3 (September 1901): 304–19.

Minto, John. "Antecedents of the Oregon Pioneers and the Light These Throw on Their Motives." *Oregon Historical Quarterly* 5:1 (March 1904): 38–63.

_____. "From Youth to Age as an American." *Oregon Historical Quarterly* 9:2 (June 1908): 127–72; 9:4 (December 1908): 374–87.

Oliphant, J. Orin, ed. "Thomas S. Kendall's Letter on Oregon Agriculture, 1852." *Agricultural History* 9:4 (October 1935): 187–97.

Rees, Willard H. "Annual Address." In *Transactions of the Seventh Annual Re-Union of the Oregon Pioneer Association*, 18–31. Salem, Ore.: E. M. Waite, 1880.

"Report of Lieutenant Neil M. Howison on Oregon, 1846." *Oregon Historical Quarterly* 14:1 (March 1913): 1–60.

Roberts, George B. "The Cowlitz Farm Journal, 1847–51." *Oregon Historical Quarterly* 63:2–3 (June–September 1962): 101–74.

Rockwood, E. Ruth, ed. "Letters of Charles Stevens." *Oregon Historical Quarterly* 37:2 (June 1936): 137–59; 37:3 (September 1936): 241–61; 37:4 (December 1936): 334–53; 38:1 (March 1937): 63–91; 38:2 (June 1937): 164–92; 38:3 (September 1937): 328–54.

Schafer, Joseph, ed. "Documents Relative to Warre and Vavasour's Military Reconnoissance in Oregon, 1845–6." *Oregon Historical Quarterly* 10:1 (March 1909): 1–99.

Scott, Harvey W. "The Pioneer Character of Oregon Progress." *Oregon Historical Quarterly* 18:4 (December 1917): 245–70.

"Slacum's Report on Oregon, 1836–7." *Oregon Historical Quarterly* 13:2 (June 1912): 175–224.

"Smith, Thomas." In *Transactions of the Eighteenth Annual Reunion of the Oregon Pioneer Association for 1890*, 75–80. Portland, Ore.: A. Anderson and Company, 1892.

Sperlin, O. B., ed. "Our First Official Horticulturist—Brackenridge's Journal of the Willamette Route to Caifornia, 1841." *Washington Historical Quarterly* 21:3 (July 1930): 218–29; 21:4 (October 1930): 298–305; 22:3 (July 1931): 216–27.

Victor, Frances Fuller. "The Oregon Indians, Part 1." *Overland Monthly* 7:4 (October 1971): 344–52.

Wells, William V. "Wild Life in Oregon." *Harper's New Monthly Magazine* 13:77 (October 1856): 588–608.

Wilkes, Charles. "Report on the Territory of Oregon." *Oregon Historical Quarterly* 12:3 (September 1911): 269–99.

Williams, Ira A. "The Drainage of Farm Lands in the Willamette and Tributary Valleys of Oregon." *Mineral Resources of Oregon* 1:4 (June 1914): 3–81.

Wood, Tallmadge B. Letter. *Oregon Historical Quarterly* 3:4 (December 1902): 394–98.

_____. Letters. *Oregon Historical Quarterly* 4:1 (March 1903): 80–85.

Government Documents

Beckham, Stephen Dow. *Cultural Resource Overview of the Siskiyou National Forest, Western Oregon*. Vol 1. Portland, Ore.: U.S. Department of Agriculture, Forest Service, Pacific Northwest Region, Siskiyou National Forest, 1978.

Boule, Marc E., Nancy Olmsted, and Tina Miller. *Inventory of Wetland Resources and Evaluation of Wetland Management in Western Washington*. Olympia: Washington State Department of Ecology, June 1983.

Brown, E. Reade, ed. *Management of Wildlife and Fish Habitats in Forests of Western Oregon and Washington*. Part 1, Chapter Narratives; Part 2, Appendices. Portland, Ore.: U.S. Department of Agriculture, Forest Service, Pacific Northwest Region, June 1985.

Bryant, Richard L., Leslie Conton, Robert E. Hurlbett, and John R. Nelson. *Cultural Resource Overview of the Mt. Hood National Forest, Oregon*. Vol. 1. Eugene, Ore.: Pro-Lysts, Inc., for the U.S. Forest Service, Region 6, 1978.

Dahl, Thomas E. *Wetland Losses in the United States 1780's to 1980's*. Washington, D.C.: U.S. Department of the Interior, Fish and Wildlife Service, 1990.

Dodwell, Arthur, and Theodore F. Rixon. *Forest Conditions in the Olympic Forest Reserve, Washington.* Professional Paper no. 7. Washington, D.C.: Government Printing Office, 1902.

Jermann, Jerry V., and Roger D. Mason. *A Cultural Resource Overview of the Gifford Pinchot National Forest, South-Central Washington.* Reconnaissance Reports no. 7. Seattle: University of Washington Office of Public Archaeology, Institute for Environmental Studies, March 1976.

Langille, H. D., Fred G. Plummer, Arthur Dodwell, Theodore F. Rixon, and John B. Leiberg. *Forest Conditions in the Cascade Range Forest Reserve Oregon.* Professional Paper no. 9. Washington, D.C.: Government Printing Office, 1903.

Maser, Chris, Robert F. Tarrant, James M. Trappe, and Jerry F. Franklin, eds. *From the Forest to the Sea: A Story of Fallen Trees.* General Technical Report PNW-GTR-229. Portland, Ore.: U.S. Department of Agriculture, Forest Service, and U.S. Department of Interior, Bureau of Land Management, Pacific Northwest Research Station, September 1988.

Minor, Rick, with Paul W. Baxter, Stephen Dow Beckham, and Kathryn Anne Toepel. *Cultural Resource Overview of the Willamette National Forest: A 10-Tear Update.* Report no. 60. Eugene, Ore.: Heritage Research Associates, 1987.

Newell, William A. *Message of William A. Newell, Governor of Washington Territory, to the Legislative Assembly, Session of 1881.* Olympia, Wash.: C. B. Bagley, 1881.

————. *Message of William A. Newell, Governor of Washington Territory, to the Legislative Assembly, Session of 1883.* Olympia, Wash.: C. B. Bagley, 1883.

O'Callaghan, Jerry A. *The Disposition of the Public Domain in Oregon.* Washington, D.C.: Government Printing Office, 1960.

Oregon. *Annual Reports of the Game and Forestry Warden.* 1899–1908.

————. *General Laws.*

Quimby, L. B. W. *First and Second Annual Reports of the Game and Forestry Warden to the Governor for the Years 1899 and 1900.* Salem, Ore.: W. H. Leeds, 1900.

Reports of Explorations and Surveys to Ascertain the Most Practicable and Economical Route for a Railroad from the Mississippi River to the Pacific Ocean, 1853–5. Vol. 12, bk. 2, pt. 2, Botanical Report. Washington, D.C.: Thomas H. Ford, 1860.

Reports of Explorations and Surveys to Ascertain the Most Practicable and Economical Route for a Railroad from the Mississippi River to the Pacific Ocean, 1854–5. Vol. 6, pt. 1. Washington, D.C.: Beverley Tucker, 1857. Vol. 6, pt. 2, Geological Report. Washington, D.C.: Beverley Tucker, 1857. Vol. 6, pt. 3, Botanical Report. Washington, D.C.: Beverley Tucker, 1857.

Salomon, E. S. *Biennial Message of Governor E. S. Salomon to the Legislative Assembly of the Territory of Washington, at Its Third Biennial Session.* Begun and Held at the City of Olympia, the Seat of Government, on Monday, Oct. 2, 1871. Olympia, Wash.: Prosch and McElroy, 1871.

Southard, Michael D., ed. *Archaeological Investigations on the Western Flank of the South-Central Cascades, Lane and Douglas Counties, Oregon.* Cultural Resource Series no. 7. Portland, Ore.: U.S. Department of the Interior, Bureau of Land Management, 1991.

Steen, Harold K. *The Beginning of the National Forest System.* FS-488. Washington, D.C.: U.S. Department of Agriculture, Forest Service, 1991.

Stevens, Isaac. *Governor's Message of the Territory of Washington.* Delivered in Joint Session of the Council and House of Representatives of Washington Territory, Wednesday, December 3d, 1856. Olympia, Wash.: Geo. B. Goudy, 1865.

U.S. Department of the Interior. *Eighteenth Annual Report of the United States Geological Survey to the Secretary of the Interior 1896–97.* Part 2, Papers Chiefly of a Theoretic Nature. Washington, D.C.: Government Printing Office, 1898.

————. *Nineteenth Annual Report of the United States Geological Survey to the Secre-*

tary of the Interior 1897–98. Part 5, Forest Reserves. Washington, D.C.: Government Printing Office, 1899.

_____. *Twentieth Annual Report of the United States Geological Survey to the Secretary of the Interior 1898–99*. Part 5, Forest Reserves. Washington, D.C.: Government Printing Office, 1900.

_____. *Twenty-First Annual Report of the United States Geological Survey to the Secretary of the Interior 1899–1900*. Part 5, Forest Reserves. Washington, D.C.: Government Printing Office, 1900.

U.S. Geographical and Geological Survey of the Rocky Mountain Region. *Contributions to North American Ethnology*. Vol. 1. Washington, D.C.: Government Printing Office, 1877.

U.S. House of Representatives. *Indian Affairs in the Territories of Oregon and Washington*. 35th Congress, 1st sess., 1858, H. Ex. Doc. 39, Serial 955.

_____. *Report of the Secretary of the Interior*. 44th Congress, 1st sess., 1875. H. Ex. Doc. 1, pt. 5, Serial 1680.

U.S. Senate. *Message of the President of the United States*. 35th Congress, 2d sess., 1858. S. Ex. Doc. 1, pt. 1, Serial 974.

Washington (State). *General Laws*.

_____. *Report of the State Fire Warden*. 1905–1908.

_____. *Report of the State Fish Commissioner*. 1890–1921.

_____. *Report of the State Forester*. 1914–1920.

_____. *Report of the State Forester and Fire Warden*. 1911–1912.

Whistler, John T., and John H. Lewis. *Rogue River Valley Project and Willamette Valley Investigations Irrigation and Drainage*. Department of the Interior, U.S. Reclamation Service, February 1916.

Williams, Gerald W., ed. *Judge John Breckenridge Waldo: Diaries and Letters from the High Cascades of Oregon 1880–1907*. U.S. Department of Agriculture, Forest Service, Pacific Northwest Region, Umpqua National Forest, April 1989.

SECONDARY SOURCES

Selected Books

Barman, Jean. *The West Beyond the West: A History of British Columbia*. Toronto: University of Toronto Press, 1991.

Beckham, Stephen Dow. *The Indians of Western Oregon: This Land Was Theirs*. Portland, Ore.: Glass-Dahlstron, 1977.

_____. *Land of the Umpqua: A History of Douglas County, Oregon*. Roseburg, Ore.: Douglas County Commissioners, 1986.

_____. *Requiem for a People: The Rogue Indians and the Frontiersmen*. Norman: University of Oklahoma Press, 1971.

Boag, Peter G. *Environment and Experience: Settlement Culture in Nineteenth-Century Oregon*. Berkeley: University of California Press, 1992.

Bowen, William A. *The Willamette Valley: Migration and Settlement on the Oregon Frontier*. Seattle: University of Washington Press, 1978.

Boxberger, Daniel L. *To Fish in Common: The Ethnohistory of Lummi Indian Salmon Fishing*. Lincoln: University of Nebraska Press, 1989.

Buan, Carolyn M., and Richard Lewis, eds. *The First Oregonians*. Portland: Oregon Council for the Humanities, 1991.

Corning, Howard McKinley, ed. *Dictionary of Oregon History*. Portland, Ore.: Binford and Mort Publishing, 1989.

Cosgrove, Denis, and Stephen Daniels, eds. *The Iconography of Landscape: Essays on the Symbolic Representation, Design, and Use of Past Environments.* New York: Cambridge University Press, 1988.

Cowdrey, Albert E. *This Land, This South: An Environmental History.* Lexington: University of Kentucky Press, 1983.

Cronon, William. *Nature's Metropolis: Chicago and the Great West.* New York: W. W. Norton, 1991.

Crosby, Alfred E., Jr. *The Columbian Exchange: Biological and Cultural Consequences of 1492.* Westport, Conn.: Greenwood Press, 1972.

Dana, Samuel Trask. *Forest and Range Policy: Its Development in the United States.* New York: McGraw-Hill, 1956.

Davis, Richard C., ed. *Encyclopedia of American Forest and Conservation History.* Vol. 2. New York: Macmillan Publishing Company, 1983.

Dodds, Gordon B. *The American Northwest: A History of Oregon and Washington.* Arlington Heights, Ill.: Forum Press, 1986.

———. *Oregon: A Bicentennial History.* New York: W. W. Norton, 1977.

Dunlap, Thomas R. *Saving America's Wildlife: Ecology and the American Mind, 1850–1990.* Princeton: Princeton University Press, 1988.

Fairbanks, Carol. *Prairie Women: Images in American and Canadian Fiction.* New Haven: Yale University Press, 1986.

Ficken, Robert E. *The Forested Land: A History of Lumbering in Western Washington.* Seattle: University of Washington Press, 1987.

Ficken, Robert E., and Charles P. LeWarne. *Washington: A Centennial History.* Seattle: University of Washington Press, 1988.

Fisher, Robin. *Contact and Conflict: Indian-European Relations in British Columbia, 1774–1890.* Vancouver: University of British Columbia Press, 1977.

Franklin, Jerry F., and C. T. Dyrness. *Natural Vegetation of Oregon and Washington.* Corvallis: Oregon State University Press, 1988.

Gibson, James R. *Farming the Frontier: The Agricultural Opening of the Oregon Country 1786–1846.* Seattle: University of Washington Press, 1985.

———. *Otter Skins, Boston Ships, and China Goods: The Maritime Fur Trade of the Northwest Coast, 1785–1841.* Seattle: University of Washington Press, 1992.

Hamer, David. *New Towns in the New World: Images and Perceptions of the Nineteenth-Century Urban Frontier.* New York: Columbia University Press, 1990.

Harris, Larry D. *The Fragmented Forest: Island Biogeography Theory and the Preservation of Biotic Diversity.* Chicago: University of Chicago Press, 1984.

Hays, Samuel P. *Conservation and the Gospel of Efficiency: The Progressive Conservation Movement 1890–1920.* New York: Atheneum, 1969.

Heilman, Paul E., Harry W. Anderson, and David M. Baumgartner, eds. *Forest Soils of the Douglas-Fir Region.* Pullman: Washington State University Cooperative Extension Service, 1979.

Hunn, Eugene S. *Nch'i-Wana, "The Big River": Mid-Columbia Indians and Their Land.* Seattle: University of Washington Press, 1990.

Hussey, J. A. *Champoeg: Place of Transition.* Portland: Oregon Historical Society, 1967.

Jensen, Merrill, ed. *Regionalism in America.* Madison: University of Wisconsin Press, 1954.

Johannsen, Robert W. *Frontier Politics on the Eve of the Civil War.* Seattle: University of Washington Press, 1955.

Johansen, Dorothy O., and Charles M. Gates. *Empire of the Columbia: A History of the Pacific Northwest.* New York: Harper and Row, 1957.

Johnson, David Alan. *Founding the Far West: California, Oregon, and Nevada, 1840–1890.* Berkeley: University of California Press, 1992.

Kimerling, A. Jon, and Philip L. Jackson, eds. *Atlas of the Pacific Northwest*. Corvallis: Oregon State University Press, 1985.

Kline, Marcia B. *Beyond the Land Itself: Views of Nature in Canada and the United States*. Cambridge, Mass.: Harvard University Press, 1970.

Kolodny, Annette. *The Land Before Her: Fantasy and Experience of the American Frontiers, 1630–1860*. Chapel Hill: University of North Carolina Press, 1984.

Kruckeberg, Arthur R. *The Natural History of Puget Sound Country*. Seattle: University of Washington Press, 1991.

Lears, T. J. Jackson. *No Place of Grace: Antimodernism and the Transformation of American Culture 1880–1920*. New York: Pantheon Books, 1981.

McEvoy, Arthur F. *The Fisherman's Problem: Ecology and Law in the California Fisheries, 1850–1980*. Cambridge: Cambridge University Press, 1986.

McNeill, William H. *The Great Frontier: Freedom and Hierarchy in Modern Times*. Princeton: Princeton University Press, 1983.

Marchak, Patricia. *Green Gold: The Forest Industry in British Columbia*. Vancouver: University of British Columbia Press, 1983.

Maser, Chris. *The Redesigned Forest*. San Pedro, Calif.: R. and E. Miles, 1988.

Merchant, Carolyn. *Ecological Revolutions: Nature, Gender, and Science in New England*. Chapel Hill: University of North Carolina Press, 1989.

Minor, Rick, Stephen Dow Beckham, Phyliss E. Lancefield-Steeves, and Kathryn Anne Toepel. *Cultural Overview of the BLM Salem District*. University of Oregon Anthropological Papers no. 20. Eugene, Ore., 1980.

Mitchell, Lee Clark. *Witnesses to a Vanishing America: The Nineteenth-Century Response*. Princeton: Princeton University Press, 1981.

Nash, Roderick. *Wilderness and the American Mind*. New Haven: Yale University Press, 1973.

Norse, Elliott A. *Ancient Forests of the Pacific Northwest*. Washington, D.C.: Island Press, 1990.

O'Donnell, Terence. *An Arrow in the Earth: General Joel Palmer and the Indians of Oregon*. Portland: Oregon Historical Society, 1991.

Peterson, David, ed. *Big Sky, Fair Land: The Environmental Essays of A. B. Guthrie, Jr.* Flagstaff, Ariz.: Northland Press, 1988.

Pyne, Stephen J. *Fire in America: A Cultural History of Wildland and Rural Fire*. Princeton: Princeton University Press, 1982. Paper, 1988.

Richards, Kent D. *Isaac I. Stevens: Young Man in a Hurry*. Provo: Brigham Young University, 1979.

Ronda, James P. *Astoria and Empire*. Lincoln: University of Nebraska Press, 1990.

Ruby, Robert H., and John A. Brown. *The Chinook Indians: Traders of the Lower Columbia River*. Norman: University of Oklahoma Press, 1988. Paper edition.

Schwantes, Carlos A. *The Pacific Northwest: An Interpretive History*. Lincoln: University of Nebraska Press, 1989.

Sherwood, Morgan. *Big Game in Alaska: A History of Wildlife and People*. New Haven: Yale University Press, 1981.

Steen, Harold K. *The U.S. Forest Service: A History*. Seattle: University of Washington Press, 1976.

Suttles, Wayne, ed. *Northwest Coast*. Vol. 7 of William C. Sturtevant, ed., Handbook of North American Indians. Washington, D.C.: Smithsonian Institution, 1990.

Sutton, Dorothy, and Jack Sutton, eds. *Indian Wars of the Rogue River*. Grants Pass, Ore.: Josephine County Historical Society, 1969.

Thomas, Duncan W. *Changes in Columbia River Estuary Habitat Types over the Past Century*. Astoria, Ore.: Columbia River Estuary Study Taskforce, July 1983.

Throckmorton, Arthur L. *Oregon Argonauts: Merchant Adventurers on the Western Frontier.* Portland: Oregon Historical Society, 1961.

Tucker, Richard P., and J. F. Richards, eds. *Global Deforestation and the Nineteenth-Century World Economy.* Durham: Duke University Press, 1983.

Washburn, Wilcomb E., ed. *History of Indian-White Relations.* Vol. 4 of William C. Sturtevant, ed., *Handbook of North American Indians.* Washington, D.C.: Smithsonian Institution, 1988.

White, Richard. *It's Your Misfortune and None of My Own: A History of the American West.* Norman: University of Oklahoma Press, 1991.

_____. *Land Use, Environment, and Social Change: The Shaping of Island County, Washington.* Seattle: University of Washington Press, 1980.

_____. *The Middle Ground: Indians, Empires, and Republics in the Great Lakes Region, 1650–1815.* Cambridge: Cambridge University Press, 1991.

Williams, Michael. *Americans and Their Forests: A Historical Geography.* Cambridge: Cambridge University Press, 1989.

Winks, Robin W. *The Relevance of Canadian History: U.S. and Imperial Perspectives.* Toronto: Macmillan Company, 1979.

Winther, Oscar Osburn. *The Old Oregon Country: A History of Frontier Trade, Transportation, and Travel.* Lincoln: University of Nebraska Press, 1969.

Worster, Donald. *Dust Bowl: The Southern Plains in the 1930s.* New York: Oxford University Press, 1979.

Zelinsky, Wilbur. *The Cultural Geography of the United States.* Englewood Cliffs, N.J.: Prentice-Hall, 1973.

Articles and Unpublished Sources

Abbott, Carl. "Regional City and Network City: Portland and Seattle in the Twentieth Century." *Western Historical Quarterly* 23:3 (August 1992): 293–322.

Abdill, George B. "The Hide Hunters." *Umpqua Trapper* 41 (Spring Hunt 1968): 7–13.

Alverson, Edward R. Telephone conversation with the author, March 29, 1993.

_____. "Use of a County Soil Survey to Locate Remnants of Native Grassland in the Willamette Valley, Oregon." In *Ecosystem Management: Rare Species and Significant Habitats*, 107–12. Bulletin no. 471. New York: New York State Museum, 1990.

Ball, Georgiana. "The Monopoly System of Wildlife Management of the Indians and the Hudson's Bay Company in the Early History of British Columbia." *BC Studies* 66 (Summer 1985): 37–58.

Benner, Patricia. "Historical Reconstruction of the Coquille River and Surrounding Landscape." Draft copy, n.d.

Blok, Jack H. "The Evolution of Agricultural Resource Use Strategies in the Willamette Valley." Ph.D. dissertation, Oregon State University, 1973.

Boule, Marc E., and Kenneth F. Bierly. "History of Estuarine Wetland Development And Alteration: What Have We Wrought?" *Northwest Environmental Journal* 3:1 (Winter 1987): 43–61.

Boyd, Robert. "Strategies of Indian Burning in the Willamette Valley." *Canadian Journal of Anthropology* 5:1 (Fall 1986): 65–86.

Boyd, Robert T., and Yvonne P. Hajda. "Seasonal Population Movement Along the Lower Columbia River: The Social and Ecological Context." *American Ethnologist* 14:2 (May 1987): 309–26.

Buechner, Helmut K. "Some Biotic Changes in the State of Washington, Particularly During the Century 1853–1953." *Research Studies of the State College of Washington* 21:2 (June 1953): 154–92.

Cartwright, Charlotte Moffett. "Glimpses of Early Days in Oregon." *Oregon Historical Quarterly* 4:1 (March 1903): 55–69.

Clark, Colin W. "The Economics of Overexploitation." *Science* 181:4100 (August 17, 1973): 630–34.

Cole, Douglas. "Early Artistic Perceptions of the British Columbia Forest." *Journal of Forest History* 18:4 (October 1974): 128–31.

Cox, Thomas R. "Lower Columbia Lumber Industry, 1880–93." *Oregon Historical Quarterly* 67:2 (June 1966): 160–78.

Cumbler, John T. "The Early Making of an Environmental Consciousness: Fish, Fisheries Commissions, and the Connecticut River." *Environmental History Review* 15:4 (Winter 1991): 73–91.

Darris, Dale C., and Scott M. Lambert. "Improving Native Cool Season Grasses for Conservation Use in the Pacific Northwest." Unpublished paper, February 11, 1990.

Davenport, T. W. "An Object Lesson in Paternalism." *Oregon Historical Quarterly* 4:1 (March 1903): 33–54.

Doig, Ivan. "John J. McGilvra: The Life and Times of an Urban Frontiersman, 1827–1903." Ph.D. dissertation, University of Washington, 1969.

———. "John J. McGilvra and Timber Trespass: Seeking a Puget Sound Timber Policy 1861–1865." *Forest History* 13:4 (January 1970): 7–17.

Erickson, Kenneth A. "The Morphology of Lumber Settlements in Western Oregon and Washington." Ph.D. dissertation, University of California, Berkeley, 1965.

Feeny, David, Fikret Berkes, Bonnie J. McCay, and James M. Acheson. "The Tragedy of the Commons: Twenty-Two Years Later." *Human Ecology* 18:1 (March 1990): 1–19.

Ficken, Robert E., with William R. Sherrard. "The Port Blakely Mill Company, 1888–1903." *Journal of Forest History* 21:4 (October 1977): 202–17.

Finger, John R. "A Study of Frontier Enterprise: Seattle's First Sawmill, 1853–1869." *Forest History* 15:4 (January 1972): 24–31.

Frenkel, Robert E., and Eric F. Heintz. "Composition and Structure of Oregon Ash (*Fraxinus latifolia*) Forest in William L. Finley National Wildlife Refuge, Oregon." *Northwest Science* 61:4 (1987): 203–12.

Gadgil, Madhav. "Diversity: Cultural and Biological." *Trends in Ecology and Evolution* 2:12 (December 1987): 369–73.

Gates, Charles M. "A Historical Sketch of the Economic Development of Washington Since Statehood." *Pacific Northwest Quarterly* 39:3 (July 1948): 214–32.

Geer, T. T. "Incidents in the Organization of the Provisional Government." *Oregon Historical Quarterly* 2:4 (December 1901): 366–80.

Habeck, James R. "The Original Vegetation of the Mid-Willamette Valley, Oregon." *Northwest Science* 35:2 (May 1961): 65–77.

Hammond, Lorne. "Marketing Wildlife: The Hudson's Bay Company and the Pacific Northwest, 1821–49." *Forest and Conservation History* 37:1 (January 1993): 14–25.

Hardin, Garrett. "The Tragedy of the Commons." *Science* 162:3859 (December 13, 1968): 1243–48.

Head, Harlow Zinser. "The Oregon Donation Claims and Their Patterns." Ph.D. dissertation, University of Oregon, 1971.

Hobucket, Harry. "Quillayute Indian Traditon." *Washington Historical Quarterly* 15:1 (January 1934): 57–59.

Johannessen, Carl L., William A. Davenport, Artimus Millet, and Steven McWilliams. "The Vegetation of the Willamette Valley." *Annals of the Association of American Geographers* 61:2 (June 1971): 286–302.

Johansen, Dorothy O. "A Working Hypothesis for the Study of Migrations." *Pacific Historical Review* 36:1 (February 1967): 1–12.

Johnson, David A. "Migration, Settlement, and the Political Culture of Oregon, 1840–1880." Paper delivered at the Western Historical Association meeting, September 10, 1990.

Kirkwood, J. E. "The Vegetation of Northwestern Oregon." *Torreya* 2:9 (September 1902): 129–34.

Lamb, W. Kaye. "Early Lumbering on Vancouver Island: Part I, 1844–1855." *British Columbia Historical Quarterly* 2:1 (January 1938): 31–53. "Early Lumbering on Vancouver Island: Part II, 1855–1866," 2:2 (April 1938): 95–121.

Lang, William L. "An Eden of Expectations: Oregon Settlers and the Environment They Created." *Oregon Humanities* (Winter 1992): 25–29.

Lawrence, William E. "Field Book #3." Unpublished paper, Herbarium, Oregon State University, n.d.

Lowenthal, David. "The Pioneer Landscape: An American Dream." *Great Plains Quarterly* 2:1 (Winter 1982): 5–19.

McKinney, F. Ann. "Kalapuyan Subsistence: Reexamining the Willamette Falls Salmon Barrier." *Northwest Anthropological Research Notes* 18:1 (Spring 1984): 23–33.

Marchak, M. Patricia. "What Happens When Common Property Becomes Uncommon?" *BC Studies* 80 (Winter 1988–1989): 3–23.

Moir, William, and Peter Mika. "Prairie Vegetation of the Willamette Valley, Benton Co., Oregon." Unpublished paper, Herbarium, Oregon State University. 1972.

Morris, William G. "Forest Fires in Western Oregon and Western Washington." *Oregon Historical Quarterly* 35:4 (December 1934): 313–39.

Norton, H. H., E. S. Hunn, C. S. Martinsen, and P. B. Keely. "Vegetable Food Products of the Foraging Economies of the Pacific Northwest." *Ecology of Food and Nutrition* 14 (1984): 219–28.

Olsen, Michael Leon. "The Beginnings of Agriculture in Western Oregon and Western Washington." Ph.D. dissertation, University of Washington, 1970.

"Oregon Range Plants." Unpublished paper, Oregon State University Extension Service, Plant Materials Center, Corvallis, Oregon, n.d.

Pavel, Michael D., Gerald B. Miller, and Mary J. Pavel. "Too Long, Too Silent: The Threat to Cedar and the Sacred Ways of the Skokomish." *American Indian Culture and Research Journal* 17:3 (1993): 53–80.

Peck, Morton E. "Invasion of Exotic Plants and Their Economic Significance in Oregon." *Northwest Science* 22:3 (August 1948): 126–30.

Pisani, Donald J. "Forests and Conservation, 1865–1890." *Journal of American History* 72:2 (September 1985): 340–59.

Powell, Fred Wilbur. "Hall Jackson Kelley—Prophet of Oregon." *Oregon Historical Quarterly* 18:1 (March 1917): 1–54; 18:2 (June 1917): 93–139; 18:3 (September 1917): 167–223.

Rakestraw, Lawrence. "A History of Forest Conservation in the Pacific Northwest, 1891–1913." Ph.D. dissertation, University of Washington, 1955.

Reagan, Albert B. "Uses of Plants by West Coast Indians." *Washington Historical Quarterly* 25:2 (April 1934): 133–37.

Robbins, William G. "The 'Luxuriant Landscape': The Great Douglas Fir Bioregion." *Oregon Humanities* (Winter 1990): 2–7.

Ronda, James. "Calculating Ouragon." *Oregon Historical Quarterly* 94:2–3 (Summer–Fall 1993): 120–40.

———. "Essay Review. 'The Writingest Explorers': The Lewis and Clark Expedition in American Historical Literature." *Pennsylvania Magazine of History and Biography* 112:4 (October 1988): 607–30.

Rostlund, Erhard. "Freshwater Fish and Fishing in Native North America." In *University of California Publications in Geography*, 9:305. Berkeley: University of California Press, 1952.

Rymon, Larry Maring. "A Critical Analysis of Wildlife Conservation in Oregon." Ph.D. dissertation, Oregon State University, 1969.

Schalk, Randall F. "Estimating Salmon and Steelhead Usage in the Columbia Basin Before 1850: The Anthropological Perspective." *Northwest Environmental Journal* 2:2 (Summer 1986): 1–29.

Schwartz, E. A. "Blood Money: The Rogue River Indian War and Its Aftermath, 1850–1986." Ph.D. dissertation, University of Missouri, Columbia, 1991.

Sedell, James R., and Judith L. Froggatt. "Importance of Streamside Forests to Large Rivers: The Isolation of the Willamette River, Oregon, U.S.A., from Its Floodplain by Snagging and Streamside Forest Removal." *Verhandlungen: Internationale Vereinigung für theorelitche und angewandte Limnologie* [International Association of Theoretical and Applied Limnology] 22 (December 1984): 1828–34.

Shively, David D. "Landscape Change in the Tualatin Basin." Unpublished paper, Department of Geosciences, Oregon State University, 1993.

Spies, Thomas A., and Jerry F. Franklin. "Old Growth and Forest Dynamics in the Douglas-Fir Region of Western Oregon and Washington." *Natural Areas Journal* 8:3 (July 1988): 190–201.

Sprague, F. LeRoy, and Henry P. Hansen. "Forest Succession in the McDonald Forest, Willamette Valley, Oregon." *Northwest Science* 20:4 (November 1946): 89–97.

Steen, Harold Karl. "Forestry in Washington to 1925." Ph.D. dissertation, University of Washington, 1969.

Taylor, Joseph E. "Steelhead's Mother Was His Father, Salmon: Development and Declension of Aboriginal Conservation in the Oregon Country Salmon Fishery." M.A. thesis, University of Oregon, 1992.

Teensma, Peter Dominic Adrian. "Fire History and Fire Regimes of the Central Western Cascades of Oregon." Ph.D. dissertation, University of Oregon, 1987.

Thilenius, John F. "The *Quercus Garryana* Forests of the Willamette Valley, Oregon." *Ecology* 49:6 (Autumn 1968): 1124–33.

Towle, Jerry C. "Changing Geography of Willamette Valley Woodlands." *Oregon Historical Quarterly* 83:1 (Spring 1982): 66–87.

———. "Woodland in the Willamette Valley: An Historical Geography." Ph.D. dissertation, University of Oregon, 1974.

Vickers, Daniel. "Competency and Competition: Economic Culture in Early America." *William and Mary Quarterly*, 3d ser., 47:1 (January 1990): 3–29.

Warren, James Ronald. "A Study of the Congressional Debates Concerning the Oregon Question." Ph.D. dissertation, University of Washington, 1962.

Williams, Ira A. "The Drainage of Farm Lands in the Willamette and Tributary Valleys of Oregon." *Mineral Resources of Oregon* 1:4 (June 1914): 3–81.

Wolf, Donald. Letter to Robert R. Bunting. August 19, 1994.

Woodward, C. Vann. "The Age of Reinterpretation." *American Historical Review* 66:1 (October 1960): 1–19.

Yonce, Frederick J. "Lumbering and the Public: The Era of Disposal." *Journal of Forest History* 22:1 (January 1978): 4–17.

Zybach, Bob. "The Great Fires of the Oregon Coast Range: 1770–1933." Unpublished paper, May 1, 1988.

INDEX

Abortion, 17
Abrams, William Penn, 125
Abundance unlimited myth, 2, 4, 36, 42, 43, 155, 162
Acculturation, 64, 70
Acorns, 9, 13, 109
"Act for the Protection of Fish and Game, An" (1883) (Washington), 112
Agriculture
    crops, 104–5
    effects of, 38, 78–80, 89, 110, 161
    growth stages, 101
    mechanized, 90–92
    mixed, 106
    monoculture, 96, 105, 106
    and transportation, 91, 92
    See also under Douglas-fir bioregion; Euroamericans; Oregon; Washington
Agriculture, Department of
    Division of Forestry, 150
    forest reserves, 157
Air pollution, 84, 161
Alaska, 5
Albatross, 5
Albion (British ship), 140
Alcohol, 31, 54, 56, 65
Alder, 8, 10, 73, 74, 78, 81, 136, 158
Allen, Beverly S., 61
Allen, E. T., 156–57
Allen, Joseph S., 96, 105
Alsea Agency, 67
Alsea River, 67
American Association for the Advancement of Science, 150
American Forestry Association, 154
American Fur Company, 26, 27
American Society for Encouraging the Settlement of the Oregon Territory, 39
American vetch, 73
Amerindians in North America, 5
Ames, F. E., 116
Anadramous fish, 145. *See also* Salmon
Animals (indigenous)
    displacement, 1, 38, 89, 110, 111–12, 160–61
    as predators, 112–13
    See also Hunting; Livestock

Animism, 18, 20
Applegate, Jesse A., 13, 43, 80, 99, 100
Applegate Rogue Indians, 65
Apples, 90
Arkansas, 40
Ash (tree), 10, 37, 73, 74, 78, 136
Ash fertilizer, 13
Ashland Forest Reserve (Oregon), 151
Asian imports, 4
Aspen, 37, 78
Assimilation policy, 69
Astor, John Jacob, 26
Astoria (Oregon), 25, 26–27, 36
Atkinson, George, 137, 149
Audubon Society, 177

Baker, Mount, 32
Bald eagle, 111
Ball, John, 6, 17, 39, 41, 44, 55
Barley, 104
Barter. *See* Exchange economy
Baskets, 9, 10
Bass, 109
Beargrass, 9
Bears, 7, 9, 13, 112
    population decrease, 5, 113, 115
Beaver, 5
    dams, 7
    ponds, 78
    population, 29, 33, 34, 35, 79
    skins, 26, 33
Beebe, R. C., 117
Beeson, John, 57
Beets, 104
Bellingham (Washington), 130
Benton, Thomas Hart, 98
Bering-Chukchi platform, 5
Berries, 8, 10, 13
Bethel Colony (Aurora, Oregon), 91
Bigleaf maple, 73
Biodiversity, 118, 149
Bioregions, 3. *See also* Doulgas-fir bioregion
Birds, 1, 5–6, 111, 112, 113
Black bears, 9, 113
Blackberries, 90
Black cottonwood, 73
Black oak, 73

Black-tailed deer, 9, 111, 114
Black walnut, 148
Blain, Wilson, 57
Blanchet, François, 31
Blinn, Marshall, 138
Blok, Jack H., 101
Bluegrasses, 108
Blue wildrye, 74
Boag, Peter G., 189(n46)
Bobcats, 9
Bonneville Dam (Oregon), 160
Booth-Kelly Lumber Company, 155
Border states. *See* Settler society, places of
    origin
Bottle deposits, 159
Bounty contracts, 64–65
Bourgeois values, 44, 54
Bowers, Edward A., 154
Bowles, Samuel, 40, 73
Bows and arrows, 9, 10
Bracken, 8, 13
Brackenridge, William Dunlop, 12
Bradbury, Clement Adams, 122
Brants, 5
British Columbia (Canada), 3, 23, 34, 36, 55,
    60
Brown, Joseph Henry, 81, 93
Browne, J. Ross, 65, 75
Bruceport (Washington), 131
Buckskin, 9
Buffalo, 6, 163
Bull Run Forest Reserve (Oregon), 151
Bunchgrass, 74, 107
Bureaucratization, 4, 36, 152, 157
Burners, 145, 147
Burnett, Peter H., 39, 43, 44, 89, 122
Buttercup, 73
Butter prices, 123

Cabbage, 104
Calapooya Mountains, 11
California, 3, 9, 37, 160
    economy, 92
    forests, 136
    gold rush, 77, 123
    governor, first, 44
    lumber market, 122, 129
    mining, 107
California black oak, 73
California condor, 111
California danthonia, 74
California hazel, 73
California oatgrass, 74
California Stage Company, 86
Camas, 8, 9, 11, 13, 37, 62, 70, 74, 109
Canadian North West Company, 23
Canadian thistles, 108

Candlefish. *See* Eulachon
"Canoe Indians," 59
Canoes, 10
Capital investments, 36, 87, 88, 94
    external, 94, 95, 102, 126, 129
    internal, 94–95, 103
Capitalist ethos, 2, 101
Car emissions, 161
Carp, 109
Carrots, 104
    wild, 13
Carrying capacity, 106, 118
Cascade Locks, 126
Cascade Range, 3, 5, 9, 14, 33, 73, 83, 127
    pastures, 110, 113, 151
Cascade Range Forest Reserve, 85, 152
Catlin, George, 41
Cattail, 9
Cattle, 36, 37, 38, 106, 107, 109, 110
Cedar, 3, 10, 73, 82, 128, 136
    bark, 9
Celery, wild, 8
Celilo Falls (Columbia River), 10
Chehalis River, 77
Cherry, 73
Chicago, Milwaukee, and St. Paul Railroad,
    86
Chicken pox, 30
Chickens, 106
China, 23
Chinese thistles, 108
Chinese workers, 81
Chinookan speakers, 11
Chinook Beach (Washington), 146
Chinook Indians, 16, 30, 54
Chinook Jargon, 28
Chinook salmon, 11, 78
Chinquapin, 26
Christianity, 69, 70
Chum, 78
Civic virtue, 47, 93
Clackamas River, 124
Clams, 5, 11
Clark, William, 6, 24, 30, 39, 114
Clarke, Samuel A., 60, 83
Clatsop County (Oregon), 43
Clatsop Indians, 30
Clearcutting, 147, 148
Cleveland, Grover, 152
Climate change, 151
Clover, 74, 108
Clyman, James, 72, 109
Coast Range, 3, 14, 67, 73, 127
Coast strawberry, 73
Cody, Robin, 160
Coho salmon, 8, 79
Colonial dependency, 3, 159

Columbia (ship), 23
Columbia County (Oregon), 78, 108
Columbia District, 28, 32–33
Columbian (Olympia), 96, 141
Columbia River, 5, 19, 24, 38, 73
    commercial fishery, 11, 145, 202(n43)
    falls, 10, 122
    floodplain, 76
    name, 23
    pollution, 145
    sandbars, 126
    sawmills, 125, 145
    transportation, 84, 122, 126
    wetlands, 78, 79, 114
Columbia Slough, 124
Commencement Bay (Tacoma), 126
Concomly (Clatsop leader), 30
Condor, 111
Congregationalists, 39
Coniferous forests, 73, 74
    fire, 14–15
    and habitat stability, 8, 149
    litter, 14
    root system, 149
Conservationism, 4, 85, 115–18, 124, 150–58,
    162
    media campaign, 155
    preservationists, 152–53
    utilitarians, 152, 153–54, 156–58, 162
Constant, Isaac, 39
Cook, James, 22–23
Coonse, Henry, 56
Cooper, J. G., 48, 54
Cooper, James Fenimore, 41, 56
Coos Bay (Oregon), 126, 127, 131, 141
Coquille River, 8, 90
Corn, 70, 104
Cottonwood, 73, 74
Cougars, 112, 115
Cowlitz (Washington), 31, 37, 38, 121, 140
Cowlitz Falls, 11
Cowlitz Indians, 11
Cowlitz River, 70
    Valley, 46
Cow parsnip, 8
Cox, R. F., 155
Cox, Thomas R., 129
Coyotes, 112
Crab apples, 90
Cranberries, 90
Crane Prairie, 110
Cranes, 6, 78, 79, 111
Cranfill, Isom, 124
Crappie, 109
Crawford, James, 146
Cronon, William, 130
Crop rotation, 38, 105

Cucumbers, 104
Curlew, 78, 79
Cutthroat trout, 7

Dairying, 38, 108
Dandelions, 108
Danthonia, 74
Dart, Anson, 62, 92, 125
Dawes Act (1887), 68
Day, L. P., 65
Deady, Matthew P., 73, 81, 123, 124
Deciduous trees, 8, 81, 149
Deer, 1, 6, 9, 13, 78, 111, 114
    conservation, 118
    population increase, 118
    population loss, 56, 111, 112, 113, 115
Deforestation, 80–85
Dentalium, 5
Depression (1837), 94
De Smet, Pierre-Jean, 6, 31
Devil's club, 26
Diapers, 10
Dickson, Roy, 116
Diking, 78–79, 184(n31)
Dioxins, 161
Diphtheria, 55
Disease, 29–31, 54–56
Division of labor, 16
Dodwell, Arthur, 110
Dolbeer, John, 147
Donation Land Law. *See* Oregon Donation
    Land Act
Donkey engine. *See* Steam donkey
Douglas, David, 12, 13, 33
Douglas, James, 25, 28, 31, 37, 48
Douglas County (Oregon), 115
Douglas fir *(Pseudotsuga menziesii)*, 9, 15, 73,
    81, 82, 83, 85, 126, 136, 156, 158
Douglas-fir bioregion, 1, 3–4
    agriculture, 36, 37–38, 87
    agriculture, effects of, 38, 78–80
    and Amerindians, 5, 15, 20–21 (*see also*
      Native Americans)
    climate, 42, 89
    economic development, 62, 87, 179(n50)
    Euroamericans, 20, 22–25 (*see also* Fur
      trade; Industrial society; Settler society)
    exploration, 22–23, 96
    feelings about, 42–50
    forests, 75
    genetic diversity, loss of, 1, 89
    land acquisition, 97, 98–99
    livestock, 36, 37, 38
    livestock, effects of, 38
    mammalian species, 9
    and national markets, 87–88
    timber industry, 4, 26

Douglas-fir bioregion, *continued*
  tree clearing, 25–26
  See also Oregon; Washington
Draining, 78–80, 110, 161
Drift jams, 7
Dryer, Thomas Jefferson, 49
Ducks, 6, 78, 79
Dugan, Joseph A., 77
Duwamish River, 77
Dysentery, 30, 55

Eagles, 111
Eagon, Joseph P., 41
Earth Lodge cult, 70
Ecological damage
  and agriculture, 38, 78–80, 89, 110, 161
    (*see also* Plants)
  and animal population loss, 1, 38, 89, 110,
    111–12
  to fish, 109, 144, 145–47, 149, 161
  and forest fires, 80, 81–85, 148, 154, 161
  and forest fire suppression, 81, 85,
    154–57, 161
  and habitat imbalance, 118, 149
  and land grants, 99–100
  and lumber industry, 144, 145–47, 158, 162
  and mining, 62
  and public policy, 162–63
  and railroads, 86–88, 101–2, 133–34
  and timber industry, 144, 147–50, 161
  warnings about, 149–50
  to wildlife, 111–17, 148, 149, 160–61
  See also Air pollution; Settler society, and
    transformation of landscape; Water
    pollution
Ecological revolution, 72, 182(n1)
Economic development, 53, 177(n10)
Ecotones, 14
"Edge" environments, 13, 75
Edwards, Philip L., 39
Elderberry, 74
Electric lights (1880s), 126
Elk, 1, 7, 9, 13, 114
  conservation, 118
  population increase, 117
  population loss, 56, 111, 112, 113, 115
Emerson, George, 147
Emery, W. G., 117
English bluegrass, 108
Environmental determinism, 44, 100
Environmental Protection Agency, 162
Estuarian habitat, 8
  and draining and diking, 78–79, 184(n31)
Ethnobotany, 9, 10, 18
Eucha Port Orford Indians, 65
Eugene (Oregon), 73
Eulachon, 6, 10

Euroamericans
  agriculture, 15, 37–38
  and Native Americans, 1, 2, 3, 15, 17, 21,
    27–28, 29–30, 35, 36, 47, 51
  settlement, 1, 35 (*see also* Settler society)
  See also Fur trade; Industrial society;
    Lumber industry; *under* Douglas-fir
    bioregion
Evans, Edward, 54
Evans, Elwood, 52, 133
Everett (Washington), 134
Evergreens. *See* Coniferous forests
Exchange economy, 94, 125
Extinction, 1. *See also* Animals, displace-
  ment; Plants, displacement
Extractive industries, 3, 87. *See also* Fishing,
  commercial; Logging; Milling; Mining;
  Timber industry

Fairchild, J. H., 66
Fallow fields, 105
Farm size, 99, 100–101
Fences, 104, 107, 110
Fernow, Bernard, 154–55
Ferns, 8, 26, 74, 77, 82–83
Fescue, 74
Finance capital, 4. *See also* Capital
  investments
Finley, William L., 116
Fir, 3, 9, 73, 74. *See also* Coniferous forests
Fire, 12–15, 48, 73, 80–85
  crown, 14, 85
  ground, 14
  suppression, 81, 85, 154–57, 161, 162
  surface, 14–15
  tree clearing technique, 82
  See also Smoke; *under* Forests; Grasslands
Firewood, 9, 82, 120
Fish, 6, 11, 78
  and hydroelectric dams, 161
  imported, 109
  indigenous, displacement, 109
  logging impact on, 144, 149
  sawmill impact on, 145–47
Fish hatcheries, 146–47, 161
Fish hooks, 6
Fishing
  commercial, 11, 69, 75, 145–46, 161,
    202(n43)
  recreational, 83, 161
  rights, 69, 160
Fish ladders, 145
Flat Heads. *See* Chinook Indians
Flattery, Cape, 127
Flax, 108
Floats, 10
Flooding, 7, 8, 41, 74, 77, 124

Flowers, 48
Floyd, John, 40, 96, 98
Flumes, 136
Food preservation, 10, 11
Forage, 9, 109, 110
Forbs, 73
Forest Reserve Act (1891), 151
Forests, 49
  accessible, 137, 147
  Atlantic coast, 123, 133, 149
  attitudes about, 120, 124, 136–37, 149, 151
  conservation, 124, 139, 150–58, 161–62
  denseness, 26, 75–76, 120
  ecosystem, 8, 9, 150, 158
  fires, 12–15, 80, 81–85, 148, 156, 161 (see also Fire, suppression)
  gallery, 74
  Great Lakes, 133
  litter, 7, 14, 149
  Midwest, 136, 149
  new growth, 148
  old growth, 1, 18, 156
  prescribed burns, 161–62
  private ownership, 2–3, 85, 134, 141, 142
  in public domain, 137–41, 142–43, 152, 157, 162
  reserves, 85, 151, 152, 154, 157
  riparian, 73–74, 149
  and road travel, 26
  scientific management, 156, 157, 158, 162
  settlement avoidance, 75–76
  in South, 133
  tidewater, 126
  wise use, 156
  See also Coniferous forests; Douglas-fir bioregion; Logging; Lumber industry; Timber industry
Fort Astoria (Oregon), 26–27, 38
Fort Clatsop (Oregon), 24
Fort Colville (Oregon), 107
Fort Davis (Washington), 72
Fort George (Oregon), 27, 33, 38
Fort Langley (British Columbia), 36
Fort Nisqually (Washington), 37
Fort Vancouver (Washington), 30, 33, 36, 38
  sawmill, 121
Foxes, 9
France, 23
Fraser River, 36
  gold strike (1858), 77, 107
French Canadians, 97
French Prairie (Oregon), 73
Fruit, 8, 90, 104
Fuller, Andrew, 149
Furniture, 136
Furs, 4, 26
Fur trade, 23, 24, 120

American, 26–27
British, 24, 26–27, 28, 32–33
decline (nineteenth century), 23, 33, 37
middlemen, 27–28
and Native Americans, 27, 28, 57
and settlement, 36, 39
trade goods, 27, 28
Fur trappers, 3, 29

Gaines, John P., 61
Game drives, 9
Game wardens, 116, 117
Gardened, systematized landscape, 47, 73, 98, 111, 115, 118
Garry oak, 73
Geer, Ralph C., 40
Geese, 6, 112
General Land Office, 139, 141
General Revision Act (1891), 152
Genetic diversity, 1, 7
Ghost Dance, 70
Gill, John, 114
Gill nets, 6
Glaciation, 5, 76
Glendale (Oregon), 115
Goble (Oregon), 77
Gold, 77, 105, 123
Gold Beach (Oregon), 116
Goodell, J. W., 72
Grand Coulee Dam (Washington), 160
Grand fir, 73
Grand Mound prairie (Washington), 47–48, 57
Grand Ronde Reservation (Oregon), 64, 66
  non-Indian settlement on, 68
Grant, Ulysses S., 69
Grape, 74, 90
Grasses, 73, 74, 78, 106, 108
Grasshoppers, 14, 81
Grasslands, 13, 37–38, 74
  fires, 80, 83, 110
  overgrazing, 106–8, 110–11
Gray, Robert, 23
Gray plover, 79
Grays Harbor (Washington), 126, 147
Gray wolves, 9
Grazing. See under Livestock
Great Britain, 22, 23, 140
  Navy, 27
  See also Fur trade, British; Hudson's Bay Company; Treaty of 1846
Great Lakes timberlands, 133
"Great Migration" (1843), 40
Great Northern Railroad, 86
Great River of the West. See Columbia River
Greeley, William B., 137
Grizzly bears, 113

Grouse, 9
Grover, L. F., 92
Gum, 10
Guthrie, A. B., Jr., 49

Habitat
   imbalance, 118, 149
   stability, 8
   variety, 7, 148
Hancock, Samuel, 55
Hanford Nuclear Plant (Washington), 160
Harbor porpoises, 5
Harbor seals, 5
Harden, Absolom B., 43, 49, 55, 82, 106, 121, 136
Hardin, Garrett, 34
Hardwoods, 136
Harper's New Monthly Magazine, 58, 100
Harpooning, 6
Harris, P. T., 116
Harvesters, self-binding, 90
Hastie, Thomas, 83
Hawaii (formerly Sandwich Islands), 122
Hawaiian workers, 121
Hay, 106
Hayden, Mary, 41
Hazel, 73, 136
Hazelnuts, 13
Hazing, 110, 112
Hemlock, 3, 9, 15, 82, 126, 137
Herons, 6
Herring, 6
Hickory, 136
Hides, 37, 113, 114, 115
Hines, Gustavus, 40, 49, 55, 57, 74
Hogs, 106, 109
Holden, Horace, 75
Homestead Act (1862), 97, 143
Honey, 14
Hood, Mount, 49
Hops, 70, 104
Horn, 9, 113
"Horse Indians," 59
Horses, 31, 32, 37, 106, 109, 135
Horsetail, 8
Hough, Franklin B., 150
Howison, Neil M., 19, 100, 111, 112, 136
Huddleston, James, 115
Hudson, Joseph (Kalapuyan), 60
Hudson's Bay Company, 19, 24, 25, 27
   and agriculture and livestock, 37–38, 120–21
   blankets, 28
   and country south of Columbia River, 32–33
   Cowlitz establishment, 31, 37, 38
   distillery, 38
   extermination of fur mammals, 32, 33–34
   land, 51, 76
   and retired workers settlement, 36–37
   sawmills, 121
   and settlement support, 38
Hume brothers, 202(n43)
Humus, 83
Hunn, Eugene S., 18
Hunt, Henry H., 121, 122, 123
Hunting
   commercial, 113–14, 115, 117
   recreational, 83, 113, 114, 118
Hunting dogs, 112
Hunting season legislation, 112
Huntington, C. A., 64
Huntington, J. W. Perit, 66–67
Hydroelectric power, 160, 161
Hydrology, 79
Hydropower, 90, 121, 122, 124, 125, 129

Idaho, 107
Idaho bentgrass, 74
Illinois, 40
Incense cedar, 73
Independence, 92, 93, 95, 101
Indiana, 40
Indian agents, 57, 61, 62, 64
Indian reservations, 61, 62, 63, 64–67
   agriculture, 69, 70
   and Christian churches, 69
   land rights, 67
   livestock, 69
   settlement by non-Indians, 67–69
   sites, 66–67, 68
Indian Shakerism, 71
Indian treaties, 61–62, 63–64, 69, 96
Indian War (1855–1856), 62–63, 179(n50)
Individualism, 53–54, 152, 153
Industrialization, 1, 36, 87, 101, 147, 152
Industrial society, 36, 59, 86, 102, 134, 158
   and forest fires, 83, 84
   and forests as market resource, 120
   See also Lumber industry; Timber industry
Infanticide, 17
Influenza, 30
Interior, Department of the, 139, 157
Intermarriage, 36, 57
Iowa, 40
Ireland, T. A., 115

Jacksonville (Oregon), 57, 107, 123
Jeffers, Joseph, 64
John (Applegate Rogue chief), 65, 66
John Day River, 107
Johnson, David Alan, 93
Joseph (Nez Perce chief), 59

Juan de Fuca Strait, 5, 22, 76, 127
Judson, Phoebe Goodell, 40, 47, 57–58, 82, 112

Kalapuyan Indians, 11, 13, 55, 109
Kanim, Hetley (Snoqualmie), 56
Keil, William, 75, 91
Kelley, Hall Jackson, 39
Kellogg, Spencer, 139
Kentucky bluegrass, 108
Kitsap County (Washington), 75
Kittredge, William, 162
Klamath mountain province, 3
Klickitat Indians, 31–32
Klondike gold rush (1890s), 102
Kuhelamit Indians, 19

Labor, 91, 92, 94. *See also under* Native
    Americans
Labor theory of value, 51
Ladlam and Company, 67
Lambs, 109
Lamprey, 6
Land, surveyed and unsurveyed, 142
Land Conservation and Development Com-
    mission (1973), 159
Landfill, 145
Land grants, 40–41, 96, 97–98, 139, 141,
    142–43
    effects of, 99–100
    universities, 142
Lane County (Oregon), 155
Langille, H. D., 83
Largemouth bass, 109
Laws, John, 161
Lee, Jason, 39
Legumes, 108
Leighton, Caroline C., 46, 48, 60–61, 130
Lettuce, wild, 108
Lewis, Meriwether, 24, 33, 39
Lewis County, Washington, Agricultural
    Association, 96, 105
Licorice, 8
Lightning, 14
Linn, Lewis, 98
Linnton (Oregon), 43
Litter, 7, 14, 149. *See also under* Logging
Little, A. C., 109, 116, 146
Livestock, 36, 37, 38, 69, 89, 106, 109
    grazing, 62, 105, 106–8, 110–11, 113
    groundwater pollution, 110
    mining markets, 107, 108
Locust trees, 136
Logging, 1, 75, 122, 124
    contract, 142
    fires, 83
    litter, 83
    railroads, 147

range, 135
    techniques, 144, 148
    waste, 148, 151
    workers, 125, 130
    See also Timber industry
Log holding dams, 145
Log jams, 7, 26, 79, 136
Loons, 6
Love, Lewis, 124
Lowenthal, David, 45
Lower Coquille Indians, 57
Luark, Michael, 40, 44, 77, 81, 82, 90, 94, 100,
    109
Lumber industry, 15, 36, 87–88, 94, 121, 123,
    125
    effect of, 145–47
    markets, 122–23, 124, 127, 129, 131
    mechanization, 147
    prices, 121, 122, 124, 132
    production, 122, 134, 135
    progressive wing, 158
    technology, 125, 147
    transport, 121–22, 125
    workers, 130
    See also Sawmills; *under* Oregon;
        Washington
Lummi Indians, 71
Luse, H. H., 141
Lyman, H. S., 101, 102
Lynx, 112

McCall, Tom, 159, 161
McGilvra, John J., 137–38
McGraw, John, 155
Machinery, 90, 91–92
Mackenzie, Alexander, 23
McKenzie River, 11
McLeod, Alexander, 12
McLoughlin, John, 28, 32, 33, 36, 121
McNeill, William H., 4
Madrone, 73
Maine, 129
Makah Indians, 5
Malaria, 30, 41
Manifest destiny, 40
Manufacturing, 87
Maple, 10, 37, 73, 74, 81, 136
Marchak, Patricia, 124
Marine invertebrates, 5
Marino, Cesare, 71
Marion County (Oregon), 105
Market economy, 54, 91, 92, 94–95
    effect, 104, 158
Marmots, 9
Marsh, George Perkins, 149
Marshland, 73, 74
    draining and diking, 15, 79

Marx, Leo, 36
Masks, 10
Matlock, W. T., 124
Mats, 9
Mazzard cherry, 73
Measles, 30, 55
Medicinal plants, 9, 10
Medicine Creek Treaty (1859), 62
"Mediterranean of the Northwest." *See*
    Puget Sound
Meeker, Ezra, 70, 104
Methodists, 39, 40, 121
Metropolitan control over hinterlands, 36,
    159
Metzger, J. R., 114
Mickey, Ross, 162
Mid-Atlantic states immigrants, 40
Miller, Perry, 4
Milling, 75, 77, 83, 91. *See also* Sawmills
Miners, 62, 77, 105, 123
Mining, 75, 77, 83, 107, 108
Minto, John, 39, 41, 48, 78, 79–80, 112, 114,
    122
Missionaries, 39, 51, 121
Mississippi River, 41, 74
Missouri, 40
Missouri River, 74
Mix, Charles E., 67
Mollusks, 5
Montgomery, J. B., 155
Moore, W. B., 78
Morse, Eldridge, 130
Mosses, 9
Mowers, 90
Muir, John, 110
Murphy, John, 115
Murray, William, 115
Muskrats, 7, 79
Mussels, 5

Nash, Wallis, 87, 105
National identity, 152
National Park Service, 162–63
Native Americans (Pacific Northwest)
    agriculture, 69, 70 (*see under* Settler society,
        and Native Americans, "reform" of)
    birth control, 17
    bounties on, 64–65
    clothing, 9
    cosmology, 18–19
    cultural and physical adaptation to envi-
        ronment, 11, 18, 20
    culture, 15–20, 56, 65, 69–71, 160
    disease, 29–31, 54–56
    displacement, 1, 21, 51, 52, 57, 61, 98 (*see
        also* Indian reservations)
    early, 5

    Euroamerican perception of, 29, 51, 56
    fire, use of, 12–15, 48, 73, 80, 98
    fishing techniques, 6, 9, 13
    and forest and stream environment, 1,
        5–15, 20
    and fur trade, 27, 28, 35, 57
    gift giving, 16–17, 19, 27
    groups, 5, 11, 19, 30, 31
    healers, 70
    horses, 31, 32
    horticulture, 15, 51, 62
    hunting techniques, 9, 13
    as labor, 51, 63, 69, 70
    land use boundaries, 11, 31–32
    and missionaries, 52
    as nonagricultural, 5–20
    plant use, 9, 10
    population reduction, 56, 98
    resource limitation practices, 12, 13,
        17–18, 19–20, 29, 35
    ritual, 10, 11, 14, 18, 70–71
    romanticized, 59–61
    settlement, 10, 11
    social ordering, 16
    tools and utensils, 9, 10
    trade, 27
    trade language, 28
    twentieth century, 159–60
    and U.S. military, 63
    villages, 10, 11
    water transportation, 6
    women, 70
    worldview, 18–20
    See also Indian treaties; Indian War; *under*
        Euroamericans; Settler society
Nature as capital resource, 2, 4, 153
Neah Bay (Washington), 55, 63–64
Needlegrass, 74
Nesmith, James W., 66–67
Nestachee River, 126
Nestucca River, 126
Nets, 6, 9, 10
Newell, William A., 68
New England, 23, 160
    emigrants, 40, 87, 94, 99
Newsom, David, 105
New York Herald, 39
Nez Perce Indians, 59
Nisqually (Washington), 37–38
Nisqually Plains, 104
Nisqually River, 37
Nooksack Indians, 71
Nooksack River wetlands, 78
Nooksack Valley, 77
Nootka Sound (Vancouver Island), 22
Northern Pacific Railroad, 86, 134, 139
North Santiam River, 11

Northwest Forestry Association, 161, 162
North West Fur Company, 24, 27, 33
Nuts, 10, 13

Oak openings, 73, 75
Oaks, 37, 48, 73, 81, 136
Oats, 79, 104, 105, 106
Ohio, 40
Ohio River, 41
Ohio Statesman (Columbus), 39
Olympia (Washington), 49, 84, 86, 87, 146
Olympic Forest Reserve (Washington), 85
Olympic mountain province, 3, 9
Olympic National Park (Washington), 118
Olympic peninsula, 111
Onion, 104
    wild, 13
Open-range management system, 106, 109
Oregon
    agricultural land, 78, 99–101, 184(n31)
    agriculture, 36, 77, 91, 92, 93, 100, 103,
        104, 123
    biologist, 118
    Board of Fish Commissioners, 116
    bottle bill (1971), 159
    and California gold rush, 123
    climate, 89
    deer and elk, 9
    economy, 92, 93, 100, 103
    fish and game laws, 116, 145
    forest fires, 80, 83, 84, 155, 161
    forest reserves, 85, 151, 152
    forests, 1, 10, 75, 85, 127, 136, 140
    forests, private ownership, 143–44
    gold, 123
    government (1843), 97, 99, 112
    governor, 116
    grasses, 108
    harbors, 126
    hunting legislation, 116
    hydroelectric power, 160
    Indian reservations, 64, 65, 67
    industry, 87, 101, 102
    land grants, 97–98, 99
    land rights, 97
    livestock, 36, 106, 107, 108
    lumber industry, 121–22, 123, 124, 125,
        126, 127, 131, 134, 141
    mining, 107
    Native Americans, 11, 13, 30, 57, 59, 62,
        64–65, 113
    overgrazing, 106, 107
    population (1850s), 123
    population (1880–1890), 86, 93, 101, 103
    population, homogeneous, 159
    railroads, 86, 101–2
    roads, 98

rural, 102, 159
sawmills, 125, 126, 127, 141
school teacher, first, 29
settlement, 39–41, 43, 44, 49, 77, 86–87,
    92–93, 101, 111, 172(n1) (*see also*
    Willamette Valley)
stagecoach service, 86
Territory (1848), 97
thistle law, 108
timber industry, 77–78, 127, 140
tourism, 159
twentieth century, 102, 159
urban, 87, 93, 101, 159
water rights, 97
wetlands loss, 78, 79, 184(n31)
wildlife conservation, 116, 118
wildlife loss, 79, 184(n31)
wildlife scalp bounty, 112–13
Oregon ash, 10, 73
Oregon City (Oregon), 10, 86, 121, 124, 126
Oregon Conservation Commission, 156
Oregon Development League Convention
    (1906), 153
Oregon Donation Land Act (1850–1855), 93,
    97, 98, 99, 123, 189(n46)
Oregon grape, 74, 90
Oregonian (Portland), 51, 84, 101, 109, 110,
    143, 145, 151
Oregon Spectator (Oregon City), 122, 123, 124
Oregon Statesman (Salem), 44, 61, 67, 95, 100,
    106, 140
Oregon Trail, 39
Oregon white oak, 73
Oregon yew, 136
Otters, 5, 26, 33, 35
Ox-drawn stage, 86
Ox-drawn wagons, 135, 136
Oysters, 5, 67, 131

Pacific madrone, 73
Pacific Northwest, 5, 22, 25, 34, 159
    exploration (sixteenth to eighteenth cen-
        turies), 22, 23, 24–25
    geology, 3, 4
    myth of, 1, 4, 163
    See also Douglas-fir bioregion; Oregon;
        Washington
Pacific Ocean, 5
Pacific Rim, 129, 131
Palmer, Joel, 32, 62, 69
Parkman, Francis, 41
PCBs (polychlorinated biphenyl), 161
Peas, 70, 104
Peck, Abraham, 115
Pennoyer, Sylvestor, 116
Perch, 109
Pesticides, 161

Pigs. *See* Hogs
Pinchot, Gifford, 155
Pine, 3, 10, 13, 37, 73, 133
Pioneer and Democrat (Olympia), 54, 129
Pioneers, The (Cooper), 41
Plains, 37, 48
Plants
  catalog, 109
  displacement, 38, 89, 106, 107, 108, 160
  exotic, 108, 160
  imported, 104, 108
  indigenous, 8, 13, 73, 74, 90, 109
Plimpton, Silas Bullard, 40, 57, 63, 89, 93
Plover, 78, 79
Plummer, Fred G., 110
Point Defiance Mill Company (Tacoma), 147
Political party system, 53
Polk County (Oregon), 80, 105
Ponderosa pine, 73
Pools, 7, 8
Pope, Andrew, 138
Pope and Talbot steam mill (Port Gamble, Washington), 125
Poplars, 37
Porpoises, 5
Port Gamble (Washington), 125
Portland (Oregon), 86, 87, 114, 121, 124, 125, 159, 179(n50)
Port Orford (Oregon), 57, 64
Possum, 160–61
Potatoes, 70, 91, 104, 123
Potlatch, 17, 18, 20, 70
Prairie, 37, 47, 48, 69, 73, 74, 78, 80–81
Prairie oak, 136
Preemption Act (1841), 97
Presbyterians, 39, 57
Progressive movement, 85, 159
Protestants, 51
Puget Sound, 23, 37, 76, 127, 160
  forests, 137
  navigation, 147
  sawmills, 125, 126, 128, 131, 147
  tideland diking, 78
Puget Sound Lumber Company, 144
Puget Sound Trough, 76
Puget's Sound Agricultural Company, 37, 38
Pull-tab cans, 159
Pumpkins, 104
Putnam, Roselle, 43, 55, 92
Puyallup River, 37, 77
  Valley, 104
Pyne, Stephen, J., 85

Quileute Indians, 5, 68
Quinault Indians, 5
Quinault Reservation (Washington), 68

Raccoons, 9
Ragwort, 108
Railroads, 36, 86, 95–96, 136
  impact of, 86–88, 101–2, 133–34
  land grants to, 139
  logging, 147
  See also Transcontinental railroads
Rainbow trout, 6, 109
Rainfall, 5, 89
Rainier (Oregon), 40
Rainier National Forest (Washington), 85, 116
Raspberries, 90
Reapers, 90
Red alder, 8, 73
Red fescue, 74
Red-top, 108
Redwoods, 136
Reed, Cyrus, 125
Reforestation, 1, 83, 151
Regionalism, 3, 160
Republicanism, 47, 53, 92, 93, 98, 102, 152
Rhizomes, 8
Rhododendron, 26
Richardson shingle mill (Olympia), 146
Riddle, George W., 13, 39, 58, 90
Riddle, William, 39
Riffles, 6, 7, 149
Riseland, John, 147
River otter, 5
Rivers, 5. *See also* Streams; Water transportation; *individual names*
Rixon, Theodore F., 110
Roads, 85–86, 98, 136
Rod and gun clubs, 117
Rogers, John R., 155
Rogue River Indians, 13, 62, 65, 66
Rogue River Valley, 9, 75
Root fibers, 100
Ross, Alexander, 19, 25, 28–29, 33, 135
Russia, 5, 22, 23
Russian thistles, 108
Rye, 104

Sacramento (California), 86, 129
St. Helens, Mount, 49
St. Louis Reporter, 39
Saint Paul (Minnesota), 86
Salal, 26
Salem (Oregon), 48, 73, 81, 108, 114, 123
Salmon, 1, 8, 10, 11, 12
  and Native American ritual, 19
  population decrease, 114, 145, 146, 161
  run (July), 11
  species, 6, 8
  stream habitat, 7–8, 78–79, 144, 145–46
Salmonberry, 74

Salomon, E. S., 154
Sam (Rogue Indian), 66
Sandwich Islands (now Hawaii), 122
San Francisco, 67, 84, 94, 131, 132
San Juan Islands, 77
Sargent, Charles Sprague, 150
Saskatoon serviceberry, 73
Sauvie's Island (Oregon), 32, 38, 39
Savage, George, 26, 56
Sawdust, 145–46, 147
Sawmills, 121, 122, 123, 124–26
    impact, 144, 145–47
    log size limits, 135
    size, 141–42
    steam-powered, 125, 128 (see also
        Hydropower)
    stumpage fee, 138–39
    workers, 125
Scalp bounty, 112–13
Scappoose Plains (Oregon), 73
Scarlet fever, 55
Schurz, Carl, 139
Schwantes, Carlos A., 160
Schwarz, C. Frederick, 156
Scientific management, 153–54. See also
    under Forests
Scotch broom, 108, 160
Scott, Harvey, 51, 101, 102, 103
Sea lions, 5
Seals, 5, 114
Sea mammals, 5
Sea otters, 5, 26
Seattle, 86, 87, 130, 159
Seattle Post-Intelligencer, 151
Sea urchins, 5
Sediment, 7
Seeds, 10, 13, 15
Sequoias, 136
Serviceberry, 73
Settler society (1840s–1880s), 4, 36, 37–39,
    72, 172(n1)
    attitudes, 54, 72, 89, 92–93, 95–96, 98,
        99–100, 101, 102–3, 104, 115–17, 133,
        158, 189(n46)
    boosterism and reasons to emigrate,
        38–40, 41–42, 49–50, 77, 92, 93, 97, 134,
        175(n25)
    cultural diversity (see Washington)
    cultural homogeneity, 93, 103 (see also
        Oregon)
    distances, 91
    and forests, 75–76, 90, 120, 136
    intermarriage, 36, 57
    labor scarcity, 91, 92
    land rights, 51, 52, 58, 61
    land titles, 92, 98, 189(n46)
    market economy, 91, 94–95
    and Native Americans, attitude toward,
        47, 50, 51–53, 54, 56–63, 65, 66, 69
    and Native Americans, "reform" of, 63–64,
        66–67, 68, 69 (see also Indian reservations)
    places of origin, 40, 41, 74, 87, 99
    rural, 40, 76, 87, 90, 91
    and transformation of landscape, 45–50,
        52–53, 62, 72, 80, 86–88, 89, 96
    urban, 40, 59, 87, 91
    water resources, 90
    See also Oregon; Washington
Shakerism. See Indian Shakerism
Shamans, 56
Shane, Carlos, 149
Shaw, William, 41, 92
Sheep, 37, 38, 106, 110–11, 112, 113
Shellfish, 5
Sheridan, Philip, 70
Shields, Benjamin F., 115
Shoalwater Bay (Washington), 90, 131
Shrubs, 73
Sierra Nevada range, 9, 107
Siletz Reservation (Oregon), 65, 66
    settlement by non-Indians, 67
Siletz River, 67
Simmons, Michael T., 41, 76
Simpson, Benjamin, 124
Simpson, George, 16, 28, 32, 33, 38, 121
Sitka spruce, 10
Siuslaw River, 67
Skagit River, 26, 78
Skagit Valley, 77
Skidding, 135–36
Skinner, Alonzo A., 61
Skipanon Creek, 78
Skunk cabbage, 8
Slacum, William, 29, 30, 34
Slash and burn, 82
Slavery, 41
Slocum, John, 71
Smallpox, 30, 54, 55
Smelt, 6
Smith, F. M., 57
Smith, Isaac, 75, 81, 106, 107
Smith, Margaret, 75
Smith, Thomas, 89, 122
Smoke, 84, 145, 161
Snipes, 78, 79
Snohomish City (Washington), 130
Snohomish River wetlands, 78, 79
Snohomish Valley, 77
Snoqualmie Indians, 19, 55
Snoqualmie River, 19
Snowberry, 73
Soil
    alluvial, 174
    compaction, 105

Soil, *continued*
   drainage, 74, 105
   erosion, 148–49
   fertility, 38, 74, 105
   and fires in logged areas, 83
   moisture, 83
   nutrients, 7, 15, 148
   sandy, 76
   tideland prairie, 78
South America, 122, 131
South Santiam River, 11, 114
Spain, 22, 23
Spawning beds, 7, 144
Splash dams, 144, 145
Spruce, 3, 10, 82, 126, 128, 137
Squash, 104
Squaxin Indians, 71
Stagecoach service, 86
Starr, Frederick, 149
Stayton (Oregon), 100
Steamboats, 77, 84
Steam donkey, 147, 148
Steelhead trout, 7
Stevens, Charles, 89, 93, 94
Stevens, Isaac I., 62
Stillaguamish Indians, 15
Stillaguamish tide flats, 78
Stinging nettle, 8
Strait of Juan de Fuca, 5, 22, 76, 127
Stratton, Riley Evans, 67
Strawberry, 73, 90
Streams, 5, 90
   embankments, 144, 149
   flow, 7, 151
   freshwater, 8
   obstructions, 7–8, 26, 79
   organic matter, 7, 8, 149
   polluted by mines, 62
   polluted by sawmills, 145
   pools, 7, 149
   siltation, 149
   temperatures, 149
Strokes, 30
Stumpage fee, 138–39, 148
Stump removal, 25
Sturgeon, 6, 10
Sugar, 8
Sugar pine, 10, 13, 73
   sweetener substance, 10
Sunflower, 73
Superintendents for Indian affairs, 62, 67
Swamps, 79
Swan, James G., 52, 84, 125, 131, 145
Swans, 6, 13, 111
Swine, 36
Swordfern, 8, 73
Syncretic religion, 70–71

Syphilis, 31
"Systematized landscape," 36. *See also* Gardened, systematized landscape

Tacoma (Washington), 86, 126, 130, 147
Tallow, 37
Tansy ragwort, 108
Tarweed, 13
Teal, Joseph Nathan, 156
Technology, 87, 90–92, 135, 147
Teller, Henry, 139
Temperate rain forest, 1
Tennant, Paul, 17
Thermal cover, 9
Thistles, 108, 160
Thrashing machine, 90
Tichenor, Ned, 140
Tillamook Bay, 126
Tillamook County (Oregon), 92
Tillamook River, 67
Timber and Stone Act (1878), 98, 142, 143
Timber Culture Act (1873), 143
Timber famine, 149, 151
Timber industry, 4, 75, 135
   effect of, 144
   and Indian reservations, 68
   production, 135
   technology, 147
   theft from public domain, 137–38, 139–41, 142
   transport, 126, 129, 135–36, 144
   See also under Oregon; Washington
Timber Trespass law (1880), 139
Timothy, 108
Tobacco, 167(n27)
Tolmie, William Fraser, 19, 26, 30, 33, 37, 46, 49
Tomatoes, 104
Tourism, 83, 153
Townsend, John Kirk, 30, 47
Trade centers, 87
Trading vocabulary. *See* Chinook Jargon
"Tragedy of the commons," 34
Transcontinental railroads, 36, 86, 102, 126, 133
Transportation. *See* Railroads; Roads; Wagon transport; Water transportation
Trask River, 126
Travel guides, 39
Treaty of 1846, 51, 96, 127
Trees, 37
   clearing, 25–26, 74, 75, 80–83, 135, 148
   downed, 7, 8, 26, 82
   fire clearing technique, 82
   food use, 10
   medicinal use, 10
   root systems, 149

worm infestation, 13
See also Firewood; Forests; Logging; Lumber industry; Timber industry; Wooden implements and construction materials; *individual names*
Trout, 6, 7, 78, 109, 147
Trumpeter swan, 111
Tualatin Basin, 79
Tualatin Plains, 39, 86, 106
Tubers, 8
Tufted hairgrass, 74
Tumwater (Washington), 76
Turnips, 70, 104
Tuttle, B. B., 139
Typhoid fever, 30
Typhus, 30

Umpqua Indians, 13, 55
    Cow Creek band, 62
    at Grand Ronde reservation, 64
Umpqua River, 32, 36
Umpqua Valley, 43, 55, 75, 104
Union Pacific, 86
University of Washington, 142
Upper Mississippi lowlands, 74
Urbanization, 36, 53–54, 87, 152
U.S. Commissioner of Indian Affairs, 67
U.S. Fish and Wildlife Service, 163
U.S. Forest Inspector, 116
U.S. Forest Service, 116, 157, 161, 163
U.S. Indian Superintendent, 32

Vancouver, George, 23
Vancouver Island, 5, 22, 36
Vegetation, 8, 26, 73, 118. *See also* Plants
Venereal disease, 30, 31, 55–56
Victor, Frances Fuller, 82, 99, 105, 107
Victoria (British Columbia), 55
Villard, Henry, 86
Vine maple, 81
Vision quest, 18
Vitamin C, 8
Volcanic eruptions, 14

Wagon transport, 86, 135
Waldo, Daniel, 113
Waldo, John Breckenridge, 102, 110, 151
Walker, Joel P., 40
Walker, Joseph, 40
Walnut tree, 136, 148
Wapato, 8–9, 29, 70
War of 1812, 27, 54
Warren, Daniel Knight, 122
Warren, David, 78
Washington
    agricultural land, 76, 77, 184(n31)
    agriculture, 79, 91, 104, 105, 132

biotic change, 118–19
deer and elk, 9
economy, 94, 101, 103, 127, 130, 131–32, 159, 160
fire wardens, 155
fish, 109
fish and game legislation, 112, 116, 145
Fish Commissioner, 116, 144, 146, 147
forest conservation, 155
forest fires, 84, 154, 155
forestland, private ownership, 2–3, 142–43
forest reserves, 152
forests, 1, 3, 75–77, 85, 134
harbors, 126–27
hydroelectric power, 160
Indian reservations, 68
industry, 87, 94, 102, 132
land commissioners, 155
land grants, 97–98, 142
livestock, 106, 107
lumber industry, 94, 102, 121, 125–26, 127–32, 138–43, 147, 157
military-industrial complex, 159, 160
mining, 77
as modernizing, 103
Native Americans, 5, 11, 31, 52, 55, 62, 64, 71
overgrazing, 106, 107
population (1880–1890), 86
population diversity and growth, 94, 101, 102, 103, 159
prairie, 77
railroads, 86, 102
rural, 94, 159
sawmills, 125, 127–28, 130–31, 134
settlement, 44–45, 47, 49, 54, 72, 75, 77, 83, 86, 94, 111
statehood (1889), 132
Territory, 62, 68, 125–26
thistle law, 108
timber industry, 77, 94, 127, 128, 134, 137–38
timber trespass, 140
urban, 94, 130, 159
U.S. District Attorney for, 137
western bioregion, 78
wetlands, 78, 79, 184(n31)
wildlife conservation, 117
Washington County (Oregon), 100
Washington Forest Fire Association, 155
Washington Pioneer (Olympia), 132
Washington Standard (Olympia), 46, 58, 59, 77, 107, 128, 132, 137, 143, 146, 150, 158
Waterfowl, 5–6, 7, 9, 78, 111, 114, 116
Water pollution
    nineteenth century, 62, 110, 145
    twentieth century, 161

Watershed protection, 151
Watershed storage, 7
Water transportation, 6, 26, 77, 85
    canoe and scow, 85
    difficulties, 126, 136
    and forest fire smoke, 84
    and log jam clearing, 79
    for logs, 126
    ocean-going, 85, 127
    steamboat, 77, 84, 85
Watson, C. B., 153
Weeds, 108
West, Chris, 161
Western buttercup, 73
Western expansion, 4, 36, 40, 41, 53, 134
Western Forestry and Conservation Association, 155, 156
Western red cedar, 10, 73
West Shore (journal), 42, 99, 149
Wetlands, 7, 78–80
Weyerhaeuser, Frederick, 2–3, 134
Whales, 5
Wheat, 37, 91, 104, 106, 108, 123
    as dominant crop, 105
    rust, 105
    yields, 105
Wheeler, George P., 76
Whiskey, 38
White, Richard, 28
White crappie, 109
White oak, 73
White River Valley, 104
White-tailed deer, 9, 111, 114
Whitman, Marcus, 52
Whooping cough, 30
Whooping crane, 111
Wigle, Andrew J., 92
Wilderness, 1, 2. See also Forests; Fur trade; Settler society; Wildlife
Wildlife
    conservation, 115–18
    loss, 111–17
Wilkes, Charles, 9, 27, 31, 34, 37, 43, 48
Wilkes Expedition (1841), 12
Willamette Falls, 10, 11, 121, 126
Willamette–Puget Sound Lowland province, 3
Willamette River, 11, 38, 73, 125
    floods, 74–75
    pollution, 110, 161
    transportation, 126
Willamette Valley, 11, 12, 25, 29, 48, 76
    agriculture, 99–100, 101, 104, 105, 108, 123, 161
    beaver population, 33, 79

dairying, 108
fences, 110
flood (1849), 124
floodplain, 74, 105
forests, 73, 81, 137
game species loss, 111
"garden," 73
grass species, 13, 73, 74, 108
lumber industry, 121, 124, 125
marshlands, 73
Methodist mission, 121
Native Americans, 13, 61, 67
oaks, 73
overgrazing, 106
prairies, 73, 74, 75, 81
riverine woodlands, 73
sawmills, 121, 124, 125
settlement, 39, 40, 73, 74, 75, 99
soil, 74, 105, 107
upland, 74, 75
vegetation, 73, 81
wetlands, 78–80
wheat production, 105
–Yaquina Bay route, 67
Willapa Bay (Washington), 52, 84, 126, 147
Willapa River forest area, 75–76
Willapa Valley, 91
Willopah Indians, 55
Willow, 73, 78
Windthrow, 148
Winks, Robin W., 45
Winthrop, Jonathan, 42
Winthrop, Theodore, 42, 46, 49, 125, 135
Wolves, 9, 112, 113
Wood, Tallmadge, 43
Woodcock, 78
Wooden implements and construction materials, 9, 10, 23, 120, 123
Woolly sunflower, 73
Work, John, 55
Worster, Donald, 2
Wright, Benjamin, 64
Wyeth, Nathaniel J., 39, 47

Yachats district (Oregon), 117
Yaquina (female Indian chief), 60
Yaquina Bay, 67
Yaquina River, 67
Yellow perch, 109
Yellow pine, 10, 133
Yeoman independence, 92, 137
Yesler, Henry, 125
Yew, 10, 136
Yonce, Frederick J., 138
Yreka (California), 107, 123